Connecticut Yankee

An Autobiography

Wilbur L. Cross

Introduction by Justin Zaremby

City Point Press

Westport, Connecticut

Paperback reprint published in 2019 under license by

City Point Press

P.O. Box 2063

Westport CT 06880

www.citypointpress.com

Distributed worldwide by Simon and Schuster

Cover and text design by Barbara Aronica-Buck

Paperback ISBN 978-1-947951-16-7

eBook ISBN 978-1-947951-17-4

Manufactured in the United States of America

Dedicated to the memory of my wife
Helen Baldwin Avery
And to our children and grandchildren

Contents

PART III

Governor Wilbur L. Cross, Democrat, Connecticut (1931–1939)
Courtesy of the Connecticut State Library, State Archives

Revisiting Wilbur Cross's *Connecticut Yankee*
Justin Zaremby, PhD, JD
Yale College Class of 2003

I n 1938, Governor Wilbur Cross issued his final Thanksgiving proclamation. As in his earlier proclamations, Cross summoned the lively
and crisp New England autumn to express a sense of pride in the
state. 1938 had been a year of loss. Connecticut suffered tremendous damage in the rampant destruction wrought by a hurricane that swept the
Eastern seaboard. The hurricane of 1938 would leave an indelible mark
on the memory and history of Connecticut's environment and citizens.
In addition, earlier that month Cross, who was first elected in 1930, lost
his final bid for the governorship amidst a series of scandals that implicated
both major parties. The proclamation opened as follows:

> As the colors of autumn stream down the wind, scarlet in sumacs
> and maple, spun gold in the birches, a splendor of smoldering fire
> in the oaks along the hill, and the last leaves flutter away, and dusk
> falls briefly about the worker bringing in from the field a late load
> of its fruit, and Arcturus is lost to sight and Orion swings upward
> that great sun upon his shoulder, we are stirred one more to ponder
> the Infinite Goodness that has set apart for us, in all this moving
> mystery of creation, a time of living and a home.

Cross declared a day of public Thanksgiving, and sought thanks for "the
further mercies we have enjoyed, beyond desert or any estimation, of Justice, Freedom, Loving-kindness, Peace."[1]

The contemporary reader imagines two potential responses to these
words during a year of turmoil. For some, the poetry would be hard to
read—a reminder of a more halcyon time that had been ripped away, like
so many old-growth forests in the face of the hurricane. The clouds of

war were gathering in Europe, and the lasting impacts of the Great Depression were still felt in Connecticut's towns and cities. At that moment, the horrors of the hurricane would have felt like purposeless and divine retribution. For others, Cross's words would, however, provide solace. They would serve as a nostalgic paean to a timeless vision of Connecticut—comforting words from the wise scholar-politician who was ending his term of service.

Cross concludes *Connecticut Yankee* with the 1938 proclamation. It is fitting that he should end his autobiography with poetry; after all, so much of his life was shaped by a love of the written word. As a Yale professor, writer, and editor, Cross devoted himself to the English language, and specifically to understanding how novels were capable of capturing the human condition. *Connecticut Yankee* is, in many ways, a novel itself. The protagonist is Cross and the plot is his education. In *Connecticut Yankee*, Cross explores the development of his character from childhood to old age through a combination of memory, hearsay, fact, and likely fancy. To read *Connecticut Yankee* is to be welcomed into Cross's Connecticut— from the quaintness of his childhood home to the rigors of Yale, where he studied and served as an influential dean, and the tumultuous politics of Hartford. Equal parts nostalgic, witty, self-serving, and frank, *Connecticut Yankee* is an entertaining and informative memoir of the state and a scholar who shaped it.

When Wilbur Cross accepted the Democratic nomination for the governorship of Connecticut in 1930, he reflected upon how his home state had shaped him. "I have not been a militant candidate for the nomination," he said. "But I owe my career to the social and educational institutions of the State, up from the red schoolhouse on the country hillside, through the public high school, and on to a university founded by the colonists far back of the first days of the Republic. As a poor return for these benefits I stand ready in the present crisis to give to my fellow citizens such services as they may ask of me provided nothing is asked beyond my abilities."[2] The "present crisis" was both economic and political: Connecticut was beginning to face the struggles of the Great Depression while the state's Democratic Party struggled to return to power after decades in the wilderness. Cross was an unlikely candidate to reclaim a place for Democrats in Hartford. He had spent his career at Yale, where he was professor of English and dean of the graduate school. He was a respected scholar of the English novel and an adept academic administrator, but had no experience in state politics. Nevertheless, the "dear old gentleman down at Yale" won a narrow victory for the Democrats in 1930.

The early twentieth century was an unsuccessful era for the Democratic Party in Connecticut. The Democrats had held the governor's chair for two decades at the end of the nineteenth century, until the nomination of William Jennings Bryan in 1896 caused a rift in the party. Bryan's promise to reject the gold standard made him a popular figure around the country, but not in Connecticut. The Connecticut Democrats largely rejected his candidacy, splitting the party and leading to a Republican victory in Hartford. The wounds within the party would not quickly heal. As the state's population grew at the beginning of the twentieth century, the Republicans gained increasing support across the state while the Democrats engaged in brutal infighting between recently arrived Irish and Italian immigrants and descendants of colonial settlers. The presence of immigrant voices in the Democratic Party raised suspicions across the state of foreign influence, and this internal strife provided a boon to the Republicans. Indeed, before Cross was elected, the only Democrat to serve as governor in the twentieth century was another Yale professor, Simeon Baldwin, who was a lawyer and retired Chief Justice of the Connecticut Supreme Court. Baldwin was elected for two terms in 1910, in large part due to conflict among the Republicans.

Wilbur Cross had always been interested in politics. In *Connecticut Yankee*, he explains that as a child "when I was hardly out of the cradle, I had to tell my father, whenever he asked for it, who was the Governor of Connecticut, whether he was a Democrat or a Republican. In my imagination, a Governor was a very exalted person, a sort of superman, who ranked very little below God and the angels."[3] However, other than academic politics, which consumed much of his career, Cross had no active engagement with politics until he became a candidate. Most of his political participation came during Thursday evening cocktails and discussion at the

Graduates Club in New Haven. At these meetings, Cross notes, "[n]o politician, however high he climbed, was spared in the talk about him."[4]

It was at the Graduates Club that someone suggested that Cross run
for office. In 1930, the Democratic Party was divided with respect to the
politically influential Democratic State Central Committee. An upstart
group within the party, known as its "New Guard," pushed for Cross's
nomination. With no candidate of its own, the Old Guard was forced to
give way. However, if the state politicos felt that the politically inex-
perienced professor would be easy to control, they were mistaken. At the
state Democratic convention, a battle was waged over whether the neo-
phyte Cross and his allies would be able to choose who would lead the
campaign. At four o'clock in the morning, Cross was awakened in his
hotel room to join the fray. Following a bitter argument, in which Cross
was accused of "being not a Democrat but a Republican in disguise,"
Cross emerged victorious. One headline read: "Delegates meet Dean
Cross in his pajamas and lose their shirts."[5]

Cross campaigned to clean up state government and to repeal national
prohibition. He recounted stories of his childhood and his deep ties to
the state and its history. During a period of economic unrest following
the stock market crash of 1929, Cross's steady, folksy charm appealed to
independent voters in the face of a powerful Republican machine. Candidate Cross won with a majority of over five thousand votes.

As governor, Cross made strong efforts to reorganize state government,
instituting a merit system for political offices. He signed legislation to
improve conditions for workers. He presided over the tercentenary of the
state in 1935 and over the opening of the Merritt Parkway in 1938. He
managed labor unrest and coordinated the state's responses to natural disasters, including devastating floods in 1936 and the hurricane of 1938.

During his years in office, Governor Cross occupied an uncomfortable
middle ground between the progressive policies of the Roosevelt years
and his own commitment to a less interventionist, laissez-faire politics of
his youth. According to one scholar, "As a Democrat who served during
the New Deal, Cross labored conscientiously throughout the 1930s to
establish himself as a 'liberal.' But his commitment to New Deal liberalism

was uneasy and ambiguous. The public speeches of Governor Cross revealed a self-conscious debate between the historical conservative and the uncomfortable liberal, an interior dialogue between the values of his heritage and the casualties of a depressed urban and industrial society."[6] Although never fully trusted by either party, he deftly maneuvered numerous political crises by relying on his "skills of accommodation, conciliation, and gentle persuasion."[7]

Although Cross was beloved by many as a wise spiritual leader for the State, a series of corruption scandals (with guilty parties from both major parties) ultimately cost him his position. Although Cross was innocent of these scandals, he lost the governorship in 1938 to the liberal-leaning Republican Raymond Baldwin. Cross returned to private life in 1939. He made an unsuccessful attempt to be nominated as governor in 1940, and in 1946 he was defeated by Raymond Baldwin in an attempt to fill a vacant seat in the U.S. Senate. Two years later he died.

Cross published his autobiography in 1945, seven years after he left office. It is striking that by the time Cross wrote *Connecticut Yankee*, not only Connecticut but the nation had undergone dramatic transformation. By 1945, the nation was enmeshed in the final days of the Second World War, and American influence worldwide had never been greater. Yet, in telling his story, Cross is mired in nostalgia. He expresses nostalgia for the simplicity of his childhood, nostalgia for his time at Yale, and even some nostalgia for the political maneuverings of Connecticut politics. Cross was raised in the Protestant, rural, and socially conservative Connecticut known commonly as the "land of steady habits." As governor he helped oversee a state with growing urban and industrial needs during the New Deal. In between, he helped transform Yale from a somewhat provincial institution into a leading research university.

Throughout *Connecticut Yankee*, Cross's nostalgia is rooted in the concept of the "Yankee." Indeed, whether in the opening chapter, in which he traces his lineage to early settlers in Massachusetts and Connecticut, or through stories that demonstrate witty repartee, clever schemes, or loyalty to school and state, Cross's connection to New England, and a sense of distinct Yankee spirit, is the strand that ties together the path he took from

Gurleyville to Hartford. For Cross, being a Yankee is as much a matter of heritage as it is a way of approaching the world. Understanding the Connecticut Yankee is therefore key to understanding Wilbur Cross.

The definition of a Yankee is elusive. For the British, the term encompasses any American. For the Southerner during the Civil War, the term referred to Northerners. And among Northerners, it refers to New Englanders. The term is a source of both pride and derision. To his fans, the Yankee is a descendant of colonial settlers who represents a strong connection to early national history. The Yankee is high minded, humble, steady, and inventive. To his detractors, the Yankee is clever, manipulative, self-serving, deceitful, and ultimately dedicated to undermining American mores. The Yankee in Mark Twain's *Connecticut Yankee in King Arthur's Court* was a conflicted and troubling figure. He was wise and scheming—an ardent democrat in a medieval monarchy who actively (and sometimes violently) uprooted the established church while bringing science and industry to Camelot. Like Twain, Cross recognized in the Yankee a complicated hybrid of innovation and conservatism.

Wilbur Cross takes pride in the term "Yankee," and in his autobiography he frequently characterizes his own decisions, or the decisions of others, as Yankee. Cross's Yankee is curious and practical and develops these characteristics through the stories he hears in institutions such as the small-town general store and the august university. He never reflects deeply on the meaning of the term, assuming a common understanding and common admiration for the Yankee. In doing so, of course, Cross assumes a particular readership of potentially like-minded individuals for whom his points of reference and language would be familiar.

Cross was born in 1862 in Gurleyville, a district in the town of Mansfield. Cross presents Gurleyville as the archetype of rural America. He pieces together his memories of the village—its economy, its people, and their adventures—with the earnest focus of a child. The stories are mundane, but filled with the excitement of youthful discovery. He first encounters irony when, upon catching his first trout, the barb caught his own finger and needed to be removed as it would be removed "from the mouth of a fish."[8] Shortly thereafter he was kicked by a horse, "which hurt me less but frightened me more."[9] Cross recalls his grandfather's clock, which was "so intimate a part of him that when it stopped an hour before his death there was great excitement in the household, for the clock's behavior was regarded as a clear omen that the end of life for grandfather was near at hand."[10]

In Gurleyville, Cross learned "as I could not have learned in a city, the ways of mankind as they were manifest in simple and naïve acts and words; there I gained a rudimentary knowledge of business, of legal procedure, of local government, and of the art and wiles of politicians, which has been of use to me in reading the minds and motives of men in my dealings with them."[11] Cross worked at his family's general store, where he overheard the talk of the village. He listened to the whispering of teenagers and gossips and the politicking of Republicans and Democrats. In what he called a "House of Commons," Cross discovered a matter-of-fact tone that permeates much of his writing.

> It was a variable group of men who came in for their mail and sat on until somebody said it was time to go home. . . . In their talk there was little or no reserve. They spoke frankly about themselves, their families, and their neighbors; and their comment on what was occurring outside their little world, in Hartford or in Washington, was marked by shrewd common sense. They were unsophisticated people such as a novelist likes to depict because they said what was really in their minds. As a rule they were honorable and truthful men except in horse trades, where it was understood that the better liar is the better man. As a boy I was most interested, except for politics, in horse trades, funny stories, and what are now called wisecracks.[12]

Cross describes an education in books and conversation. He fondly recalls reading the *Hartford Courant* and *Robinson Crusoe* and his school's assigned reader. The reader, with its samples of poetry and prose, inspired in him "a love of words for their own sake and the rhythms and cadences of prose as well as of verse which I must have felt as I read the selections aloud."[13] He acknowledges rather idealized memories of his one-room schoolhouse, despite the fact that "[i]t was almost a crime to put children no more than four years old in a one-room school where little was provided for them to do."[14] His education was practical. With respect to mathematics, he explained: "As befitting the Yankee's desire to see his savings increase, there was considerable practice in computing compound interest over periods long enough to double or triple the original capital."[15]

Gurleyville also exposed Cross to war. As a child he "learned of the past not from books but from the lips of men and women."[16] His family and his community introduced him to men and women who were born before the surrender of Cornwallis at Yorktown. He therefore was connected to a pre-revolutionary America even as he witnessed the transformations in American politics and society after the Civil War. That war, of course, loomed even larger in his memory. During his time at the general store, he heard the stories of middle-aged men who had fought the South. They spoke of "their experiences in this and that battle or in the prison at Andersonville when they were captured, or of the fun they had in camp, or of their fraternizing with the Rebs when on picket duty, swapping matches for tobacco, and smoking together, and hoping that the war would soon end."[17] He remembers learning about horrible battles at Shiloh and Antietam, which were "embedded" in his memory.

As Cross matured into adulthood, the homogenous society in which he was raised was changing. New immigrant groups were beginning to replace the original settlers of English and Scottish descent, and Connecticut's march to the twentieth century brought new economic and political challenges. When Cross matriculated at Yale College in 1881, he may not have realized that the world of his childhood was on the decline, but by the time he wrote *Connecticut Yankee*, he describes his home with deep longing. Gurleyville embodied a "Yankee ambient" from which he brought away "the gift of self-dependence, an imbedded conviction that in any undertaking a man must go on alone, if his associates fail him, to its completion. This was a Yankee gift of which I was then unaware."[18]

Cross arrived in New Haven for the first time in September 1881 to sit the entrance examinations for Yale College. He "entered upon [his] studies with the utmost zeal, trying to do as well in one as in another, on the theory, now abandoned in education, that a study which a student finds hard for him is as essential as the study he finds easy if his aim is the development of a well-balanced mind adequate to cope with a world where things are hard as well as easy."[19] The curriculum in that era was largely prescribed. While Harvard had begun to experiment with the radical notion of elective courses, Yale remained dedicated to a largely classical curriculum. Cross reflects fondly on his education: "It is quite likely," he explains, "that if Latin and Greek had been purely elective studies I should have chosen them as the best foundation of the literary life which I was already vaguely hoping to lead."[20] This knowledge would become vital to his work as a scholar. "What would now be, I ask myself, my outlook on life and literature had I no direct knowledge of Homer and Vergil, Demosthenes and Cicero, Plato and Aristotle, Thucydides and Tacitus, and above all, no knowledge of the Greek dramatists?"[21] While the elective system only began to be implemented toward the end of his time as an undergraduate, Cross had the opportunity to learn from leading figures of the era, including the geologist James Dwight Dana, the political economist William Graham Sumner, and law professor (and later Ambassador to the Court of St. James's) Edward J. Phelps.

Outside of the classroom, Cross seems to have fully engaged with college life. Evenings were spent in conversation, smoke, and song while perched on windowsills and the iconic Yale College fence. Students dined on grim meals at their eating clubs and were required to attend compulsory chapel ("an institution as old as Yale itself, it was taken for granted would never die") at 8:10 each morning.[22] Dormitories lacked bathtubs or showers, and Cross displays delight in describing the difficulty of being clean in "that unwashed age."[23]

Cross's interest in literature was kindled in secondary school, but was firmly established during his time in college. He won numerous prizes for his written compositions and the college's top prize for oratory as well. In addition, he studied with the leading English professors of the era, Henry A. Beers and Thomas Lounsbury, who largely revolutionized the study of English. Instead of focusing on the study of the English language to understand grammar and syntax, their courses explored concepts of character and plot in literature. Cross began his studies at a moment when literary studies were adopting a new rigor, and Cross embraced that rigor with excitement. In describing a course taught by Lounsbury, he writes:

> One of my courses with him was on the English dramatists contemporary with Shakespeare. Whatever the play, whether by Ben Jonson or by Beaumont and Fletcher, or by someone else, the first thing he expected of us was that we should have an intimate knowledge of it from beginning to end. Then came the discussion of the play in parts and as a whole. There was never any talk about plot as something apart from the characters which could be represented in the formal German manner by a curve showing the beginning of the action, the climax, and the end. With him characters were the thing. By their emotions and consequent behavior in crucial circumstances plot is determined. By them one's knowledge of human nature is broadened. And by them only is a play or a novel remembered.[24]

Like the education he received at the "House of Commons" in Gurleyville, his Yale education was an education in character and personality. With faith in the ability of literature (and literary scholarship) to reflect the human condition, it is, perhaps, no surprise that after a brief period serving as the principal of Staples High School in Westport, he would return to Yale for graduate school and most of his career.

Cross began his graduate studies in 1886. He studied not only English but also Spanish, French, German, and Norwegian literature. After completing his doctoral work in 1899, he spent five years teaching at a secondary school in Pittsburgh. That year, he married Helen Baldwin Avery, with whom he would raise four children (Helen died in 1928, before Cross became governor). Cross returned to Yale as an instructor in English at the Sheffield Scientific School, Yale's scientific division. Along with William Lyon Phelps, Cross became one of the first professors in the country to offer a course on contemporary novels in the university environment. At the time, the idea of teaching contemporary literature was considered radical. Indeed, the idea was so revolutionary that Cross was forced by the administration to withdraw the course the first time it was offered. When his old classics professor came to inform him of the administration's demand, Cross revealed his impish side:

> I acceded immediately to a request which, expressed in plain language, was a demand, remarking by the way that relief from graduate instruction would give me more time to complete a book which I was then writing on the English novel. But I added that if fiction were to be placed under a taboo, the *Odyssey* would have to go, for that wonderful epic was a skipper's tale filled with folklore and primitive sex notions. So would the *Iliad*, in which the motive for the war with Troy was the intrigue between Paris, son of Priam, King of Troy, and Helen, the wife of Menelaus, King of Sparta. Professor Seymour, of course, endeavored to correct my perverse views on the motivation of sex in Greek literature.[25]

He became known on campus as "Uncle Toby" from a character in Laurence Sterne's novel *The Life and Opinions of Tristram Shandy, Gentleman*. The name seems to have been indicative of how people perceived Cross's character—gentle, quixotic, and a bit disconnected from the world. Cross once described Uncle Toby as "the innocent gentleman who knows nothing of the world" whose "heart goes out in sympathy for all in misfortune and distress."[26] Whether Cross agreed with the moniker, he certainly embraced it, although his gentleness of spirit belied a talented political mind.

Cross developed a reputation as a widely regarded campus administrator. He edited *The Yale Review*, a literary journal that flourishes to this day, as well as Yale's editions of the complete works of Shakespeare. He also served as president of Yale's Elizabethan Club, a society for students and faculty devoted to the arts and letters. Perhaps his lasting legacy at Yale, however, was as a transformational dean of the graduate school. Before Cross's appointment as dean, graduate education at Yale was largely an afterthought—it lacked the organizational support and political capital held by Yale College. Indeed, when Cross became dean in 1916, his colleagues asked him why he had accepted an "empty title."[27] However, although the job offered little prestige or power initially, Cross set to work to shape the institution. With a "personality, compounded of salty humor, shrewd insight, and massive self-confidence" and an "exceptional ability to outguess and outmaneuver those who opposed his designs," Cross restructured the school, establishing institutional structures to empower the graduate school in relation to the rest of the university, and to develop its own robust faculty, curriculum, and admissions standards.[28] Indeed, according to Edgar S. Furniss, who served as dean of the graduate school while Cross was governor, Cross had an uncanny ability to get what he wanted. According to one report, the dean of Yale College was once deeply bothered following a conversation with Dean Cross during which Cross had "overreached" him. When asked how, the college dean replied, "I don't know exactly and that's what bothers me. I have just finished a luncheon conference with Uncle Toby about a matter in dispute between the College and the Graduate School; he agreed to everything I proposed; so it stands to reason that I've been overreached."[29]

When not teaching, Cross devoted himself to his scholarship. His published his first book, *The Development of the English Novel*, in 1899. The book reflected his wide command of literature. In it he explored the evolution of literature from medieval romance to a range of modern authors including Henry Fielding, Laurence Sterne, Walter Scott, Charles Dickens, George Eliot, Henry James, and Rudyard Kipling. For Cross, the evolution of the novel was a story of tension between two basic psychological impulses—"We are," he wrote, "by nature both realists and idealists, delighting in the long run about equally in the representation of life somewhat as it is and as it is dreamed to be. There is accordingly no time in which art does not to some extent minister to both instincts of human nature."[30]

Cross would explore this tension throughout his scholarly work. Among other things, he wrote biographical studies of important English novelists and wrote essays on the dangers of relying on autobiography to understand an individual's life. "The view a man takes of himself," Cross once wrote, "though he has all the facts, must be partial and one-sided;

he puts into the account and leaves out what he pleases with equal uncon-
cern; usually he does not see his career in true perspective, and he often
deceives himself on the why and wherefore of his conduct at the crucial
points of his history."[31]

In reading *Connecticut Yankee* it is worth considering the extent to which
that tension between realism and idealism permeated Cross's writing about
himself. In 1921 he wrote an essay for the *Yale Review* in which he
explored the pitfalls that confront both the biographer and autobiogra-
pher. Reflecting on why he wrote biography as a scholar of English literature, Cross explained:

> When a man (or a woman) accomplishes something worth while
> in art, letters, science, statesmanship, or business, I try to find out
> what I can about his life and personality. Behind this desire which I
> have with the rest of the modern world is more than mere curiosity.
> Life for most people is a rather difficult piece of business. So we
> want to know not only how others have turned the trick against
> fortune; we want to know also all the details of the game as they
> have played it.[32]

Biography not only provides information, but allows the reader to
expand his own understanding of the human experience. Biography serves
as a "sort of Life Extension Bureau" which allows the reader to acquire
"a fairly good working knowledge of human nature, though he may never
have mastered the Freudian psychology or wandered very far from a small
university town."[33] It allows the reader to live vicariously through another.

More than seventy-six years after Cross published *Connecticut Yankee*,
the landscape of the state has dramatically changed. When speaking of
Yankees, people are more likely to speak of baseball than New England.
The form of Yankee pride that Cross took for granted has been replaced
with a more ethnically, religiously, and socially diverse vision for Connecticut. His vision of the state and his identity seems tinged with a combination of fact and fiction and at times can seem quaint and foreign. In
addition, Cross's tone may strike the modern reader as impersonal. Unlike

today's memoirists, Cross's autobiography largely eschews emotion and even discussion of family. *Connecticut Yankee* is very much the story of one man at a particular time and place.

During his own life, Cross seemed to be a man slightly out of step with time, mired in nostalgia yet still capable of advancing change in his scholarship, at Yale, and as governor. Nevertheless, Cross's narrative remains both enjoyable and informative. It provides a lens for understanding the education of one man and the transformation of a state. Cross's path from town to city, from schoolroom to statehouse, and from civilian to politician remains relevant and compelling.

Notes

(In all instances, CY in these notes refers to the text of this edition.)

1. CY 420.
2. CY 225.
3. CY 217.
4. CY 218.
5. CY 224.
6. Robert L. Woodbury, "Wilbur Cross: New Deal Ambassador to a Yankee Culture," *The New England Quarterly* 41, no. 3 (Sept. 1968): 331.
7. Ibid., 337.
8. CY 16.
9. Ibid.
10. CY 17.
11. CY 57–58.
12. CY 29.
13. CY 21.
14. CY 25.
15. CY 23–24.
16. CY 12.
17. CY 31.
18, CY 58.
19. CY 62–63.
20. CY 65.
21. Ibid.
22. CY 79.
23. CY 78.
24. CY 75.

25. CY 117.

26. Wilbur L. Cross, *The Development of the English Novel*, New York: The Macmillan Company (1899), xi.

27. Brooks Mather Kelley, *Yale: A History*, New Haven and London: Yale University Press (1974), 338.

28. Edgar S. Furniss, *The Graduate School of Yale: A Brief History*, New Haven: The Graduate School (1965), 46–47.

29. Ibid., 127.

30. Cross, *The Development of the English Novel,* 74.

31. Wilbur Cross, "From Plutarch to Strachey," *The Yale Review* 99, no. 3 (July 2011): 45.

32. Ibid., 42.

33. Ibid., 42–43.

Part I

I. A Roomful of Ancestors

When a man views a long life in retrospect, it looks to him like a dream—sometimes as one continuous dream; at other times as a succession of dreams imperfectly fused in his imagination. In either case the events of his life are seen through a glimmering haze which obscures many rough and hard edges. Dreams usurp reality. With this illusion in mind Calderón, a great Spanish dramatist, once wrote a play which he called "Life Is a Dream." So if I am to give here a true and clear account of myself I must by a strenuous effort wake out of dreams that have played the deuce with me as with all men. I should rid myself of one particular illusion that haunts me. As I read the books and addresses which I have written they often appear as the work of someone else with whom I am unacquainted. Where and how did I ever get the facts and stories therein related? Whence came the opinions therein expressed? They must have come from me, for I have always been too poor to employ a ghost writer. I sometimes imagine that they came from another self. For did not Plato say in *The Republic* that every man has two selves, the one being in command of the other as circumstances vary? And yet, if there be two selves, they must be merged to make life whole.

Great men whose lives or works I have read have felt that they were guided in their careers by some mysterious power not themselves. Many have simply called it fate. Socrates and Goethe regarded it as a beneficent daemon, meaning an indwelling genius or guardian spirit who was born and died with them. Washington attributed his dramatic career to destiny. Shakespeare let Hamlet say:

> There's a divinity that shapes our ends,
> Rough-hew them how we will.

In our present realistic age, H. G. Wells, letting his mind run over his career, has inquired, "What is the *drive* in me?" It was a tremendous drive in a boy who first jumped the counter of a draper's shop and afterwards as a man kept on jumping through science and literature at the rate of several volumes a year. In the view of Conrad and Galsworthy, a man's character and to an extent his career also are in some mysterious way determined by family and racial inheritance as moulded by environment. Conrad stressed race, Galsworthy stressed heredity as exemplified in the Forsyte family which was in large essentials his own family.

Though I am not of this great company, I sometimes wonder what characteristics of myself may be discovered by a survey of my family history. Once in a while I receive an inquiry from some part of the earth in regard to the family and the origin of the name I bear. Not long ago a Harvard friend thought I would be interested to know that when Elihu Yale was Governor of Fort St. George at Madras he ordered a groom named Charles Cross to be hanged for stealing a horse. The implication was that there may be some remote relationship between myself and that unlucky thief in far-off India. Several correspondents have endeavored to give martial and religious dignity to the family name by suggesting that it was first used to designate men who carried the Cross in one of the Crusades to the Holy Land. For enlightenment they have appealed to me in gilded words of flattery as "a learned scholar." Some of them do not appear to be satisfied with what I have been compelled to tell them. Although the name antedates the Third Crusade, in with Richard Coeur de Lion played an adventurous part, it is in origin merely a placer name given to men who lived in houses situated near the village, town, or wayside Cross at a time when crosses, often with a crucifix, were common throughout England. Some of those beautiful crosses, built of stone instead of wood, survived the Protestant Reformation and may still be seen here and there as in Bristol and Winchester. In the manor lists of the thirteenth century one finds many names like "John atte Cross," meaning literally John at the Cross or, as we should say now, John living near the Cross. John and all others like him were small tenant farmers holding lands from the lord of the manor. Thus, like other members of my family, I must be content with this humble descent from the common people of England.

The first New Englanders of the name were a part of the Puritan

immigration to Boston Bay. Several of them were among the earliest settlers at Ipswich, which came to be regarded as the New England home
of the family. The first man of the name to reach the Connecticut River
Colony, then comprising Windsor, Hartford, and Wethersfield, was William
Cross who may have come by way of Ipswich. It has been surmised that
he was a Londoner. He was in Wethersfield in the spring of 1637 when
the Pequots in a surprise attack killed a few men and women working in
the fields, with the result that the General Court declared war against the
tribe. On May 11 William Cross, with other men of Wethersfield, Hartford, and Windsor, enlisted in the war under Capt. John Mason and thus
had a share in that terrible massacre of the Pequots in their fort at Mystic.
One day, while Governor of Connecticut, I had an opportunity to apol-
ogize to the few surviving Pequots on parade in full feather for what one
of my ancestors did to their ancestors. In return they laughed and gave
me their war whoop. Some time after the war was over William Cross
purchased a house and land in Wethersfield; and the next year he was fined
by the General Court of Connecticut forty shillings for selling wine in
that house without a license. Perhaps in a desire not to live too near the
seat of government where laws are more strictly enforced than in remote
places, he removed to Fairfield where he died in 1655, leaving his estate
involved in debt, as often happened in those days in the case of men
engaged in trade or in the purchase and sale of land. William Cross, I rather
think, was a seafaring man who wanted to try his luck in various parts of
Connecticut. Beyond reasonable doubt my branch of the family is in
direct descent from this Puritan soldier.

A son or grandson named Peter Cross (?1653–1737) first came into
view (so far as records go) in Norwich, where he married Mary Wade,
the daughter by a second marriage of Robert Wade, one of the founders
of Norwich. This Robert Wade, who early enters the Cross picture, first
settled in Dorchester, Massachusetts, where he lived for five years; thence
he moved on to Hartford and stayed there for another five years. Then he
went down the river to Saybrook where in 1657 he obtained from the
General Court a decree of divorce from his wife Joan on the ground that
she had deserted him fifteen years before. It may be observed that Robert

Wade has the distinction of being the first man in the Connecticut Colony to receive a decree of divorce from that honorable body. In granting the divorce, the General Court denounced Joan for her "unworthy, sinful, yea, unnatural carriage towards . . . her husband, notwithstanding his constant and commendable care and endeavor to gain fellowship with her in the bond of marriage."

Two years after the divorce Robert Wade arrived in Norwich with his second wife named Susanna, the mother of Mary, destined to be the wife of Peter Cross. At the age of twenty-two Peter Cross enlisted as a volunteer in King Philip's War (1675–76) and afterwards shared with his fellow soldiers in the division of land on the Rhode Island border in a district now known as Voluntown. By 1693 he had settled with his wife, her mother, and other members of the Wade family in that part of Windham which was named Mansfield Street or Mansfield Center sometime after the town of Mansfield was incorporated in 1703. As one of the original proprietors of the town he took an active part in its affairs and in the organization of the First Congregational Church of Mansfield. For protection against wandering bands of Indians he built a stockade on a site near the Natchaug River which afforded a clear view up and down the stream and across the meadows.

Nine children were born to Peter and Mary of whom the youngest, Wade Cross (1699–1773), was the first of our family to become identified with that part of Mansfield which is now the seat of the University of Connecticut. He lies buried in the old graveyard by the Second Congregational Church at Storrs. He was known as a gentleman-farmer who took for his wife the daughter of "Isaac Hall, Gentleman," who in turn was the son of Capt. William Hall, one of the very first settlers in Mansfield. The inventory of Wade Cross's estate indicates that he was partial both to blue coats and blue stockings. In family history Wade Cross serves as in interesting link between Peter Cross who married Mary Wade and his only son Peter Cross (1740–1808) who married Alice Warner of Ashford, sixth in descent from William Bradford, who was for thirty years Governor of the Plymouth Colony. Like his father, Peter Cross was a small farmer, who was also a maker or pedlar of earthenware, a good specimen of which, bearing the inscription "P. Cross Hartford," now stands in the hallway of my house in New Haven. Peter Cross was active in military affairs during and immediately after the Revolution, being appointed by the General Court first as ensign and then as lieutenant in the 13th Company or Trainband in the 5th Regiment of Connecticut. Tradition has it that he was a convivial companion who loved a jest and a good story whether he told it himself or heard it told by another.

Peter's youngest son, Eleazer Cross (1783–1836), was my grandfather; he lived on the family homestead with its open fields and meadows in the Fenton Valley, a scant mile north of Gurleyville, where I was to be born. In character and habits he appears to have resembled his father. As he died in middle life, twenty-six years before I was born, all I know of him comes from casual remarks I heard from members of my family and others who remembered him. The last person to see him alive was Eunice Storrs, a sister of Augustus and Charles Storrs, who gave a large tract of land to the State of Connecticut for an agricultural school which has since developed into the University of Connecticut. Though only seventeen years old, Eunice Storrs was at that time the school ma'am in the little red schoolhouse on a Gurleyville hill. Eleazer Cross was very fond of children and often came into her school to talk to them. After one of these visits on a beautiful May morning he started on his way home and was found dead by the roadside. He was in his fifty-fourth year.

Eleazer's wife, Hannah Williams, brought into the Cross family two interesting collateral lines of descent. One of her grandfathers, for instance, was Maj. Joseph Storrs who took a conspicuous part in local and state affairs, and as one of the proprietors of the town of Hanover, New Hampshire, gave to Dartmouth College 110 acres of land. Her other grandfather, Capt. William Williams, was cousin to Rector Elisha Williams who served as President of Yale College from 1726 to 1739. This, I may say, is as near as anyone related to the Cross family ever came to Yale before my admission to the Freshman class of Yale College 142 years later.

My father, Samuel Cross (1823–76), was the youngest of seven children born of Eleazer Cross and Hannah Williams. During a large part of his boyhood he lived with his maiden aunt, Eleanor Cross, doing chores for his board and clothes. Late in his teens he taught school for a winter or a year in a nameless town somewhere in Rhode Island and then joined the crew of a whaling vessel, sailing from New Bedford, which took him round Cape Horn to the Northern Pacific. In this adventure he was following almost precisely the example of an elder brother Franklin who also ran away to sea. In each case, however, before setting sail they sent letters home to tell the family what they were going to do. Unlike Franklin, who soon rose to the rank of captain and followed the sea for twenty-five years, Samuel returned to Mansfield at the end of one voyage of three years. After an interval of farming, he married the girl who was to become my mother. Her name was Harriet Maria Gurley, the only child of Lucius Gurley and Abigail Shumway.

The miller's house in Gurleyville, where Wilbur Cross was born. (People unidentified.) Photo ca. 1910.
Courtesy, Mansfield Historical Society

The original home of the Gurleys was Inverness, Scotland. The Mansfield branch of the family is in direct descent from William Gurley who, it is related, came to Massachusetts in 1679 at the age of fourteen with the family of an English clergyman who settled in Northampton. Eight years later he was accidentally drowned in the Connecticut River, a fortnight before his wife Hester Ingersoll gave birth to a son who was named Samuel (1687–1760). Not long afterwards, his widow married again. Her second husband and two of their children were slain before her eyes in an Indian massacre near Northampton in 1704. Her house was ransacked and burned and she herself was taken as a captive to Canada where she died the next year in great mental distress.

Stricken with terror by this awful massacre, her son Samuel Gurley with other young men migrated to North Coventry where there was little or no danger of Indian attacks. Thence he moved eastward into Mansfield, setting at Spring Hill which gave him a wide range of pasturage for his cattle. By his marriage with Experience Rust, also formerly of Northampton, he was the father of ten children, one of whom, the elder Jonathan Gurley, was the friend and adviser of Governor Jonathan Trumbull at the outbreak of the Revolution. Through that son and his son, the younger Jonathan, Samuel became the great-grandfather of my great-grandfather, Ephraim Gurley (1765–1845), after whom Gurleyville was named. It is a pleasant village stretching along a narrow plain above the meadows east of the Fenton River. Geologically the plain is a terrace left by the receding waters of the last glacial period. It is still marked here and there by potholes, which we boys who used to play about them, called Indian wells. Coming down from the hills, Ephraim Gurley acquired a long stretch of this terrace of varying width. More than half of the houses on each side of the road, all but one of which are still standing, were built by him and his son, Lucius Gurley (1797–1872), who was my grandfather. A hundred years ago a neat Methodist church was built commanding the highway, upon land given by Ephraim Gurley.

In my childhood Gurleyville with its two stores was the center of a community comprising nearly three miles of the valley of the Fenton River.

East of the village the land rises for more than a mile over hills and small brook valleys with roads, and, when I was a boy, with lanes and footpaths connecting one farmstead with another, all survivals of the Colonial Period. These lands and paths have long since disappeared under the growth of bush and trees; and of many of the old farmhouses nothing remains but cellar holes. West of the river rise steep woodlands, with here and there an intervening clearing of arable land, until you reach the hilltops.

Though most of the Gurleys hitherto had been farmers, Ephraim Gurley was a keen businessman and a skilled mechanic who saw the industrial value of the Fenton River. At the foot of a steep hill down by the river he built a shop equipped with trip hammers for making bits, screw augers, steelyards, and other tools which found a ready market not only in Connecticut but also in adjoining states. My grandfather who grew up in the business carried it on for a short time after the death of his father; but in 1848, a month after the marriage of his daughter, Harriet Maria, to Samuel Cross he gave it up and bought in the name of himself and his son-in-law an old stone gristmill with attached saw and shingle mill down another steep hill by the river. Not long afterwards the property passed by deed to my father, Samuel Cross. Near by on the other side of the road was a comfortable red house where I was born April 10, 1862. Except for an addition to the kitchen the interior of the house remains nearly as it was in my boyhood, though its exterior has been changed almost beyond recognition by a veranda which was built on two of its sides some twenty years ago.

Like many other boys of the time I was named Wilbur after Wilbur Fisk, a Methodist leader and first President of Wesleyan University. When I reached maturity and learned about my family history I keenly regretted that I was not the Peter Cross of my generation. What a wonderful name that would have been for me on entering a public career! "Peter Cross the Governor of Connecticut!" It would have been good for thousands of votes.

A quarter of a miles away from my birthplace my grandfather, Lucius Gurley, lived in the center of the village in a house which he had built on rising ground, where he had a good view of all that was going on in front of the two stores as farmers and their wives drove in from a distance to make their purchases and at the same time to hear and tell the news.

The Lucius Gurley house in Gurleyville, where Wilbur Cross's family later lived. Lucius Gurley was Wilbur Cross's maternal grandfather. Photo ca. 1910. *Courtesy, Mansfield Historical Society*

Sometimes he might see a good horse trade which was one of the glories of Gurleyville. In imagination I see him yet sitting at leisure by his favorite window as if he were the lord of a manor. Lucius Gurley had the reputation of never being in a hurry. There was a story that while he was eating his noon dinner one of his men came running in to tell him a fire had broken out in his shop. He asked a few questions and then remarked that after he had finished his dinner he would go down and put it out. And he did put it out. Sometimes when as a small boy I was playing about the grist- and sawmill he would take me home for dinner with him. Although I was hardly tall enough to reach his hand, I could easily keep up with him as his gait was very slow. In some way I must have acquired that slow gait, for when I was walking along the dusty road even after his death not only boys but older people would shout out "Hello, old uncle Loosh!"

Occasionally I stayed over night with him and my grandmother. The day always began with family prayers as I knelt between his knees. After prayers we had breakfast. Then he would open a cupboard and break off a small piece of leaf tobacco and put it in his mouth. He made a little ball of it, no larger than a pea or a blueberry which he quietly rolled about in one or the other cheek all the morning wherever he might be. It was his intimate companion. On Sundays the Methodist minister, who was an Englishman, used to come in for luncheon between the morning and afternoon sermons, each one an hour in length. On those occasions grandfather would go to another cupboard and bring out a bottle of yellowish liquid, a little of which he would pour into two glasses, one for the minister and the other for himself. It must have been good, for both smiled and smacked their lips and the minister usually asked for another. He got it and grandfather got one too. The tobacco grandfather grew in his garden solely for his own use, and years before he had made the rum, which had mellowed with age, in a still he built beneath a small cliff in the rear of the house lot. As with rum and tobacco, he cut at the roots of costs in all things. When toolmaking ceased to be profitable he moved the shop up the hill near his house where it might be available for making and sharpening such tools and utensils as were needed on his little farm. Even the charcoal for his forge he made in his own kiln from wood that grew on his own land. A woodshed he once turned into a pretty dwelling which may still be seen. He also built a mill for threshing out clover seed at the foot of a fall of water on a brook flowing into the Fenton River and, when the farmers in the district were supplied with all the clover seed they wanted, he took down the mill and used the timber so far as it would go for building a large house opposite his own. In June the roadsides and fields of Gurleyville were bright with red clover.

Once he deposited in the Hartford Society for Savings $150 to be kept there for an emergency. When the emergency came and the deposit was withdrawn for him fourteen years later by my brother George, it amounted to $317.25. As the teller pushed the money through the window he remarked that they say money doesn't grow but this seems to have. On leaving the bank I asked my brother what the man meant by saying that my grandfather made money grow. I was thinking of how God makes the grass grow. Outside of real estate my grandfather invested in nothing but bonds and bank stocks. The first time I saw him cut a coupon from a bond I thought that it might be a shinplaster. Still he did not look quite like a shinplaster, so I asked him what he called it. Lucius Gurley, I daresay, never lost a cent on any investment.

And here I am. I have looked back over three centuries of ancestors who were very human men and women. Something of what I have said has come down by tradition in the Cross family. Three centuries is traditionally a long time, but to me for various reasons it seems but yesterday. When a boy I often sat by and overheard the conversation between my father and his sister Eunice when she came on a visit from her home twenty miles away. Brother and sister talked of the two Peters and of their great-grandfather Wade as if they were still living. They seemed to be amused by anecdotes they repeated about the second Peter and they spoke of Wade, "the gentleman," with great respect. As I was very young the details of their talk have mostly passed from memory. But from time to time my father used to tell me about King Philip's War and he once showed me where the first Peter built his stockade to drive the Indians out of the Natchaug Valley. He was equally familiar with the Pequot War, though so far as I remember he never mentioned the name of William Cross. Nevertheless he regarded Windsor, where William Cross owned land as well as in Wethersfield, as the home of the family.

Being the child of my father, the members of the Cross and related families all along the chain have seemed to be almost alive for me also. I can imagine meeting any one of them and looking him or her over to see what traits of character and behavior are mine also. What about William Cross, the adventurer? In what sense, I may ask myself, am I an adventurer too? What about the first Peter Cross? I feel sure that if I had lived in his time I should have enlisted as a soldier in King Philip's War. In changed circumstances what battles have I fought in civil life? Instead of having a bullet put through my head, I have been consigned to hell by a considerable number of political enemies. What about Wade Cross in his blue coat and blue stockings? If he stepped into my room, I should have to tell him that as a Yale man I loved a particular shade of blue. What about the second Peter, the teller of tales? Haven't I told many tales in which imagination has played its full part? What about my grandfather Eleazer? I was for three months a teacher in the Gurleyville school where he gave his last talk to children. What about my great-grandfather, Ephraim Gurley? I should have to say to him that I have no mechanical skill whatsoever, though I have been intensely interested in reading such sheets of his account books as have survived, which have told me a few things about his business transactions. What about my grandfather, Lucius Gurley, whose daughter was my mother? Here I must pause and think over what I have just said about that grandfather. Does the slow pace I was reputed to have acquired from him indicate a mind like his which moves forward "without haste but without rest"? It may be that I have also inherited the Scot's thrift which has kept my budget in balance. But in these times I can hardly grow my own tobacco or distill my own liquor so that they may cost me not much of anything. The best I can do is to limit (financially, at least) my indulgence in both.

My intimate association with my grandfather and my acquaintance with still older men greatly foreshortened for me the three centuries of family history. All through childhood I learned of the past not from books but from the lips of men and women. Several of them were born before the surrender of Cornwallis at Yorktown. I recall visits with my father to Daniel Fuller, the last innkeeper of the Fuller Tavern at Mansfield Four Corners. He was born in 1778 and was then ninety-four or ninety-five years old. On one occasion we sat with four generations of the Fullers while the old innkeeper, who had become as blind as a bat, told stories of the old coaching days along the turnpike which Washington had traveled from Boston to New York. Several times my father took me on a long trail through the woods to call on Asa Simons who was born five years before the Declaration of Independence. He was the great-grandfather of Bruce Simonds, Dean of the Yale School of Music. My father usually brought along old newspapers from which he read to Asa Simons and his wife as they sat in rocking chairs smoking clay pipes. There was much talk about old and new things. When I last saw Asa Simons he was in his hundredth year. His dwelling, barn, and sheds were in a field from which a grassy lane led to a narrow dirt road more difficult to travel than the lane itself. His nearest neighbor dwelt in a similar field but with another way out to another road. In fact the whole of that part of Mansfield was but a network of lanes and bad roads impassable in the snows of winter and the floods of spring.

Besides taking me on visits to see old men, my father loved the old ways of life not much different from the life of the first settlers who came into the wilderness. His heavy cowhide boots, for example, he often had made by an old shoemaker who when a young man used to go from house to house making and repairing boots and shoes for families on his route. Occasionally, too, he wore a suit of wool spun by the wife of an old farmer and made by the farmer himself, who had been a tailor. It may be that the wool had been shorn from sheep in the farmer's own fold. In traveling my father preferred the stagecoach to the railway, if one were available. On my first trip to Hartford we walked two miles before daybreak to catch a stagecoach which took us as far as Bolton Notch, where we boarded a train for the rest of the journey. My mind, alert for all that was going on, was thus unconsciously creating for itself a background of a far-distant past as if I had been a part of several generations.

I have here traced the two main streams of my lifeblood back to the earliest settlements in Massachusetts and Connecticut, not out of any particular pride so much as out of curiosity to discover whence I came. This is not to deny that as a Governor of Connecticut I felt it an honor to be in descent from the great Governor Bradford, who came over in the *Mayflower*. This fact, however, I never proclaimed to the citizens of my native State, remembering too well the remarks of Will Rogers that his ancestors met the boat. He reckoned that he was "about one eighth cigar-store Injun." On that basis perhaps I could qualify as an Indian, for I have been adopted in the Iroquois Tribe as "Big Chief," entitled to a piece of land on one of their reservations whenever I desire to go into retirement.

II. A Lost Village

When I came on the scene Gurleyville was in the heyday of its prosperity. The entire Fenton River Valley was then alive with the silk industry. How this came about is an interesting story. Midway in the eighteenth century the cultivation of silkworms began in Connecticut and other colonies. Mansfield was one of the first places anywhere in the New World to see what silk might contribute to the material welfare of the people. For a long time the industry was carried on in private houses where the cocoons were raised and the silk was reeled from them by hand. This phase of silk culture had not come quite to an end when I was a boy. I used to climb mulberry trees whose leaves had once fed silkworms, and once I saw the silkworms at work on the garret of a farmhouse. The transition in the manufacture of silk thread from the home to the mill came soon after 1800 when Horatio Hanks invented the double wheel head for spinning silk. In 1810 Horatio and his brother Rodney built their little silk mill well up the hill on a plain in the Fenton River Valley where a small stream provided sufficient waterpower. This was the first silk mill, it is agreed, to be built in America. In appearance it looked like a very small house. As the business grew a larger mill became necessary, but the old mill was moved a short distance to higher ground where one of the Hanks boys, a few years older than myself, installed a hand printing press. With this first silk mill in the United States I have a slight connection in that I there learned how to set type. A few years ago the building was purchased by Henry Ford and carried away to his industrial museum in Dearborn, Michigan. There one may see the processing of silk done in the Mansfield manner of more than a hundred years ago.

The Hanks' mill set an example for three mills on the Fenton River, one of which displaced the tool shop of Ephraim Gurley. With the decline of silkworm culture in garrets, which became unprofitable by 1840, importation of raw silk from China began and silk manufacturing was placed upon a wider and firmer basis. The three mills were all enlarged from time to time and the steam engine eventually became necessary to supplement the water wheel. Boarding houses were built for young men and women who came in from distant farming districts to carry on the work. The business was hardly retarded by the depression in the 'seventies. All through my boyhood Gurleyville flourished almost as a community sufficient unto itself. The farm and the silk mill were held in almost equal balance. Farmers exchanged their products at the two stores for what they did not grow themselves: for sugar, molasses, flour, crackers, confectionery, patent medicines, kerosene oil, nails, ribbons, dress goods, boots, shoes, etc., on to the end. In turn workers in the mills, then called "help," bought at the stores not only these products which came from afar but also the immediate products of the farm such as butter, eggs, cheese, fruits, potatoes, turnips, and other vegetables. Convivial members of both groups were ready customers for beverages bearing names like Plantation Bitters, Orange Grove Bitters, and Quaker bitters, on each bottle of which was a Quaker in broad-brimmed hat and knee breeches. It was, you see, a happy as well as a prosperous community.

There was a brisk demand for sewing silk manufactured in the Gurleyville district, which was run off on spools by pretty girls who easily found husbands. These girls were nicknamed "spoolers." Down to the time of the Civil War and somewhat later sewing silk from the Gurleyville mills was distributed by local pedlars, many of whom were young men who wanted to see the world outside of Mansfield as well as to make a little money. I can imagine them as they set out on foot, with flowered carpetbags filled with silk, one in each hand, for neighboring towns within the State or across the borders. Their customers were housewives and small country stores. One of these pedlars I knew well when he had reached middle life. He liked to tell how he once drew a prize of $5,000 in a lottery over in Providence; but he always regretted that he had to pay a man $500 to collect the money from him. This was an old trick of sharpers in lottery days. So easy was it to sell silk thread that a young man who failed to make good was called a "good-for-nothing" for the rest of his life. One such fellow came back from a fortnight's trip with his carpetbags as well stuffed as when he started out. "What," his father asked him, "have you got in them bags?" "Silk," was the reply. "Didn't you sell any of that silk?" "No," replied John. "Were there in inquiries?" "One man," replied John, "asked me what I had got in them bags, and I told him it was none of his damn business." Everybody laughed whenever that story was told.

As the manufacturing of silk grew, the product was distributed in larger quantities by pedlars with horse and wagon, who drove north to the Canadian border and south as far as Georgia. Of these pedlars on a large scale, none was more successful than Ebenezer Gurley, a cousin of my grandfather's, whose shrewdness led him on to a fortune. Out of his profits as a pedlar, he accumulated enough funds to become a middleman between the importer of raw silk from the Orient and the manufacturer. On one occasion he was able, with the assistance of a New York importer, to get control of all the raw silk on the market and all that was on the ocean due to arrive in port. By this corner of the market he made a comfortable fortune, and settled in Mansfield as a farmer on spacious lands by the graveyard of his Scottish ancestors, all of whom he had outstripped in the virtues of his race. Ten years after Ebenezer Gurley's clever stroke, the speculator and pedlar, except for sporadic instances, had disappeared and silk manufacturing had assumed the regular channels of trade. I was then playing about in the roads and fields of Gurleyville.

For the first nine years of my childhood the family lived most of the time in the house where I was born by the river. There I opened my eyes on the old stone mill with its large wooden water wheel, on the up-and-down saw which made boards out of logs, and on the stages of converting corn on the cob into meal or buckwheat into flour. Men and boys of all ages brought in small loads of grain and waited for it to be ground amid talk and jokes and laughter. My first trout I caught in a dark pool under the bridge below the mill. In taking him off the hook, the barb caught me in the forefinger and I yelled till my father came and removed it in the same way that it would be removed from the mouth of a fish. Near the same time I received a smart kick from a horse hitched to a post in front of the mill which hurt me less but frightened me more.

Many memories of the household come back to me, one by one. On two evenings in succession I walked in my sleep, coming out into the sit-ting room where my mother waked me up. Never before and never since have I so lost myself; it is agreed that as a rule I have known what I was doing. Sometimes my mother had a girl with a long nose come in late in the afternoon or early in the evening to do the ironing. Once, I remember, as darkness was coming on, the girl had difficulty in finding the best spot on the table for a large lamp. She tried it here and she tried it there, moving it back and forth all over the table. Amused by her perplexity, I asked my mother and sister Adelaide, who were watching the process, why the girl didn't hang the lamp on her nose. This seems to have been my earliest attempt at a wisecrack. I was then four years old. Sometime before that, while I was in dresses, my sister Adelaide made me a beautiful brocaded coat and short trousers. She and my mother tried them on me to see how they would fit. Soon my mother made a move to take them off, saying that I was not old enough yet to wear a boy's suit. There ensued a lively squabble which was quieted by my sister who persuaded my mother to let me wear the flowered suit until bedtime if I would agree to stay indoors. By this incident perhaps I learned that it is sometimes better to compromise on a question at issue than to run the risk of certain and disastrous defeat.

A few months later Adelaide, of whom I was very fond, fell into a quick decline and died in my grandfather's house. She was only seventeen years old. When she died on a cold winter morning I was in school a little dis-tance up the hill learning to read. As if frightened out of his wits my older brother John rushed into the schoolroom and shouted "Adelaide is dead." The schoolteacher wept and at once dismissed the children. Ten minutes later I was lifted up on the bed to see for the last time a delicate and beau-tiful face lying quiet on the pillow. This was my first sight of death. Two or three days afterwards six boys of the village bore Adelaide on their shoulders to the churchyard a quarter of a mile away. For months and months thereafter one friend or another would call on my mother to tell her that Adelaide had appeared to them as in life, walking along the road or coming up the pathway towards their house, only to vanish suddenly as if a spirit. Visions of that sister in life and in death began to haunt me also. And they haunt me still.

In my tenth year my field of observation began to be greatly widened in ways that were to prove most significant. On the death of my grandmother, Abigail Gurley, in the spring of 1871, the family moved up the hill into the house of my grandfather so that my mother might look after him, for his health was beginning to break. He died after a short illness the next year. My father sold the saw- and gristmill, and thereafter until his own death in November, 1876, devoted himself to improving the land and buildings which my mother had inherited. Our habitation was now in the center of a lively village.

The foremost of the Lares of the family was a beautiful clock which my grandfather bought soon after he built the house in which we were living. As a lesser household divinity there hung by its side an English bull's-eye watch of his youth. Visitors admired the clock and asked questions about it. Sometimes my grandfather took off the dial for them so that they might have a look at the wonderful works within. But I never saw anyone except him touch the clock until I touched it myself. It was so intimate a part of him that when it stopped an hour before his death there was great excitement in the household, for the clock's behavior was regarded as a clear omen that the end of life for grandfather was near at hand. Not understanding the mysterious words, I stole into the room where the clock sat silent on its shelf and quietly opened the lower door to see what had happened. To my amazement I saw that the clock, which my grandfather had wound up eight days before, had simply run down. I did not dare tell anyone what I had discovered.

No man could give himself more completely than my father to the work that lay before him. There were times when he managed both gristmill and sawmill single-handed, early mornings and long evenings being occupied in running the up-and-down saw through logs so that all the daylight there was could be given to grinding grain for customers coming in. This often meant a sixteen-hour day. But after he had disposed of this business and we were all settled in grandfather's house his work became less strenuous. In fact there was leisure for him provided he would take it. Even then, however, he sometimes listened to a call to return to the mills for a week in an emergency. About once a year he would say on an evening that the next morning he was starting out for Windsor to visit Earl Simons, a friend of his youth and a son of Asa Simons. He usually stayed on for a month assisting in the management of a famous old gristmill dating back to 1636. In these years of comparative leisure he was engaged when at home in all sorts of work such as clearing waste land and repairing old buildings, rarely going out of an evening except to visit a relative or friend.

He had a few books which he read over and over again. At that time they were for me unrelated books, some of which seemed to have no special connection with his personal history. Now as I look back upon them I become aware that they were really a part of the man himself. The Bible was always with him, particularly the Old Testament, the stories of which he told his children long before they were able to read. Of the three other books, the most significant was *The National Preceptor*, comprising selections in prose and poetry by Jesse Olney, a popular educator, a native of Connecticut who served for ten terms in the General Assembly and for one term as Comptroller of the State. This was an excellent collection, having extracts from some of the best verse and prose in the English language. Large space was given to Shakespeare, and even Sterne was represented in his sentiment and humor. *The National Preceptor* was designed not only to place good literature in the hands of the student but to give him practice in reading aloud. A large part of this book of more than three hundred pages my father, it seemed to me, had committed to memory, for he was ready to recite anything I asked of him. It was the foundation of such general culture as he possessed and from it he may have derived his effective manner of speech. *The National Preceptor* thus harks back to the time when he was teaching school over in Rhode Island. One of the poems which he liked to declaim carried him back to his life on the sea. It was called "The Mariner's Dream," and described the visions of home which the sailor boy sees as he lies asleep in his hammock at midnight, only to be awakened by storm and wreck which bear him to death beneath the waves.

As an antidote to nostalgia, if he felt any, he kept by him an illustrated book on the natives of Hawaii, whom, like other sailors, he called Kanakas, I used to watch him as he read on and on and smiled. Once I asked my uncle Franklin, who on his voyages always stopped at Hawaii on his way to and from the Northern Pacific, about the Kanakas. He told me that the natives took him prisoner, as the captain of the vessel, when he landed in Honolulu, placed him for safekeeping in a fort near the entrance to the harbor, and then left him alone as darkness came on. On a visit to Hawaii I saw the shallow little fort all grown over with grass and so was not surprised that my uncle was able to creep out towards morning and signal his ship. In spite of this hostile incident he, too, smiled when he talked about the Kanakas.

By another book of my father's I am still more or less perplexed. It was a descriptive treatise on astronomy with maps of the northern and southern heavens. Did he take this book with him around the Horn as a guide to a study of the stars? At any rate I learned about the stars from him as we watched the heavens on summer evenings.

Not long afterwards my father placed in my hands from some unknown source a copy of *Robinson Crusoe*, which begins with the account of a boy who like my father ran away to sea. It was not the *Robinson Crusoe* abridged and rewritten in words of two syllables for children; it was one continuous narrative just as Defoe left it with all its hard words and with no division into chapters. Nevertheless I puzzled my way through it. Before that time I had read Sunday School books telling stories about good boys and good girls who always obeyed their parents and so grew up into fine men and fine women, with here and there a bad and disobedient boy or girl who while stealing cherries from a neighbor's tree fell and broke one or both arms. I had read, too, romantic love stories without understanding them in the *New York Ledger* and the *Saturday Night* which my older brothers brought home. But *Robinson Crusoe* I regard as the first real book that I ever read. It never occurred to me that it was a story spun out of someone's head; for me it was a true account of a sailor who was shipwrecked on a desert island and lived there in a stockade, like the stockade of Peter Cross, all alone with his goats until he saw the footprints of Friday on the sand. So great was the impression made upon me by *Robinson Crusoe* that when I had an opportunity nearly forty years afterwards to edit one of forty books in a series I chose this one. At that time my son

Wilbur who was reading the novel drew for me a map of Robinson Crusoe's voyage to be published in the edition I then brought out of the great
classic, which, remarked Daudet, the French novelist, "is as nearly immortal as any book can ever be."

Men who have to do with writing professionally are expected to say
that they cannot recall a time when they were unable to read. This claim,
for instance, Conrad made for himself. Were Conrad and the rest posing
or did God endow them with poor memories? At any rate I can make
for myself no such claim as theirs, for I remember the first stages in learning to read, in accordance with the "antiquated" method which has long
since been cast aside. First I was taught the alphabet at home and shown
how to print both big and small letters. Then at a time when there were
no kindergartens in Mansfield, I was set when four years old to the little
red schoolhouse where my father and mother had learned to read. The
schoolteacher, who that first summer was a woman, would have five or
six of us children stand round her three or four times a day and ask us
what words we would like to learn to spell. Then she had us spell them
in chorus, and afterwards it was her custom to print them on the blackboard so that we might see how they looked. They were usually names of
simple objects about the room like ink, stove, and desk, or such as we
could see from the window like grass, hill, and road, or such as were familiar to us in our homes like dog, cat, and fire. I still remember when I
learned to spell the hard word "rock." After we had acquired a vocabulary
of a hundred or more words which we could spell as well as recognize at
sight, there came the primer and in my case at least storybooks which my
mother bought for me and a younger sister. Well I remember one story
which for a time I read every day. It was called *The Three Little Pigs*.

A year or two later I was reading or beginning to read everything at
hand. As a test, I suppose, my father sometimes asked me to read aloud the
headlines in the *Hartford Courant* (to which, though a Democrat, he was a
subscriber). On one occasion the headline concerned a lively caucus held
by one of the political parties. When I came to the word "caucus" I hesitated for a minute, and then pronounced it "ca-u'-cus." That must have

been in very early childhood, before I had learned either how to say it or what politicians did with it.

My mispronunciation of "caucus" indicates that children in learning to spell were taught to break up words into syllables, a practice which has since unfortunately gone out. In this oral manner we went through Webster's Spelling Book up to the lists of words at the end which were so difficult that they were known as jawbreakers. In all spelling classes the members stood in line for a match of wits, moving up or down as the case might be. To go from the head to the foot of a class on any word was so deep a humiliation that it sometimes caused an outburst of tears and hiccups. But I have no regrets that I learned to spell in the old way.

Nor have I regrets that I was put through courses in formal English grammar, which has since given me a touchstone for determining the grammatical correctness of any sentence I may write, however careless I may often have been in applying a test at my disposal. It was an unfortunate day when a decade later Richard Grant White convinced the schools that "English is a grammarless tongue." His contention initiated a style in writing characterized by billowy sentences having neither beginning nor end. Perhaps I put a slight brake upon this movement when long afterwards, in 1906, I insisted as chairman of a Committee on Uniform Requirements in English for Entrance to Colleges, that English grammar of a somewhat different kind should be restored to its former place in the curriculum of secondary schools. The requirement has happily been continued.

In the midst of grammar and spelling as taught in the Gurleyville school, I went on apace in reading. At that time the most popular books in Connecticut for secondary schools were a graded series of Readers edited by George Stillman Hillard. I went through them all with avidity. The *Sixth Reader* became my companion much as *The National Preceptor* had been my father's. There I had within the compass of a single volume of moderate size a wide variety of verse and prose, much of which by frequent reading I committed to memory without being aware of it. Some titles and short passages I have never forgotten. What, I ask myself now, has been the influence of this book upon me? It was, I surmise, a love of words for their own sake and the rhythms and cadences of prose as well as of verse which

I must have felt as I read the selections aloud. This is my conclusion, because I have the habit, as a rule, of reading sentences I write aloud or silently before I let them stand. The first word I was charmed by though I had no idea of its meaning, was "eloquence," often used by Hillard in his Readers. Until corrected by my father I pronounced it "e-lo'-quence."

The Sixth Reader had a long introductory treatise on elocution by Mark Bailey of Yale, to which no attention was paid by my teachers, though I read and studied it as well as I could by myself. Quite different, however, was the attitude of the School Visitor who quizzed and addressed us at least three times a year. He was a highly respected citizen of Mansfield, very formal in dress and manners and most precise in speech. He was the last gentleman of a type upon whom children looked with awe as if he were closely related to God himself. Yet children had no fear of him, he was so kind and considerate towards them. This visitor, then sixty-odd years old, whose name was Nelson Conant, always read to us a selection in the *Sixth Reader*, showing us what words should be emphasized and giving us the proper tone for reading the passage as a whole. Twice, I recall, he called upon me to read a piece in the way he had read it. Once it was an address by Henry Ward Beecher on the pleasures of autumn, beginning "Once more I stand upon this serene hilltop." At another time he asked me to read after him Lincoln's "Address at Gettysburg." He closed the exercise with a disquisition on the boyhood of Lincoln who he told us, once attended for a short time a school much like ours and then had to go out and make a living. In conclusion he said that some one of us boys might sometime become President of the United States. As he spoke this last sentence he laid a hand upon my head. The children looked on with sober faces as if a prophet had spoken. That night I related the incident to my father and mother. "Did Nelson Conant say that!" exclaimed my father, and smiled. My mother laughed for pleasure.

Hillard prefaced his selections with brief biographies of their authors, which were pretty interesting to one who had no knowledge of literary history. Graduates of Harvard and other writers like Longfellow associated with that institution were so well represented that I imagined Harvard to be the literary hub of the universe. There were in the book, I think, no more than two or three things by Yale men. When several years afterwards it was decided that I might go to college, this exalted view of Harvard as against Yale still held sway over me until a Yale student of the Class of 1878 informed me that Mr. Hillard was a Harvard man, who would, in his original sin, naturally favor Harvard at the expense of Yale. I was disenchanted. The Yale undergraduate probably claimed for Yale a long line of writers including contemporaries such as "Ike Marvel" and N. P. Willis. He also told me that Mark Bailey, who wrote that "wonderful" introduction on elocution was a Professor at Yale. I was torn between Yale and Harvard and very likely I eventually chose Yale because New Haven was only sixty miles away from Mansfield. Had I decided the other way I am fairly sure that I should have been very happy in my college career there. When Harvard in 1933 conferred upon me an honorary degree, that act freed me from my childhood dilemma by making me both a Yale man and a Harvard man to my perfect joy and satisfaction. As a matter of fact, Hillard treated Yale justly enough, for Yale was then at the nadir of her literary fame. Sinclair Lewis, Thornton Wilder, Archibald MacLeish, and Stephen Vincent Benét, for example, were not yet born.

After I entered Yale I was to become rather well acquainted with Mark Bailey in and out of the classroom. In Sophomore year he gave a required course in elocution with practice in reading and declamation. I was not a little disconcerted to observe that his lectures appeared to follow the general lines of his introduction to Hillard's *Sixth Reader*. Unsophisticated as I was, I was yet to discover that some college professors revamp year after year material a quarter century old. When a young man, Mark Bailey worked out an ingenious system of upward and downward "slides" of the voice in reading or reciting verse and prose. In training us, one by one, in declamation, he gave most attention to the emphatic downward slide at the end of the declamatory sentences, where many speakers like myself fail to let the voice fall. This slide he humorously named the "Amen slide," very appropriately too, for most people in uttering the word "Amen" come down with a bang as if all were over. If a student insisted upon keeping his voice on a level or on raising it, when he should come down hard with it, Mark Bailey used to jump up from his seat and bring his arms down with all the force he possessed, shouting, "Amen. Amen. Good God, Francis, can't you do any better than that?" He had, too, an elaborate system of gestures for appropriate emphasis in public speaking. To a student who let a hand drop down in front of him while orating, Mark Bailey would shout, "Stop that. No fig leaf gestures here." This was the jolly good fellow whom I knew only name when I was a Mansfield schoolboy, but who was destined to try to make an orator out of me!

With the fundamental processes of arithmetic I had very little difficulty. As was then the common custom, the multiplication table was sung by the class in chorus to a simple tune. Decimal numbers were used much less than now. As befitting the Yankee's desire to see his savings increase, there was considerable practice in computing compound interest over periods long enough to double or triple the original capital. In this and other computation involving interest, weights, and measures I became an adept. But I had a great dislike for intricate problems concerning the time it would take for A to do a piece of work with the aid of B and often with the further aid of C. This hostile attitude, I surmise, had its origin in the fact that a boy several years old than myself used to get me to do a large part of his manual work, such as throwing a big pile of wood into a shed, by threats that otherwise he would tell his guardian who ran a store, that I had stolen things like sticks of candy from jars on the shelves. Eventually I went on strike against this young blackmailer. And once a boy in school asked for assistance on a problem to determine the length of time required for A, B, and C to do a piece of work under certain conditions. Well I remember my relief at the reply of the teacher, who had a moderate sense of humor: "Don't bother about A, B, and C. How long does it take a goose to trot a mile?" But all through my schooldays A, in my view was a bad boy who imposed upon B and C as his victims. This I had learned from experience.

To one teacher, who was an older cousin of mine, Madison Cross, I owe a lasting debt for the practice he gave us in mental arithmetic. It is astonishing how far one can go in this method which is, of course, a survival of the time when paper and lead pencils cost money. Now head, paper, and pencil have been supplanted, where strict accuracy is required, by the calculating machine. Still, I have kept my head, which has been of very great value to me. When I was Governor of Connecticut I was given, in 1937, control over the administration of the budget, my head served me well in seeing how income and expenditures were moving along. Only when the margin was close did I have to ask Dr. Whitaker, an expert Budget Director, what his machines had to say.

Not long before I came along geography had been added to the traditional three R's of the curriculum of Connecticut common schools, though "reading, 'riting, and 'rithmetic" continued to hold the first places. The study of geography kept close to the plan set by Jesse Olney of *National Preceptor* fame, in his *American Geography*, a pioneer book, in which boys and girls were to learn first of their town, county, and State. Thus at the age of six I was bounding Mansfield and Connecticut, and naming the capitals of the State (of which there were then two), and the counties and county seats. The next step was to name and bound the other New England States and to name and locate their capitals. Thence we traveled through all the States and Territories of the Union, with brief accounts of their settlements, products, and industries. *Cornell's Geography*, more comprehensive than Olney's, which was used in the Gurleyville school would doubtless be strange reading now. There were then ten Territories, not counting Alaska; and as illustrations showed, buffalo were roaming over the plains and gold was being washed from the sands of mountain streams.

Less attention was given to Canada, Central and South America, and still less to Europe, Asia, and Africa. But they came into a general survey. Particularly valuable was a continuing study of the world as a whole with the aid of a globe, on which one saw at once the relative positions of continents, islands, oceans, and seas. It was fun to take the parallel of latitude running through New York City or Washington or London or Rome, and to follow it round the earth and observe the unexpected places it would hit. The knowledge of the earth which I got in this way afterwards served me in good stead. At that time Yale had not yet abandoned an entrance requirement in geography. When on a June morning in 1881 I read the entrance paper in geography which was handed to me, I smiled as I saw there a question on the course a parallel of latitude, getting its start at some American city, would take in going round the world. No such questions, I daresay, are now asked and answered anywhere except in some odd information coming over the radio. The earth now appears to be well-nigh lost for the majority of men and women who live upon it despite the conquest of land, sea, and air since my boyhood. That kind of knowledge which once came from the terrestrial globe may sometimes be appreciated in the Americas if a hostile nation ever gains a foothold well up on the western shore of Africa.

Very likely the picture I have drawn of the village school where I obtained my elementary education is lacking in dark shadows which have mostly faded out of my memory. No one of all the teachers—sometimes there were three in a single year, a different one for each of the three terms—was trained for the profession they had undertaken. Such qualifications as they possessed may be credited to temperament and experience only. Some were good and some were thoroughly bad. It was almost a crime to put children no more than four years old in a one-room school where little was provided for them to do. Four of us, I recall, sat on one long bench with a desk before us which concealed what might be going on below. We spent most of the time in pinching one another and in whispering to the disturbance of recitations which were being conducted near us. One master carried a pair of horse's bits in his pocket, which he used to toss on our desk when we got too noisy, where they struck with a rattle that silenced all other sounds. After a recitation was over he would put the bits into the mouth of one of us. Not a bad way to stop whispering throughout the entire school for that day.

During recess periods there were often quarrels on the little playground of which the master had a clear view from a window. Any quarrel that might occur he settled immediately after the school reconvened by bumping two heads together. Once my head got a good bumping against the head of a boy with whom I used to fish for trout and shoot gray squirrels. On another occasion, when I was six years old, a boy named Herbert Hopkinson tripped me in a friendly wrestling match, and I fell on a large rough rock, breaking my left arm above and below the elbow and putting

the elbow out of joint. It took four persons to set that arm while I sat in
a chair. One man held my legs, another man held my right arm, and the
surgeon had his wife press my head to the back of the chair as he restored
the bones to their proper places. I wept, I yelled. But it was all over in
three minutes, so skilled was the young surgeon, Julian N. Parker, a graduate of the Yale Medical School the year before.

Women teachers confined their discipline to the ferule which, as it hit
the palm of a hand, hurt worse than head bumping. Once I pulled my
hand away when the teacher came down with her ferule so that it hit
only the air. She, however, got the hand back and gave it the hardest strokes
it has ever received. But all in all, corporal punishment was more or less a
farce. As it was expected it did not disturb us much. And it was sheer
amusement when the other boy got the licking.

The real weakness of the rural school, as I have said, was that it did not
keep us busy. This was true mainly because its studies could be only loosely
graded on account of the short tenure of the teachers. Frequently a new
teacher did not go on in a study from the point where the previous
teacher left off but would go back to the very beginning of the book.
Constant review of this kind held in check the natural forward movement.
In my own case there was, however, some compensation., for I used my
unoccupied time in listening to the recitations of boys and girls older than
myself. In this way I kept the whole school going on in my mind.

With all its shortcomings I remember with keen gratitude a little red
schoolhouse built on the side of a hill, where the summer heat might be
so intense that teacher and children adjourned to the shade of huge walnut
trees by the side a brook in a neighboring pasture, and where winter
snows sometimes almost obliterated the building from sight and the door
could be reached only by digging a tunnel through drifts ten feet high.
What I learned there was to admit me easily into an excellent high school;
and the arithmetic and geography were to enable me later to pass the
examination in these studies for entrance to Yale College.

While yet a schoolboy, I was also living in the world of men. It happened in this way. In the summer of 1872 my brother George became of

age and in anticipation of that event my grandfather Lucius Gurley helped
him to buy out a general store, well situated across the road from the Gurley house, with a wide approach where customers found room for their
horses and buggies and oxen and carts. My grandfather dying before the
transaction was complete, my mother, who was his sole heir, assumed all
the obligations he had incurred. George soon married a good-looking
Irish girl of North Ashford, one of the spoolers in the largest silk mill,
and settled in the little house next door, the former woodshed which my
grandfather had transformed. My brother John took a job as spinner in
the silk mill near the site of the shop where my great-grandfather had
once set up his trip hammers for making tools. Though I was but ten years
old I was given free access to the store to help out as much as I liked
before and after school hours, on Saturdays, and during vacations.

Two parallel counters ran the entire length of the main store with a
wide space between for customers. Behind one counter were shelves for
light groceries, chewing tobacco, and patent medicines. On the counter
rested a showcase for assorted candies and another for cigars. At the ends
of the counter stood cracker and sugar barrels, while along in front of it
ran a row of nail kegs with their tops knocked in. Behind the other
counter were the shelves for a good variety of cotton goods including
beautiful domestic calicoes for ladies' dresses. On this counter a large
showcase made a display of ribbons and all things worn as ornaments by
factory and other girls. Boots, shoes, and crockery lined shelves in the rear.
A door led to a back room where a great hogshead of Porto Rican
molasses lay on a stout frame near a large cask of beef in brine, a small
cask of pickled mackerel, and a pile of dried codfish, at a safe distance
from a barrel of kerosene oil. A trap door took one into a dark and poorly
ventilated cellar, where were stored butter and eggs.

Outside the double-door entrance stretched a roofless veranda, on the
edge of which boys and young men from the silk mills found good
enough seats; for older men a row of rickety chairs was provided. Here
was the usual scene for horse trades. On winter evenings the crowd gathered within the store, sitting on counters, barrels, and nail kegs. Well back
in the space between the counters a large sheet-iron stove was set up as a

protection against the winter's cold; in front of it lay an old raisin box filled with sand or moist sawdust for the benefit of tobacco chewers. An expert could easily hit the box from the cracker barrel on which he was perched. Ten feet away was a sure shot. By this stove I learned the ways of men and women too.

As soon as I was permitted, I jumped into the midst of things, with both eyes and both ears wide open to see and hear everything. Within a year, at the age of eleven, I was often left alone to manage the business when my brother was out taking orders; and within two years I was keeping the books of the concern, sitting in glory on a high stool before a high desk. All sorts of people came in for trade, some playing in cash, others paying in barter with eggs, butter, cheese, and potatoes, and in season with strawberries, apples, and huckleberries. They were always talking to one another; they were newsmongers; they told racy stories in low voices which they thought I did not overhear; girls whispered secrets to one another which they thought I could not possibly hear or at least not understand. They were all mistaken. If I did not understand at once, I soon learned to understand. But I kept my mouth shut.

These whispering girls in their teens amused me. They cultivated small feet, claiming that the shoes they wore were of the size marked 3½. Not to be exposed, they used to come in for their shoes when I was alone in command of the store. I would look their feet over and pick out a pair of shoes that would fit. Then they would ask me what the size was. A direct answer to this question I had to evade pleasantly by saying that no dependence could be placed upon any marks the shoes might bear; and the sale was quickly made, though the shoes really belonged to the 5 or 5½ class. Likewise I was amused by a confidential conversation between the chairmen of the Republican and Democratic town committees a few days after the presidential election of 1876. They spoke in very low voices not far away from me. I learned that of the 450 voters in the town they bought 54 in all, paying on the average $5 a piece. I learned further that each chairman kept in his own pocket about $150 of the cash that was sent him from the headquarters of his party in Hartford to pay "the legitimate expenses" of getting out the voters. Neither of these thrifty Yankees,

I concluded, was in politics for the fun of it.

A "House of Commons," as it was sometimes called, assembled late in the afternoon or early in the evening either on the veranda or inside the store, depending on the season or on the weather. It was a variable group of men who came in for their mail and sat on until somebody said it was time to go home. (My father, though a good mixer, was for some reason never there.) In their talk there was little or no reserve. They spoke frankly about themselves, their families, and their neighbors; and their comment on what was occurring outside their little world, in Hartford or in Washington, was marked by shrewd common sense. They were unsophisticated people such as a novelist likes to depict because they said what was really in their minds. As a rule they were honorable and truthful men except in horse trades, where it was understood that the better liar is the better man. As a boy I was most interested, except for politics, in horse trades, funny stories, and what are now called wisecracks.

It is a late summer afternoon. A man nicknamed Toot drives up before the group seated on the veranda, cutting as he does so a wide circle, with reins held tight. As he jumps from his buggy someone says: "I see, Toot, you've got a new hoss." "Yes, sir." "Where did you get him?" "None of your damn business." Another asks: "How old is he?" "Going on nine." Everybody laughs. And another asks: "May I look into his mouth?" "You may look into him anywhere you damn please. But look out that he don't bite you." After inspecting the horse's teeth the man shakes his head and smiles; and as he walks slowly back into the crowd, someone inquires: "What did you find?" The inspector of the horse's teeth directs his reply to the whole company: "I guess he is of age all right. I guess Toot has to cut his hay pretty fine for them teeth." Toot's retort is that the horse is nearer eight than nine years old and that he sold his feedcutter long ago. Still another man asks: "Any objection, Toot, to my feeling that off hind leg? Unless I am blind there is a spavin there." "You may feel of his legs or of his tail if you want to get kicked in the guts." The man rubs his right hand along both hind legs for a long while and soberly announces that the horse is badly spavined in both hind legs. With a profusion of profanity

Toot gives him the lie and offers to poke him in the face. As soon as quiet is restored, a newcomer who has hitched his horse and buggy near Toot's and has listened in without yet saying anything, turns to Toot with "How about a trade?" "No more hoss trades for me," Toot replies in a decisive tone. "I've got here just the kind of hoss I have been looking for all my life. Young. Sound as a dollar. With no outs except that he is rather hard on the bit. I'll keep the cuss until he dies on my hands." By this time everybody is laughing. Soon the newcomer breaks in again: "Any objection, Toot, to my taking a little turn with the hoss down the road and back?" After a minute's hesitation Toot replies to the courteous request: "Not alone. I'll go along with you. I'll drive and you set on the seat with me." In fifteen minutes they return. Not a word is spoken by anybody. The crowd is just looking on to see what may happen. Toot and the newcomer alight. Each begins to take the harness of his own horse to transfer him to the thrills of the other buggy. That was one kind of a horse trade. No cash, of course, was involved. It was clearly an even swap.

It did not take me long to make the acquaintance of most of the horses within several miles of the village as I observed them and heard tales about them. Many of them had tricks which a driver had to guard against for his safety on the road. My brother George had his troubles with horses of this kind. His first horse on beginning business was a mare which he kept in a stable behind the store. Whenever I went into the stall to lead her out she started to kick and bite unless handled very gently. A year or so afterwards she caught the "epizootic," a violent and nasty influenza, and at the same time developed a bad case of scratches on two legs, which lamed her terribly. On a day when a trade was imminent it was my job to curry her off and to loosen up her legs by running her round the backyard while the terms of the trade were being discussed in the store. After I had finished with her she looked pretty well as she stood in the shed with the scratches partly concealed by the hair of her fetlocks. My brother and the other man came out to take a view of her. In reply to several questions indicating some suspicion on the part of the other man, we assured him that the epizootic was disappearing and that the application of arnica for another week on her sore legs would effect a perfect cure. He appeared to be fairly well satisfied with this prognosis, and the trade was made after some haggling over what my brother should pay to boot—whether it should be $15 or $20. When the transaction was over, each party seemed to be the happiest man in the world. Each thought he had fooled the other. And it was so in a sense neither anticipated.

My brother had got in exchange for the old mare, who went to the boneyard a year later, a young Canuck, a name then common for a rather small horse bred in French Canada. He had taken him on a wild gamble, having never seen him before the trader appeared. As soon as the old mare was out of sight my brother asked me if I thought the Canuck had any outs. I told him that when I led the horse towards the stable he acted as if he didn't want to go there and that when I finally coaxed him into the stall he was so nervous that he shook all over. That was so bad an omen that my brother shook all over like the horse. He proposed that we go out and hitch the Canuck into the buggy for a trial of his speed. With great difficulty we got the Canuck, who kept whirling around, between the thills and at last we were able to fasten the traces to the whippletree. Then we jumped into the buggy, my brother holding the reins. The Canuck reared, plunged forward, and then backed us round all over the yard, while George kept exclaiming, "Sold again, by God."

In course of time the Canuck was swapped for a large and beautiful horse who had the trick of throwing his tail over one of the reins and then running at full speed. In turn he was swapped for a very gentle horse who, while trotting along, stepped on a rolling stone and fell to the ground breaking a thill and throwing me over the dashboard among his heels. These were the kind of horses I associated with. In a boy's way I tried to train them out of their tricks, which, however, I kept as secret as I kept the size of shoes worn by girls in the community. Also I used to ride bareback and always rode my father's mare in that way. I loved horses of all sorts and learned from them characteristics of behavior not very remote from the characteristics of some men and women I have had to deal with in private and public life. There is very little difference between tricks of horses and tricks of men.

In school a boy learns from books; in a store of the old village type he

learns, as I have intimated, from the conversation of men who have lived
and are still living. Men, then in middle life, who had fought through the
Civil War in different regiments were always telling of their experiences in
this and that battle or in the prison at Andersonville when they were captured, or of the fun they had in camp or of their fraternizing with the Rebs
when on picket duty, swapping matches for tobacco, and smoking together,
and hoping that the war would soon end. The dreadful scenes on the fields
of Shiloh and Antietam were embedded in my memory. Naturally as a boy
I was entertained by the lighter side of war such as raids on sutlers who
followed the army with provisions and whisky which they sold to the
troops at high prices. I liked to hear a big jovial Irishman tell how he was
"kilt" at the battle of Shiloh for twenty minutes. Apparently he had been
stunned by a stray bullet and lay unconscious for a time he estimated to
have been twenty minutes. We did not know that "kilt" is a Celtic word
meaning "stunned," having no relation to English word "killed." So we
thought he claimed to have been killed for twenty minutes. The best liar
among the veterans was a man who lost a leg at Antietam. Like a Sir John
Falstaff he boasted, when he had a chance, of the number of Rebs he had
killed in hand-to-hand fights. No one believed his impossible stories but
we listened and encouraged him to go on.

Another good liar, who had been in several hard battles, used to claim
that nothing in war ever frightened him so much as the strange things
that were happening in the haunted house where he was now living. Last
night, for example, while he was reading the *Hartford Times* he heard
screams coming from the cellar. "I lighted a candle and went down the
cellar stairs. All was still until I got back to the top of the stairs and then
the screams began again louder than ever. I was skeered, you bet. I picked
up the newspaper again, and then there was a noise in the hall as if someone had dropped from the top of the stairway a barrel which fell all to
pieces as it struck the floor. I went out into the hall but there was no
barrel there. So me and my wife decided to go to bed. But as soon as we
got into bed the bedstead began to rise until the posts touched the ceiling;
then it slowly came down again. By that time my wife was skeered too."
While he was telling his story his young wife, who, he said, was afraid to

stay in that haunted house alone, sat on a counter smiling. At this point someone inquired of him what kind of whisky he was drinking nowadays. "Nothing," he replied, pointing to a shelf, "but Plantation Bitters. George, let me have a bottle to take home to put me and my wife to sleep tonight." The evening's entertainment, with the audience sitting on counters, nail kegs, and cracker barrels, might close with a short disquisition by a malapropian gentleman on the origin of the Civil War. He invariably began: "When old Boreeguard turned his guns on Fort Smutter, that meant war."

Sessions of the House of Commons were enlivened by jests and ribaldry. There was one story which I have several times repeated in addressing medical associations. On a Friday evening when there was a full house, a man, known for short as Captain, who had come in from a distance, inquired for the news and was told that "old man Storey" up on the hill was sick. "What is the matter with him?" "I don't know exactly, but he has a fever of some sort." "Is he round the house or is he in bed?" "He's in bed." "Who's his doctor?" "Dr. Richardson." "God he's in for a fit of sickness all right." Dr. William Henry Richardson, an early graduate of the Yale School of Medicine, had the reputation, quite undeserved, of prolonging the illness of his patients for the increase of his earnings. A more obvious characteristic of him was a strong sense of fear for himself. He feared catching cold. On a hot summer day he might be seen driving through the village in overcoat and muffler. He was afraid also to come near a patient who might have a contagious disease. Once when I was severely poisoned with ivy he was called in. He entered the door of a large room at the other end of which I was lying on a couch. He took a step and stopped. He took another step and stopped and looked, and so on till he was within two feet of me. He thought I might have the small-pox of which there were a few cases in the State.

It was inevitable that I should now and then try my hand at a jest. One of them I recall, doubtless because I received a reprimand for it from my brother George. It was a rainy afternoon; I was left in sole charge of the store. Among a dozen or more men sitting about and gossiping was a short stout young fellow called "Tubbydub." Generally hard up, he was slow in paying his bills. On that rainy day he began looking over the whips which hung from a rotating circle fastened to the ceiling. He took one down; and stepping out in the middle of the floor, he gave it a hard crack. In the same way he tried out two more whips. By that time I was getting a little nervous and remarked: "You know, Tubby, it don't do them whips any good to snap them like that." He took down no more and walked away from them amid the smiles of the audience, as I asked him pleasantly whether he couldn't find the kind of whip he wanted. His replay was that none of them was long enough to reach his hoss's ears. As I had come near the mark with my first shot from my popgun, I now aimed at the bull's-eye, "Well, I guess, Tubby, if you took one of them whips home on tick it would be long enough before you paid for it." The next morning I was warned, half seriously, by my brother to whom Tubbydub had complained, never to say anything that would drive away customers.

Humor and rough jests played a part as a relief even in the most acrimonious political discussions and debates, which rose to their height during state and national campaigns. I faintly recall the presidential campaign of 1868 (I was six years old) when young Republicans formed an organization called Boys in Blue, wearing on their coats ribbons which bore the names of Grant and Colfax; and young Democrats in a similar organization were all dressed in white, with ribbons inscribed with the names of Seymour and Blair. Both Blues and Whites were picturesque groups, rather highfalutin in talk and manner. I had not yet come to understand that there was any political antagonism between these local groups who were very friendly whenever I saw them together, drinking something out of bottles which they carried in their hip pockets. I looked on and wondered. But intimations of what political parties meant were not long a coming after that. During my first campaign for Governor, in 1930, doubts were thrown by political orators on whether I was really a Democrat, or only a Republican who was posing as a Democrat. Henry Hanks, then a man ninety years old, who had known me from childhood, came to my rescue with a story to show that I had been a Democrat almost from birth. Though he exaggerated in some details he gave of the story, as when he said that it spread all over Mansfield, he was not far out of the way. It is a good story, which I will retell in my own way.

There was a farmer about half a mile from the village named Jefferson Dunham who, despite the name given him by his parents, was so ardent a Republican that he named his son, a year or two older than myself, Frémont in honor of General Frémont, the first Republican candidate for the presidency of the United States. About once a week or fortnight Frémont and I used to play together about the farm and in season gorge ourselves with watermelons and muskmelons, sitting in the shade of the field where they grew, after he had finished his morning tasks with my help. It was understood that I was to stay for noon dinner. As soon as we came into the house Frémont's father, seated in a big chair, would shout out in a sharp voice humorously intended to frighten me: "Wilbur, come here." Then holding me tight as I stood between his legs facing him, he would put me through a series of questions with answers which he taught me to give. "Who was the first man?" "Robert Carr"—who, though not very old, looked older than he was. "Who was the first woman?" "Sally Carr," who had been my nurse. "Who was the first President of the United States?" "George Washington." "Who is President now?" "General Grant." "Who is the Governor of Connecticut?" "Marshall Jewell." "That will do." And I would be released from the clasp of those knees, with a loud laugh that resounded through the house.

All went well with answers, true and false, until 1870 when Marshall Jewell of Hartford, the Republican candidate for Governor, was defeated by James E. English, a New Haven Democrat. Soon after the election, perhaps the next day, I was in the village store where my brother George was then but a clerk. A few men, mostly Republicans, began talking about the election while I was listening in. Unexpectedly Philo Hanks appeared, an older brother of Henry Hanks, and the most active Democratic politician in the town. Presently Philo turned to me and said, "When Jeff Dunham asks you who is the Governor of Connecticut tell him that his name is James E. English." He made me repeat it several times over in a loud voice, to the amusement of the Republican spectators. When Jeff Dunham next put me through his quiz I shouted, as I was instructed to do, "James E. English." "Who told you that?" he asked. I replied, "Philo Hanks." And Jeff shook with laughter. Before he let me go he asked me whether I was a Republican or a Democrat. He got in return, "I am a Democrat. Philo Hanks says you are nothing but a Black Republican." I was but eight years old when I thus first announced to the world that I was a Democrat. Jeff Dunham as well as Philo Hanks spread the story, but Jeff quizzed me never more.

Such was the earliest background for my political education which really began two years later when I was acting, with many interruptions, as clerk in my brother's store. There could have been no better place for such a course in politics, for the village store was a microcosm of the whole United States. Nor could there have been a better period for directly observing political history. The question whether "To the victor belong the spoils" still had its reverberations. So, too, the impeachment proceedings against Andrew Johnson continued to be a live issue between the two leading parties. Likewise opinion was divided on the Fifteenth Amendment to the Federal Constitution granting suffrage to Negroes. Though President Grant was of stainless character, he was without political experience and without administrative ability. As a consequence he was duped by politicians; and corruption crept into his very cabinet of advisers. In the name of reform Horace Greeley, whose *New York Tribune* all Republicans in Connecticut read, ran against Grant for President in 1872, on a fusion ticket of Democrats and liberal Republicans. Immediately after his nomination by two parties many men donned the tall gray Greeley hats, more or less for sport, but they soon laid them aside. Greeley never had a chance. He went down to defeat and death. Corruption still went on apace, mightier than ever, in Congress and in the executive branch of the Federal Government. Under the battle cry, "Turn the rascals out," Tilden and Hendricks were pitted against Hayes and Wheeler in 1876. It was a hot campaign through which the Republicans swung high the bloody shirt. On the face of the returns the Democratic ticket won. But the election was contested by the Republicans. After an investigation by an Electoral Commission, on which the Republicans had a majority of one member, Hayes and Wheeler were declared elected by one electoral vote. From the Democratic point of view Tilden and Hendricks were counted out. Besides all these vents, the country sank under a deep economic depression aggravated by an inflated currency. In Connecticut as elsewhere men who had lost their jobs turned tramps, roaming through country districts, begging, stealing, robbing, and breaking into houses and stores for food to keep them alive. In those laissez-faire days, neither Federal, state, nor local governments felt any obligation to look after the unemployed. The only resting place for tramps was jail or prison. What a wonderful opportunity I had for hearing all the questions rising out of this unstable, ever-changing social scene canvassed and debated by a House of Commons improvised by a group of Connecticut Yankees!

There was no parliamentary restraint in that Yankee House of Commons. Everyone spoke the language to which he was accustomed, however profane or indecent it might be. Never before not since have I heard so many double negatives for emphasis; never before so may allusions to sexual and other functions of the human body or to the hencoop or barnyard. It was the raciest speech God or Satan every put into the mouth of man. At times eyes flashed and fists doubled up, though no blows were ever struck. Some of the liveliest sessions were when Ozro Hanks, the son of Philo Hanks, a clever, sassy boy no more than twenty years old, got into an argument with the local Justice of the Peace, a man of sixty, who, once a Democrat, went over to the Republican party in protest against the Dred Scott decision. No one interfered with that hot give-and-take, for all liked the fun too well for that.

The Justice of the Peace, Emory B. Smith, was one of the most substantial and highly respected citizens of the town. He began his career as a silk pedlar "across the Hudson" in the State of New York, but when I came on the scene he had become owner of one of the silk mills. A steady, conservative businessman, he had his humorous side also. He was, I think, the first to refer to the company that assembled for debate at the village store as a House of Commons. To enforce his arguments he used to quote Josh Billings or Artemus Ward or Brick Pomeroy. This was my first introduction to professional humorists. "As Brick Pomeroy says," he would so often begin his talk that his youngest son, Edward, was nicknamed Brick. Another son, Frank Clifton Smith, of my own age, was my most intimate chum. Later we were to prepare for college in the same high school and go to Yale together. It was through this companionship that while a schoolboy and a clerk I gained entrance to the court over which Frank's father presided. It was a rare chance to see so early in life how country justice was administered.

The court convened in the largest room in the house of the Justice, who sat at the head of a long table, with a lawyer, in important cases, on each side halfway down. A constable or occasionally a sheriff might be sitting at the foot of the table next to the man he had arrested. Spectators lined the wall. Frank and I usually took seats near a door opening into another room through which we might escape if the proceedings failed to interest us.

Most of the cases were of a criminal character involving, as a rule, assault and battery. Two men, for instance, get into a fight in which one is knocked senseless; or a man insults another while they are shingling a house and is kicked off the roof. A wife has her husband arrested because he takes her across his knees and spanks her and then boxes her ears. A blacksmith has his wife arrested because she plays an accordion over his head so that he cannot sleep while he lies, very tired, on a lounge in the sitting room after a hard morning at the forge. When he gets up and drives her to the other end of the room she throws a flatiron at his head, leaving bad cuts on his face which he shows to the court. Family troubles were occasionally settled then and there on the advice of the Justice; but invariably, so far as I can remember, the plaintiff won in all other cases, to my disappointment, for I had no use for anyone who squealed when he was licked. I did not yet know that there was in those days no fee for either justice or constable when a decision went in favor of the defendant; so I could not measure the influence which this fact may have had on the administration of justice.

The courtroom, like my brother's store, was a place of entertainment for boys long before Disney arrived with his Mickey Mouse. Nothing else was ever quite so entertaining as the cross examinations and browbeatings of witnesses or the scandalous abuse that passed between the lawyers. I remember the thrusts two lawyers once gave one another. The cleverer of the two was a Democrat and Episcopalian. The other was a Republican and Methodist. The first lawyer, who had been divorced, was on very friendly terms, it was whispered, with a woman whose husband had recently divorced her. The second lawyer, whose wife was the daughter of a Methodist minister who had presided for three years over the Gurleyville parish, had been, not long before, the administrator of a certain physician's estate which everybody supposed would turn out to be very large but which proved to be hardly anything at all. During a lull in the battle of tongues across the table, the Republican and Methodist asked the Democrat and Episcopalian how Mrs. . . . was getting along, naming the grass widow. The Democrat and Episcopalian replied that he didn't know anything about that; but that he did know that he hadn't got any of the doctor's estate. Whereupon the Republican and Methodist jumped up, struck his fists on the table and shouted: "Are you insinuating that I have taken for myself any of that doctor's estate?" "Oh, no, I am insinuating nothing about nobody. I merely remarked that I hadn't got any of Dr. . . . .'s estate."

Events were already occurring, however, which made me take a less comic view of a local court and a village store. I saw that business, however small, had its risks. One day my brother was informed that the property of which his store was a part had been bought by a father for a son who had a smaller store in the village. When it looked as if all were over with my brother, the Justice of the Peace, who was a friend of the family, came to his assistance by providing him with a store in a new building which he erected on land my mother sold to him at a low price. We were all happy again. On an afternoon when I was alone at the desk I wrote my first rhymes to help on the sale of the stock before our removal. I printed the lines in large letters on a big sheet of manila paper which I tacked to a shelf where they could be seen by everybody:

> Come on, come all, both small and great,
> And buy these goods before it's too late.
> They must be sold by April next,
> For Austin Royce this place expects.

A year or so afterwards, as I was running down to the new store early on a July morning to open up shop, I saw at once that the building had been entered during the night by breaking through a back window. I gave the alarm to my brother and the Justice of the Peace. A cursory examination showed that the money drawer had been cleaned of such shinplasters and coins as had been left there the night before, that there were missing some cigars and chewing tobacco, candy and sugar-coated cathartic pills, and that a gallon jug had been drained of its alcohol. Though the value of all the money and luxuries stolen was probably less than $25, it was a burglary. Who were the burglars? That was the question. I told the little company of investigators that on yesterday afternoon, while I was sitting outside, three tramps passed by and kept their faces towards the store as if they were looking it over. The Justice asked their approximate height, age, and dress, and the color of their hair. Posters were sent to all parts of the State offering a reward of $100 for their arrest and conviction.

Two weeks later, without any advance notice, the sheriff of Windham County, two of his deputies, and a so-called detective drove up to the store with the three men in handcuffs. I immediately identified them as the ones I had seen. That night the three tramps were put through the third degree with no result until something unexpected happened. Some years before, on looking through three large wallets of my great-grandfather, Ephraim Gurley, I had found among receipted bills several old colonial coins. One was a copper halfpenny and another was a silver sixpence. These and other rare coins I kept in an envelope at the bottom of the money drawer. In searching the tramps the officers of the law found them in a pocket of the youngest of the three, a boy only eighteen years old. On being confronted with this evidence against him, he collapsed and confessed to his part in the crime. The next morning the other two tramps were arraigned before the Justice of the Peace; they pleaded guilty and were bound over to the Superior Court of Tolland County, which met in September, when they were sentenced to State Prison for three years. In the meantime the boy, who was set free by the Justice of the Peace, stayed on in the village during the summer as a material witness for the State against his companions at their trial before the county court. For his support plenty of work was at hand in the hayfield at a good wage.

It so happens that I remember his name. It was Everett Herman Burgess. He was not a boy of the criminal type. He belonged to that great army of the unemployed who tramped the country during a business depression hitherto unprecedented. He had fallen in with older men who led him into crime, not as a way of life but as a way to live. We younger boys—thirteen or fourteen years of age—took Everett into our games as one of us. We played ball, pitched quoits, and swam in the river together. Never did I hear from him a profane word or a vulgar tale. I asked him to tell me the story of his life from childhood. Besides doing this, he gave me a good course of instruction in amateur burglary, describing the necessary tools, the various ways to break into a dwelling, office, or store, or how to deal with an ordinary safe. This knowledge I have never put to a practical test, though not long ago I did show a friend who had lost his keys the easiest way to break into a house. He stared at me when the feat was quickly accomplished with my advice and assistance.

On a little knoll between the new store and the house where we lived stood the Methodist Church, as much a social as a religious institution, which my mother regularly attended with her children while my father might walk off by himself to the Congregational Church, more than a mile distant. Sometimes I went with him. A church service consisting of an hour's sermon and a long prayer with hymns before and after made very little appeal to me. But I loved the Sunday School where we committed to memory verses from the Bible; and at short intervals "spoke pieces" at school exhibitions given on Sunday evenings. I liked to attend prayer and conference meetings in which many took a part and to hear men shout "Hallelujah" or "Amen" or "That's good, brother." Occasionally I was permitted to go into "Class Meetings" which were regularly held on Saturday evenings. They were public confessions, where the members of the class gave accounts of their "experiences" during the past week, and a lay brother in return gave them religious advice to help them over their difficulties. The minister was never present. For him to have taken any part would have made this experience meeting look too much like a confession to a priest of the Church of Rome. Above all, I was held spellbound by the last of a series of "protracted meetings" in the church when the new converts related, so far as they might desire, the story of their sinful lives, not forgetting the sins they had seen committed by others. If they did not tell everything, they told enough for a boy to understand what kind of lives were being lived by some men and women in the community. I was thrilled when one man told how he once quarreled with another man at a dance and tried to shoot him but missed fire. It is clear that in these early formative years I had developed very little interest in religion except for the light it threw upon secular matters.

My view of the clergy was the same. They were human beings like my father, though they wore better clothes on week days. That clerical friend of my grandfather who loved too well a pipe and a drop of something was soon taken care of by the presiding elder of the district who objected to his habits as unbecoming to a clergyman. He was presently succeeded by an unmarried man, who, though still in his thirties, was called "an old bachelor." To us boys he was a dude. We stood and looked at him as he walked along on the other side of the road, just as now and then we stared at a girl from New York who affected the Grecian bend. We did not understand why he wore gloves on warm days or needed a cane, for he was neither old nor lame. The exotic gentleman, however, was pursued by the girls of the parish; and in this connection a story of him that went the rounds redeemed his character at least for me. One day his landlady remarked at dinner that several people had inquired of her whether he was "engaged." "What did you tell them?" was his response. "Why," she said, "I had to tell them that I didn't know." "That is right," he said, "keep on telling them so." This minister lasted for only a year. When he took his leave he carried away with him as wife not a girl of the parish but a girl who was just a summer visitor there with her grandmother.

Another minister, near the end of the series, was by trade a painter before his "conversion." He repainted the inside of the church, relieving the monotony of the while walls with bright colors. He became rather well known in Mansfield for his eloquent sermons. The secret of this man's eloquence, which I came upon by chance, I never betrayed, perhaps because I liked to hear him talk. The tale may now be told. My mother once received as a gift a cheap edition of sermons by the famous preacher, Thomas De Witt Talmage, which I read through immediately. This minister derived his texts, his ideas, and his eloquent speech all from Talmage. Though he never divulged the source of his sermons, he was likely not aware of any wrongdoing. Both Addison and Franklin, you know, advised country parsons to repeat sermons of the great masters rather than attempt "laborious compositions of their own." It was a pleasure for me to listen all summer to sermons cribbed from a master of emotional eloquence, read in a clear voice by a local minister. From them I learned something about what was going on in the wide world.

The minister just before this one brought with him besides his wife two sons and two daughters. How, one may wonder, was he able to support this large family and keep a horse and carriage with two seats on a salary of $500 a year! This he accomplished with the aid of some, though not many, gifts. It was a cultivated family which had a good influence on the community. The weakness of the preacher was that he relied too heavily on the promise, "Open thy mouth wide and I will fill it." So after reading his text it was his custom to open wide and twist a very large mouth and wait for the words to come. When the words began to flow, it was essentially the same stream which had flowed for an hour on the previous Sunday from a different text. On the other hand, another minister often cut his sermons short because he had a canker in this "thrut." On the whole, the minister whom boys and girls liked best was a well-educated man who, after serving in larger parishes, was assigned, as he desired, to Gurleyville because of approaching old age. Once a month he visited the village school on Friday afternoon for an hour or more by request of the teacher, pleasantly advising us about our studies and making their purport clear to us as no one else could do so well. He used also to come into the store on afternoons when I was alone, for more intimate conversations, never on religion or conduct, always on books, reading, and general knowledge. It may be that he was turning my mind towards a college education.

Before him, in the series, were two evangelical ministers who set the community on fire. The first of them had been a "horse jockey," who had made a precarious living by dealing in horses until his "conversion" by "Elder Swan," about whom he had much to say. After that he took up the ministry as his vocation. He was a tall man, over six feet in height, of pale face and scattered reddish hair, who, I can now see, was the worse for wear in a dissipated world. Emotionally he was a wreck. He almost always wept at some point in his sermons so that tears would run down his cheeks. Why I could never guess. For three winters he conducted "revivals" with the assistance of a professional revivalist who had a fine baritone voice for solos like "Ninety and Nine." He kept a close watch on his converts lest they should backslide during the summer and so have to be reconverted the next winter. As a rule, he often repeated, the slide backward begins when a convert returns to the sin he last gave up, such, for example, as smoking cigars or playing cards. Just before he left for another parish, the devil getting the better of him, he made so sharp a horse trade with one of his parishioners as to make one gasp at his cleverness. This trade delighted us boys as the man who was laid low was a "tightwad" who in prayer meetings sang with great gusto, "I'm glad salvation's free."

The second of these evangelicals was a big, brusque, dark, and heavy man, with a frontpiece so large that he could not bend over far enough to lace a shoe. He evaded this difficulty by wearing shoes with elastic bands at the sides. Sometimes, when his shoes were in dire need of a shine, he walked over to the store and asked me to help him out. For about a year I was his occasional bootblack. He never dropped me a nickel. He did not go in much for converting miscellaneous sinners for the reason that such an effort, he said, would be useless before the church members had undergone a second religious experience which would keep them free of any temptation to sin and thus assure them of "full salvation." So he put in his time "whipping" his congregation, as it was called, out of every sinful desire. The king, queen, and jack on playing cards he denounced as "painted demons" and the rest of the pack as "hellspots." A cigar he picturesquely called "The tip end of the devil's tail," meaning thereby that if you just touch the tail of the devil for a smoke, he will eventually get full control over you and stamp you to death under his cloven hoofs.

His hardest punches he gave his congregation the Sunday after nearly everybody in the village—men, women, and children, myself among them—went to Barnum's Circus in Willimantic, eight miles down the road. He took as his text a sentence from the Old Testament, probably from the Book of Judges: "They went a whoring after other gods." At any rate it was something like this. You say, he shouted in substance, that you went to the circus so the children might see the animals. You know that you didn't go there for the animals. You went there to hear clowns sing. You went there to see girls in tights, almost naked, jump through hoops, and so on. After each blow he repeated twice over, pounding the pulpit, the first part of his text: "You went a whoring." Then he enlarged his illustrations by accusing merchants of giving short weights and short measures, three quarts for a gallon, twelve or fourteen ounces for a pound, three pecks for a bushel, etc. When you do any of these things, "you go a whoring, you go a whoring." But for the intervention of the presiding elder, that ranting minister would have been driven out of town. For us boys it was as good a show as the circus.

I had, it is evident, no particular reverence for the clergy. Their behavior I observed in the same objective manner as I observed the behavior of lawyers, doctors, schoolteachers, farmers, millowners, and workmen. They were all one to me. I had a great curiosity about the ways of men and women. I did not get far behind the show of things into the real character of anyone. It may have seemed strange to my generation that I had no understanding whatever of the significance of so-called "religious experience." More than once has the memory of those early years come back to me as I have read about the conversion of great Christian philosophers and teachers: about Saint Paul on the Damascus road, when there "shined round about him a light from heaven"; about the strange voice Saint Augustine heard in a garden twice commanding him to open the Bible and read (*tolle lege, tolle lege*) the first verse that should meet his eyes; and about John Wesley, who on hearing one in a company of friends read Luther's preface to the Epistle to the Romans, felt his "heart strangely warmed" and received the assurance that he was saved "from the law of sin and death." When I read these great scenes in religious history and am thrilled by them I wonder whether those men and women with whom I associated in boyhood and early youth were not after all made better by their emotional religious experiences, even if many of them rapidly slid backward into their old ways.

Though my brother's store was the center of my life for five or six years, it should not be inferred that I was steadily employed as a clerk for more than short periods, even during long summer vacations. As a rule, my brother had a more regular clerk. I was in and out much as I pleased, receiving for my services $2 a week. In no appreciable way did the store interfere with the pastimes of childhood and youth. I decided when I had reached the age of twelve that I might well try a little business on my own account. At that time a local farmer used to expatiate as he sat by the big stove in the store on the profit he was making by hatching out chickens in a warm place such as a kitchen early in March and selling them as broilers in June or July. This phrase of the chicken business, of course, would have been impossible in my case. But it occurred to me that I could make a little money by dealing with hens primarily for the eggs they might lay. Neither father nor mother had any objection to my making the trial by using for the purpose some $25 which I had saved from picking and selling huckleberries the summer before. They were surprised that I had so much ready cash, as I had kept it safely locked from their sight in a tin box on a shelf in my bedroom. All went well. As soon as spring arrived I erected against a ledge, with the assistance of several other boys, a rough henhouse out of slabs from the sawmill with a large window in front which I discovered somewhere. To me the building was a thing of beauty.

To start the business, I bought seventeen hens of mixed breed and a chanticleer as their companion and protector, paying 60¢ apiece for them. My profit over all for the first year fell but little short of $40. The next year I increased my stock and employed a carpenter to build for me a model henhouse, painted all over in white. So well I prospered that I began to see happy visions. Already I had subscribed to the two leading American poultry journals and had bought a little book "giving a complete description of all the recognized varieties of fowls," and that I might see with my own eyes some of the rare varieties therein described I visited several poultry yards in eastern Connecticut and attended a big poultry

show in Hartford. By this time my own barnyard fowls were for me a
sorry-looking lot. I asked myself: Why shouldn't I as well as others become
a "poultry fancier," breeding only very rare or exotic varieties, selling eggs
for hatching purposes, not at 30¢ a dozen by at $3 a dozen; hens and roost-
ers not at 60¢ apiece but at $5 or more apiece. This was the vision.

To make so important a transition from mongrel to full-blooded stock
required large additions to the henhouse with provision for separate pens
and runs for different breeds, and a preliminary outlay of $125 for fancy
fowls and eggs for hatching my own chickens. This necessary expenditure
was underwritten by my mother. Though I experimented with a dozen
different varieties, I soon reduced the number to three or four of the
rarest, for which there was a good demand among poultry fanciers. These
very rare birds I advertised in poultry journals and built up a trade, as
extant correspondence shows, extending as far south as Richmond, Virginia, and as far west as Fort Wayne, Indiana. No one who dealt with me
from such distances had any notion that he was corresponding with a boy
of fourteen or fifteen years. I advertised myself as "W. L. Cross, Proprietor
of the Gurleyville Poultry Yards." One of my correspondents usually put
"Esq." after my name on envelopes, perhaps because of the dignity displayed in my letters to him. Involved in the joy I felt when so addressed
was likely the jest of playing myself up as a full-grown man.

Certainly it was all a jest to those who watched me in the business. In
killing ordinary fowls for the market I adopted a new technique. The traditional way was to hold them by their legs on a block and chop their
heads off with an axe, letting the headless animals run and flop about until
they bled to death. Instead of doing this, I used to string a row of them
by their legs on a stout wire between two posts and, walking along the
line with a sharp knife, take off a head at each step. "Gawd," drawled an
old farmer as he saw one head after another go in quick succession,
"Gawd, look at that."

A few times I tried my skill as a surgeon on a valuable cock or hen
which had developed some disturbance of the digestive process whereby
grain stuck in the crop, never getting any further. These "crop-bound
birds," as they were called, always died if left to themselves. I wondered

whether they could not be saved by a surgical operation. As boys and men stood round, I occasionally opened a swollen crop with a very sharp knife, thoroughly cleaned it out, and then sewed it up with fine silk. The victim, though temporarily relieved, always died in the course of a week. This, however, did not matter much. I had performed my great showpiece as a poultry fancier. That was what counted.

While I was picking up here and there a few grains of amusing human knowledge in a byplay with cocks and hens, I made in 1876 a decision, all my own, which was ultimately to determine my career. That year was observed everywhere as the Centenary of the Declaration of Independence. I had attended town and county celebrations. But my heart was set on a trip to the Centennial Exposition in Philadelphia, the wonders of which were being told by returning visitors. My father promised to take me with him in September. It was to be a three weeks' visit with cousins living near Philadelphia whom I had never seen. But on an evening late in August, my father remarked, as the family were at supper, that next month a young lady was going to open a private school in a long-unoccupied school building in a place we now call Storrs, a mile and a half up the hill. My father and mother agreed that they would like to have me and my sister Agnes attend the school through the pleasant autumn months, but that it could hardly be arranged this year as I was to be away in Philadelphia, and my sister, only twelve years old, was too young to walk three miles a day unless her brother were with her. The talk, I now surmise, was adroitly drifting along in this manner so as to give me a chance to speak up, as they knew I would speak up before the meal was over. Without hesitation I chose the school as against the Corliss engine and all the other mechanical marvels of the great exposition. This was, in Dante's phrase, the Great Decision of my boyhood.

Whitney Hall, where the school was to be conducted, was for me a large, mysterious building, haunted by a strange story which I had heard many times over. It appears that just after the Civil War a young man named Edwin Whitney, a graduate of the New Britain State Normal School, opened a private school in a large rambling house south of the

Congregational Church of North Mansfield. In this undertaking he was assisted by Charles Storrs. The school started out well with some thirty boys and girls, among whom was my sister Adelaide. Not long after, however, the school was converted into an Orphans' Home, partly under the supervision of the State, for the benefit of orphans of veterans of the Civil War. Unfortunately, Mr. Whitney admitted under pressure an incorrigible boy, who set fire to the farmhouse, which was burned to the ground.

The story of this bad boy is among my earliest recollections. It was first told me in all its details by Mrs. Eunice Anderson, a sister, as I have said elsewhere, of Charles Storrs, or by her husband, Dwight Anderson. For several years afterwards I never saw either Mr. or Mrs. Anderson without asking that the story be repeated. Sometimes I would ask each of them to tell it, one after the other, as their versions differed in some respects. Before either of them began the story I had to describe at some length what an orphan is and undergo a half-serious quiz on my own behavior towards my father and mother. The bad boy, who had no father or mother, they said, was always in rebellion: he would obey none of the rules of the institution, he would not work, he would not study his lessons, he found fault with the best food that could be provided, he would tear up his warm bed and throw sheets and blankets out of the window. One day towards evening he stole a card of parlor matches and lighted a pile of shavings in a woodhouse attached to the main building and everything went up in a blaze. That night all the children except him were gladly taken in by the neighbors. No one wanted the bad boy. Finally the kindhearted Mrs. Anderson said that he might stay at her house for one night. That evening he refused to eat a nice supper which she prepared for him. At eight o'clock she tried to persuade him to go to bed. He said he wouldn't go to bed and sulked in his chair. At nine o'clock she tried to have him go to bed again with the same result. A little later she asked him if he wouldn't like a bowl of bread and milk and he "reckoned" that he would. When it was brought to him as he sat by the table, he just tasted of it, made up a face at it, and then poured it all down the chimney of a lighted kerosene lamp. In the darkness bread and milk flowed all over the table and all over the floor, which Mrs. Anderson would say his wife always kept as bright and clean as a mirror, in which you could see your face. This was the climax of a perfectly told story. "Wasn't he a bad boy?" I was always asked. "Yes, he was an awfully bad boy," I was trained to reply.

When on a September morning in 1876 I walked for the first time into the schoolroom of Whitney Hall, built on the site of the old farmhouse, I saw not the bad boy but a young woman who, I thought, must be the most beautiful woman in the world. She had a plain name, Sarah Ann Smith, but that did not occur to me. She had just graduated from Lasell Seminary. *O dea certe.*

Miss Smith greeted us with a short address in a voice that sounded like the song of a bird. Then she proceeded to take each one of us in hand for a brief oral examination. Before the day was over we were all assigned to classes in such studies as she deemed most appropriate. There was nothing in this schoolroom that resembled a village district school. There was no turning backward to review studies which we had several times gone over. The look was forward to new fields. Apparently taking it for granted that I would some day go to college, she told me that I should begin Latin and algebra at once. There will be also, she added, lessons in spelling, practice in English composition, and in reading aloud prose and verse. All her advice I accepted with glee. When my father returned form the Centennial Exposition I told him what studies I had selected without being able to consult with him, and he seemed pleased. Evenings he quizzed me on the work of the day, and he was so much interested in algebra that he took it up himself.

As algebra and Latin were entirely new subjects, the class moved on slowly, but we moved nevertheless. Towards the close of the term we were reading *Aesop's Fables* in Latin. Never before had I written a composition. Now I was encouraged to write a brief one every other day during the first month, and later once a week on topics agreed upon by Miss Smith and myself. Some of these crude little pieces I preserved, usually because of the teacher's written comment on them. Everybody was then talking about the Indians, for General Custer and all his men had been killed during the summer in a campaign against the Sioux. One of my two compositions on the Indians was marked "good." On one entitled "Hard Times" Miss Smith wrote in pencil: "I like this particularly well as it sounds original and very sensible." At her suggestion, I wrote a composition, now lost, on my choice of a career, if I could have my own way. I took as my title: "A Writer," meaning an author of books and essays. She commended my ambition as "laudable," but said no more.

Miss Smith, who had a well-trained voice, often recited for us the most musical of poems such as Poe's "The Bells" and "The Raven" in the hope, I daresay, that we would catch the rhythms. So impressive to me was the grave rhythm of Bryant's "Thanatopsis," as she rendered it, that I learned the poem by heart. But when I recited it to her in private, she shook her head and made a true remark, that I did not grasp the meaning of the poem. So she advised me to take for my next declamation something much simpler which had a boy in it, like a sentimental poem attributed to Walter Colton, a Yale man, beginning "Old Ironsides at anchor lay," in which "little Hal, the captain's son" is the hero. So well I learned this poem that it has never left my memory.

One morning late in the term there appeared in the schoolroom with Miss Smith a smartly dressed young man who wore gold-rimmed eyeglasses fastened with a silk cord to a buttonhole of his vest. Young as I was I knew what that meant. On a day in "chill November," a teacher whom we all loved and admired bade us good-by.

A few days later my father died. The last time I saw him in life was early on a bright frosty morning, November 16, 1876. We met in a path in the "mowing" behind the house. He was returning from the barn for breakfast, and I was on the way out to look after my fancy poultry. We stopped and said "Good morning." He remarked that he was going down to the gristmill after breakfast to help out the miller for the day, but that in the evening we could talk over a plan he had in mind for continuing my studies now that Miss Smith was giving up her school. What that plan was I never knew. For about noon a messenger from the gristmill came running into the house to announce that my father was dying. Within five minutes I was at the mill. My father had fallen unconscious as he was carrying a small bag of meal in his arms through the door to throw it into a wagon. Within a few minutes after my arrival he died as I stood with others by him. It was written of my father: "No pleasanter spoken man resided within the town . . . his friends were many; and the universal saying was a good and honest man was gone." To me for the moment it seemed as if the light which was to guide me onward had gone out, leaving me in darkness.

It so happened that the village school for that winter, 1876–1877, was to have as its teacher a cousin of my father's the William Williams of that time, who in his youth ad acquired some knowledge of algebra and Latin. He carried me on a little further in these subjects until September when I entered the Natchaug High School of Willimantic with the definite aim of preparing for college. This was a good arrangement, for my brother George had sold out his store in Gurleyville and moved to Willimantic, and taken up a new business there. I was to board in his family for the five school days of the week. As it turned out, I usually walked the long eight miles to Willimantic early on Monday mornings, whatever the weather might be, and picked up a ride home on Friday afternoons. For more than a year I also kept the chicken business going at full speed, and then gradually disposed of my fine stock to other poultrymen. Thus ended an interesting business experiment. I was no free to five all my time to my studies, without any entangling outside alliances.

The Natchaug High School was not an independent institution. It was no more than an extension of a graded district school above primary and intermediate departments. Over all was one Principal, who, however, had the whole district school so well organized that he could give a large part of his time to the high school, which he conducted with the aid of one or two assistants, who were very well qualified young women of college training. There was an enrollment in the high school of about a hundred students of whom some eight or ten took the college preparatory course, although not all of them intended to go to college. For this group the main studies were Latin, Greek, and mathematics, in which all the instruction was given by the Principal, John B. Welch, a graduate of Wesleyan University, who had been a Professor of the Classics at the Episcopal

Academy of Connecticut at Cheshire, near New Haven. Mr. Welch was one of the best teachers I have ever seen in action. He knew well the subjects he taught; and he knew equally well how to keep his students steadily at work. And yet he was not a drillmaster. Rather, he assisted his students in laying good foundations in mathematics and the classics. I cannot overestimate the debt I owe to his inspiring guidance.

Mr. Welch was also so much interested in science that he put the whole school through a descriptive course in physics and chemistry with some opportunity for experimental work. Incidentally, he made arrangements for us to gaze at the first electric arc lamps installed in the town; to converse through the telephone; and to talk into a phonograph which squeaked back our voices. Everything about these new inventions was explained to us. One of his assistants took us all in physical geography and physiology, saying little or nothing, however, about the kidneys, for in the Victorian era it was indelicate to mention in the presence of boys and girls glands which excrete urine. A short course in ancient history was provided for students in the college preparatory group; and there was a year in French as an elective course, which I was able to work into my curriculum. English began with a drill in grammar and proceeded to elementary rhetoric, which Mr. Welch supplemented with a brief history of the English language. In looking into such notebooks as I have kept, I see, to my surprise, that I made for him a little study of Chaucer so that I could read the poet's verse accurately. The many extant compositions which I wrote, several of considerable length, show no knowledge of paragraphing either on my part or on the part of the instructor who read them. A declamation once a term was required of each student, and a contest for prizes in declamation always formed a part of the exercises at Commencement.

By a happy chance I heard, probably in 1878, an address on temperance by Wendell Phillips, when he was in Willimantic on one of his lecture tours. While condemning overindulgence in alcoholic liquors, Phillips took a lenient attitude towards "the moderate drinker" on the ground that most people feel the need of some sort of stimulant in order to make their way through a hard and difficult world. For me it was a merry thesis. And I watched closely his manner of speech, which was quite unlike the

noisy oratory to which my ear had been accustomed. He spoke, with a
few gestures, in a clear persuasive voice, bringing home the points he
wished to make, often with cutting irony. To listen to Wendell Phillips
once was better training in oratory than any school could give.

At Commencement in June, 1878, I entered the annual declamation
contest and received honorable mention. The next year I won the first
prize. The prize, which was a copy of Hudson's *Shakespeare: His Life, Art,
and Characters*, in two volumes, led me to wider reading on my own initiative of books outside the school curriculum. The next year I read, with
Hudson as a guide, ten plays of Shakespeare, and during the same period
a number of novels, among which were *Ivanhoe, David Copperfield, Adam
Bede,* and *Middlemarch.* My prime interest was still in words and phrases
and in wise and witty sayings, as is shown by the list I made of Hudson's
literary expressions, which I had never seen before, and by my copying in
a notebook such short passages from Shakespeare as made a special appeal
to me. As yet I had no conception of the structure of a play or a novel as
a whole. But my mind was being drawn towards the way in which characters were introduced and developed, particularly in fiction. Of the
novels, *Middlemarch* was then my favorite; it may be because I saw certain
resemblances between some of the inhabitants of an English midland town
and the men and women whom I knew in Mansfield and elsewhere. And
I learned from one of the characters in the novel a convenient answer
whenever I am asked for my views on a subject I know nothing about.
"Much may be said on both sides of the question," I remark gravely.

At first I had difficulty in adjusting myself to the way of Natchaug.
I did not feel at home there. The main reason why is now evident to me.
Since the death of my father I had been on the verge of a nervous breakdown, if indeed I had not gone over the precipice. Doctors said that I was
"in a decline." I read all the patent medicine advertisements in the newspapers and imagined that I had every disease they described. I attended
now and then in Willimantic a spiritualistic séance, open to the public, in
which departed spirits tried to converse through professional mediums
with their friends in the audience. I certainly was in a bad way. Though I
did not die, as I feared would soon happen, the general average of my

studies for the first term in old Natchaug was only 49 on a scale of 100. The report handed to me showed that I had passed in nothing but deportment and declamation. Very likely Mr. Welch privately told me to brace up or quit. I did not quit. I braced up, coming out in the second term with an average rating of 80 in all my studies. After that I attended public séances merely for relaxation and entertainment.

Once in control of myself, I went on improving still further in my scholastic record until I hit in my Senior year a general average of 99. This meant that I would be the valedictorian of my class. I chose as the subject of my Commencement Oration in June, 1880, "The Influence of Poetry," in which, among other things, I developed the commonplace distinction between science and poetry—that the one addresses the intellect and the other addresses the emotions. Perhaps it all sounded better than it really was.

Three members of the class were destined for Yale. No one of us, however, was yet fully prepared in Latin and Greek. I was short by nearly a year's work. It was arranged the Principal Welch would take two or three of us during the fall and spring terms on mornings at eight o'clock, an hour before the school opened, in the Homer and Vergil requirements which we had not yet completely covered, and that if we stayed out during the winter term we must read by ourselves three more of Cicero's orations which were necessary to qualify for Yale. This plan suited me perfectly, for, though but in my nineteenth year, I had been assured of my appointment as teacher in the Gurleyville district school for the winter term on a salary of $6 a week. It was for me a happy year, as I was with my mother and sister over week ends in the autumn and spring and with them all the time during the winter.

Those three orations of Cicero I read with equal pleasure and profit, sitting on cold winter evenings by a wood fire and a sputtering kerosene lamp and facing my grandfather's clock. Cicero I had known only as a master of vituperation such as we have him in the orations against Catiline, "the arch conspirator," though he was not so terrible as Cicero claimed him to be. Now I was to make the acquaintance of another Cicero, the orator of superb eloquence, who in the Roman Senate thanked Caesar for recalling Marcellus from exile, and in the Forum extolled the character and military achievements of Pompey. It seemed marvelous to me that language could reach these heights in compliment and praise. But the oration which took full possession of me was Cicero's glorious tribute to Archias, the Greek poet, who had been one of his instructors in youth. Herein Cicero reveals his own habits of study through days when others feasted and through nights when others slept, and lets his mind roam over a wide realm of knowledge with comment and conclusions which as a boy I marked on the margins as "True." Cicero then taught me what literature and philosophy may mean in the life of man.

The old red schoolhouse had been torn down, and a new and larger one, painted white, had been built on land then owned by my mother. There I was having my first experience in teaching boys and girls of all ages, some of whom were but a year or two younger than myself. The minds of backward children I sought to stimulate by awakening in them new interests, and good minds I endeavored to keep going at full capacity. As a result, there rarely arose any question of discipline at a time when corporal punishment was not yet outmoded. Naturally I was very much pleased when I read in the next annual report of the School Visitors that "Mr. Cross showed marked capabilities as a teacher."

Thus ended the career of my childhood and early youth. I say career, for it *was* a career. I went from one thing to another as if I enjoyed perfect freedom. That, of course, was an illusion. My parents, it is now evident, watched over me, rarely prohibiting me from doing this or that, but guiding me, sometimes, I daresay, with amusement. The word "shan't," however much it might be used in other families, was never heard in ours. I remember once, when I was seven or eight years old, going into a house some distance away, where a girl, twice my age, had a piano. She started to play a tune for me, whereupon her father, who was in the yard, came rushing in, exclaiming in an angry voice: "You shan't play that piano any more today." With this command he closed the piano and sat upon the lid while his daughter protested and in tears left the room. Frightened by this man who with his big bushy whiskers looked like a picture of Bluebeard or a pirate, I jumped up and ran out of the road and raced off home.

Many times I passed that house afterwards, but I never again stopped to go in. In tone and temper this household was the extreme reverse of my own home.

To my mother, as well as to my father, I was attached by deep affection. In her girlhood scarlet fever impaired her hearing; and by middle life she became so deaf that others in talk with her raised their voices to a shout. Observing one day that a loud voice, which she could not hear, acutely distressed her, I discovered on a chance trial that if I spoke slowly to her eyes she could read my lips. After this discovery we were able to carry on quiet conversations interrupted only by laughter. The whole or a part of every summer I passed with her thereafter until she was overtaken by a mental illness just preceding her death in 1898, in the seventy-first year of her age. I sat by her till the end.

On the death of my mother, the Gurley homestead of my grandfather passed to my sister Agnes and her husband George Dimock, who lived there until their death in 1934. On my visits with them long hours were spent in talk of old times. George had been one of the gayest young men in the House of Commons in its last days, brilliant in repartee. As he had the reputation of being the strongest man in the community, the crowd was struck speechless when he once shook his fists in the face of the village squire. We tramped woods, pastures, fields, and lanes over the hills, stopping to look at old cellar holes where lilacs bloomed in the spring. Sometimes in October afternoons George would throw a gun over his shoulder, occasionally shooting a partridge to show me that he was still a good shot at the age of seventy. As we sat by my grandfather's window, looking over the offset down on the village, one or the other of us would point out where the tin pedlar used to stop on his rounds or where an itinerant photographer every summer drew up his wheeled gallery and stayed on until he had taken tintypes of everybody around at 25¢ apiece.

A visit with George and Agnes often ended with a walk to the churchyard by the river, where, as we passed from one headstone to another, I would ask questions about the later life of an old acquaintance. Coming one day to the grave of "young Toot," the son of "Toot" the horse trader, I remarked that I always supposed he would never die. "Well, he has lain there for eight years, you see," was the reply. I said: "I remember that he married when hardly eighteen years old and became the father of three children by the time he reached twenty-one and that his wife ran away with a blacksmith the next year." "You have got a damn good memory." "What did he die of?" "He hanged himself." "Why did he do that?" "You know, young Toot married again and became the father of several more children. His oldest daughter, about eighteen, had a feller that young Toot didn't like, and he told his daughter that if that feller ever came to the house again he would shoot him. She laughed in his face. The feller came again one night and young Toot, sneaking under the window, saw them sitting together in the parlor. He went and got his shotgun and fired at the guy's head through the window, and then, getting skeered, he ran off and strung himself up under a railroad bridge. But the damn fool didn't hit the guy. And they were married." "Where does Toot's wife live now?" I asked. "Oh, she don't live anywhere. She got discouraged a while ago and turned the gas on." "But I don't see her grave here." "No, she left word that she didn't want to be buried by the side of Toot."

By that time the old life under which we grew up was but a reminiscence. It had slowly and almost imperceptibly faded into nothing under influences mainly economic. Those four silk mills proved to be only the first phase in the development of a great industry which required large capital, abundant water power, and the transportation facilities of railroads near at hand, not several miles away. And yet, in spite of every disadvantage, silk manufacture lingered on with diminishing output in the Gurleyville district until near the close of the last century. Then came the collapse. Of the four silk mills two were burned to the ground; one was converted into a button factory; and one still stands empty with all its machinery as a silent monument to past and unrecoverable years.

Along with the silk mills the three stores began their downward course. As I have related, my brother closed out his stock of groceries and dry goods as early as 1876 because he could no longer make both ends meet. In the next decade the oldest store of all somehow caught fire on a dark night and went up in a blaze while the proprietor and his neighbors stood by watching the flames, none daring to come very near because a keg of powder in the building, it was said, might blow up any minute. The third store, in front of which were made those famous horse trades for the entertainment of the village, lived on precariously for business with the farmers well down into the present century. That building, as the ell of a dwelling house, still facing the highway with its wide doors, has apparently closed up forever. Its death knell was struck by the automobile, for every farmer now has his car; and if he wants anything badly he can drive to Willimantic in twenty minutes over a road which took me two hours and a half to walk, even if I ran some of the way.

Long before the demise of the third store the House of Commons went, with its brisk debates, shrewd remarks, and lies so cleverly told as to look like true tales. The members dwindled to three or four graybeards and then all disappeared from the earth, leaving at last only their memory in the mind of a boy who sat in and listened. As that boy, I recall a clash between two well-known men of the time in one of the last sessions I attended. It was a debate between a deacon of a Congregational Church and a militant Baptist on infant baptism. The Baptist kept repeating that the command of the Master was "believe and be baptized," not "be baptized and afterwards believe." When the debate began to wax hot another man, from up the hill, broke in, "There ain't nothing," he suddenly fired at them, "in what you are talking about. If you are going to say anything, you have got to begin somewhere and end somewhere. The man whoever he was, who said that you should 'believe and be baptized' meant that you should do both. It don't make a damn bit of difference which you do fust." Another man, who sided with the deacon, remarked that Jesus was baptized before he had a chance to believe in anything. The retort of the Baptist was, "That may be so, but he was not sprinkled by a Congregational minister; he was immersed by John the Baptist in the River Jordan." Here the debate ended in laughter.

With the passing of the graybeards, who with few exceptions, I hope, have long since taken up their everlasting rest somewhere in Paradise, the old social order came to its end. For three generations Gurleyville and its environs had been a homogeneous society. All the families were Yankees of English and Scottish descent, and most of them were closely interrelated, the Dunhams and the Gurley predominating. All along young men of these large families had been migrating to other parts of Connecticut and across the borders and at last as far westward as the frontiers receded. Like their fathers they became pioneers in a new land. But enough of the young men remained at home to carry on the farms and to keep the silk mills going. They lived comfortably on the land and usually made sufficient provision for old age. If they did not live too long, they left small estates running from $3,000 to $6,000 to be divided among their children. Anything above that was rare. When the estate of a man who had been in the silk business was appraised after his death at $20,000, the company who gathered at the village store were dumfounded. The method by which he made so large a fortune was discussed on a night when I saw there on a nail keg. A small farmer who owned a few acres of land and a horse and buggy remarked, "Give me $10,000, and I would give a goddam for nobody."

This idea of competence or wealth, however, was on the wane. The time was at hand when nearly all young men like myself in the Gurleyville community sought pastures new and rarely came back. A contributory cause was a gradual decline in the silk industry, which had been a large factor in the prosperity of the farmers. As soon as the old folks at home died, the Yankee families met their doom. At first their farmsteads were acquired here and there by Irish and German immigrants; and then in the 'eighties and 'nineties of the last century came an invasion of Russian Jews who took up much of the land, not usually for mixed farming, but for the chicken industry. In turn they and their children have largely disappeared, like the Yankees before them, by death and migration to the cities. Though a few still remain on, they have been supplanted for the most part by other people. A Polish family now cultivates the soil on the old farm of my grandfather Eleazer Cross. A family of German descent now lives in the house of the Justice of the Peace where fines were imposed for assault and battery when a coward squealed who had been licked. A Bohemian manufactures buttons in the old silk mill down by the river. And another Bohemian runs the grist- and sawmill once owned by my father, where I worked and played as a boy. The schoolhouse, built in my youth, though still standing, has been abandoned. The village store has been partly converted into a woodshed. Some years ago the little church on a rocky knoll closed its doors never to be opened for worshipers again. Its roof and steeple beaten in my wind and rain, it is up for sale as old and half-decayed lumber. The house, however, which was built by my grandfather, Lucius Gurley, on land purchased by his father, Ephraim, 160 years ago has always remained in the family, and is now owned and occupied by Leon Dimock, a son of George and Agnes. Except for that house and land, still kept in prime condition, the home of my childhood and youth is now a lost village, the like of which can never exist again.

But if as Wordsworth wrote, "the child is father to the man," that lost village lives on in me, be it for better or for worse. There I learned, as I could not have learned in a city, the ways of mankind as they were manifest in simple and naïve acts and words; there I gained a rudimentary knowledge of business, of legal procedure, of local government, and of the art and wiles of politicians, which has been of use to me in reading the minds and motives of men in my dealings with them. Of all the gifts I brought away from that Yankee ambient the chief was the gift of self-dependence, an imbedded conviction that in any undertaking a man must go on alone, if his associates fail him, to its completion. This was a Yankee gift of which I was then unaware.

Part II

III. Yale College Sixty Years Ago

With these antecedents I entered Yale College in September, 1881. Late in the previous June I took my entrance examinations in New Haven with the friend of my boyhood, Frank Clifton Smith, whose father, the Gurleyville Justice of the Peace, had been my guardian since the death of my own father. As neither Frank nor I had ever been in New Haven, we arrived a day or two before the examinations so as to look over the university and get our bearings.

In one of our walks across the Green we saw that something was going on in the historic Center Church. We stopped and entered, finding only standing room by the door in a crowded audience. All eyes were turned towards the pulpit platform where stood a man speaking with a flow of words such as I had never heard before. Though he was not so incisive in his speech as was Wendell Phillips, he spoke with a persuasive eloquence. Within a few minutes his form and features became fixed in my mind with photographic detail. He was a tall man as straight and lean as a top rail on a Mansfield fence. He was immaculately dressed in black; and wore, instead of a collar, a stock like my grandfather Lucius Gurley's. In appearance he resembled a country deacon dressed in his best Sunday clothes. On inquiry a bystander told us that he was William M. Evarts, the great international lawyer, who had been Secretary of State under President Hayes, and that he was giving the Commencement Address to the faculty and graduating class of Yale Law School. I was thrilled.

When in my boyhood I used to frequent the local court my interest in the administration of the law extended far beyond that particular court. In 1875, for example, a sensational lawsuit was brought against Henry Ward Beecher, the most famous preacher of that time. Evarts was one of the lawyers for the defense. The details of the long trial, so far as they were reported in newspapers, I read with avidity. Mr. Evarts' cross examinations of the witnesses for the plaintiff seemed to me, a boy of thirteen, to represent the most acute intelligence that God had ever vouchsafed to a man.

The intellectual idol of my boyhood, who was then but a name to me, I now saw as a man alive and in action. He was, too, a Yale man talking to Yale men. Aglow with the eloquence of William M. Evarts who exalted, very likely far beyond desert, the character and achievements of Yale men, I felt more certain than ever that I had made no mistake in my resolve to join sometime that glorious company.

The next morning I appeared in old Alumni Hall to take the Yale entrance examinations which were to last for three days. As we sat, a hundred and fifty or more of us, at little octagonal tables, strange faces from the portraits on the walls—they were great Yale men of old—kept looking down upon us, in one instance with a hand uplifted in warning, while a dozen tutors zigzagged slowly among us to see to it that there was no cribbing. I went through translations from Latin and Greek easily, though I was unexpectedly confronted with a Latin passage which I had never seen and was also required to turn into Latin or Greek, I forget which, a brief sketch of Epaminondas, a Theban general and statesman, of whom I had never heard. I failed, however, to pass in algebra and plane geometry, though I had gone in these subjects considerably beyond the Yale requirements. The trouble was that I had looked into no book on either subject since I completed them in high school one or two years before. During the summer I found time to review both of them, to read several more plays of Shakespeare, and to work a month in the hayfield at 20¢ an hour. The last week in September, 1881, I was admitted to Yale College as a full-fledged Freshman without any conditions whatever. I was happy beyond measure.

College was for me a great adventure. Much is being said and written in these days on the difficulties many students have in making the transition from school to college. As for myself, I was aware of no difficulties. True, the college routine and environment were new and strange to me. They were, however, but the background of an unknown adventure, the conditions of which must be met if I were to succeed. I questioned nothing. I took it for granted that God was in his heaven and that all was right with the college world. I mixed with my classmates, making a few close friends and becoming more or less acquainted with them all within three months. When I went home for Christmas and looked in on the village store, I was adjusted to a new life, though still mindful of the old.

I entered upon my studies with the utmost zeal, trying to do as well in one as in another, on the theory, now abandoned in education, that a study which a student finds hard for him is as essential as the study he finds easy if his aim is the development of a well-balanced mind adequate to cope with a world where things are hard as well as easy. After a probation period of six weeks, I was assigned to the highest ranking division of my class and I stayed there until scholarship divisions, at the end of two years, were no more.

During those first two years we were all put through a fixed course of study in Latin, Greek, and mathematics, which was based upon equally fixed requirements in those subjects for entrance to the Freshman class. The implied purpose was to cast our minds all in the same intellectual mould. In this endeavor primary stress, I soon saw, was placed, to my delight, on the literary masterpieces of ancient Greece and Rome. Still, I was almost equally interested in pure and applied mathematics which brought us to the threshold of calculus. Euclid, which had been in the Freshmen curriculum for generations, fascinated me, not because it added anything new to my knowledge of geometry, but because of the art displayed by the old Greek mathematician in proving by a strict deductive method the truth of propositions which anyone might see were true at a glance. It was like traveling over a beautiful road to the foreseen end of one's journey. Likewise, in a course in analytical geometry with "Andy" Phillips, we played with the curves of algebraic equations which fell into strange and wonderful patterns, rivaling anything I have ever seen in the most fantastic designs of wallpaper. Though drawn in the first instance to higher mathematics by a kind of artistic sense, I maintained a secondary interest in mathematics as the foundation of science. The more difficult the problem, the more intense was my desire to attempt its solution.

The rigid curriculum of Freshman and Sophomore years was pleasantly relieved by declamations in connection with gay lectures on elocution by Instructor Mark Bailey, and particularly by a course in rhetoric given by Professor Cyrus Northrop, soon to become President of the University of Minnesota. Northrop was an outstanding personality in appearance and character. His nickname was Gutsy, as he was beginning to grow too round for his height. He usually wore a low-cut waistcoat which gave ample room to display a stiff shirt front, in the center of which sparkled a diamond. He was the faculty's best extemporaneous speaker by all odds, whether the subject were light or grave. His manner, his voice, and his whimsical smile were captivating. The course he conducted in rhetoric was a forum for the discussion not only of literature and style but of politics, morals, and religion. The two characters in English literature whom he liked most to talk about were Hamlet and Colonel Newcome—the one he regarded as supreme in drama and the other as supreme in fiction. If we wanted to know whether Hamlet was mad or not, he advised us to go and see Booth tomorrow night. Thackeray he had actually seen with his own eyes, when President Woolsey brought the novelist into the College Chapel on his first American tour. Northrop, then a Freshman sitting in a back row, thought that Thackeray, with bushy head and beard, looked as he strode on his long legs up the aisle like a Norse god who had come on a visit to Yale.

In quizzing the class on the book in rhetoric which we were studying, Northrop adopted a modernized Socratic method; that is, he set traps for us in which we were certain to be caught with a direct contradiction in statement or opinion unless we kept our minds alert. One day he sprung a cleverly contrived trap on a member of the class, leading him on to express two directly opposite opinions on the same subject. Amid the stillness that fell upon the class Northrop called out my name and I rose to my feet, with my hands close to my sides, determined to go warily in an encounter with a Tartar.

"Mr. Cross, what was Macaulay's method of composition?" "According to the book, he wrote rapidly, paying little attention to details, and afterwards put everything into shape." "Is that the correct way?" "It was Macaulay's way." "Yes; but is it the correct way? Is it *your* way?" "I have never written anything except a few high school compositions. I can't write fast—without thinking. I have to think out in advance what I want to say and then try to say it."

All through the colloquy the class laughed and Northrop, beginning with a smile, laughed too. His final comment was: "There is no one way to write. Much may be said for the Macaulay way. Much may be said for the Cross way. It all depends upon the kind of mind one has. Certainly you should think out ahead of time what you intend to say." The next year Northrop awarded me two prizes in English composition.

By this time reverberations of a rather noisy controversy over the traditional college curriculum were sounding against the walls of Yale. It was, with some differences, a revival of the eighteenth-century dispute between the ancients and the moderns. President Eliot of Harvard was the leader of the moderns who, with few restrictions, would make all studies in the college curriculum elective, giving preference to none. President Porter of Yale, in so far as he entered the debate, was for maintaining the ironclad college curriculum in prime essentials. He was in particular a staunch supporter of the program of classical studies, such as we had a Yale, which the reformers would make elective, partly on the ground that a classical education interfered with acquiring wider and more general knowledge necessary for success in a professional career.

To this claim Lord Chief Justice Coleridge of England on a visit to Yale in October, 1883, took exception in a notable speech which he gave in Battell Chapel while President Porter sat looking at him with a smile of delight. We all listened intently to Lord Coleridge's defense of the classics. We liked his looks and his voice. But the general impression made by his speech upon the students was, I think, accurately stated by the class historian, who was to become a Congregational clergyman: "Somehow we believed in what he said, but were willing to let him read the classics as much as he pleased. We felt as though we had got enough."

As I have remarked, I accepted the college curriculum as it was without wasting any time over whether it might be better or worse. It was my business to saw the wood so long as there was any wood to saw, whether soft or hard. Now, after the lapse of years I can take a saner view of a classical education than when I was in the midst of acquiring it. I have no regrets for the five or six years I spent on Latin and Greek in school and college. I do not feel that the long time was wasted. Destined as I was to become a Professor of English and to follow, to some extent, a literary career, I am glad that I could cast my anchor in the two great ancient literatures which have made a large contribution to the moral and intellectual ideals on which our modern civilizations have been built. What would now be, I ask myself, my outlook on life and literature had I no direct knowledge of Homer and Vergil, Demosthenes and Cicero, Plato and Aristotle, Thucydides and Tacitus, and above all, no knowledge of the Greek dramatists? I wonder just how I should have got on without this knowledge.

It is quite likely that if Latin and Greek had been purely elective studies I should have chosen them as the best foundation of the literary life which I was already vaguely hoping to lead. So whether the classics were required or not required for the first two college years hardly concerned a small group of students of which I was one. But the question was of vital concern to the large majority who were looking forward to law, medicine, and the ministry, or to business as a career, all of whom had for some time felt that a prolonged student of Latin and Greek, with certain other absolute requirements, was curtailing the time they ought to give to modern subjects such as English, French, German, history, economics, and the natural sciences.

It was becoming clear that a classical education for all was well on the road to eventual doom soon or late, for the simple reason that it had ceased to interest the general body of students. Some of the instructors were distinguished scholars, while others were tutors of the traditional type who conducted classes in both Latin and Greek and might be called upon to take a class in a wholly unrelated subject like mechanics. Limited in their knowledge, several tutors had a hard time, I afterwards learned, in keeping more than a week ahead of the reading they assigned to their students. One of them, I heard, used to walk over East and West Rock by night in order to quiet his nerves before meeting his class at eight-thirty in the morning. With incidental exceptions, the instruction, whoever gave it, was primarily grammatical. True, there were placed in our hands a little red primer on the history of Greek literature and a similar red primer dealing with Roman antiquities. But both primers were dull and hardly understandable because of their brevity. They furnished a basis not for enlightenment on ancient civilizations so much as for mere questions and answers. So, with asides like this, we were fed on Latin or Greek grammar day by day for two years.

Class statistics of the time show that English translations were employed in varying degrees by four fifths of the men as welcome if not necessary assistance in reading Latin and Greek in preparation for another reading and quizzes in the classroom. This percentage held even for members of Phi Beta Kappa, who resorted to a horse or a pony or a trot when hard pressed for time. Down towards the bottom of a class there was always a considerable group of men who were wholly dependent upon a horse to ride through any Latin or Greek text whatever.

Though an official frown was cast upon the horse and the crib, professors and instructors of all grades often made a joke of their use if only to raise a laugh in the classroom. It was a sort of sardonic humor which we rather enjoyed. Once when I was asked by the instructor to translate a very fine passage in the *Electra* of Sophocles, I tried to render it in the best English at my command. There was a general smile when the instructor said without quiz or comment: "That will do, Mr. Cross." The inference was that I had cribbed the translation from some unknown literary source. On another occasion I read aloud a translation from the *Agricola* of Tacitus. Again I was asked to sit down by the instructor, who remarked that I must have a different Latin text from the one the rest of the class was using. Everybody laughed. A little riled, I replied ironically: "That is true, sir. The *Agricola* I have in my hand was edited by a former Yale professor now dead. The text may be faulty but the type is large; and there is a preface which tells all that is known about the life of Tacitus and also gives an extended account of his other books." In no way offended by my retort, the instructor later apologized for his insinuation and we were afterwards the best of friends.

One instance more. Professor Northrop once set a day when the men in the first scholarship division were to appear in class ready to make a short extemporaneous speech on some man whom for one reason or another we admired. I chose Socrates about whom we had been reading with a Greek instructor in Xenophon's *Memorabilia*. No sooner did I mention the name Socrates than everybody laughed. Nevertheless I went straight on. At the end, Professor Northrop, though he was smiling, commended my choice of a hero. This scene summarizes the attitude of the best students of the 'eighties to Greek or Latin literature. To them the *Memorabilia* was but another Greek text to be translated. They missed the realistic portrait of Socrates as if it were not there, for nobody called their attention to it.

Unknown to us the faculty of Yale College under the leadership of Professor Sumner and a few others were already insisting upon a comprehensive revision of the curriculum. Towards the end of my Junior year they partially succeeded against the emotional protests of President Porter. Hitherto elementary or advanced French and German could not be taken until Junior year. They were now pushed back into Freshman and Sophomore years where they belonged. In order to find room for them there, it was necessary to cut down the required studies in Latin and Greek by nearly a half. Likewise prescribed courses of study in Junior and Senior years had to give way, with some irritating exceptions, to an elective system which provided a wide latitude in the choice of subjects for study. This revolution came in time for the class of 1885 to reap its benefits in our last year. "Never before," our class historian wrote, reviewing our Senior year, "has work been so conscientiously and well done."

As the elective system for Junior and Senior classes did not go into effect until the academic year 1884–85, my studies in Junior year were mostly still prescribed, with just enough leeway, however, for the choice of such courses as I particularly desired in elementary German, advanced French, and English literature in place of Latin and Greek which I discontinued. In Senior year there were only two prescribed courses—one in psychology and the other in ethics, which were retained, it was understood, in deference to President Porter. Outside this restriction, a student was free to roam to his heart's content.

The prescribed work of the Junior class covered a good range of courses, as many as eight, most of which were short courses running for two hours a week through a half year, occasionally for a still briefer period, while a few extended throughout the entire year. There was no grouping of studies for concentration of work in the same or related fields. The old idea lying behind a program of dispersed studies was that a college student should have a chance to look here and there into various parts of the whole realm of knowledge. Then, after graduation, he might be classed as a liberally educated man. The real break in this old conception of a college education came when the elective system was introduced in the studies of Senior year.

My memory returns with pleasure to most of the studies of the last two college years, whether prescribed or elective. Many of my associates, however, who had no knowledge of elementary science did not take kindly to the natural sciences, which were compulsory for all. With their attitude I sympathized in a measure. We doubtless expected to learn from astronomy all about the stars in God's heavens. But the course in that subject as conducted by a professor in mathematics was mainly mathematical, consisting largely in the solution of spherical triangles under unusual difficulties, for it was hard to find where the triangles were. There was, it is true, an occasional opportunity to look through a telescope at the moon and some of the planets. That was all.

On the other hand James Dwight Dana whom we had in geology took us on long Saturday tramps for miles around in the New Haven district so that we might learn within a limited area something about the earth which God had made through the ages. Surrounded by a group of us he talked all the time. It was a remarkable experience. Curiously enough, this eminent geologist accepted Darwinism reluctantly. Every year he used to give in the Old Chapel a Sunday evening address to show that the theory of evolution did not upset, except perhaps in one or two details, the story of Creation as we have it in the first chapter of Genesis. I never missed being there. The college pastor, a Scotsman, who sat by Professor Dana's side in a happy mood, always dismissed the audience with the same formula: "You see, gentlemen, that when the right kind of a man of science and the right kind of a theologian come together there is no dispute between science and religion."

The geologist's son, Professor Edward S. Dana, known familiarly as "Eddie," conducted for a part of the time the required course in physics which extended through the entire Junior year. The book used was a translation from the French of *Ganot's Physics*, which, though called an "elementary treatise," ran on and on to more than eight hundred pages of small type. The principles of physics as stated in this big book it was our business to master and to stand a test on by discussion over which the instructor presided. Students as a rule were asked to reproduce on the blackboard drawings from the book to prove this or that principle. The only apparatus ever brought into the classroom consisted of several machines, including the complicated one bearing the name of Holtz, for developing electricity. The action of these various machines students were called upon to explain in detail. Most of us wished that those "damn machines" had never been drawn from their resting places. It was nevertheless a good course in descriptive physics. Eddie was a genial gentleman who knew his subject well and was ready to answer all questions we might throw at him. Towards the end of the year "Buffalo" Wright, the senior Professor of Physics and Chemistry, regaled us with spectacular experiments in both subjects. At that time Yale had two professors named Wright. To distinguish one from the other, A. W. Wright, who wore a long black beard, was called Buffalo, while Dean Henry P. Wright, Professor of Latin, whose cheeks and chin were always closely shaven and whose head had lost most of its hair, was known as Baldy.

To complete the required work in the natural sciences, Buffalo Wright gave a short course in chemistry, which was a failure simply because the few weeks assigned to it did not give time enough to do anything with chemistry. It was profitable to me, however in one sense. When the time was approaching for the term examination, one man after another asked me to help him "get by" in a subject he knew nothing about. It was arranged that I should coach a squad of fifteen men for two hours on each of three successive evenings. They were to come to my study with textbook and pads and take down such notes as I might give them and read such pages as I might designate. If they would do that, I guaranteed that all would go well with them. The price I put on each of their heads was $3, provided they got by. If they didn't, the price was lifted. In the end I took on a second squad. As soon as the results of the examination were reported thirty men paid the price.

To step from traditional courses of study into the large room of the Old chapel for recitation, half lecture, half quiz, by William Graham Sumner, Professor of Political Economy, was to step into a new and enlarged world. It took but three minutes to make the transition to this wide realm where land and population, capital, currency, banking, taxation, economic history, and political science were explored. I elected Sumner's so-called long course in political economy covering a year and attended his lectures on the political and economic history of the United States which ran for two years. No other teacher of those days exerted so profound an influence upon his students as did Professor Sumner. It was tremendous. True, some thought him too dogmatic in his opinions and convictions as he stood behind his desk and pounded ideas into our heads. But the blows of his hammer awakened our minds. He never shut down upon free discussion. He seemed to like to have students ask questions of him, which he answered immediately as one who knows. That after all was what most counted.

Professor Sumner was then in the very prime of life. He lived a mile out in the suburbs. On the morning of a lecture it was his custom to walk in to his class, stopping at the post office on the way for his mail which he brought with him into the lecture room ten or fifteen minutes before the hour set for meeting his students. I liked to watch him as he sat at his desk examining letters and miscellaneous mail. Much of it he threw into a wastepaper basket. A few letters and periodicals he carefully laid aside to take home with him. Picking up a metropolitan newspaper, he would rip it out of its wrapper, let his eyes run over all headlines, and finally scan for a minute or two the editorial page. If he found an editorial which had some bearing on the special subject for the day he would tear it out and like as not show up its fallacies as a part of his lecture. By this and other adroit means he made alive everything he touched.

In a larger manner he was, first of all, a coördinator of knowledge. For example, if he were discussing the American banking system, he would have nearly as much to say about the British banking system, comparing or contrasting the one with the other, pointing out their good and bad features. He helped us to think things through. Quite apart from anything

I may have learned of economics or of political science, in listening to "Billy" Sumner I learned that knowledge is not disparate; that in any particular field of knowledge one part is related to other parts, so that in trying to go through that field it is well for a man to look on each side of himself and as far ahead as he can see.

The economic and political theories which Professor Sumner sought to inculcate were essentially those of John Stuart Mill (whose *Principles of Political Economy* we all read), and of Richard Cobden and John Bright, all of whom were militant advocates of laissez faire in general and of free trade with other countries in particular. Protective tariffs he damned as class legislation for the benefit of the few and so against the economic welfare of the many. The doctrines he was teaching aroused a good many captains of industry to denounce him in turn as a man who seemed to regard it as his mission to "poison the minds" of a whole generation of Yale students. We understood that they tried to persuade the President and Fellows of Yale University to oust him. But a professor of the first rank, they discovered, could not be removed even by the arms and suckers of an octopus, then the familiar designation of an industrial corporation. When in an open discussion one of my classmates asked Sumner to give the arguments for protection, he replied that he could not give them, for there were none. Nevertheless, Yale found an economist who defended protection and engaged him for a course of lectures to appease the hostile critics of Sumner. He was Robert Ellis Thompson, a Presbyterian divine and professor in the University of Pennsylvania. He served the purpose. That was all. Billy Sumner stayed on.

Not so, however, in the case of Frank B. Tarbell, who though primarily an Assistant Professor of Greek, gave one or two courses in logic. His affectionate surname was "Balls." Despite the fact that he had been out of college eight years when our class came in, he looked as young as if he were one of us. He was tall and so thin that someone described him as a mathematical straight linen having neither width nor thickness. Within that slim body of Tarbell was a mind that came closer to pure reason than any other I have ever known. Logic as ordinarily taught is a subject as dry as dust. But Tarbell made it a most interesting and valuable study by applying its methods to social science and to morals, thus coming near to religion. The powers that be took the alarm; for Tarbell was not quite orthodox in his religious views, which, so far as I could make them out, were very much like those of Matthew Arnold who lamented that the sea of faith, once at the full, was receding down the "naked shingles of the world."

The crisis came in the consulship of Timothy Dwight after my class was out. It was a foregone conclusion that there could be no reconciliation between the religious views of Timothy Dwight, a fundamentalist with some reservations, and Frank Tarbell, a liberal who kept his mind wide open for new ideas. Both of them, I daresay, took their religion too seriously for their comfort. Tarbell left Yale at the expiration of the term of his appointment as Assistant Professor. He eventually migrated to the University of Chicago, where he had a brilliant career in Greek archeology.

Professor Arthur M. Wheeler's general history courses, which I attended, took a wide sweep through Tudor England and through Europe of the nineteenth century, with a background of French history just before and during the French Revolution. His lecture on the battle of Waterloo which he first gave in the classroom, was famous. He repeated it on compulsion every year to the whole body of Yale students in Carll's Opera House across Chapel Street where we had all seen Booth in the rôle of Hamlet and Brutus. Ever afterwards he had no other name on the college campus than "Waterloo Wheeler."

The most picturesque member of the faculty was Edward J. Phelps, Kent Professor of Law, one of the well-known international lawyers of the period. After his graduation from college in 1840 he spent, I afterwards heard him say, a good deal of time in Washington with his father, Samuel S. Phelps, who served for thirteen years as a Senator from Vermont. As his father's son he saw much of the immortal trio—Webster, Clay, and Calhoun; and when Webster became Secretary of State in the Fillmore Cabinet, the young man, then in his thirtieth year, was appointed Second Comptroller of the United States Treasury. In manners, dress, and bearing he came upon us as a gentleman of the old school, such as we may have seen in portraits but never in the flesh with our own eyes. As he walked up the aisle of the lecture room to his desk in Prince Albert coat and with silk hat in his right hand, we looked at him at first in wonder. Before sitting in his chair he laid his silk hat on the desk, bottom upwards and gazed at it for a moment as if he were taking a short leave of a dear friend. Then, seated in his chair, he began his lecture in a grave and slow voice so that we might take notes upon it if we so desired.

His subject (by whatever name it may have been called) was the fundamental principles of law, each one of which he stated so clearly and illustrated so well in a series of lectures that a student of ordinary ability could not fail to understand and remember them. The end of the course came abruptly in the midst of it when Professor Phelps was appointed by President Cleveland as Ambassador to the Court of St. James's. We felt our loss but we were pleased with the honor conferred upon him and Yale.

Near the same time Professor E. J. Phelps was persuaded to give to a university audience a political address which revealed at the full the charm and humor of his personality, particularly in his description of the devious ways by with political sergeants are able to march the intelligence of the country to the polls on election days. He told us that there would likely be times when, whatever our political party, we would be justified in taking a walk. Somewhere in his address, he said: "The coming man is the independent voter. Independence in politics is the part of true manliness, and, if I am a judge of the future, the part of true policy." As I now read again the newspaper report of this address, I am astonished at the number of political ideas which I must have derived from it and which I long afterwards reiterated in different words in inaugural messages and miscellaneous speeches.

Of President Noah Porter I have pleasant and lively memories. In those days the president of a college or university was chosen not so much for his administrative abilities as for his learning and success as a teacher. Whenever I had occasion to consult President Porter in his office in the old Trumbull Gallery, I found him seated at the end of a long table with pen in hand and paper and manuscript lying before him. All was quiet and serene as if he were sitting not in the center of Yale College but in some remote monastery far from the haunts of men. In such an ambient he must have written *The Human Intellect*, concerning which it was often said, in varying words, that only God who inspired it and Noah Porter who wrote it could understand so learned a book. As a matter of fact there were no depths in *The Human Intellect* that the intelligence of even a college student could not sound. On it as a basis President Porter gave twice a week lectures which laid open a field of knowledge hitherto unknown to us. He was so well read in English literature that he could bring to bear on his subject illustrations from countless poets and novelists. He rarely quizzed us in the classroom. Rather it was his custom to assign us a choice of one of the few subjects for brief essays before he began his lectures. Well I remember how in one of these essays I gave free play to my own mind irrespective of what *The Human Intellect* said. When I finished that essay I felt for the first time that I had discovered myself. Hereafter I was to be my own man. It was "a great awakening."

Though I neglected no subject of study in favor of another, my mind by Junior year was moving more and more towards English literature as the center of my interests. My English compositions and more formal disquisitions were well received and I entered the competition for the coveted Junior Exhibition Prize in composition with a eulogy on Charles Sumner. I lost out in the contest but came in second. Go into literature seemed to be the categorical imperative. I was particularly fortunate, when I was making my decision, to have as my guide Professor Henry A. Beers, who was rightly regarded as "the most literary man" on the Yale faculty. A graduate of Yale in the Class of 1869, he had returned to Yale as a tutor in 1871 after trying out and giving up the study of the law. The year before I entered college he had been promoted to a professorship in English literature at the age of thirty-two. I distinctly remember my first sight of him in Freshman year as we used to pass each other on the campus. He looked like a boy, perhaps a member of the Senior class, who had come from some strange country. He dressed like no one else at Yale. He wore a conspicuous checked coat and trousers, a tight fit, a low-crowned derby hat, and shoes of patent leather, I think, with pointed toes. He walked straight ahead at a good gait, looking neither to the right nor to the left. I did not then know that he was so nearsighted that he had to watch his steps.

This smartly dressed young man in conjunction with Professor Louns-bury, over in the Sheffield Scientific School, had revolutionized the study of English at Yale and elsewhere. Hitherto in the study of English stress had been placed upon grammar as in Latin and Greek. Such verse or prose as was assigned for study was read aloud by students in the classroom, who one after another were asked to name the part of speech of this or that word or to "construe" this or that sentence. This minute study of grammar Professor Beers scrapped. In place of it he substituted a manual on the history of the English language which Professor Lounsbury had recently published.

He was saturated with literature. He lived among the great English writers as if they were his familiar friends. He read with ease French and German. Nor had he lost his knowledge of Greek and Latin. Greek literature was for him "the light of morning" which ushered in all the literatures of the modern world. All this was evident in the courses of study I took with him. He wrote beautiful verse and prose, serious and humorous. Though he had not yet come into his own with *The Ways of Yale* and *A Suburban Pastoral and Other Tales*, which belong to the next decade, he had already begun his studies for the *History of the English Romantic Movement*, parts of which he incorporated in lectures which I attended.

One of my courses with him was on the English dramatists contemporary with Shakespeare. Whatever the play, whether by Ben Jonson or by Beaumont and Fletcher, or by someone else, the first thing he expected of us was that we should have an intimate knowledge of it from beginning to end. Then came the discussion of the play in parts and as a whole. There was never any talk about plot as something apart from the characters which could be represented in the formal German manner by a curve showing the beginning of the action, the climax, and the end. With him characters were the thing. By their emotions and consequent behavior in crucial circumstances plot is determined. By them one's knowledge of human nature is broadened. And by them only is a play or a novel remembered.

As an aid in the interpretation of dramatic characters, I had but to walk over to Carll's Opera House, where in one season or another I might see the great contemporary actors: Booth and Barrett, Irving and Terry,

Modjeska or Bernhardt, or Joe Jefferson (a favorite of the students). It may have been in New York that I first saw the elder Salvini in the rôle of Othello. Was it then or later that Gilbert and Sullivan's operas came to town? I thank God that the visual age was in the far distance when novels and plays were to be washed out with pictures on a screen.

In another course with Professor Beers we ran along down the stream of verse and miscellaneous prose, apart from fiction, of the nineteenth century. Of the poems we read he often recited passages from memory, sometimes not quite accurately, for he had the habit of throwing in here and there a word of his own in place of the original, perhaps because he preferred his own word to another's rather than because of any lapse of memory. In this course I first became acquainted with the beautiful prose of Cardinal Newman and the critical essays of Matthew Arnold which helped me to gain a point of vantage for viewing the field of literature. It was a memorable day towards the close of Senior year when Professor Beers, disturbed because we had not read *Faust* in our elementary course in German, remarked that he would read and translate it for us himself, for none of us should leave Yale without a direct knowledge of Goethe's masterpiece. The next week he began. He read the German text slowly, scene by scene, thus making it easy to follow him with open books. Then came the translation, likewise scene by scene, with comment as he proceeded. So ended a course in English literature with the great German who overshadowed all the other writers we had read.

The extreme literary cosmopolitan of the time was Matthew Arnold who, for his generation and ours also, defined the function of criticism as "a disinterested endeavor to learn and propagate the best that is known and thought in the world," irrespective of race or language, as a means of establishing "a current of fresh and true ideas" in the whole realm of thought. I can now almost relive the emotions I felt when in my Junior year I heard that Matthew Arnold was coming to Yale on his American tour. His New Haven address (he called it a "discourse") was on "Numbers." It was good but not one of his best. He read it with eyes close to his manuscript in a pronounced Oxford dialect such as I had never heard before. The next morning he came into Battell Chapel with

President Porter, who introduced him in a neat speech. Arnold rose, threw his arms about him in an awkward manner, smiled upon us, and after a few incoherent sentences, sat down. The only complete sentence I could make out was: "I suppose you all heard me last night." It was difficult to imagine this gaunt and bewhiskered man as the author of verse and prose which for beauty, rhythm, or eloquence had entranced me.

It was while under the spell of Matthew Arnold that in Senior year I entered into competition for the DeForest Gold Medal, which was to be awarded "to that member of the Senior Class who shall write and pronounce an English Oration in the best manner." As I have remarked, I lost out the year before in the Junior Exhibition Prize by a hair, and now came a chance to redeem myself if I could. When the list of subjects from which the contestants were to make their choice was announced, I saw there to my surprise and delight the name of Sainte-Beuve, whom Arnold had eulogized as the creator of the best modern literary criticism. In going out of English or American literature for my subject very likely I felt that I was following an example that Arnold had set in his early critical essays. All went well with me, for I quickly discovered that Matthew Arnold was in good measure the English counterpart of Sainte-Beuve. By a close shave I won the DeForest Gold Medal against five competitors, all of whom were members of Yale's oldest Senior Society.

As I now take leave of my instructors of all grades I have one word for them all. There seems to be an opinion that the faculty of Yale College in those days kept aloof from their students. Nothing could be further from the truth. It is true that we did not live together in colleges. Nor was there any organized system of counselors. But every member of the faculty was available for consultation in his office. Dean Wright, whom I saw as often as once a fortnight, kept in touch with my general studies; Professor Seymour with my Greek; Professor Wheeler with my history; Northrop and Beers in turn with my English; and so on along the line. They all advised me in talk as familiar as that between father and son. My last word to their memory is that they were a delightful and noble race of omen.

Life on and around the Campus was much simpler in the good

old days than it is now in the luxurious new quadrangles. The entire
enrollment of Yale College ran not far about six hundred. This meant
room enough on the Campus to house the three upper classes, while
Freshmen lived mostly in little congenial groups on adjoining streets. The
four classes really formed a single compact community. Many Seniors and
Juniors who could afford it had rooms respectively in Durfee and Farnam
Colleges; but the center of the most lively as well as the most primitive
dormitory life was in the Old Brick Row where for the last three years I
took up my quarters with Walter F. Frear of Honolulu, who was to be
sometimes Chief Justice and Governor of the Territory of Hawaii. The
suite (study and bedroom) which we two last occupied was heated only
by a small half-open stove for which the coal was stored in a dark hole of
a bin reached by a small door. The bedroom was a narrow oblong with
two bedsteads placed foot to foot. Water for washing face and hands had
to be brought up from a lavatory on the ground floor.

Not a bathtub nor a shower was there in any of the Yale College dormitories, not even in crack Durfee. As a substitute for a good full-length
stretch under water or for a good cold spray from head to foot, a professor
of the School of Medicine, who gave us a series of lectures in Freshman
year on "How to Keep Well," advised anyone who wished to go further
than face and hands in the morning washup to purchase a small sponge
and to do the best he could with sponge and washbowl. Most Freshmen
tried the experiment for the rest of the year. There were, however, tubs
and sprays in the gymnasium; the tubs, though not the sprays, were available for us, at hours when they were not preëmpted by athletes, at a cost
of 25¢ apiece. A few of my classmates, who were accustomed to a bath
oftener than once a week, discovered that the Divinity School had two
bathtubs for the hundred young men who were preparing for the ministry
and that it was quite easy to steal a bath over there with little chance of
being caught in that unwashed age. Water for drinking might be brought
in pitchers from the lavatory of a dormitory or from the Old South Pump
on the Campus, with whose undefiled waters generations of Yale men
had quenched their thirst. Sometime afterwards this old wooden pump
with its long squeaky handle fell into disrepute and it had to go.

Instruction on how to keep well included other things besides sponge baths and the source of the water we should drink. The professor from the Medical School, though temperate in his habits, was not a strict water drinker; once when I was a little rundown he prescribed a tablespoonful of *spiritus frumenti* three times a day before meals for a fortnight. This may have been the first time, though I doubt it, that I had ever tasted whisky. It was so pleasant a medicine that I kept it up for a second fortnight. He warned us all against swallowing grape seeds because they were liable to lodge in the appendix. To avoid the danger I stopped eating grapes altogether. The medical professor stressed exercise, of course. Very soon Freshman rooms were provided not only with small sponges but also with Indian clubs and dumbbells, in the manipulation of which we received proper training over in the gymnasium.

In the recommendation that we take long walks, many of us anticipated advice. For in my time a Freshman on his first Saturday or Sunday in New Haven climbed East Rock, walking along the edge as closely as he dared. The next week he took in the longer tramp over West Rock, where with others he climbed the split rocks of Judges' Cave, the hiding place of the two regicides, Goffe and Whalley. From these high points which overlooked the City of Elms, I began my exploration of New Haven and its lovely environs, and with classmates sailed along the shore, east and west, in a catboat.

As I now write, I am sitting by my study window where I have a good view of the red cliffs of East Rock, which was first seen of white men in 1614 by Adriaen Block, who named it "Rodeberg," or "Red Mountain." The Dutch navigator, I daresay, felt the same urge to climb to the top of Red Mountain as has since been felt by thousands of Freshmen when they first came to Yale and saw its red face glittering in September sunshine.

No Yale dormitory was provided with a lounge for talk and smoking in easy chairs. But we did not miss what we had never had. We crowded into one another's rooms, sitting, when chairs were filled, on window sills, beds, and floor, with pipes and cigarettes, talking endlessly, never however, saying anything about our studies, for that was taboo. Some suites were consecrated to poker, in which several members of my class were experts.

In spring and autumn we all gathered towards evening by the fence on the corner of Chapel and College Streets. The top rail, which was round, made a comfortable seat, and another round rail below was a good resting place for feet. On warm evenings the crowd was so large that many had to stand. If anyone wanted a bunch of Sweet Caporals (the favorite cigarette) or a lime-and-soda (the favorite drink) all he had to do was to step across a narrow street to Beers' Drug Store. Singing always started up spontaneously. Those old songs were the voice of Yale as it had been and as it yet was in my own time. In the morning we had to be out of bed by seven o'clock if we were to get to Battell Chapel for prayers at 8.10. Compulsory chapel, an institution as old as Yale itself, it was taken for granted would never die. As a jest someone might remark that prayers ought to be put among "the elective studies," but most of us in reality thought it well to begin the day with a recognition that the Lord still reigned in heaven if not on earth. One feature of the service, however, was quite unpopular. Several tutors were assigned to high seats where they could look down through the pews and spot students who might be taking a last look at their morning lesson while their heads were bowed low during President Porter's five-minute prayer. The names of all transgressors whom the tutors caught were sent to the Dean, who usually gave them a certain number of black marks for disobeying college rules. One day Dean Wright summoned me to his office and remarked with sober face: "Mr. Cross, you were reported for studying in Chapel yesterday morning. Were you?" At once I acknowledged my guilt with a "Yes, sir." When came, with relaxed face, the penalty: "I shall have to give you give marks. Don't do it again. Next time the marks will be more." A good thing about compulsory chapel was that it brought together all the students of Yale College once a day. When they were dismissed, the members of each class walked side by side in conversation to their recitation or lecture rooms. Chapel, like the fence, meant quick acquaintance for us all.

Against the democracy of a closely knit community life on a single Campus disruptive forces, though they existed in a mild form, had very little effect. There was, indeed, a faint line of social division between members of the college Societies and students who were left on the outside. This line of division almost disappeared in the case of the Junior Societies as a large majority of Juniors were taken into either Psi Upsilon or D.K.E. I was a member of Psi U, where I had a good time with intimate friends on an evening once a week. Even now a classmate sometimes asks me if I remember my excitement on a November night in 1884 when, as the returns of the national election were coming in, it looked as if Grover Cleveland would win against James G. Blaine. I rather think the story is true that I put a lighted cigarette over my right ear instead of a pencil and did not discover the mistake until a classmate shouted out that my hair was on fire.

Members of the three Senior Societies wore their pins a little too conspicuously in their neckties for the eyes of the envious classmates. Some prestige was lost by the Senior Societies because they passed over two outstanding scholars in my class who were to become valedictorian and salutatorian. At this very time, however, an impetus was given to scholarship by the revival of Phi Beta Kappa, which, once Yale's leading society, had met an ignominious death back in the 'fifties when it abandoned its fine traditions and made itself the rendezvous of a group of social lights almost exclusively. Set on its feet once more with the applause of President Porter and other members of the faculty, Phi Beta Kappa soon recovered its old honorable place in Yale College as a touchstone of broad, liberal scholarship in its best sense.

It was an era of "eating clubs" which served as a good mixing bowl for the class as we migrated, sometimes in rapid succession, from one of these clubs to another. My first eating club, consisting of a number of Freshmen, was run by a pale anemic widow who fed us on an anemic diet. As usual, breakfast at seven o'clock (oatmeal and weak coffee, one egg, no fruit); dinner at one (codfish cakes or dried beef); supper at six (prevailing dessert stewed prunes, tenderized by letting them soak in cold water for a few hours). We all quickly got out and started on the rounds of cheap places, stopping for a long time at a white house on the High Street side of Campus, which had formerly been the College Commons. There we ran into a group of classmates. The food was good enough for the price we paid, four dollars a week, and I could get there my favorite dessert, which was apple pie, coffee, and cheese; or coffee, cheese, and apple pie. In the course of time I was enticed away by a classmate who was managing a club of his own; and from that one I passed on to other similar clubs out of which some classmates were making profits that materially helped them through college.

The man in the class who seemed to have been born for a business career was Benjamin Kaye Heaton, who not only made a big success with an eating club, but midway in our college course laid the foundation of the Yale Coöperative Corporation, which he afterwards organized, for the sale of books and everything else college students need in their work. The year before coming to college he had proved his ability as a canvasser on the road for an illustrated subscription book. Towards the end of Freshman year he casually remarked to a group of us that he was going out again as soon as college closed and advised any of us who were hard up to try our luck during the summer with a very remarkable book which he had selected for himself. Several of us fell for the proposal and were duly trained as canvassers by an agent of the publisher who knew how to do it. The book was a compilation called *The Museum of Antiquity*, describing the wonders of Ancient Rome, Pompeii, Troy, and the Near East generally as revealed by recent excavations. Heaton, who chose his field of action with skill, returned to Yale in September with the spoils of a high-powered salesman. My roommate, Walter Frear, chose East Greenwich, Rhode Island, where without making much of an attempt to sell the book of wonders, he settled down for a good rest somewhere on the shore of Narragansett Bay. I took, as the scene of my first and last experience as a book agent, West Greenwich, for the most part a farming district, where before the summer was over I was threatened with being tarred and feathered if I did not get out of my own free will.

My very first sale was made in a farmhouse kitchen, where I explained to the farmer and his wife that I had called upon them first of all because I had been told they were readers of good books. Thereupon I pulled out a prospectus which hung concealed under my coat and began to set forth the marvelous things of the ancient world. While I was telling the story of the eruption of Mt. Vesuvius and the destruction of Pompeii, I noticed that the farmer kept shaking his head as if from some nervous affliction.

But I soon discovered that there was nothing the matter with his neck, for when his wife took pencil in hand to put her name down for a copy of the book, he jumped up and shouted that everything I had said was a lie, you couldn't get ashes enough to bury a city, and he wouldn't have the book in the house. His wife reduced him to silence by saying that she was buying the book for herself, not for him, that she had money of her own to pay for it, that the house and land were hers, anyway.

As soon as the quarrel seemed to be over, I shook hands with the wife, tried to shake hands with the husband, and so departed, happy over a sale on my first trial. In my innocence I was only amused by the scene, not anticipating that tinder had been lighted in that kitchen which would set the town on fire against me. For three weeks thereafter I tramped over the hills of West Greenwich, miles upon miles, with one excursion into Voluntown across the border in Connecticut. By that time I had decided to quit business. To make easy a release from my agreement with the publishers, a young local physician, with whom I passed a pleasant hour, kindly certified that on examination he found me greatly debilitated physically and mentally, partly owing to long tramps under a hot sun, and that I should be unable to go back to college unless I gave up the job and took a long rest in the shade.

I still had to return to deliver some sixty copies of the book to subscribers. It had been arranged that one of them, an intelligent and substantial farmer named Benjamin T. Gorton, was to drive me through his part of the town to leave the books with subscribers and collect my money. When I arrived at his house with the books one evening three weeks later, he turned a cold shoulder on me, even refusing at first to take me in and urging me to get out of town as quickly as I could. I asked him what it was all about. "Well," he said, in substance, "two years ago a man came over here from Providence and sold the farmers in the town a receipt for a substitute for paint. Some of them who tried it out found that it cost more than lead paint and that one good rain washed it all off their houses. If that man should ever show himself here again, he would get tar and feathers and a rail. My man [the manager of his farm] who goes over to the store most every day, says that they are all ready for you because you're

a worse liar than the man who sold them the receipt for a worthless paint."
I certainly was a bit skeered.

I had some difficulty in persuaded Mr. Gorton to let me stay over night,
but at last when his wife intervened in my behalf, he consented. The next
morning I had a talk with his man, who brought in the ringleader of
the opposition before the day was over. The ringleader, to whom I had
sold no book, came with fire in his eyes. I greeted him cordially and
showed him the book. We went over it together. I assured him that it contained no lies. He got interested as I turned page after page and read here
and there. Finally I gave him a damaged copy. We clasped hands and he
went away with the book under an arm. Within a day or two I had similar
talks with others in the posse. The result was that the next week I delivered
all the books, with the aid of Mr. Gorton and his horse and buggy.

In order to bring my nerves back to normalcy I stayed on for another
week, and listened to my host's racy stories of the countryside, which ran
back to training days when he was an officer in the militia. Nor should I
forget Mrs. Gorton who knew how to manage her house as well as her
husband. We began the day with a nourishing breakfast, starting with three
fingers of hard cider for Mr. Gorton and myself and a teaspoonful of sal-
eratus added to make it foam; then delicious johnnycakes with maple
syrup—I forget the rest.

One Campus with fence and chapel for all, a common curriculum for
all during the first two years and for a large majority during the last two
years, and migratory eating clubs, taken together, assured social and educational unity for each of the four classes for the whole body of students
so far as that is humanly possible. Over all was the tremendous influence
of athletics which held us bound together with "hoops of steel."

The gymnasium on High Street across from the Campus would now
be considered hopelessly inadequate for athletic training. On the main floor
was a narrow padded running track with some miscellaneous equipment
intended primarily for Freshmen. In a basement were two or three rowing
machines and at the foot of a stairway four bathtubs and two showers for
the athletes. The crew, however, was provided with a boathouse down East

Chapel Street on New Haven Harbor, ample for these boys though it and a successor have since been abandoned as out of date and out of place. But not until my Senior year did Yale have a fully developed athletic field of her own. Before and sometimes even after that year intercollegiate baseball and football games, when played in New Haven, were played in Hamilton Park, a mile and a half out Elm Street or Edgewood Avenue, which, I assume, was leased by the Yale Athletic Association. That is all, except headquarters for the crew on the Thames. And yet Yale never had a more brilliant career in baseball, football, rowing, and track athletics than when the Class of 1885 was doing its part in these competitive sports.

The Class of 1885 was baptized by immersion in the noisy waters of the Yale spirit on May 20, 1882. On that day our Freshman nine met Harvard's on the battlefield of Hamilton Park. Ordinarily Freshmen were not allowed to sit on the college fence. But in case they won the annual May contest with Harvard Freshmen, they were to be given eight sections of those sacred rails, at the tag end of the line on College Street. A great issue was thus at stake; for on the winning of this game depended where we could sit for the rest of the college year. We came out for the game in full force, occupying a large bloc of seats on the stand, and all about us were groups of upper-classmen, watching every move in the game and jeering at every misplay. At the end of the seventh inning, the score stood four to two in favor of Harvard; but after that Harvard made no more runs. The game was tied in the 9th inning, and won by Yale in the 11th inning by 5 to 4.

At once bedlam broke loose. We embraced one another and threw hats and umbrellas into the air as we jumped to the ground to put up the victors. The scene grew wilder when the Sophomores pounced upon us for their last rush. It was not the cut-and-dried rush of later degenerate days when under the light of torches the two classes stood in ranks and watched wrestling matches between their representatives. It was a spontaneous "shirt rush" of the good old days, where everybody ran in and tackled the first man of the enemy he could lay hands on and threw him to the ground if he were able, where hats were smashed and trampled into the dust, where coats were ripped up the back and shirts were torn into shreds. The scrimmage, rough but good-natured, was kept up for some distances on the road. Suddenly quiet fell upon the scene and we Freshmen, as if it had been so arranged, were permitted to fall in line for an orderly march to the fence, which we took in the midst of a large crowd of undergraduates, while a group of girls looked on from the balcony of the New Haven House. The eventful day closed with the most popular old songs by the Freshman Glee Club, who had been practicing them for weeks in anticipation of the victory. Upperclassmen who had never before heard our Glee Club sing listened in curiosity and loudly applauded. As we sat on the fence near the Sophomores in friendly conversation, we felt that we had no further occasion to worry. We were now on the map literally; for the *Yale Daily News* "at great expense" published a sketch of the fence on the front page of the next issue. Freshmen were requested to purchase a copy to send home to "their delighted parents," to give them "an idea of the kind of thing their victory has brought them."

Wild as was this scene, I was to have a part in a wilder scene two years later. In the college year 1883–84, Yale gained a triple victory, winning the intercollegiate championships in football and baseball, and the boat race with Harvard on the Thames. Only the championship in intercollegiate athletic games was lost, though Harry Brooks of our class had previously broken all intercollegiate records as a sprinter and had won the championship of America in the 220-yard dash. Victories on the gridiron and the diamond were easily won, the score in the last football game of the season with Harvard being 23 to 2 in favor of Yale. But as the time was approaching for the boat race, few if any of us expected that the crew could win. Our minds doubtless reverted too much to the race of the year before when, on the advice of a professional, a very high stroke was adopted, with the result that Harvard beat Yale by 15 lengths. No recovery from so great a disaster seemed possible within a year. But Harry Flanders, of our class, who was elected captain for the nest year, carefully trained his crew, without talking about it, to a longer and lower stroke and won over Harvard by 4 lengths. He had achieved the impossible and was a hero to every one of us.

The news of that memorable day (June 27, 1884) came over the wire just before six o'clock. Within a few minutes the chimes of Battell Chapel were set a ringing and the Campus by the fence was quickly crowded with students shouting and jumping with joy. Soon horns were blowing and cannon crackers were bursting at our feet and over our heads; while a wild procession of students began a march around the Campus to the noisy music of drums. By that time the excitement was spreading through the city. The chimes of Trinity Church struck up "Here's to Good Old Yale" and the bells of Center Church and the First Methodist Church rang out the victory. Before darkness came on, merchants along Chapel Street decorated their stores with bunting and the stars and stripes were flung to the breeze.

An immense throng of students met the returning crew at the railway station and, led by a brass band, escorted them, as they sat dressed in white flannel suits in open carriages, all the way to the college fence, burning Roman candles and red lights in front of them as if they were demigods. When they reached the fence the Campus was ablaze with a huge bonfire of tar barrels, and a cannon installed on the Green was firing a salute while hoarse voices were sending up cheer after cheer in a continuous volley. On a signal the noise subsided and a leader, stepping into the street, proposed "Three times three for Captain Flanders" and after that a long cheer for each member of the victorious crew. Then under the glare of red lights the crew were taken over to the New Haven House for supper and a brief rest, to return an hour or two later to the Campus for a celebration which lasted until the break of morning.

As I took my last look at the Campus flooded with light from the bonfire, rising and falling through giant elms and over the face of the long brick row, I felt an exhilaration which transcended the glare and noise of a celebration over an athletic victory. Did my imagination vaguely transmute the real scene into a vision of historic Yale where generations of young men have come in their search for the light of truth, and afterwards departed with gifts that Yale bestowed upon them? *Lux et Veritas*. I do not know. All I know is

> Bliss was it in that dawn to be alive,
> But to be young was very Heaven!

IV. High School Principal

Of course, most students as well as members of the faculty had nicknames. The one which has stuck to me through life is "Senator." It was given to me in the second term of Freshman year by a classmate whose room was near mine in a dwelling house where a group of us Freshmen had quarters together. He complained, half seriously, that I kept him awake nights by declaiming orations in the Websterian manner. The fact is that I was trying to commit to memory Burke's long address to the electors of Bristol, not so much for its political philosophy as for its logic and eloquence. Still, it may be that if my financial resources had not been exhausted after I graduated from Yale, I might have entered the Law School and ended my career as a Senator of the United States. This, however, is only a wild surmise, for I began to imagine, as I have noted, that nature had cut me out for a literary career. When I broached the subject to President Porter and Professor Beers, they both warned me that literature was a precarious profession if undertaken without some means of livelihood such as teaching in school or college. I followed their advice and armed with their testimonials and a certificate of my success as a teacher in a rural school I began a canvass of Connecticut prep and high schools in the hope of finding one that wanted a teacher of my "character and caliber."

So I come now to the tale of how I landed a job in the days when it is assumed that there was a job for everybody for the asking. A month after graduation I received word from Secretary Hine of the Connecticut State Board of Education that the Principal of the Staples High School in Westport had resigned; and that if I wanted the position I had better go to Westport for a conference with Mr. Horace Staples, the founder of the school. I took the first train that afternoon and called on Mr. Staples, a deaf octogenarian, to whom I explained my business through the mouthpiece of a yard-long ear trumpet. Mr. Staples greeted me with cold civility, saying that though no appointment had actually been made it was practically agreed that the call would go to an Amherst graduate whom he described as "a Cape Cod man." The appointment of the Principal I learned rested with an Executive Committee (really a Board of Trustees of the school), consisting of twelve members, of whom eight were local clergymen; and of the eight three were Episcopalians like myself.

Leaving Mr. Staples, I inquired the way to the parsonage of the first Episcopal clergyman on the list, the Reverend Alonzo N. Lewis, Rector of Holy Trinity. As soon as I told Mr. Lewis who I was, he told me he was a Yale graduate of the Class of 1852 and like me a member of Psi Upsilon. Soon I was accepting his hospitality for the night. After supper with his family we retired to his library, where we sat talking and smoking corncob pipes, occasionally sipping hard cider, until two or three o'clock in the morning. Mr. Lewis gave me a very intimate account of Yale life and customs, such as the hilarity over the burning of Euclid in the consulship of President Woolsey. He described Dickens and Thackeray, both of whom he had heard when they visited New Haven. A good mimic, he imitated their speech, even to the cockney dialect from which Dickens could never get quite free.

The business in hand, though it became incidental, during the ambrosial night I passed with Mr. Lewis, was never quite lost. Mr. Staples, I learned, was held in awe as one of the two or three richest men in the town. He was president of the First National Bank of Westport and owned most of its stock. He had acquired in business, principally as a dealer in grain, coal, and lumber down by the dock, a fortune of towards half a million dollars, which was mostly invested in railway bonds and New York bank stocks, giving him a return of 6 or 7 per cent. He was sharp, though not unscrupulous, in trade. But he was a close-fisted old man who never let a cent slip from his fingers, even for charity. In short, he was a rugged individualist. This was the common view, though not, as I was to learn, a just view, of Mr. Staples' character.

Naturally Westporters were taken by surprise when without solicitation he built a high school for their children, with the intention of turning it over to the town as a gift, perhaps with an endowment. The school had been running for only a year, under the general supervision of an

Executive Committee and with James H. Tufts, an Amherst man, as Principal. Tufts had had a hard time with Mr. Staples and had come out of the ordeal with typhoid fever. This story Mr. Lewis told me as a warning, but it only made me more eager for the adventure.

The next day Mr. Lewis took me on a round of visits to the clerical members of the Executive Committee, all of whom gave me a cordial reception. Forthwith the chairman of the Executive Committee, the Reverend B. J. Relyea, the genial and whimsical pastor of the Congregational Church at Greens Farms, called a meeting of the entire Committee and Mr. Staples to be held a fortnight hence in Mr. Lewis' study in the close of Trinity Church. I was invited to be present so that the lay members might look me over. On the appointed day I presented myself for inspection and a glare from Mr. Staples, who was surprised to see me there. After some general talk, Mr. Relyea picked up the end of the old man's trumpet and told him that the members of the Executive Committee were ready to ballot for a Principal, but that before they proceeded they would like to know whether he regarded himself as having the power to veto their decision. Mr. Staples replied that he would not veto any action they might take but "You all know that I want the Cape Cod man." As they were preparing to vote I started to take my leave, but was requested by the chairman to remain, for it was to be a secret ballot. When all was over Mr. Relyea picked up the ear trumpet again and informed Mr. Staples that Mr. Cross had been unanimously elected Principal. "I hope that it will turn out all right," the old man said, "but you know I wanted the Cape Cod man."

That evening I called on Mr. Staples, at his request, to talk over matters pertaining to the school as a business proposition. He had not invited me to supper, he remarked, because his housekeeper was away and he could find nothing in the pantry to eat but bread and butter and fig pie. He had, however, a cask of excellent cider in the cellar and proposed that I should go down and drawn a pitcherful while he held a candle at the head of the stairs to light me to the spigot. I climbed the steep stairway with the cider, appalled as much as amused by the prospect of having hard cider as a companion for another night in Westport.

As we talked over the cider Mr. Staples' manner to me mellowed noticeably. Yet despite his appeasement he proceeded to drive a hard bargain with me, which he said was similar to the one he made with Mr. Tufts the year before. Nothing had ever been said about the salary I was to receive as Principal. It now turned out that I was expected to take over the school on the basis of a sort of partnership with Mr. Staples. He would agree to pay the salary of an assistant, who was to be Miss Cynthia H. Whitaker, a competent and popular teacher, who had held this position the previous year. He was ready also to contribute $600 towards the running expenses of the school, and I was to have all the tuition fees which, on an anticipated enrollment of sixty students, would amount to $800. On the other hand, I was to pay the cost of heating the building, estimated at $400, and of a part-time janitor who could be had for $300. That is, if all went well, there would be left $700 for my services. At this point we began to dicker, a young Yankee against an old Yankee, who in the end promised to pay for the janitor.

The school opened auspiciously on August 31, 1885, with an increase in enrollment, owing perhaps to the prospectus of the Staples High School (picture of the building and a description of courses of study) which was widely distributed in the surrounding towns. This improvement in business pleased the old man. Very soon I was visiting him for a little while on an evening once a week; and on every Friday afternoon he came down to the school, midway between Westport and Saugatuck, to see for himself how things were going. At the founder's urgent request, I conducted a course in bookkeeping and commercial arithmetic for a group of special students during the winter. Mr. Staples did not want the school to neglect the boy who was looking forward to a clerkship in a store or a bank.

The main instruction, all the same, was given in the old established studies. I took the courses in Latin and Greek and in geometry; and introduced a course in English literature at a time when the student of English in high schools rarely extended beyond grammar and composition. I used to recite or read aloud to the class great passages in Shakespeare, Milton, Wordsworth, Byron, Keats, and Shelley, and encouraged the boys and girls to commit to memory something from every poem they read so that they might feel the rhythm of words. Once I asked the class to memorize the first twenty-five lines of Milton's *Paradise Lost* for the next lesson a week after. Nearly all of them stumbled through the twenty-five lines. As I was about to dismiss the class, I asked whether anyone could go on further. A girl raised her hand and I told her to start in. She went on and on, amid first grins and then wonder, until I called a halt to ask where the end would be. The end, she replied, was the end of the first book—793 lines. The beautiful verse often bogs down into lists of heathen divinities; but the music of their names carried her on. It was a marvelous display of memory such as I have never encountered in another of my thousands of students.

In order to conduct a course in English literature with full profit to a class, a few reference books at the very least are necessary. Not one such book was in the school There was, for example, no encyclopedia, no Webster's dictionary, either unabridged or abridged, no map except an old torn one of Westport. One evening I called upon Mr. Staples to lay the situation before him. I found the man of thrift sitting in all his glory. He had just taken from a coat pocket a large roll of postage stamps which the heat of that day had solidly stuck together. While I watched him picking off a stamp here and there, I made the impertinent remark that a man of his wealth ought not to be wasting his time on two-cent stamps. He said that he was never happier than when he saved not two cents but one cent. I ventured the suggestion that if he wet the roll the stamps would come off easily. "Yes," he rejoined, "but what about the gum?" I had to admit that he would lose the gum. I smiled as I said this and he smiled as he laid aside the damaged stamps.

I broached the subject of my mission. I told Mr. Staples that I wanted to lay the foundation of a little library in the school comprising a few reference books and a hundred or more miscellaneous volumes as a supplementary reading for the class in English literature. The whole would cost $600. After smacking his lips two or three times, he said, "I'll tell you what I'll do. I will give you $300 if you raise the other $300 from the parents of the students in the school." This seemed to be a hopeless proposal. But at the suggestion of a friend I called at five o'clock the next day on a generous woman who had contributed largely to the building and support of Trinity Church, and gave her a full account of my conference with Mr. Staples. "That," she remarked, "is just like Uncle Horace," as she drew a check in my name for $300. "Be sure," she added, "to show the check to Uncle Horace and tell me what he says." An hour later I threw the check on his table. He looked it over and asked me what it was for. I told him what it was for. He squirmed in his chair and said he did not suppose that Mrs. Page would do anything like that. I assured him that she had done just that, and I stayed on until Mr. Staples also did just that.

The thrifty octogenarian was a skillful if beneficent chiseler. By a clever device he had cut down the cost of those books to himself from $600 to $300. As he viewed the transaction he had saved $300. The device which worked well in procuring books he tried out with less success on expenditures in connection with the school building. Some of the rooms were left partly unfinished. Whenever I asked Mr. Staples how or why this had happened, he always said that he was leaving a few things for the town to do when the school became its property.

Once the chisel slipped in his hands. He had intimated that he would like to have me arrange for a public celebration of his eighty-fifth birthday, to be held at the school on Monday, February 1, the day after his birthday. I duly submitted for his approval a program to consist of recitals by the students and addresses in his honor by well-known men in and outside Westport. His face glowed with delight as I related what I had in mind, only to take on a sober hue when I told him that the program could not be carried out unless he built a stage in the assembly hall of the school. To this proposal involving an expenditure of $100 or more he issued a positive, almost angry, No. Nevertheless I went on with the preparations for the celebration in the expectation that after a few days he would see the necessity of having a stage for the exercises. But a month passed and he still stood adamant. In this crisis I took action so daring that I yet wonder at my nerve. I let the job out to a contractor, telling him to send the bill to Uncle Horace, on the understanding that if he didn't settle it I would. It so happened that Mr. Staples visited the school while the work was going on and demanded an explanation. I said that I was in the dilemma of having engaged five or six men to come there next week to extol what Horace Staples had done for Westport and having no place where they could stand high enough to be heard by the audience. He asked me who the five or six men were and when I gave him their names he was surprised at their prominence. He walked across the hall for a short talk with the contractor and when he came back said he would take care of the bill. I learned afterwards that he imagined he had got a reduction of $25 on it.

The celebration the next week in honor of Mr. Staples and the school he had founded was a day of wide interest to the community. At noon Mr. Staples gave a dinner to a large group of distinguished guests. Two hours later the assembly hall of the school was crowded to the doors with men and women not only of Westport but of neighboring towns. The program for the students was so devised as to form a comprehensive picture of the work they were doing. After that was over, ten or twelve men, one of them from as far afield as Stamford, paid their tributes to Mr. Staples in five-minute speeches for establishing the first high school in Westport; and in behalf of his fellow students the orator among them presented Mr. Staples with a pair of gold-rimmed spectacles. But the address which commanded the most attention was the octogenarian's general reply to all the eulogies he had listened to through his uplifted ear trumpet. The audience was astonished that he could speak so well, for none of us knew that in his youth he attended the Free School in Easton, once one of the leading college preparatory schools in New England, founded by a distant cousin, Samuel Staples, and that for six years afterwards he taught in the district schools of the neighborhood. But he really startled us by his frank confession of the prime error of his long life:

"All you that hear me today, let me entreat you to resolve to do some good at once. Be assured the first good act will lead you to want to do good to the end of your days. Be sure and not wait until you have seen fourscore years, but act at once and rejoice in doing good."

A week or two later I put his confession to a test. I told him that I wanted to try out a course in elementary physics and chemistry which would require some apparatus for simple experiments. He inquired, as was his way, how much the apparatus would cost. I replied that my estimate was $300. Though the man of thrift tightened his lips, another man within him authorized me without more ado to go ahead. There was no word about splitting the cost with somebody else.

At the end of that academic year I felt that I must leave the school to take a fellowship at Yale which would enable me to go on with advanced studies in English literature, and to some extent in philosophy. On my recommendation Thomas C. Stearns (Yale 1886) was appointed as my successor. There was at the time some comment on the tough, cross, and stern names borne by the first three Principals of the Staples High School, though in fact none of us wore severe faces. Mr. Tufts, who was to become a Professor Philosophy in the University of Chicago, married Miss Whitaker, the assistant teacher; and Mr. Stearns, who after a while shifted from education to a business career, married one of the girls under his instruction; while I alone, who refrained from flirtations, escaped "fancy-free."

My last official meeting with Mr. Staples and his Executive Committee took place in a lower room of the High School. They had assembled to consider the appointment of my successor and to wish me Godspeed. We all sat near shelves filled with the books I had procured for a library. In the rear of the room I had arranged for their inspection the new apparatus designed to illustrate some of the fundamental principles of physics and mechanics. Curious to hear what Mr. Staples would say, I picked up a vacuum tube containing at one end a feather and a nickel, and, tilting the tub, let him see nickel (perhaps it was a dime) and feather hit the other end at the very same instant. He was puzzled and asked me to explain the trick. I told him that it was no trick, for in a vacuum the velocity of all falling bodies is the same. He shook his head as if he were displeased with the sad behavior of a coin in a contest with a feather.

V. Student in the Yale Graduate School

My return to Yale in September, 1886, was in many ways like returning home. Twelve of my classmates were still in residence as students in the Graduate and Professional Schools of the University, of whom, incredible as it may now seem, seven were enrolled in Theology. Besides these, two other classmates were permanently settled in New Haven for business careers. There were also with us several Sheffield men of our time with whom we had been closely associated. As a body we formed a sort of microcosm of the Class of 1885. As '85 men dwindled their places were taken by '86 and '87 men with whom I was well acquainted, among them William Lyon Phelps, my lifelong friend and colleague on the Yale Faculty.

With the march of time my circle of friends grew wider and wider. By a curious chance I joined an eating club in a house on Wall Street, where as a Freshman five years before I had been fed on prunes once or twice a day. It was a large club in which divinity students predominated. There was no question now about having enough to eat except on one day in the great blizzard of March, 1888, when we were forced down to a diet of buckwheat griddlecakes flooded with butter and maple syrup. Here in Zion life went on smoothly among familiar and new faces amid serious talk relieved by wit and raillery which sometimes took the form of improvised verses.

The fellowship to which I was assigned by the faculty of Yale College for advanced studies in English literature involved certain services which I was to perform under the direction of a member of an Executive Committee of the Graduate School. The member who first took me under his wing was Hubert A. Newton, Yale's leading Professor of Mathematics, who informed me that I was to act as one of the supervisors of Freshman entrance examinations and to read all the entrance papers in Latin. To my consternation he added that I would be expected to take his class in calculus whenever he was away. I protested that I had only a very slight knowledge of the subject. After some talk, it was arranged that I should begin the study of calculus at once by myself with the privilege of calling on him for assistance if I met with any difficulties. Meeting with difficulties, I called on him many times. Twice I took over his class, once for a week in November and again for a week in February. After that he asked me no more. I grew very fond of Professor Newton, who liked young men. Years afterwards I learned that Josiah Willard Gibbs, Yale's great mathematical physicist, consulted with him, week by week, sometimes day by day, while engaged in epoch-making discoveries in the field of thermodynamics.

The next year Professor Newton released me to Professor Tracy Peck, Yale's foremost scholar in Latin, who let me alone until a few weeks before Commencement, when he asked how I was getting along with the essay I was writing for him as my adviser. This was the first time, I replied, that I had ever heard of such a requirement being attached to the fellowship I then held. Since the time was too short to write a suitable essay, I requested that he accept, in lieu of an essay, a Latin translation of Lincoln's "Address at Gettysburg" which I had made when an undergraduate. In the emergency he accepted it.

My translation of Lincoln's speech on the battlefield of Gettysburg served me well in an hour of need more than forty years afterwards when I incorporated part of it in an address before a distinguished international audience where others spoke in French, German, Italian, and Spanish as well as in Latin and English. I quoted Lincoln to show that in some mysterious way the political ideals of Cicero and Demosthenes received a new birth in Lincoln's great speech. The occasion was the observance, under the auspices of the American Academy of Arts and Letters, of the two thousandth anniversary of Vergil's birth.

Soon after coming into residence as a Graduate Fellow I was appointed a proctor, a minor officer of Yale College, just below the rank of tutor, whose first duty was to keep in good order the students in the dormitory where he was provided with a suite of rooms. It was further understood that a proctor would be available to give regular instruction in his own field of study whenever a tutor for any reason, such as illness or resignation, dropped out of the ranks. Thus for a part of my last two years as proctor I substituted for J. Ernest Whitney, a promising young Instructor in English who fell a victim to tuberculosis. During the long period of anxious suspense, his work was divided between me and Edward T. McLaughlin, a brilliant tutor in English. I read half of the Sophomore compositions, and met the men individually for conference. Of Mr. Whitney's courses of study, I was permitted to choose the one in Elizabethan literature. This was my first real experience in college teaching. Though it retarded the pace I had struck in my own studies, I made up for part of the loss by intensive work through an intervening summer.

Thank God, graduate studies in English literature at Yale as elsewhere were not yet organized in specialized courses of which a student must take a fixed number, reckoned by lecture or conference hours, in order to qualify for a degree. At that time Yale had in English only two professors of the first rank—Professor Beers of Yale College and Professor Lounsbury of the Sheffield Scientific School. A student might choose either of these two men as his responsible director. Naturally I chose Professor Beers as he had been my former teacher and also because my fellowship was under the jurisdiction of the faculty of Yale College.

His advice (almost a command) was to read, read, read, along lines which we agreed upon. On this carefully designed reading program I was to take notes and then submit them to him as a basis for general discussion as we sat by a little table in his office, sometimes with cigars. More than once he told me that when I came to a great author I should read all his published works, some perhaps rapidly, but most of them, in the words of Lord Bacon, "with diligence and attention." In short, I should box the compass of the principal writers on whom my studies were to be based.

This view of literary study is well illustrated by a course of reading which Professor Beers laid out for me in the summer of 1885 just before my departure for Westport. The program was to cover the leading English romantic poets in the first years of the nineteenth century, with Wordsworth as the center. I was to read everything in the six-volume edition of Wordsworth, not omitting the Ecclesiastical Sonnets, so that I might see, I assume, both how high the poet could rise, and how low he could sink.

I was also to read in the same large way, Coleridge, Scott, Southey, Byron, Keats, and Shelley. In addition to all this, I was to read a mass of criticism, serious, light, and humorous, which had grown up around these poets while they were still living. This course of reading formed a coherent whole, and yet it was so varied in its parts as to keep me awake nights after long days of teaching.

In conference with Mr. Beers it was now decided that I should start in on a three-year course in reading, to begin with Elizabethan literature and to proceed in a wide sweep down through the next two centuries to Wordsworth and his compeers. The first book Professor Beers asked me to read, it may be curious to tell, was Lyly's *Euphues* (1579), whose strange and affected style created a sensation in its day.

When I reached the middle of the eighteenth century, I enlarged my field of study still further by including French literature of that period, with the result that I chose as the subject of my dissertation for the Ph.D. degree the interrelations of English and French fiction, with some excursions into other literary forms.

The cosmopolitan urge carried me on into several literatures. I learned a little Spanish under Professor William I. Knapp, my former instructor in French. I attended Professor Alfred L. Ripley's small Senior class in Goethe's *Faust* and lyrics; and with a few others was invited to his apartment to read Goethe's *Iphigenie* and Lessing's *Laokoon*, dealing, by way of contrast, with the art of sculpture and the art of literature. In a class with Professor George Bendelari I learned enough Italian to read before the year was over the most famous cantos in Dante's *Divina Commedia*. Subsequently I made by myself essentially the same kind of study of Dante that I had made of Wordsworth. While I was reading Dante and Goethe, a Norwegian Divinity student, named Olaus Dahl, awakened my interest in Ibsen and Björnson, then the contemporary high lights in Norwegian literature. With Mr. Dahl as tutor I embarked on Norwegian grammar and went on until I was able to make my way through Ibsen's *Brand*, which had not yet been translated into English. Of this tremendous dramatic poem I wrote an account, which two years later appeared in the *Arena* (a magazine long since defunct) for December, 1890. This was the first article I ever submitted for publication off the Yale Campus. In high glee I flourished the check for $25 in the faces of my friends. A little later I contributed an article on Ibsen's social plays to the *New Englander and Yale Review*, a magazine which I was destined to reorganize and edit twenty years later.

This rather wide reading in various foreign languages, which at first satisfied a mere inner craving for knowledge as such, created for me ultimately a good background for the study of all forms of English literature in relation to similar forms in other literatures. It was doubtless a desire to have a look into the foundations of literature that led me into philosophy. As an undergraduate student I had taken with Professor George T. Ladd a general course in philosophy which surveyed the main field from the Greeks down through the nineteenth century. Now as a graduate student I had an opportunity to look more closely into the philosophy of three master minds which have had immense influence on modern thought. To each of them a year's study was devoted, in a course of lectures given by Professor Ladd who met the class twice a week. In order first came the transcendental philosophy of Kant, with its a priori conception of time and space. Then came Lotze, who brought into philosophy the fresh mental equipment of a physiologist. He endeavored to reconcile the mechanistic view with the idealistic view of man and nature, much as philosophers are still trying to do. In this attempt he wrote a book, called the *Microcosmus*, of more than fourteen hundred pages in the English translation. Lotze's philosophy made a strong appeal to Professor Ladd, the theologian, for it appeared to smooth out any apparent contradictions between science and theism. For me the *Microcosmus* was an almost boundless realm for thinking through as well as I could specific questions in science and metaphysics with their literary bearings.

Most interesting to me in those formative years was Schopenhauer's *World as Will and Idea*, fifteen hundred pages of it in Lord Haldane's remarkable translation from the German. With the thoroughgoing pessimism of Swift and other great writers I was familiar; but in Schopenhauer I was first confronted with pessimism as an uncompromising philosophic system. Up to a certain point, Schopenhauer was an idealist like Kant.

That is, the world of man and nature in which we live and move is, objectively considered, only a creation of our minds; it is built up from sense perceptions which we generalize in consciousness as ideas and ultimately as one great Idea. But behind this phenomenal existence there is something real, which Kant called "the thing in itself" without being able to define it. Schopenhauer proceeded to define this "thing in itself" as Will, not the will of a conscious spiritual being, perhaps a God, such as was assumed by Bishop Berkeley, but unconscious Will working aimlessly through the blind forces of nature and the actions of mankind. This is the basis of philosophic pessimism, pure and simple. Schopenhauer did not make a pessimist out of me, but he held my rapt attention by the skill with which he developed his metaphysical assumptions and by the wealth of his quotations. He ridiculed the claim of Leibnitz that this is the best world that God could create out of the materials at hand. A world worse than this one, he declared, could not possibly exist. It is true, he admitted, that the planets move in harmony in their orbits under the force of gravitation, but let there be some disturbance, however slight, among them, and the whole universe would blow up. A very moderate increase in heat would dry up all the waters of the earth. Any great alteration in the atmosphere would extinguish all life. As it is misery lies at the foundation of all human life. The lower classes work seven days a week in order to live; the middle classes work six days a week and pass the seventh day in ennui; the upper classes, who live in ennui for seven days a week, are the most miserable of all. Ennui is misery. At best there is just enough pleasure in life to keep some of us from suicide. Notwithstanding the contention that there could be no worse world, I felt as I was reading Schopenhauer that he must have been, while writing his book, one of the happiest men who ever lived. He was too gay in his *obiter dicta* for a pessimist. For me he was primarily a man of letters whose metaphysical gymnastics stirred up the muscles of my mind.

VI. Master of English

When my graduate studies came to an end, I was twenty-seven years old. The time had come for me to embark upon the career of teaching English as my life work. It was my hope that I might obtain at once a position which would give me some leisure for miscellaneous writings of a semipopular character. During the last academic year when I was conducting one of the courses of Ernest Whitney who was ill of tuberculosis at Colorado Springs, I was enrolled without the title among Yale Instructors and Assistants in Instruction, and was thus in line, as Professor Beers informed me, for an appointment as Instructor in English, were one to be made for the next academic year. It was decided, however, to appoint a Professor in English of the first rank, who would be able to build up the work in Old and Middle English. Negotiations were begun with Professor Albert S. Cook of the University of California, who wavered for a time but finally ceased from wavering. So I was out, and had to wait five years for an invitation to return to Yale.

My proctor's rooms in Farnam College looked down upon North College in the old Brick Row across a narrow strip of the Campus. Precisely at eight o'clock in the morning a rather short and stout man wearing a silk hat would enter that building. At various times through the day he would leave for an hour or two, always to return and keep his lights burning at night until the Battell chimes struck eleven. Instantly a man rose from his desk, put on a coat and hat, and the room was in darkness. This man was William R. Harper, professor of Semitic Languages and Biblical Literature, soon to be the first President of the rejuvenated University of Chicago. During my last year in the Graduate School he seemed to be a good deal interested in my future. On reading an essay of mine, never published, on the medieval Jews as one of the avenues through which ancient learning came down into modern times, he urged me to concentrate my literary studies on the English Bible. This advice though never carried out in the way he intended, did have its effect, years afterwards, when I helped to have parts of the Old Testament introduced as an elective into the curriculum of preparatory schools.

One day Professor Harper remarked that if I were unable to find an opening as instructor in a good college, I might well consider, for the time being at least, a position in a good preparatory school. Then he told me about Shady Side Academy in the suburbs of Pittsburgh, the Principal of which was a friend of his. There were then two vacancies in the staff of instructors—one in Latin, which he thought would be taken by James J. Robinson, a Princeton man who had a Ph.D. degree from Yale, and the other in English which was still available. In the circumstances this position rather appealed to me. It seemed to me that it might be a good thing to get out of New England for a while and see how people lived beyond the Alleghenies in Pittsburgh, which I had often heard described as lurid as "hell with the roof off." On Professor Harper's recommendation I received a conditional appointment as Master of English in Shady Side Academy. Before making the appointment irrevocable the Principal wrote that he wanted to have a conference with me. In less diplomatic language I replied that I should like to look him and the school over also. His name was Crabbe (William R.), a name which might be indicative of a temperament more difficult than my own.

I made the trip to Pittsburgh by daylight, in order to get a view of the devastation wrought by the flood at Johnstown three weeks before. Mr. Crabbe met me at the station and took me to the home of Oliver McClintock, a Yale man who then had two sons in college, Norman and Walter, whom I had met in conference on their English compositions. As a guest of the McClintocks, who introduced me to their friends, I remained in Pittsburgh for several days to supervise the examination of candidates for entrance to the Yale Freshman class. In the meantime my appointment received the approval of the trustees and faculty of the Academy. There was, however, some disappointment over my church affiliations. Principal Crabbe and Mr. John C. Sharpe, the second in command, both graduates of Wooster College, an excellent Presbyterian institution in Ohio, were ardent Presbyterians in a Presbyterian community. They seemed to think that God was a Presbyterian. Still, they conceded that an

Episcopalian might be a Christian. The shadow passed and I left for home in a happy mood.

That summer, on July 17, 1889, I married Helen Baldwin Avery, a daughter of William Burrill Avery, a veteran of the Civil War, and of Helen Mar Baldwin of Mansfield. The marriage ceremony was performed in the house of her parents in Willimantic, Connecticut, by the Reverend S. R. Free, a former pastor of the Congregational Church there, who had turned Unitarian under the influence of Mrs. Humphry Ward's *Robert Elsmere*. My wife, who followed Shakespeare's advice to take for her husband a man a little older than herself, belonged to the family of Averys who had settled in early colonial times in Groton, Connecticut, where she was born, September 3, 1864. The Averys all descended from one of the founders of Groton, Capt. James Avery, who fought in the Indian Wars and took a conspicuous part in the civil affairs of the town and colony, as a friend and companion of John Winthrop, Jr., Governor of Connecticut.

The friendship between Helen Avery and myself began many years before we thought of marriage. We were students together in the old Natchaug School, where we learned our elementary physics and chemistry out of a book bearing the name of a kinsman of hers. That manual called *Natural Philosophy* had a strange introduction on the care of the eyes, which Principal Welch advised us to read and remember. My eyes, which were then farseeing, often wandered across the room where Helen had her seat. Whether it was love at first sight or at second sight, I do not remember. It was a happy marriage of one Yankee to another with enough difference in temperament to keep the household alive.

The week before we were to leave for Pittsburgh in September I received telegrams from the President of the University of Kansas offering first to appoint me as an Instructor and two days later as an Assistant Professor of English. I was thus confronted with a situation which might determine my ultimate as well as my immediate career and which, at the same time, I felt involved a question of honor, for I had made no reservations when I accepted the position in Shady Side Academy. I suggested a compromise to the President of the University of Kansas, which was that I would come to him the next year. This was impossible, he replied, as an immediate addition to his English staff was imperative. It was now or never. So I never went to Kansas.

On the way to Pittsburgh, we passed a week end in Philadelphia with the family of a cousin, James, the youngest son of Marcus Cross, who had spent his life in attempts to dethrone King Alcohol. They were all ardent admirers of John Wanamaker, who had recently been appointed Postmaster General in President Harrison's Cabinet. Mr. Wanamaker I saw in action not as a distributor of political patronage but as a religious enthusiast in the rôle of Superintendent of the Bethany Presbyterian Sunday School. Standing on a round platform in the middle of an auditorium he led an immense throng of men, women, and children in singing Gospel hymns until the roof rang, while he kept turning round on the platform, looking here and looking there, waving his arms and swinging high his hymn book. The performance resembled, I daresay, the song fests conducted by Ira D. Sankey in his early days before he became associated with Dwight Moody, the great evangelist; only, if my memory is clear, there were no solos. When it was over, the audience divided into groups who marched into adjoining rooms for a study of the Bible lesson of the day. I attended Mr. Wanamaker's class, of which my cousin was a member, was introduced to him, and listened to his fervent exposition of a passage in the New Testament.

When we reached Pittsburgh, on someone's recommendation we took temporary lodgings in the family of a Mr. Sankey who was a cousin of Ira. This Mr. Sankey could not sing any more than I could, but his daughter had the voice of a lark. He told me the story of his kinsman's life from childhood upward, remarking by the way that he was no evangelist like Ira; nor had he made so much money; in fact he was nearly down and out.

On a Sunday morning an incident occurred which corroborated to some extent what he had related of himself. Being out of cigars that morning, I went across the street to buy a few at a drugstore. I returned without any and without even seeing any, for the cigar case was covered with a dark cloth and the clerk informed me that it was against the law to sell cigars on Sunday. When I told this to Mr. Sankey, he laughed and said the trouble is that you are not yet known in these parts. He took my money, went out, and in a few minutes came back with a bunch of long, loosely rolled, cheap cigars having the strength of a Samson. While I was trying to smoke one, he remarked that the Sunday sale of alcoholic liquors was also prohibited in Pittsburgh, but there were speakeasies all over the city. My new acquaintance, who had a thirsty look, offered to take me to a speakeasy down the street so that I might see what one was. I drew the line at that. I still see a face writ all over with disappointment.

That year Shady Side Academy opened with a larger enrollment than ever before and with two new instructors besides myself; Dr. Robinson of Princeton in Latin and William Z. Morrison of Cornell in Science. Somewhat later came Hermann J. Schmitz, widely known for his success in teaching German in the summer school at Chautauqua. These new instructors, who outnumbered the other members of the faculty, naturally exerted a great influence towards a revision of the curriculum of the school in those respects which all of us regarded as desirable if not necessary. The students for whom the curriculum was designed formed a homogeneous body in that all of them were drawn from around Pittsburgh and its environs, and nearly all of them were preparing for college with Princeton and Yale in the lead. My work, more comprehensive than that of others, covered all the six Forms or six classes. In the first two Forms I subjected the boys to an intensive study of English grammar, relieved by miscellaneous reading which was to increase in amount as the class moved forward through the upper Forms. No such course in English literature was then required for entrance to college, and as a consequence none was yet provided, as a rule, in the great preparatory schools. Harvard and Cornell, however, were beginning to ask some English literature of candidates for admission. They were the pioneers. Princeton prescribed only an essay on any subject which a candidate might elect. This was no real test, for the essay might be written in advance under the direction of an instructor and then be committed to memory by the candidate. The Sheffield Scientific School prescribed an examination in English grammar, with a question on the distinction between strong and weak verbs about which few boys had ever heard anything unless they had read W. D. Whitney's "English Grammar." Yale College prescribed no examination in English of any kind. Not until 1894 did colleges agree generally on a requirement in English literature. When that time came graduates of Shady Side Academy were ready for it by five years of reading in English and American literature.

It also fell to my lot to give the instruction in English and American history, which I treated, in a measure, as the background of English and American literatures. And besides that I often took in hand for a few weeks students who were preparing for their college entrance examinations in French. I have undertaken many and various jobs in a long life. In some I have failed. In others I have met reasonable expectations. I like to think about the job I performed as Master of English in Shady Side Academy because it has the air of completeness in that no student who came under my instruction and entered college while I was there failed to pass his college entrance examination in English or history or French. That was a clean record which now awakens my admiration!

I was hardly settled as a teacher of boys before I was giving talks on literary and semiliterary subjects before various adult organizations. One which I carefully wrote out as an address on "What and How to Read" I was asked to repeat several times. The *New York World* had just come out with a Sunday edition of twenty-six pages, at a time when eight or twelve pages was the rule for most Sunday newspapers. One of the questions I raised was what should a reader do with a monstrosity or octopus of this kind? This address led to a request by a group of young women who had graduated from college or "finished" in a "female seminary" for a class to guide them in their reading. The class, when it materialized, consisted of some twenty-five women, ten of whom were in middle life. For them I laid out a course in Shakespeare, meeting them once a week for twenty weeks for a lecture and a free-for-all discussion of one play at a time. The next year we chose Charles Eliot Norton's beautiful and exact translation of Dante's *Divine Comedy* which opened a new world for them. The third year we decided upon English poetry of the nineteenth century. Then at last came a series of twenty lectures on the great English novelists from Defoe to Meredith, which made an appeal to large audiences. These lectures on the novel were all written out and adjusted to one another in such a way as to indicate the general development of English fiction for two centuries through romance and realism. Without being quite aware of it, I had no designed in rough outline a book which might be made good enough sometime for publication.

Besides these four series of lectures, I accepted numerous invitations for short informal talks before audiences of all sorts running from schools and church clubs to after-dinner speeches in which I tried to be humorous. On such occasions I was rather likely to run up against the Reverend George Hodges, of Calvary Episcopal Church, an eloquent preacher and a prime mover in measures for promoting the intellectual and social welfare of all classes of people within and without his large parish. I often had to warm my brain up to alert action, for Dr. Hodges liked to start a debate. He had a lively sense of humor. Every winter he gave at his evening services a series of informal sermons (which were not sermons) on a wide range of subjects. One evening in announcing that the plates would not be passed for the offering, he entertained his congregation with a preliminary discourse on three-cent pieces which, he remarked, the United States Government seems to have coined especially for my congregation, for several thousand three-cent pieces (he reported the exact number) had been dropped on the plates during the last year. Amid some show of merriment in the congregation he expressed a sincere hope that this practice might now end. It is true, he conceded, that a three-cent piece looks like a dime in a dim light, but when daylight comes it is only a three-cent piece. The next Sunday evening he announced that no only three-cent piece was discovered on the plates the week before.

My classes and addresses were an incentive towards literary studies that carried me far afield during the long summer vacations which were passed in Willimantic and Gurleyville by the village store, still a center of gossip and tales of rural life. There in my grandfather's house, where my mother was yet living, I read to the end Dante's *Divina Commedia* and translations of his other works and his letters. There also, my curiosity being awakened by William Morris' "Sigurd the Volsung" and "The Earthly Paradise," which I was to assign to my class of young women, I learned enough Old Icelandic to read some of the Sagas and the Younger Edda. I was fascinated by the simple, direct storytelling of the old Norsemen, with here and there a dramatic episode, just as people talk who are not trying to build up an artificial climax such as sophisticated writers strain for. It was not the literature of conscious art. It was the literature of "an art that nature makes." At the same time I learned enough modern Icelandic to read, with difficulty, a few charming contemporary peasant stories and little folk plays which were then being performed all over Iceland in barns and sheds temporarily made into theaters. Coming under the influence of Gerhard H. Balg, of the University of Wisconsin, I also turned to reading for a season the existing fragments of the translation of the Bible into Gothic made by Bishop Ulfilas in the fourth century of the Christian Era. Here I acquired some knowledge of an old Germanic language antedating in its literary monuments our own Anglo-Saxon. After summer studies like these, with a little afternoon work in the hayfields and visits to the Connecticut shore, we returned to our friends in Pittsburgh.

Among our Pittsburgh friends were Joseph R. Hunter, an elderly merchandise broker, and his wife Cornelia, who was an elder half-sister of Mrs. H. C. Frick. One evening my wife reported to me that Mrs. Hunter had proposed that we join them in renting a commodious brick house and running it on a cooperative basis with a young woman as housekeeper. Under this arrangement we passed a happy year together, but at the end of that time it seemed best for Helen and me to go our own way. Soon afterwards our first child was born, and named after his father.

Mr. Hunter was seventy-five years old while I was but thirty. Like myself he was a Democrat who swore by the ashes of the Democratic party, out of which, he used to say, had risen Grover Cleveland. Though not a college man he was among the best informed men I ever knew. His education came from long experience with men. He lived, as it were, two lives, one in the immediate present and one in the memory of the past, both functioning together. He still dressed much as he had dressed when a young man before the Civil War, except that he had laid aside the stock. On rising from the breakfast table, he always took a pinch of snuff, and then in silk hat and Prince Albert coat he boarded a trolley for his office in town. Every morning he called at a bucket shop where he speculated on a few shares of stock, usually taking the short side of the market, and then made his rounds among his customers, the wholesale merchants, who bought through him as their agent molasses and other heavy goods. Before leaving for home in the afternoon he again visited his bucket shop to collect his gains or pay his losses. When he greeted me on his return home he usually carried, under one arm, where it would stick, a copy of yesterday's *New York Evening Post*, which he read religiously for E. L. Godkin's editorials, the best in the world, he said, and for shrewd guesses on the way the stock market was likely to go the next week, up or down.

After dinner we walked into another room by ourselves, where he took his evening pinch of snuff, sometimes remarking that the only proper way to use tobacco is to snuff it. This was a preliminary act of grace before lighting a cigar with me for an hour's talk, running back, if I could lead him that way, into fifty years of political history as he had actually observed it. He particularly liked to go into details on presidential elections. He well remembered, for instance, the hard cider campaign of 1840 when the Whig candidate, William Henry Harrison, the military hero of Tippecanoe, was swept into office, only to die a month after his inauguration. During the campaign of 1848 Gen. Winfield Scott, the Whig candidate of Mexican War fame, made a speech in Pittsburgh, he said, from the deck of his steamer to a group of German and Irish longshoremen, whose votes he won by telling them how much he loved "the sweet German accent" and "the rich Irish brogue."

As correspondent of a Pittsburgh newspaper, Mr. Hunter spent some time in Washington during the administration of President Buchanan and heard the angry debates in the Senate over the extension of slavery into Kansas. He was sitting in the Senate gallery when, sometime after the election of Abraham Lincoln, Senator John C. Breckinridge, the silver-tongued orator of Kentucky, made an eloquent speech justifying secession and the Senators from the South rose from their seats and with Senator Breckinridge at their head silently walked out of the Senate Chamber, leaving the spectators breathless. I sat breathless, too, when I heard Mr. Hunter describe the scene.

By 1893 there was considerable uneasiness among the new instructors in Shady Side Academy. They felt very insecure in their positions, and the promise of later advancement looked equally dubious. Two of them resigned. Their places were easily filled at lower salaries, not with Yale or Princeton men, but from a list of candidates recommended by a teachers' agency. When I came up for my annual appointment for the academic year 1893–94, I asked for a moderate raise in salary, which was denied. I was told bluntly to take the position on the old terms or to leave it, just as I preferred. I decided to take it, on the psychological ground that it is easier to go from one job to another than from no job at all. My hope was that by 1894 something else would turn up.

Andrew Carnegie had given Pittsburgh a million dollars for a library which was building in Schenley Park. The management he placed in the hands of a large committee with most of whose members I was well acquainted. To try out my chances for appointment as librarian I canvassed them all and met in general with a cordial reception.

My last conference was with Henry Clay Frick, head of the Carnegie Steel Company, whom I had never met. The year before, during the terrible Homestead strike, an anarchist had brushed past an office boy into Mr. Frick's private room with the intent to kill him. He put two bullets into Mr. Frick's neck and slashed him with a dagger in leg, thigh, and side before he could be overpowered. As a result Mr. Frick was guarded by detectives and a large office force on the Saturday morning when I entered the anteroom of his offices in the Carnegie Building to keep an eleven o'clock appointment which had been made for me by Mrs. Frick. When I told a clerk, who stood behind a grated window, that I had an appointment with Mr. Frick, he replied that there must be some mistake, Mr. Frick was very busy and could see no one. I protested and urgently requested that my card be taken into him. There was some whispering among the clerks. Mr. Frick's secretary was called in; he looked at the card, looked at me, and immediately conducted me through several doors into the sanctum where his chief sat at a desk with a telephone at his ear. Mr. Frick beckoned me to a chair by his side. It was unnecessary for me to announce my mission, for he already knew what it was. For two hours we sat there and talked; I told him of my interviews with his colleagues on the Library Committee, of what they said and what I thought their attitude was towards my candidacy. Then the conversation turned to art, of which Mr. Frick knew more than I, and to literature, of which I knew more than Mr. Frick. During those two hours there was an interruption every two or three minutes. The telephone rang or a secretary came in with an inquiry. Invariably somebody at the steel works wanted to know what to do. Never did Mr. Frick say that he would have to think about it. He always replied immediately.

I left his office amused, happy, and edified. Tall, slight, wiry, I had been taken at first for an anarchist. I had looked in on what Mr. Carnegie called "the empire of business" and had a long talk with the man who ruled over one wide realm of that empire. The memory of that scene was with me when in after years it fell to my lot to administer the affairs of a University Dean and the State of Connecticut.

Still uncertain of my future, I attended the Yale Commencement of 1894. There under the tent by Old Alumni Hall I met Professor Lounsbury of the Sheffield Scientific School, who was complaining, not too seriously, that Professor Beers, who was sitting by, had stolen "Dolly" Smith, his one instructor in English, for the College. There was some give-and-take over the theft, during which Beers remarked, "Here's Cross, what about him for Dolly's place?" Lounsbury, turning to me, remarked, "You may have it if you want it." I took him up then and there. That day, Wednesday, June 27, 1894, was a red letter day in my career.

A fortnight later, as soon as I had cut loose from Pittsburgh entanglements, including my candidacy for the office of a librarian, I was duly appointed Instructor in English in the Sheffield Scientific School of Yale University. The next time I saw Professor Lounsbury he cooled my enthusiasm somewhat by saying that my appointment was for one academic year only, subject, however, to renewal if all went well. The only assurance he could give me, he added equivocally, was that "Yale is a good place to go from."

The five years in Shady Side Academy among friends in and out of the school have long since become a pleasant background in my memories. Incidents of those days I sometimes relive in my dreams, out of which wake, never in distress, but with a sense of contentment. Since then a young woman who attended my Pittsburgh lectures, Elizabeth Moorhead, has described in her family history (*Whirling Spindle*) her impressions of Helen and myself when she first saw us at a dinner party given by her mother: "Wilbur Lucius Cross came, a quiet and I think a rather shy young man, bringing with him his charming bride, Helen Avery, whose pink cheeks were like wild roses. She was like a flower, indeed, in her freshness and simplicity." Helen retained her beauty to the end. But somehow I lost my shyness.

VII. Instructor in English

The ways of fate are dark and peculiar. Educated in the strict classical traditions of Yale College, I found myself at the age of thirty-two thrown at one fell swoop into a scientific environment. No one who has not lived through it can understand the antagonisms then bristling between the old and the new system of education. When I was an undergraduate, faculty and students of Yale College, with few exceptions, were afflicted with a superiority complex, the manifestations of which were resented, not too openly, by faculty and students of the Sheffield Scientific School. "Darkest Sheff" was a glib half-humorous phrase heard everywhere, appropriated from Stanley's *Darkest Africa* where no light of the sun ever penetrates the deep jungles. Moreover, Sheff, because it had no chapel for morning prayers, was reputed to be a hotbed of agnosticism.

As for myself, I never took this feeling of superiority very seriously, for I had several friends in Sheff who told me about what they were doing. With one of them I visited a chemistry laboratory and saw a large group of students engaged in experimental work under the direction of a body of instructors and assistants with a professor at their head. This was something different from committing chemical formulas to memory and watching a lecturer perform a few spectacular experiments. In that laboratory I had a look into a world of which I had hitherto known nothing. Likewise while I was laboring with mathematical astronomy I spent, by invitation, hours on bright nights in viewing the planets through a telescope in the tower of Sheffield Hall. That was my first glimpse of the universe.

The German dictionary and the little grammar and reader which my class used in beginning German, I observed, bore on their title pages the name of William Dwight Whitney, America's most distinguished Sanskrit scholar, who conducted Sheff's courses in German and French. And I always took notice when William H. Brewer, Professor of Agriculture, was to give a public lecture on his experiences in California in the old days of the Vigilance Committee or to tell of visits to Panama or to Nicaragua (where in his opinion the Canal should be built). Once I went over to North Sheffield Hall to listen to an address on wages and profits by Francis A. Walker, President of the Massachusetts Institute of Technology, and formerly Professor of Political Economy and History in the Sheffield Scientific School, where he had succeeded Daniel Coit Gilman, then President of Johns Hopkins University. In the same lecture room, too, I was fascinated by a literary address by Edmund W. Gosse, who, while in New Haven on an American tour, was the guest of Professor Lounsbury.

The question may well be asked why Lounsbury and other men in the humanistic studies formed a conspicuous part of the faculty of a scientific school. It is an interesting story which Russell H. Chittenden has related at large in his *History of the Sheffield Scientific School of Yale University*.

The School had its humble origin as far back as 1847 in a little chemical laboratory set up in the old abandoned house of the President of Yale College on a corner of the Campus where the grass was allowed to grow high. Five years later experimental chemistry was reinforced by civil engineering which found a home on the fourth floor of the old College Chapel. These two scientific departments or schools grew apace and in 1860 were brought together under one roof by the financial assistance of Joseph Earl Sheffield, a wealthy and farseeing promoter of railroad construction, who bought, made over, enlarged, and equipped for the combined schools a commodious building on the corner of Grove and Prospect Streets, formerly owned by a medical institution which had chosen a site near the historic Grove Street Cemetery. In recognition of Mr. Sheffield's benefactions, which included an endowment, the School was named after him. During the next decade the School rapidly expanded until it included most of the departments in applied science, as then understood. Men of unusual ability were appointed to all the professorships, who had obtained their training in the laboratories of the best scientific minds of Germany and other countries of Europe. In 1866 a chair of paleontology was established, the first in the United States, to which was appointed Othniel C. Marsh, a who soon took his place among the foremost men of science in his generation. I used to look upon this magnificent man with that awe which only youth can feel.

With these men of science were associated humanists of a progressive type, some of whose names I have mentioned—Whitney, Gilman, and later Walker. Both groups were in agreement that specialized work in science should be preceded by or carried along with a wide range of studies in the modern languages and literatures, in history, economics, and government. They held to three years of Latin as a requirement for entrance but discarded Greek as too remote for education in a new age. English grammar and composition they regarded as an essential study for every boy either in school or college. To this they added practice in public speaking such as declamation and debate, which were called "oratory." But so far as I have been able to discover, neither they nor the faculty of any college in the United States provided a course in English literature apart from historical manuals until Lounsbury came on the scene; he once told me that during his four years as an undergraduate in Yale College he never heard the name of any English or American man of letters mentioned in the classroom. That was the age of Tennyson and Browning, Dickens and Thackeray, Longfellow, Whittier, Emerson and Hawthorne.

When Lounsbury was invited to become an Instructor in English Composition in Sheff he made one condition, which was that he should be permitted to give a course in English literature also, beginning perhaps with Chaucer and coming down through Shakespeare and later writers. The condition was immediately accepted, with particular enthusiasm, Director Brush long afterwards informed me, by Gilman. Lounsbury began his course in modern English Writers in September, 1870, and succeeded so well that he was appointed a professor of the first rank beginning with the next academic year. This in brief is the story of how modern English literature first found its way into the curriculum of institutions of higher learning. It came through a scientific school which was breaking the fetters of an educational system centuries old. During the next two decades, Mrs. Lounsbury liked to tell me, college professors from all parts of the country used to visit her husband's classroom to see "how he did it." Beers learned from Lounsbury.

To describe more clearly the scene of Lounsbury's experimentals it should be stated that all instruction in the Sheffield Scientific School was organized on a group system. There was, for example, a prescribed group of studies for men specializing in chemistry and another prescribed group of studies for men in civil engineering, though there was necessarily much overlapping in the fundamental sciences for all the groups in pure and applied science. Lounsbury put all Freshmen, whatever their group, through a stiff course in the history of the English language, and wrote for their use an admirable book to which I have referred. The next year he took them in English composition and literature. In this course he let the students choose their own composition subjects, warning them, however, not to make too free use of the *New American Cyclopedia*, for he himself had written most of the literary articles in that valuable work. More important still, he set an example for his successors, not always followed by them, of actually reading all compositions submitted to him and then of meeting in private conference the students who wrote them.

The main stage, however, upon which Lounsbury played is revolutionary rôle was in the group called for short the Select Course, in which an even balance was struck between the fundamental natural sciences in one scale and language, literature, history, and the social sciences in the other. It was with this group, organized in 1860, that Professor Lounsbury introduced his long course in English literature extending over a period of two years. With this addition, the Select Course was lifted to the plane of a liberal college of a new type in which Latin and Greek were displaced by French and German; and chemistry and physics with other experimental sciences were accorded conspicuous recognition. In all essentials the curriculum of the Select Course corresponded with the ideal of a liberal education which Huxley, the Darwinian, was soon advocating in his *Lay Sermons* for Great Britain.

When I accepted the position of Instructor as assistant to Professor Lounsbury, nothing was said about what would be expected of me. On this subject I was to have an entertaining conversation with him, which I well remember, though I can here give only a brief outline of it. "I want you to take," he said, "the short Freshman course in the history of the English language and when that is over to take the second year men in English composition, meeting with the various divisions once a week.

Is that satisfactory?" I replied that it was. When I inquired whether there was any special method he wished me to follow in teaching composition he said: "Go your own way. I have wasted the better part of twenty years in reading compositions, and now I am passing the job on to you. Good students learn of themselves from their reading how to express their ideas. You can be of some help to them in the matter of details and in comment on the manner in which they develop their themes. That is all. But poor students, who are in the majority, are hopeless. The only thing you can do for them is to get them to read in the hope that they may learn something which they will want to say."

I asked whether he thought it advisable to place a rhetoric in the hands of the students to guide them in good usage. Whereupon Lounsbury proceeded to knock down by name a half dozen rhetoricians, no one of whom was qualified to say what was good usage, no one of whom had any knowledge of the history of the English language, no one of whom had ever written a readable book. I should never have asked the question had I ever heard of the remark he made some years before on rhetoricians at a time when all through the Middle West small colleges were springing up under the name of universities. "Just as men who don't have money enough to found a college," he said, "found a university, so men who haven't brains enough to write a grammar write a rhetoric."

Naturally I was very much pleased when Lounsbury announced that after a talk with Beers he had decided to let me give the first half of his two-year course in English literature. That is, I was to have Chaucer, as much of Spenser as the class or myself could stand, Bacon's essays, and as many of Shakespeare's plays as there might be time for. At that point, somewhere in Shakespeare, he would take over the course. Again, I put in another heedless question and got a tart reply. I asked him whether I should be content with a modernized pronunciation. Quick came the sharp retort: "If you know how the English language was pronounced in Chaucer's time, you are the only man who knows. But if you want to adopt that sort of bastard pronunciation of Chaucer now current, you are perfectly free to do so."

As I was about to leave him after our first conference I inquired

whether he had ever written anything on the teaching of English literature. He silently rummaged through drawers and dusty bookshelves and
handed me the *New Englander* for October, 1870, containing an essay by
him entitled "The Study of English," in which he outlined the method
of study of English language and literature that he was trying out as a first
experiment. It included a gay condemnation of Thomas B. Shaw's *Complete Manual of English Literature.* After citing three instances where Shaw
had given grossly inaccurate accounts of poems and plays, he remarked
that if we may generalize from three examples, Shaw never read any of
the books he has described! Without the slightest doubt Lounsbury rescued the study of English literature at second hand from untrustworthy
historical manuals, of which Shaw's book was then the most popular.

On my first appearance in September, 1894, to begin work I discovered
that I had been appointed Instructor in English by the authorities, "sight
unseen." While I was walking with Professor Lounsbury in front of Sheffield Hall, we met Director George J. Brush, a distinguished mineralogist,
to whom he introduced me. the Director remarked that he thought it was
about time for him to see the man whom he had appointed. A day or
two later, when the results of the September entrance examinations had
been reported, the Director called Lounsbury and me into his office for
a conference. He was greatly disturbed over the increase in the enrollment
in the School by almost a hundred over the previous year. He wondered
particularly how so many men could be handled in English. Though there
was some talk about a part-time assistant for me, I quickly understood
that the proposal, not quite expressed, was that I should go it alone, with
a slight increase in salary. Without any ado I accepted, which meant that
I should have under my instruction two large divisions in English literature
of the Select Course, as extra division two hours a week in Freshman
English, and two hundred men of the Junior class in English composition
for two thirds of the year. It was a big job.

I well recall the first faculty meeting I attended. It was held in the
vaulted library room on the top story of Sheffield Hall. On each side of
a long table, with the Director at the head, sat the professors of the first
rank who comprised the Governing Board. At a distance behind the long

table were chairs so arranged for the rest of us that we faced the backs of the nearest row of the demigods, among whom the scientific men, like their predecessors, were nearly all members of the National Academy of Science. Here in one room were my new colleagues whom I looked at with a curious eye.

The days of that first year passed pleasantly. I was early admitted to the Graduates Club of which Professor Lounsbury was then president. In that large company I came into intimate association with members of all the faculties of the University and with professional businessmen of the city. The friendships I formed there have had a most important bearing on my career in the University and in public affairs. The free talk at the Graduates Club on all subjects became from the very first an essential part of my education. It cleared my mind of cobwebs.

There were times when, for all my University friends, I felt shut in from the outside world. The amount of instruction I had undertaken stood in the way of public addresses such as I had given while at Shady Side Academy. One address, however, I gave in a general course of lectures under the auspices of the Sheffield Scientific School on the suggestion of Lounsbury who evidently wanted to see what I could do in that line. I took as my subject George Eliot, revamping for the purpose an address which I had repeated several times in Pittsburgh the winter before. This time I had the pleasure of being mistaken for somebody else. On entering the lecture hall I was amazed at the sight. Not only were the seats filled but men and women were standing in the rear and along the side walls. I walked down the middle aisle in full dress and mounted the platform. Directly in front of me there sat a row of clergymen. There was no introduction. I began reading my address in the best manner I could command. In forty-five minutes it was all over except for the applause.

As I stepped from the platform the clergy, one by one, took me by the hand, "Glad to meet you, Mr. Cross." I could understand a cordial greeting from the clergy, for I was a very moral young man in looks, and, as quoted in a morning newspaper, I had said: "The lesson George Eliot teaches us is that our salvation is to listen to the call of duty. She insists on the awful responsibility of the individual to society . . ." But the great mystery still remained: Why so many people? The next day when I met on the street a daughter of Director Brush, who congratulated me on the fine audience, I said that I had wondered why so many people came out to hear a lecture on George Eliot by an unknown stripling. With a smile she replied that she wondered, too, until she heard a woman sitting near her say to another as I came on the platform: "That ain't George Eliot's husband, he's too young for that." So that was it, and we laughed together. Wilbur Cross had been mistaken for Walter Cross, who had married George Eliot. Of all my addresses none has every given me greater satisfaction.

It was the custom to invite young Instructors, believed to be competent, to give a course in the Graduate School. Encouraged by Professor Lounsbury I announced for the college year 1895–96 a course in the English novel from Defoe to Scott. No students enrolled for it, though two or three expressed a desire to take it on the side. Under the circumstances I decided to postpone the course until the next college year when I planned to extend it down into the nineteenth century as far as George Eliot. In the meantime, William Lyon Phelps, then a young Instructor in the College, gave a course in contemporary novels to a large body of undergraduates with success so extraordinary as to be sensational. The press generally lauded the innovation, with here and there some banter. But several of the older members of the Yale faculty looked askance on the introduction of modern fiction into the college curriculum and in particular they criticized the two or three novels in the reading list as too outspoken on the facts of sex, which were related without the traditional severe condemnation of all sexual irregularities. Unaware that Phelps had been requested by President Dwight to drop his experiment with modern fiction after his first trial, I proceeded to announce, as I had planned, my graduate course in the history of the English novel for the academic year 1896–97. The announcement, however, never got farther than the office of Dean Phillips of the Graduate School, where it caused a flutter of feathers in the dovecotes.

President Dwight sent Professor Thomas D. Seymour to wrestle with me. He doubtless chose Professor Seymour to speak for him because we were very good friends. With this distinguished Greek scholar I had read Homer's *Iliad* in Freshman year. He broached the subject most courteously by saying that Phelps was to withdraw his course in fiction and that President Dwight would like to have me withdraw mine also. I acceded immediately to a request which, expressed in plain language, was a demand, remarking by the way that relief from graduate instruction would give me more time to complete a book which I was then writing on the English novel. But I added that if fiction were to be placed under a taboo, the *Odyssey* would have to go, for that wonderful epic was a skipper's tale filled in with folklore and primitive sex notions. So would the *Iliad*, in which the motive for the war with Troy was the intrigue between Paris, son of Priam, King of Troy, and Helen, the wife of Menelaus, King of Sparta. Professor Seymour, of course, endeavored to correct my perverse views on the motivation of sex in Greek literature.

By the intervention of Professor Lounsbury, who "saw" President Dwight, Dean Phillips, and some others, the ban on the study of fiction in the Graduate School was lifted for the college year 1897–98, and I was permitted to give the course which I had been asked to forego the previous year. Among my first students were Jack Adams, John Berdan, and George Nettleton, all of whom were soon to become members of the Yale English faculty. For thirty years thereafter I went on with fiction, nobody molesting. The total number of students who made a sober study of the novel under my direction runs into the hundreds. Many of them have had notable careers in teaching and in literature. Among them I may mention, without disparagement to the others, Henry Canby, Stephen Vincent Benét, Marjorie Nicolson of Columbia, and Dean DeVane of Yale College. Bill Benét also took a similar course with me in Sheff.

VIII. Summer In England

When I was assured of my reappointment as Instructor for the next year, I began to look towards England and Scotland for the summer vacation which would soon await me. One day while rereading Lord Bacon's *Essays* in preparation for a talk to my class on this wise man's mind and character, I came to a sudden pause and read several times over a saying of his which seemed to have a special application to myself. It was: "Travel, in the younger sort, is a part of education; in the elder, a part of experience." If travel were to be for me not mere experience but an education, I mused, it was high time for me to cross the ocean to the home of these men and women whose works were my main interests as a teacher of English literature.

It had, indeed, been my habit when reading the great English writers to try to visualize them in the environment where they once lived and moved and had their being, but the scenes thus evoked were at best vague and visionary. They lacked authenticity. Wordsworth, it will be remembered, long had a vision of the Yarrow unvisited, but when he afterwards traversed that beautiful Scottish valley, with his sister Dorothy, the vision faded into another scene, real and yet as entrancing. This incident is a symbol of an age-old experience. What one sees always differs, for better or for worse, from what one has imagined. Now I hoped to see with my own eyes parts of the real land of my imaginings. Not only would I visit historic and literary landmarks, but I would take along a bicycle so that I might go into the byways and hedges where tourists rarely go but where Englishmen and Scotsmen live. For a time I would be one of them so far as they would permit it.

With this intention, I stepped aboard the S. S. *California* at the foot of 21st Street, New York, on Saturday, July 6, 1895. Though reputed the largest steamer of the Allan Line, it was of but 6,500 tons, and only 400 feet long. The ship was crowded with tourists, for whose discomfort first- and second-class passengers were thrown together; and in some cases, as in mine, cabins were improvised for four occupants, none of whom could sleep but the very tired or the very drunk. So most of my sleeping was done on deck sometimes between midnight and six a.m. The fare one way was $45; or $80 for a round-trip ticket, which I bought with the understanding that on the return voyage I should have only one companion in my cabin.

In the motley crowd that jammed the decks when the sea was quiet were groups of schoolteachers like myself, who were going to make the grand tour, several Canadian Catholic priests on the way to Rome, and a larger number of Protestant clergymen, one of whom from Brooklyn affected the dress and mannerisms of Henry Ward Beecher. So perfect was the likeness that one might have imagined that Beecher, not yet really dead, was taking, like King Arthur, a sea voyage to Avalon. The man above all others among us was Samuel Pierpont Langley, one of the great pioneers in aviation. He was a lone traveler who never spoke unless spoken to. His mind seemed to be elsewhere; perhaps on his experiments with models of machines heavier than air, which were to prove partially successful the next year.

When the winds blew and the rains descended and the ship rolled, nearly everybody went below. During one of those not very heavy storms I looked into my cabin and quickly turned away from a dreadful sight. God spared me because I did not stay. Towards evening the sun broke through in a blaze of glory; and when night came on the heavens filled with stars. No sunset, no starry night, had ever come up to what I then saw. On another day as we were passing along the rugged coast of western Ireland, with views far inland of green hills and roads reflecting the sunlight, the Irish on board who were to leave the ship on a small steamer in the beautiful Lough Foyle for Londonderry, became greatly excited and shouted loud greetings to their homeland. After leaving the Foyle, Scots, who were returning home, took possession of the upper deck. They too began to shout and jump as soon as they caught sight of the Mull of Kintyre and then of Arran and Bute, over which hovered low-lying clouds bursting into all sorts of colors when the sun tried to shine through them. I watched a black cloud moving slowly towards Holy Island, where it rested for a moment and then passed on, leaving the scene of Saint Cuthbert's labors in full sunlight. On all sides Scots and the rest were singing "My heart's in the Highlands a-chasing the deer" until we were well up the Clyde.

That night the ship anchored at Greenock and the next morning docked at Glasgow (Tuesday, July 16) in a drizzling rain. Early in the afternoon I took a train which brought me in good season to the edge of the English Lake country, where I began my zigzag journey, by rail or by bicycle, southward through the Midlands to London.

Only a few curious travelers had at the time discovered Haworth, the home of the strange Brontë sisters and their brother, children of the Vicar of the parish. From the deep valley of the Worth I climbed on foot the long steep cobblestone street of the old part of Haworth to the parsonage and beyond. On the way, near the church, I drank a glass of ale in the Black Bull, where Branwell Brontë had dissipated away a life of literary promise. The man behind the bar might have been, so far as appearance went, the very man who had once poured out glass after glass of whisky for Branwell. His hands shook; and his nose and cheeks looked as if they were on fire.

As I came out of the inn, two little girls, who had evidently seen me enter, were standing in the street to greet me. They were slight, bright-eyed girls, neatly dressed and wearing, like other children I saw there, clogs with wooden soles which rattled on the stone walk as they came towards me. They said that they were sisters, ten and eight years old, and that they lived near the Black Bull in a house which they pointed out to me. They asked if they might show me around. Never was I luckier in my guides. As we walked along together, everybody seemed to know them as well as they knew everybody. We went into the church where we saw the tomb of the Brontës, bearing the names of Charlotte and Emily. We visited a small museum which the Brontë Society had recently opened to the public, where I examined manuscripts in the beautiful handwriting of Charlotte and Emily and fantastic sketches which Branwell had made of his sisters, and many other relics and reminders of the Brontë family, including a picture of the house which it is supposed Emily had in mind when she wrote *Wuthering Heights*.

The vicar, my young guides informed me, would let nobody into the parsonage except people he knew. (Since then the parsonage has been taken over by the Brontë Society.) But the vicar was away for the afternoon, they said, and the housekeeper might let us in if I gave her a shilling. Without rapping, the two girls led me into the kitchen. When I shook hands with the housekeeper (or whoever she was), a shilling passed quietly from my palm to hers, and we four went all through the house.

Leaving the parsonage, the two girls took me higher up the hill for a view far out over the extensive moors, brilliantly green in the sunlight. On such an afternoon as this Emily, taking a stool, used to go out on those moors and sit for hours, communing with a God greater, she believed, than the God of her father's sermons. We, too, passed through a stile out on the moors that we might for a time be of them. I asked where Wuthering Heights was. The girls said that house was too far away to see, but its site was like that, as one of them pointed to a long rolling hill in the distance. It was very cold and windy they said, over there in the winter.

When I parted from the girls near the Black Bull I felt as if I had been walking hand in hand with Charlotte and Emily Brontë as they were when they were children roaming about in clogs with wooden soles.

One Sunday morning with a Harvard graduate student in English I visited Stoke Poges. We wanted to see the churchyard which inspired Gray's "Elegy Written in a Country Churchyard," and to read the famous inscription which Gray wrote for his mother's tomb: "The careful, tender mother of many children, one of whom alone had the misfortune to survive her." As we passed through the yard to the church, the congregation was breaking up into groups among which were the vicar, a curate, and a church warden, who looked curiously at us before giving us a cordial greeting. I told them who we were and why we were too late for the service. The warden took us in hand and showed us about, explaining everything as we sat in Gray's pew. In the cloisters I observed a remarkable painted window with a drawing of something that resembled a bicycle without pedals, bearing the date 1642. We concluded that as far back as the time of Milton people rode on wheel carriages, pushing them along with their feet on the ground. As we left the church there lay before us a scene of perfect loveliness and repose. No sound was heard but a slight echo of our voices, which enhanced the stillness.

Unexpectedly, as we were about to part, the warden invited us home for luncheon. We walked through the extensive Stoke Park to his house where we met his two sons, one of whom was an Oxford man. When we were seated at his table of cold meats, luscious wall fruits (grapes and peaches), and old Burgundy, he began to tell his story. He had been in the United States three times—twice in connection with Confederate loans which were negotiated through a London banking house of which he was an agent. In particular his bank had provided funds for fitting out the *Alabama*, a Confederate raider of the seas. "In that chair where you are sitting," he remarked to me, "often sat Mr. Mason when he came here to plead for more financial aid to the Confederacy." He was in the United States, he said, just after the battle of Gettysburg and had a conference with General Meade who let him through the lines on his way to Richmond. His moral sympathies, he averred, had always been with the North, though financial transactions had thrown him in with the South. On inquiry in Oxford the next day, I was told that we had been the guests of Mr. Algernon Gilliat, a member of a London investment house who had sat in Parliament as a Conservative member from Clapham.

In London I took lodgings in Guilford Street just off Russell Square over which, drab as it had become, still hung for me the enchantment of *Vanity Fair*. To please my imagination I picked out the house where Becky Sharp played her clever game with the emotions of Jos Sedly, and Amelia watched from an open window for the coming of George Osborn. I walked alone through slums such as Dickens had described, through narrow streets and lanes damp with refuse thrown from rickety old houses. Children were sprawling in the filth and all the men and women I saw were dressed in rags and almost as dirty as their children. I did no more than look into alleys, for Jack the Ripper was then in the full flush of his sanguinary occupation.

A Sunday I chose for an excursion with my bicycle, riding where I could, and walking the rest of the way, over Salisbury Plain and beyond over the downs, to Old Sarum, Amesbury, Stonehenge, Wilton (where Sir Philip Sidney wrote the *Arcadia*), and Bemerton to see the tiny little stone church of which George Herbert had once been rector. Along the small stream called the Bourne I often halted for a few words with a small farmer, partly for a pleasant greeting, partly for the sound of a strange dialect. On one occasion a man pointed to my bicycle and asked, "Did you bring *him* with you?" I encouraged him to go on talking and he never used "it" or "she." With him all genders were covered by "he," "his," and "him."

I stood alone at midday among the huge circular pillars of Stonehenge while a brilliant sun, playing with the clouds, illumined the immense plain as far as one could see. In the distance rose in clear view the lofty spire of Salisbury Cathedral. On that Sunday, for once in my life, I offered up an improvised prayer to the bright god in his heavens pouring his light upon the earth and upon shepherds here and there tending their sheep.

On my return to London after a trip to Paris I felt that I had seen enough of England for one summer. I had roamed cities and countrysides, visiting scenes memorable in the history of English literature. I had spent long mornings in the British Museum reading rare books and old manuscripts which were of prime interest to me in my profession. And at Stonehenge I had had an imaginary glimpse of prehistoric Britain as it was in the Neolithic age before the coming of Angles and Saxons or Celts, even before the land had a name. My heart turned towards Scotland for an intervening fortnight before my ship was to weigh anchor at Glasgow for home.

After a sojourn in Edinburgh and a visit to Abbotsford, I set out in a brake for a journey through the Valley of the Yarrow, redolent with the memory of old ballads and later poems by Scott, Wordsworth, and James Hogg, known as the Ettrick Shepherd, a farmer's boy who developed a genuine talent for local verse yet remembered. My main objective was St. Mary's Loch, which Wordsworth first visited with the Ettrick Shepherd as his guide. It was an early September morning that I chose for my visit. During most of the way from Innerleithen I rode through a heavy mist but as I came near the object of my desire, the sun broke through the clouds overhanging the high hills among which lay the long narrow loch. Soon I was watching Wordsworth's swans floating in waters ever changing in mist and sunlight. Aware of what that meant, I climbed to the top of one of the hills and there looked down upon the loch. Not only the swans but all the hills on the other side of the loch were reflected in the waters, light green with purple patches from the heather when the sun shone bright, dark green when a heavy cloud passed over the hills. "Not a feature in those hills," Wordsworth observed, "is in that mirror slighted."

After viewing for a long time this lovely interchange of lake and sky I descended the height for a last look into the deep waters which were so clear that the reflection of the hills extended far below the surface. Then I walked to the head of the loch for a noon dinner at Tibbie Shiels's Inn, a fishermen's resort, once famous as a meeting place for literary men. I was given a seat at a long plain table for my first straight native dinner of pea soup, mutton from the hills, biscuits and cheese, and home-brewed beer. While I was eating this dinner as delicious as substantial, a small group of men came in and took seats a little distance away. They were all Scots. When I told them that I was half a Scot myself, the ice was broken and we began to talk. One of them, well read in the history and traditions of the Yarrow, related for me many curious tales. One story he told was of an old tenant farmer of the district who, when about to die, became impatient with his friends who tried to console him by assurance that he would soon be on the road to heaven. In response to their palaver he was heard to mutter: "Give me Bower Hope at a fair rent and heaven may go to the devil." Towards evening I retraced my journey through the Yarrow. As we drove in the gloaming, long lines of sheep looking like white threads were slowly coming down the hills, while here and there a strag-gler was half visible on the braes, trees were assuming all sorts of shapes, slim and grotesque in lights and shadows. It was the fairyland of the Shep-herd of the Ettrick Forest, whose mother or grandmother (I forget which) was the last, according to local tradition, to talk to fairies and to hear their thin sibilant speech.

I had been under the impression that my boat was to leave Glasgow on Saturday, September 14. But on examining the ticket I was startled to read "Friday, September 13." Either Friday or 13 taken by itself would not have alarmed me, for I had then very little superstition about days fraught with impending disaster. But Friday and 13, taken together, did give me pause to consider whether I could face a double jeopardy. In the end I tried to laugh it off. All would have been well had I not been greeted when I arrived in Glasgow, two days before the ominous day of sailing, by a high wind that whistled through the streets and beat against the face of the hotel at which I put up.

This made me think hard for two days and two nights. I asked the steamship office when the next boat for New York would sail and was told that it would be on the next Friday. I inquired about insurance on my life for the voyage and was informed that it could not be easily obtained. In the end I concluded that insurance would be of no value anyway, for if I went down the insurance policy would go down with me. A secret voice within me seemed to say, "Hold on to your first-class passenger ticket which cost you $40. Don't lose that. Go aboard and run the risk to your life and save the $40." That was the advice of the Scot within me. I took it.

Out of the Clyde we met with heavy seas, though not dangerous. By good luck Professor C. T. Winchester of Wesleyan University was aboard, with a cabin near mine. We formed a friendship which lasted, growing more and more intimate, until his death. For me he was almost another Lounsbury or another Beers. Most of the passengers were tourists who had spent all their money in Europe, reserving only enough for drink and poker on the trip home. Among them were a number of sharpers who slaughtered the innocents, as I looked on with my pipe.

Somewhere in mid-ocean we ran into a dreadful storm and everybody was too frightened for storytelling or playing poker. Then I wished that I had not bet $40 against the perils of the sea. One dark night when the storm was at its height and we were all in our berths the engines stopped. The lifeboats, it was rumored, were being lowered. The ship rolled about helplessly in a tumult of waters. At midnight Professor Winchester crawled to my cabin to tell me to get up and put on my clothes so as to be ready for the lifeboats. We sat and talked for a while amid the roar of the storm and the crash of crockery and then turned in to await our fate. But the next day the wind—which had approached a hurricane—abated somewhat and we escaped a wet grave. Had we all gone under the waves, the Devil would have had business on his hands.

IX. Professor English, Sheffield Scientific School

Not long after my return from Europe it appeared that I was in the Sheffield Scientific School to stay. One day Director Brush casually remarked that I gave him less trouble than most instructors and that I might expect promotion a year hence. I was made an Assistant Professor of English in 1897; and in 1902 a Professor of the first rank. On Professor Lounsbury's retirement from active service in 1906, which we celebrated by a trip to England and France, part of the time together, full responsibility for English instruction in the Sheffield Scientific School was transferred to my shoulders.

In the meantime Director Brush retired. He was succeeded in 1898 by Russell H. Chittenden, who was as noted a physiological chemist as Brush was a mineralogist. I well recall my first sight of Professor Chittenden. It was at the first meeting of the faculty I attended in October, 1894. As one of the younger members of the Governing Board, he sat near the foot of the long table preempted by the demigods. He kept quiet until there arose a question on which there was disagreement. Then he spoke up, his large dark eyes flashing along the table. He was, I observed, a slight man with hair and beard as dark as his eyes. He appeared to be under forty years of age. With this man I was to be intimately associated for eighteen years.

Director Chittenden faced the problems looming before him with keen insight and indomitable courage. The most obvious problem was occasioned by the rapid increase in the enrollment of students, which rose during his first ten or twelve years in office from 570 to 1,400. In order to provide adequate instruction for this fast-growing enrollment it was necessary to double the number of active faculty members from 60 to 120. These are approximate figures. In this adjustment of faculty and students it was the Director's aim not just to maintain the current standard of teaching but to improve upon it in all departments of study by the appointment of the best available men to every grade of the faculty.

At the same time facilities for instruction had to be greatly enlarged.

Gifts and endowments were obtained for new buildings in mineralogy, mechanical, electrical, and mining engineering, for a camp of 2,000 acres for field work in civil engineering, and for a building named Leet Oliver Memorial Hall in memory of a student who was killed in an automobile accident. The difficulty of housing the students was partially met by the beautiful Vanderbilt dormitories, now merged with Silliman College.

Such was the new, maturing Sheff, of which I was a part. After I had been driven about from pillar to post, the scene of my action became Leet Oliver Memorial Hall, where all the instruction in the so-called human-istic studies was brought together. This building was designed with small rooms for private conferences between instructors and students. In this respect it almost marked an epoch, for the personal touch in teaching, which counts for more than formal lectures and quizzes in a classroom, was for Yale a new approach.

In no study was the increase in the enrollment more immediately felt than in English literature and composition. As early as 1898–99 George H. Nettleton was added to the English staff; on my transfer to the Grad-uate School in 1916 he became my successor. In 1900 came a second new appointment—Henry S. Canby, who has had a distinguished career as edi-tor and man of letters. Had English kept its former status as merely a sub-ject in the curriculum of the Select Course, the staff with these two new members would have been able to carry on in a satisfactory manner. But it did not remain there. By the will of the Governing Board of the School, English literature and composition were made essential preliminary studies in all the various scientific groups or departments, where they had been more or less incidental though important. As a result of this enlarged pro-gram the English staff, by 1911–12, had risen to nine members.

It was a rare company of young men. Besides Nettleton and Canby, it comprised Frederick E. Pierce, who had an extensive knowledge of Eng-lish and other literatures, ancient and modern; Jack Crawford, who had specialized in the drama; Walter L. Ferris, an excellent teacher with a background in philosophy; Thomas G. Wright, who, though he died near the outset of his career, had proved himself a thorough scholar in American literature; Willard H. Durham, who migrated to the University of California; and Henry Noble MacCracken, who became President of Vassar College at the age of thirty-five.

Over this brilliant corps of Assistant Professors and Instructors I kept close watch, edified and amused by what they were doing. Each one of them was an alert personality having his own particular literary interests. Each one thought that he knew what was what. No two conducted their classes in literature in quite the same way. No two assigned subjects for compositions in quite the same field. Diversification was the rule. I rarely interfered with the freedom which they regarded as their right. At most I acted as a safety valve. I left it largely to the conflict of young minds to work out their problems, of course giving advice when it was asked. The result was in a high degree good. Even in a scientific school they awakened among students an interest in literature and in trying to write English as well as they were able.

Very often Professor Lounsbury attended our dinners to listen to the talk. On one of these occasions I asked the men who had charge of English composition to describe, one by one, what they were doing. When he heard the full story, how for instance all the work in composition was related to the particular interest of each student, including even the fine arts, he threw up his hands and declared in his delightful formal manner that he was ready to take back all that he had ever said against the futility of teaching English composition.

While these young men were experimenting with ways, somewhat new, of teaching English, I was surveying as a member of regional or national committees the whole subject as it concerned colleges and schools of all kinds. Simple English grammar, so necessary for testing correct sentence structure, had as I have remarked mostly disappeared from the schools; while in many colleges the study of literary masterpieces, especially of Shakespeare's plays, remained, as it once was, merely a basis for disquisitions on historical English grammar, as if philology were the key to the world of literature.

More extraneous still to the mind and spirit of an author was the introduction in the 'nineties of the scientific study of literature, in which a poem, essay, or play was resolved into its component parts as if it were a chemical compound. In its extreme form this method was elaborated by Professor Lucius A. Sherman, of the University of Nebraska, in *Analytics of Literature* (1893). Sherman, it is worth noting, was the first man to receive the Ph.D. degree in English at Yale. His book was dedicated to Lounsbury and W. D. Whitney. Over this irony of fate Lounsbury was hot and yet amused. One day while he was denouncing Sherman as we sat in the Graduates Club, I repeated a story I had heard from Professor Francis Stoddard of New York University, who had tried out Sherman's analytic method and given it up. It required, Stoddard said, about three months to take a class through a play of Shakespeare's if every word and phrase and every peculiarity of syntax and versification were to be considered and the average number of words in the sentence was to be calculated and all put into statistical form. There was so much to do with *Macbeth*, the last play of Senior year, that the class had to stop on reaching the fifth act. A member of the class who came back for his reunion at the next Commencement gave Professor Stoddard a warm shake of the hand, remarking, "I got more out of that course in Shakespeare than out of any other. I feel that I ought to tell you so. What a wonderful play *Macbeth* was. I've always wondered how it came out." Then and there Stoddard decided to abandon the scientific analysis of literary masterpieces.

Professor Lounsbury himself has been criticized by Mr. Canby, one of his students, for a too close study of textual details of the play or poem which the class might be reading. Without doubt progress was slow through Shakespeare and Milton in whose works there are many allusions and references which Lounsbury required his students to run down and explain. In exposing their ignorance of the Bible and Greek myths he derived perennial fun. I recall a score of instances of this kind which either he or his students related to me. On one occasion he discovered in his class a Jew to whom the name of Moses was unknown. At other times he was informed that Judas Iscariot was a Greek hero, that the Pierian Spring was a watering place, and that Castor and Pollux were a pair of old heathen twin gods, one of whom killed his twin brother who had accused him of being illegitimate. With a reference to Mary and Martha, Lounsbury succeeded rather better. By questioning a half dozen members of the class the story of Our Lord's visit to the house of their brother Lazarus was pieced together with reasonable accuracy. Then Lounsbury turned to one of the students who had never before heard of Mary and Martha: "Which of these two girls do you think did the right thing?" Taking a chance, the student replied: "On the whole, I think Martha, who stayed home and looked after the old folks." "There, sir," retorted Lounsbury, "is where you and Our Lord disagree." The scene closed, the victim told me, in peals of laughter.

Young instructors of English, who were content with casual attention to allusions, nevertheless ran into another doubtful course by asking on their examination papers the location of passages they quoted from the books the class had read under their supervision. This practice, then as now, was called spotting passages. Sometimes the sole aim was to determine whether students had actually done the reading assigned to them. At the other times a passage to be located might have some significance in the development of the plot of a play. In the case of lyric poetry, it was clear, students were asked to spot snatches of verse which made a special appeal to their instructors. Against this custom I entered strong objection, not only as unfair but also as an attempt to impose upon students our own preferences. Each one of us builds up his own body of quotations in accordance with this age and temperament. What appeals to one of us at any age may make no appeal to the rest. It is of course a function of an instructor in poetry to show his students why Wordsworth's "The Solitary Reaper," for example, or Keats's "Ode to a Nightingale" is great poetry in the hope that they will commit to memory such parts of the poem as they particularly like. To accomplish this one hardly needs to do more than read the poems aloud to his class with slight comment. This I afterwards learned was Mark Twain's way of conducting a class in Browning.

Sometimes I used to turn the tables against my colleagues by asking them to spot passages which for personal reasons had long clung to my memory though probably not to theirs. For example, while Shakespeare was still living there was published in his name a poem in which occurs the stanza:

> Truth may seem, but cannot be:
> Beauty brag, but 'tis not she:
> Truth and beauty buried be.

After quoting the stanza to a small company of English professors, I put the usual question: "In what poem occur these lines?" All kept silence, even a Shakespearean scholar among us, until Professor Beers expressed surprise that anyone who had read that stanza could ever forget it. He went on to say that when he was a young man he visited by invitation Emerson at Concord one Sunday afternoon with a group of transcendentalists, and Emerson on being requested to read some of his favorite poems recited first of all parts of the poem attributed to Shakespeare, evidently regarding it as an anticipation of his own transcendentalism. I tried my friends out on another poem, which I committed to memory the first time I read it. Silence again, until Beers began reciting the entire poem.

During the 'nineties the lack of agreement among colleges as to what entrance requirements in English should be had become a pressing problem for preparatory schools. To clear the air for concerted action a National Conference on Uniform Entrance Requirements in English was called, and its recommendations were generally adopted by colleges and preparatory schools throughout the country. Soon, however, loud criticism developed against the manner in which the new English requirement was being administered in several of the large colleges and universities. The most enlightened preparatory schools felt that certain colleges were imposing upon them an analysis of English literary masterpieces such as could not be expected of boys and girls. Many college professors, including myself, agreed with them, knowing from experience the mental capacities of the best students in secondary schools.

When President Hadley received an invitation to appoint a delegate to a Conference of New England Colleges in 1906 to discuss entrance requirements, he asked me to serve in this capacity. I accepted the mission with full approval of all the English professors of the faculty except Professor Cook, who advised President Hadley to send no delegate, or, if I were sent as a courteous gesture, to make it clear that Yale had come to the irrevocable decision that no changes whatever should be made in the English requirement for admission to Yale College. Directly to the contrary, however, President Hadley instructed me to act on my own initiative, with the proviso that we confer on doubtful proposals. The final proposals of the New England colleges were presented to the National Conference at its meeting in 1908; and a report which I largely wrote and read to the National Conference the next year was adopted after some warm debate.

The changes thus initiated were more far-reaching than appeared at first sight. Our report began with a clear statement of the objectives of English instruction in the schools. It recommended that more attention be given to the essentials of English grammar and that subjects for composition no longer be confined to books prescribed for reading but "be taken mainly from the student's personal experience and general knowledge"; it greatly enlarged the list of books for reading so as to provide a wider choice; it placed in logical sequence to this reading list a restricted list of books for study, and to illustrate such a logical sequence there was appended a typical course in English covering four years, to be varied as local conditions might demand. Finally there was indicated a type of examination to be set for entrance to college which would discourage the mechanical questions on form and structure that we felt were leading schools astray. Considered as a whole the revision was a step forward towards the so-called "Comprehensive Examination" in English.

A spectacular feature of the revision was the formation of an entirely new elective group of books which was placed at the head of the lists for reading. This group consisted of selections from the Old Testament and English translations of the *Iliad*, *Odyssey*, and *Aeneid*. The practical motive for introducing these into the school curriculum was not only to acquaint the student with some of the greatest literary masterpieces of all time but also to familiarize him with those Hebrew stories and Greek myths and legends which permeate large areas of English literature, so that when he came upon them in his reading he might not lose his way in a maze of allusions. This part of the new English requirement awakened wide and favorable comment in the press.

When in 1908 I broached the question of bringing in selected narratives of the Old Testament for literary study, I was informed by the chairman of the National Conference that the attempt had already been made and abandoned because in certain states the reading of the Bible in public schools was prohibited by law. However, since the proposal was only to include the Bible among electives, the conference ended by wishing me Godspeed. During the next year I sought the advice of the clergy, Catholic, Protestant, and Jew. Though I encountered some opposition for fear that the schoolmaster was trying to supplant the minister of the Gospel in religious instruction, the clergy were mostly in favor of the proposal. A young rabbi, in reply to my first inquiry, informed me that the Jews needed no help from the schools as they had their own ways of instructing their young people in the Bible. But when I reported to him that we once had in Yale a Jew who had never heard of Moses, he wrote me "Go ahead."

The man who gave me the wisest counsel was Cardinal Gibbons who expressed deep interest in the endeavor to promote the study of the Old Testament as literature. In order to keep my literary aim clear, he advised me to include in any book of selections parts of the Apocrypha, which was once liberally drawn upon by English writers when every man sat in peace "under his vine and his fig tree, and there was none to fray them." He himself when a young man had carefully read Webster's "Speech in Reply to Hayne" to determine the influence of the Bible upon the orator's style, and at my request he had some of the notes he took on this famous speech copied for me. Nothing better could be said in favor of the Bible as literature than what the Cardinal wrote me: "Apart from its inspirational character, the Bible still remains the one means of culture." I read one of his letters to the Conference in 1909—and the Bible immediately went on the reading list for boys and girls. It has not yet been removed. Homer's two epics are still there too.

The goal towards which the National Conference began its march in 1909 was reached at the session of 1916, when provision was made for a comprehensive examination in English composition and literature as an alternative to the old plan of questions on a specified list of books. Under the new plan, which was strongly recommended to colleges, the aim was to test the ability of a candidate for admission to write clear and correct English and to discover, by questioning him on passages of verse and prose, whether he had learned to read with understanding and appreciation. In place of a prescribed list of books, there was subjoined a large list of books deemed suitable for secondary schools from which selections were to be made. No methods of study were prescribed or even indicated. In this respect schools were given perfect freedom. Results were to be measured only by examination. I was a member of the committee of the College Entrance Examination Board which set for most of the colleges the first English examination under the comprehensive plan. After that I withdrew from the National Conference for other work that was pressing upon me.

In those days teaching and administration were not such distinct functions of a Yale professor as they may be now. I soon saw that the only way to keep free of standing and special committees would be to do the work so badly that after one appointment I might be passed by in the future. But both Directors of Sheff under whom I served were too insistent upon administrative aid for this policy to be successful in my case. The result was that I was always on several committees of which some, like the Committee on Admissions, of which Professor Corwin was chairman, concerned the relations between the College and the Scientific School. Seeing that I was easy game, President Hadley also put me on various University committees, of which Secretary Stokes was often the chairman.

Of all these assignments, the one now most alive in my memory was the Discipline Committee of three professors which Director Chittenden set up for dealing with the aberrations of students in Sheff who neglected their studies or disobeyed rules or broke away from usual standards of moral conduct. Punishment for offenses might be probation for a definite or indefinite period and sometimes dismissal. In all instances, however, the aim was to save a student from the error of his ways. As a member of this committee I learned much about what was going on in the minds of young men who needed guidance more than all else. This conviction I felt strongly when as chairman of the Committee for several years I had to act alone in emergencies whenever the other two members were not available. On those occasions I learned something also about incompatible marriages in private conferences with a father or a mother of a delinquent student. The father damned his wife for her overindulgence of their son; whereas the mother berated her husband, whom she was sorry she ever married, for setting the boy a bad example by the dissipated and indecent life he was living. From the stories husbands and wives told me I acquired a good deal of knowledge of these marital quarrels which culminate in separation and divorce.

I learned something, too, about some kinds of circumstantial evidence. For instance, two dull boys were accused of cribbing from one another because in their written papers on a test in physical geography they made the very same egregious mistakes in answers to specific questions. The case against them seemed clinched by a drawing in which both placed the Torrid Zone at the South Pole. I questioned the boys singly and together. Both denied the charge against them. I discovered that in the examination room they had been so far apart as to preclude any communication. At this point I reproduced on the blackboard their drawing of the Torrid Zone at the South Pole and asked them how they both happened to make that mistake. A flicker of light passed over the face of one of the boys who explained, "Oh, I can tell you about that. We didn't take any notes on the lectures. We had one of the boys in the house do that. We crammed up for the examination from his notebook." "Where is the notebook?" I asked. He got it, and there was the Torrid Zone at the South Pole. I apologized and told the boys they should get a better man to take their notes thereafter!

Perhaps as a sign of my miscellaneous activities, I was elected to the Board of Trustees of the Sheffield Scientific School who had control over financial affairs; and for the closing months of one academic year I was appointed Director of the School while Director Chittenden was in England to attend the Darwin Centenary (1909). In these positions I cut off coupons of bonds not my own and had all the practice I wanted in auditing the accounts of others. I was long a member of the University Council and on the 100th anniversary of the School of Medicine I presented a score of candidates for honorary degrees, making my citation short and crisp as directed by President Hadley. Outstanding among candidates that year was Jean Sibelius, the great Finnish composer on whom was conferred the degree of Doctor of Music. Alas! Poor Finland!

My spare time I devoted to editing and writing books. I revised nearly all and rewrote many of the articles in English literature, as distinct from

American literature, for the *New International Encyclopedia* (1903–04). The number of articles, long and short, ran into the hundreds. Of that job I recall vividly the difficulty I had in discovering the dates when contemporary women poets and novelists were born. If for some urgent reason I have since wanted such information, I have simply inquired, "Madam, what age do you give for the record?" After that question is answered, I take a good look at her and make a marginal note. As an outgrowth of my association with teachers in school and college, when a member of the National Conference, I undertook the general editorship of a series of English classics called *English Readings*, which ultimately reached the number of forty small volumes.

In the meantime I had published a book on the English novel and a biography of Laurence Sterne and was well on in my studies of Henry Fielding. I had also assumed the editorship of the *Yale Review*. How and why I entered upon these literary ventures I leave for a later story. They are mentioned here as an indication of what I was doing in the middle years of a long life.

Some of my colleagues said that I was carrying too heavy a program of work. One day as I passed two of them on the street I heard one say to the other: "Cross can't last much longer." He judged of me by my appearance. I was lean, 5 feet, 10½ inches in height, and never weighing more than 145 pounds and at times 10 pounds less than that. I was also "a pale face." And yet, like Chaucer's Sergeant of the Law, "I seemed busier than I was." Laborious days, if such they may be called, were carefully planned with provision for an hour's sound sleep before dinner, a habit which I have never quite abandoned. It was my custom also to go out every day for a walk or for a ride with a friend on bicycles. Summers I usually went into retreat with my family somewhere either in Mansfield or in the north country. Altogether I ruled my life pleasantly and kept reasonably well.

In my forty-second year I had, however, a good scare. I came up for life insurance and was brusquely turned down. The physician who examined me put his stethoscope over my heart, listened for a minute, and remarked casually that there was no use going any further with me. I asked him to go ahead and tell me what was the matter with my heart.

After playing his stethoscope over breast and back, he announced that I had a leakage at the tricuspid valve. Having some doubts about that, I consulted a half dozen other physicians, all of whom diagnosed the case differently. At last I unbuttoned my shirt for an examination by my old friend, Dr. Oliver T. Osborn, who had had a good deal to do with Yale athletes. He asked me what I had been doing. "You have strained your heart in some way. There is a murmur at the mitral valve." He let me listen through his stethoscope, and I heard a rough sound, a sort of squeak. The strain had evidently been caused by a recent long bicycle tour over hills. I cast the bicycle aside, never to mount it again. Gradually the squeak became less pronounced; it grew faint; and disappeared. Six months later I was insured for $5,000. The physician who had first examined me now put me through some severe paces before he was ready to certify to the integrity of my heart. In all his practice, he said, he had never known a tricuspid leakage to clear up like that and thought it miraculous.

The summer after this winter of alarm the Cross family settled for a good rest at Randolph Center, high on the hills of Vermont. We took our meals at the Maplewood Hotel, with rooms outside at the Colonial Inn, the home of a Miss Martha Gilbert. The morning after our arrival a sprightly old man whose long white beard made him look older than he probably was appeared at the house, with milk and cream and eggs. He was Miss Gilbert's father, Henry G. Gilbert, a retired farmer, who lived a little distance down the road in a house by himself. After a short talk with him I saw that I had fallen in with a native humorist of the first water. I soon learned that like myself he was a Democrat, a rare bird in Vermont, and that he loved his pipe which he handled with unusual dexterity. All through the summer we rode together in his buggy over hills and through valleys. He drove leisurely while he talked on and on about himself and people who lived in this or that house, aptly describing their good and "funny" characteristics. "Funny" was his word for something sharp or rather disreputable in their dealings with their neighbors. His conversation cured me of my ills.

On our first trip I asked him why he addressed his horse as "Des." The name, he replied, was short for "Desdemona." He was proud of his mare, as fair in her youth as Shakespeare's heroine, though now past her prime. Shakespeare, he added, knew a good horse when he saw or rode one; and in proof of it he recited, to my amazement, several stanzas from "Venus and Adonis." He also recited a passage from Byron on another fine horse. He did not tell me that when a young man he used to take a part in amateur performances of *Macbeth*, as his son, the Reverend George Gilbert, has related in *Forty Years a Country Preacher*, a delightful autobiography by a devoted minister of the Gospel and a rare storyteller as well.

Before the summer was over my Vermont companion related for my edification many episodes in his life. A young man still in his teens, he drifted down into Mississippi, where for a short time he conducted a school for a planter in a windowless cabin dependent for all light on an open door. The plantation was near a nameless village lying within the fork of two converging streams. As he stepped from a stagecoach, the air was so damp, hot, and muggy between those sluggish streams that he could hardly walk or breathe. Meeting a gentleman by the roadside, he inquired the way to the cemetery of the town. At this point in the story I interrupted, "Why were you looking for a graveyard?" "To see how old people lived to be in that damnable climate." He spent an hour or two reading inscriptions on gravestones, long enough to discover that most folks down there, if they reached maturity, died in the thirties, some went on into the forties and now and then one got into the fifties. Nevertheless he went out to the plantation and stayed on in the school there until the Civil War was breaking out, when he returned home and enlisted in the Northern army.

No one except the Gilberts knew that I was a professor of English. To all others I was a New Haven man a little under the weather. My identity I concealed as a guard against requests for literary addresses or other intrusions. But Mr. Gilbert urged me to make one exception to the rule for the benefit of the little Episcopal church of which he was senior warden. Twenty-five dollars, he said, had been collected for painting the church, but $50 would be needed to put it in good shape with two coats of paint. The second $25, he thought, could be raised if I would give a lecture in the State Normal School across the road. The admission fee was to be 25¢. I agreed to the proposal on the explicit understanding that the date of the lecture should be on my last night in town. Posters designed by an "artist" at the Maplewood announcing an address on Charles Dickens by Wilbur L. Cross, Ph.D., Professor of English in Yale University, were displayed in all public places on the hill. Beneath my name, to attract attention, were caricatures of Pickwick and Sam Weller, no two of them alike. Few if anyone outside the game suspected that I was the Yale professor.

But on the morning of that eventful day, while I stood talking with the Methodist minister on the veranda of the post office, I escaped discovery very narrowly. Turning from one of the posters, the minister began, "You live in New Haven, I am told. Are you acquainted with this Professor Cross? Is he a strong man?" etc. I replied that I had just read the poster, which I thought very funny, that I lived in New Haven, that I expected to attend the lecture, that I was a little acquainted with Professor Cross but did not know whether he was "a strong man."

That evening Mr. Gilbert conducted me to the platform without saying a word by way of introduction. I caught the eye of the Methodist minister, who smiled. Others smiled, too, and stared. I told them Dickens stories, now and then reading one in the cockney dialect, for an hour and a half. They were in the mood for laughing and so was I.

There was a sequel to the tale. The next winter Mr. Gilbert visited me in New Haven on the way to see his son George, the rural parson then living in Middletown, Connecticut. I remarked that the church must shine in its new paint. "Not so fast, brother," he cautioned me. "The minister and I, you know, got into a quarrel over the color of the paint. He wanted one color and I wanted another. Well, he had his way. But he got his comeuppance, for just after we put on the second coat of paint there came up a heavy shower, wind and rain, which washed off a lot of the paint and streaked up all the rest. The church now looks a damnsight worse than it did before 'twas painted, and I'm damn glad of it."

The full flood of life in these middle years had its ebb tides of pain and sorrow. "There is nothing in life," I once wrote in fear, "more pathetic than the death of children." A daughter Elizabeth died of pneumonia in her fourth year (1903) and a son Arthur in his eighth year (1912). My devoted wife tried to conceal her intense grief, I could see, in order to mitigate mine, but for years thereafter it would break through the restraint of her strong will. As for myself I found relief only in some new under-taking which required for its success complete concentration of mental energies. In quiet hours and in dreams those children still live on in my memory as they frolicked through the house, now and then stopping to look into my study where I sat writing, as if in wonder of what I was doing. One day Arthur, who was trying to read a copy of *Robinson Crusoe*, which bore on the title page my name as Editor, asked me if I would write another story like that one. This belief of a boy seven years old that his father was the author of one of the most famous books in the English language and could at any time repeat the achievement is the highest trib-ute that has ever been paid to my literary ability. His only criticism of my *Robinson Crusoe* was that there were too many hard words in it.

During these years I was twice in England for summer vacations. In June, 1911, while reading in the Bodleian Library at Oxford I had the rare opportunity of more than casual association with Sir William Osler, Regius Professor of Medicine in Oxford University. Two years before that time on the publication of my life of Laurence Sterne, Dr. Osler had written to me about the book, and since then several letters had passed between us. He was particularly interested in my account of Dr. John Bur-ton of York, the original of "Dr. Slop," the "man-midwife" of whom Sterne played humorously in *Tristram Shandy*; and was as much amused as I was by the publication of a pamphlet by a London physician on the his-tory of midwifery, in which I was quoted as an authority on the subject.

As soon as I came to Oxford Dr. Osler called on me in my lodgings and invited me to his house in Norham Gardens to meet Mrs. Osler and some of his friends. He was not yet Sir William Osler but the title was near at hand. On Sunday, June 18, I attended a large tea party in Norham Gardens, and a few days later, on the coronation of George the Fifth, June 22, he was honored with a baronetcy.

The last time I saw Dr. Osler was in April, 1913, when he came to New Haven to give a series of six Silliman lectures on *The Evolution of Modern Medicine*. One afternoon we had tea together at the Graduates Club. Only instead of tea he asked for "sherry and sponge cake," which was, I think

the favorite refreshment of Sr. Robert Peel in the lulls of debate during
night sessions of the House of Commons. While we were sipping sherry,
he told me what had happened to several men whom I had met in
Oxford. One of them, well on in years, had died of arithmomania, a mental disorder, he explained, which manifests itself in an obsession for
counting objects or the number of acts required for doing something
which the patient has in mind to do. For example, a man afflicted with
arithmomania in the worst form, Dr. Osler said, holding up a glass of sherry,
would calculate the number of swallows he intended to take in draining
the glass to its last drop and if he made a mistake in the count, which he
was certain to do, he would be seized by a paroxysm of rage. The Oxford
man, who was one of Dr. Osler's patients, could never cross the street in
front of his house when the mania had settled upon him without first
fixing in his mind the number of steps he was going to take. If he made a
miscount he would go back and try crossing on another count, failing again
and again, until a friend appeared and helped him home. Dr. Osler
reminded me that a mild form of the mania got hold of Dr. Johnson who,
according to Macaulay, touched every post as he walked along a street and
if he feared that he had overlooked one would go back to it. I was a little
startled when Dr. Osler remarked that I had been looking at windows and
doorways while we were talking, as if I were counting them.

I retaliated by remarking that if I counted windows and doors, he
seemed to have been suffering from two fixed ideas when he wrote that
famous valedictory address given at the Johns Hopkins University on
Washington's birthday before his departure for Oxford in 1905. He spoke
then of the comparative uselessness of men after the age of forty and their
utter uselessness by the time they reached sixty when, as Trollope in one
of his novels suggested, they might well be eased into Paradise by chloro-
form. This part of the widely quoted address was composed in a mood of
sober and learned humor. The general public, however, took it seriously
and denounced Dr. Osler as a cold-blooded scientist who advocated that
sexagenarians should be quietly put out of the way. His critics did not
observe that before he finished with the subject he expressed some doubt
about the advisability of Trollope's suggestion and recommended instead

that college professors of sixty be retired on double salary.

The ages of man we discussed rather soberly, coming to the conclusion that as a rule whatever a man may contribute to his community, his country, or the world has its origin in the years before forty. Darwin in science and Dante in literature were cited among cases in point. "As for you and me," he said, "it little matters what may happen to us now." Dr. Osler was then sixty-three years old; I was fifty-one. Though I met Dr. Osler only at rare intervals, I always as in this instance fell under the spell of his wonderful personality.

X. Hadley, Beers, and Lounsbury

When I was an undergraduate Hadley was a tutor, not long back from Germany. He seemed to speak German as fluently as English. Even in those days I knew him slightly. One term while he was conducting a class of Juniors in elementary German, I was attending a class of Sophomores in Horace or Tacitus in a room separated from his by only a thin partition. I well remember that partition shook with laughter whenever he stopped to relate an incident or anecdote of his life in Berlin which had a bearing on the story the class was reading. A year later he began his lectures on Railroad Transportation, which awakened very great interest among us all. He was soon made a Professor of Political Economy.

When long afterwards he cast into the background the commanding position he had gained in a new field of economics in order to become President of Yale University, friends who thought they knew him well frankly told him that he was not cut out for an administrator. In some respects this opinion may have proved to be true. Hadley was almost sheer intellect. A short time before he was elected President I heard an address by him in which he outlined a comprehensive idea of a university. When he finished Lounsbury, one of the doubters, who was with me, remarked that if Hadley could make real his conception of a university he would become one of Yale's greatest Presidents. Twenty-two years later almost to a day I attended a meeting in New York of an association of university presidents and deans. Hadley, though there, was not on the program of speakers. I asked the chairman, Nicholas Murray Butler, if he knew that this was the last time Hadley would meet with the group, for his resignation from the presidency of Yale was to go into effect three months hence. Taking the hint, Butler called upon Hadley for a farewell speech. It was a most extraordinary performance, purely extempore. Hadley reviewed the course of university education from his youth onward and closed with a forecast of the future. These two speeches, far apart in time, showed an intellectual grasp of educational problems that had perplexed universities for a generation, which Yale had hardly considered before the period of the reorganization that was effected in his presidency.

During that period, especially while I was Dean of the Graduate School, I had many opportunities to watch the working of Hadley's mind. When any question came up for discussion in the faculty of Yale College, it was said, he would canvass it from various points of view and stop there, just short of recommending a course of action. This habit was called by the younger men of the faculty merely boxing the compass without using the instrument to steer the ship. There was a degree of truth in this. Several years later, while he was writing an article for the *Yale Review*, he complained in his prime he could see any subject from five or six points of view. This often led him to change his mind and sometimes resulted in no action at all.

I soon discovered that the best way to come to conclusions with Hadley was by quiet talks in his office when we were not likely to be disturbed by interruptions, which might unnerve him. For instance, it was agreed that a Department of Education should be organized, but opinion was divided on whether emphasis should be placed on professional training or on special studies of a research character in educational problems. I told him that, in my opinion, both aims ought to run along together in the expectation that research would finally prevail if the department was to be under the control of the Graduate School. "An excellent solution of the problem!" he exclaimed, throwing his arms into the air.

President Hadley was an opportunist in the best sense of the word. If he did not try hard to mould circumstance to educational ideas which he elaborated in eloquent speeches, such as the proper studies for a business career, he could be quick to seize circumstance for some far-reaching purpose he had in mind. Occasionally he seemed to act on momentary impulse, as when he took the bit on university reorganization by advocating, as I shall relate, the administrative control of all higher nonprofessional degrees by the Graduate School. This act, however, was not born of mere impulse. In the background lay a decision at which he had already arrived. When Caesar, standing by the Rubicon, exclaimed "The die is cast," he had long since made preparations for invading Italy at the first opportune moment.

With Beers, under whose direction I had laid the foundation of my English studies as an undergraduate, I came into increasingly close relationship as a colleague and later as Editor of the *Yale Review*. He was a scholar in a broad, liberal sense, like Henry Adams. But he was primarily a man of letters. He might have gained recognition as one of the leading poets of his time or as one of its first essayists or humorists had it not been necessary for him to hold on to his English professorship in order to support a wife and eight children. Perhaps, too, he was somewhat lacking in ambition. He seemed content with an occasional revelation of his rare literary talents, whose afterglow often lent enchantment to the *Yale Review* during its first ten years.

Inspiration for verse in the latter days of Beers's life came from moods rising out of his inner self. One day he brought into the *Yale Review* office a poem entitled, "The Dying Pantheist to the Priest," which he said had been rejected by another magazine for fear its paganism might offend readers. It was a beautiful dramatic lyric in which an ancient Roman pantheist told the priest that, though as a man he was about to die, he would live on in other forms of life through "the eternal undulations" of nature. "So take away your crucifix." I placed the poem at the head of the next number of the *Yale Review* and awaited its reception by the public. A strait-laced Puritan woman, I was told, was so shaken in her faith on reading it that she took to her bed for a week. Fortunately, after those few days of meditation she regained her faith in the religion of her forefathers.

Once a week it was Beers's custom to come into my office late in the morning, after my correspondence was out of the way, for a quiet smoke and miscellaneous talk mostly reminiscent in character. The talk lasted for just an hour or for the exact time it took to burn a mild cigar of my brand down through the stump, which he kept dry with the aid of a pointed match, one end between thumb and forefinger and the other end inserted in the stub, the part of a cigar he liked best because it had the best flavor. It happened one day that I had read in a New York newspaper a contemporary account of Lincoln's "Address at Gettysburg," which was strangely regarded as quite inferior to the long oration declaimed on the occasion by Edward Everett. Beers smiled and proceeded to tell two stories about Everett's oratory.

When a boy, he said, he heard Everett's famous address on George Washington. As the crisis of the Revolution the orator described the hard winter at Valley Forge when even Washington lost all hope of winning the war. Everything, Everett used to say, was then coming down with a crash, and, to show his audience what a crash is, he would hit as if by accident a large, thin glass of water on the desk before him, knocking it to the floor of the stage where all could hear glass jingle and see water flowing.

On another occasion Everett was the orator at an anniversary celebration of the battle of Lexington and Concord, speaking from a stage erected in the open air. Near him sat a few survivors of the embattled farmers who "fired the shot heard round the world." Just before beginning to orate Everett told those venerable men that at a certain point in his speech he was going to ask them to rise while he addressed them directly. At the proper time he paused and turned his eyes towards them. They rose. For a dramatic moment he looked them over in silence and then said: "Be seated. It is for us to stand in the presence of the heroes of Concord and Lexington." As the three or four old farmers were leaving the platform, one of them was overheard to say to his comrades: "What did old Squire Everett mean by telling us to stand up and as soon as we stood up to set down?"

When Beers had finished this story I asked him where he got that tale. He said that it originally came from Judge Hoar (1816–95) of the Supreme Court of Massachusetts, a native of Concord, who as a boy was present and heard and saw everything that took place on that memorable occasion.

The tricks of oratory, of which he related many, amused Beers. Misplaced oratory he despised. He never forgot the vitriolic attack on him by D. H. Chamberlain, that "old carpetbagger of South Carolina," because as the senior member of the Yale English faculty he made no provision in his course of study for oratory such as Yale had fostered in the old time. The only orator I ever heard Beers speak of with respect was Burke, whose entire works he set me to reading when I was a graduate student. No orator himself, Beers addressed his classes in a subdued but clearly audible voice and stopped there.

In his association with his colleagues Beers was careful to give no offense. He never stepped on their toes in order to get into a fight. He also disliked controversy because it was for him a waste of time and energy. This was the outward Beers. But there was another Beers behind the veil. One day we got to talking about an old school friend of his who was, I remarked, the most placid and kindly man I ever knew, much like Sterne's uncle Toby who would not harm a fly. "Was he like that," I inquired, "when he was in school?" "He was the only boy in school we could all lick," Beers said. "I could lick him." Beers's boyhood love of an open fight, still there in memory at least, I concluded had been washed down to an undercurrent of strong, at times violent, opinions of men and things which he would express, if in the mood for it, in intimate conversations. All that he might say was, however, tempered by humor. From him I learned what were the blind spots of many members of the Yale faculty from his student days down to the present. It was a fine collection. The pugnacious Lounsbury he was inclined to let off easy. Of him he wrote *"Heu! Quanto minus est cum reliquis versari quam tui meminisse!* (Alas! How much less happy to remain on with others than to remember thee.)

Of Lounsbury I saw more than ever after his retirement in 1906. Both of us were in England for the summer, much of the time together. I arrived the middle of June and went directly to York to visit the places in the country associated with Laurence Sterne whose biography I was then working on. Lounsbury came over on a later boat which left New York on Friday, June 13, thus putting his life in "double jeopardy," as I had once done with my own. Having finished my excursions through Sterne's Yorkshire, I went up to London to greet him as he stepped from a Liverpool train.

We put up at Cranston's Ivanhoe Hotel in Bloomsbury so that we might be near the British Museum, where Lounsbury wanted to do some work on Tennyson while I was examining Sterne manuscripts. We roamed about London for our lunches and dinners until we found a place where the coffee was satisfactory to Lounsbury, who abhorred tea. Once a week, sometimes oftener, we dined at the Oscar Wilde Restaurant in Piccadilly, where Wilde and his friends used to dine. On those occasions we ate an elaborate table d'hôte, drank a quart of Lachryma Christi, Lounsbury's favorite wine, smoked a shilling cigar, and "felt good."

After a few days in the British Museum Lounsbury was forced to curtail his stay there to an hour a morning. His head, he said, felt so queer that it could stand work for no longer a period. As a relief he proposed that we take a trip into the country. He would go with me anywhere provided I would agree to keep him out of cathedrals. We had a particularly delightful time touring western England as far as Land's End. The day we were in Bristol Lounsbury sat in the hotel while I went out to the cathedral and walked through the beautiful cloisters for a look at the mural monument dedicated to Eliza Draper, Sterne's last lady of the heart. On my return to the hotel I asked Lounsbury if he wouldn't like to walk over with me to St. Mary Redcliffe, which Queen Elizabeth praised as the "fairest" parish church in all England, and where, in the muniment room, as he well knew, Thomas Chatterton claimed to have discovered the famous Rowley manuscripts. St. Mary Redcliffe was not a cathedral; I submitted to Louns-bury the nice question whether we might not inspect a parish church together without a breach in our agreement. He conceded the point and we spent more than an hour in St. Mary Redcliffe. Lounsbury was moved by the interior beauty of the church and thanked me for taking him there. Before our return to London we visited at his request Winchester Cathe-dral, which interested him so much that it was evening before I could get him away from the precincts.

I preceded Lounsbury on the voyage home, leaving him in Paris with W. Gordon McCabe of Richmond, Virginia, one of his more intimate friends. From there he set out in mid-September for Scotland, to represent Yale at the celebration of the 400th anniversary of the founding of the University of Aberdeen. On his return to London, where he made many new friends among men of letters, he resumed his reading in the British Museum; but though his head felt better he reluctantly gave up all work and came home.

Lounsbury's frequent remark from now on that he could work for only

two hours a day without complete mental exhaustion needs some qualification. Work for him meant that kind of careful research which pervades
his prolonged studies in Chaucer and Shakespeare. Work so exacting as
this, which he was attempting in his investigation of Tennyson problems,
he was now unable to carry on with his old persistence which took no
account of time. In his best days, he told me, he used to work through a
night and sometimes through two nights and the intervening day without
sleep. That practice, he complained a year or two before we went abroad,
he had been compelled to give up. Still, he continued to extend into the
night miscellaneous work which required no close study. One day I
received from him a letter which I could hardly read. Though the lines
were straight enough, the words were abbreviated; no *i* was dotted, no *t*
was crossed. I asked him about that. He replied that to avoid strain on his
eyes he did much of his writing in darkness and corrected it in the morning. But, he added, "I had no time to waste on you."

Despite the handicap of failing eyesight, Lounsbury continued to work,
revising and enlarging for publication in books magazine articles and
addresses which in shorter form or in conception belonged to an earlier
period. Researches he had made on the early literary career of Robert
Browning he cast in the form of lectures which he gave in November,
1910, at the University of Virginia. The next year he brought out his *Yale
Book of American Verse*, notable as representative in its unusual selections
and omissions of his own personal likes and dislikes in our poetry, and
more notable still for an introductory essay in which he played ironically
with previous anthologies of American verse.

It was left for me, with the assistance of Miss Helen McAfee, to edit
after Lounsbury's death *The Life and Times of Tennyson*, which was based
mainly on lectures he had prepared as far back as 1897 for a class of forty
graduate students in English. Originally these lectures were all written
in pencil on coarse paper with wide margins for additions and afterwards
typed by Lounsbury himself. For the last chapter and some other parts
of the book I had nothing to go by except narrow strips of paper written
hastily on sleepless nights. What I had sometimes surmised I then saw
was true. Except for a few details, Lounsbury had added nothing to his

Tennyson manuscript since his return from England in 1906.

To the last Lounsbury enjoyed verbal sparring with his friends. Even while his health was breaking we often went to New York together for dinner at one of the clubs or to see a popular play. We always put up at the old Hotel Manhattan. Lounsbury did not care to go to the Authors Club, he said, because we were likely to find no authors there, nor to the Players Club because we were likely to find no players there. He was ready to go to the University Club, where he first met McCabe on "a storytelling night." But he seemed most at home at the Century Club, the rendezvous of old friends.

One night at the theater the play was *A Pair of Silk Stockings*, which in its treatment of sex was regarded as ultrasensational by respectable people who flocked to the theatre to see what it was. Coming in a little late, we saw in seats just in front of us a colleague and his rather censorious wife, who turned her startled face to Lounsbury and whispered: "Oh, Mr. Lounsbury, when I see Mrs. Lounsbury, where shall I tell her I saw you tonight?" Lounsbury's retort was quick: "Tell her, madam, that I spent the evening with you."

Lounsbury used to tell a story about John C. Calhoun. In Calhoun's time the two rival literary debating societies at Yale were Linonia and Brothers in Unity, each of which in after years claimed Calhoun for its membership when recruiting for new members among the students. To settle the dispute beyond question a member of Linonia in the Class of 1858 produced a letter purporting to have been written by Calhoun to his mother immediately after his entrance to Yale on a certain day in September, 1802. He informed his mother that he had had a conference with President Dwight, who admitted him to the Junior class, and that he had already been taken into Linonia. After the production of this old letter Brothers in Unity conceded that Linonia had proved its claim to Calhoun. Lounsbury, however, detected in the letter a clever forgery. The paper on which it was written was yellow with age and the hand which wrote it was a good imitation of Calhoun's. But the forger, Lounsbury at once saw, had made one mistake. He gave the letter a September date, whereas in Calhoun's time the academic year did not open until late in October. September then fell in the

vacation when all the students were away. After Lounsbury finished his tale
I remarked that there must have been some commotion among faculty and
students when he exposed the forgery. He replied: "I did not expose the
forgery, for I myself was a member of Linonia."

Lounsbury was the first to level attack on the kind of cigars I smoked
and handed out to friends without apology. It was a light cigar having a
Connecticut seed-leaf wrapper and perhaps a little Havana tobacco tucked
away in the interior. The story of his utter condemnation of that cigar I
still hear variously told. I will now correct the record for posterity.

Occasionally on a bright spring or autumn day Lounsbury and I took
a long ride in an open trolley car through Connecticut, stopping at a good
inn for luncheon. On our return to New Haven late one afternoon, he
inquired of me where he might get a few cigars which I could guarantee
as good. We walked across a street to a little shop which had sold me thousands of my favorite cigars. While Lounsbury was looking over Romeo
and Juliets and other Havanas of various sizes, 20¢ or 25¢ apiece, the proprietor reached down under the counter for a box of fifty cigars of my
own brand and opened them up for my inspection without saying a word.
I said "O.K." and threw out a $2 bill, and in return received not only the
fifty cigars but a dime to boot. Lounsbury who was watching the curious
transaction from the corner of an eye began to ask me about those "four-
centers." I told him that they were domestic cigars, so very mild that I
could smoke them all day without feeling any evil effects from them,
whereas one big Havana such as he smoked would knock me out completely. "No wonder that your doctor will let you smoke only one Romeo
and Juliet a day." On my invitation he took three or four of my harmless
favorites to try out.

The next evening while I was sitting at the round table in the Graduates
Club with a group of friends Lounsbury came in and began to fire at me.
"What is the name, Cross, of those cigars you gave me yesterday?" I told
him. "I don't know," he continued, "that it makes any difference what
they are called, but after dinner last night I lighted one and took a few
whiffs and threw the damned thing away."

"What about Mark Twain's cigars?" I inquired. "You once took a trip with him through the Great Lakes when somebody asked him if he smoked all the time and he replied that he had not yet learned how to smoke in his sleep. What brand of cigars did you smoke with Mark Twain?" Lounsbury avoided the trap by declaring that he did not smoke at all on that trip; in fact that he had rarely smoked a cigar until I came to New Haven and set him a bad example.

So I told the company about the kind of cigars that Mark Twain could smoke in a pinch. While I was staying one summer in a New Hampshire village the only cigars I could get at a local store were so rank that I went a whole week with only one smoke. For the same summer Mark Twain settled some distance away in Dublin, New Hampshire, where a friend of mine had taken a house for the season. This friend of mine, who smoked only a pipe, invited Mark Twain to dinner and in anticipation of his coming scurried around on his bicycle for cigars for his guest but could find nothing except those mighty cigars of the brand which had floored me— six for a quarter. After dinner Mark Twain smoked one of them to the bitter end without flinching. When he was offered another he looked it over before lighting it. My friend expressed regret that there were no better cigars to be had in the village store. Mark Twain replied, "No apology is necessary. All the time I was smoking that first cigar I wondered where you got it."

Lounsbury quizzed me rather sharply on this tale; but when I gave him the name of my friend, who was a former member of the Sheffield faculty, he concluded that the tale might be true though I must have dressed it up considerably.

Death came suddenly for Professor Lounsbury on the evening of April 9, 1915, while he was making a call on Secretary and Mrs. Anson Phelps Stokes. His wife was then on a visit in the South. Though he had been suffering for some time with mild attacks of angina pectoris, none of us thought that the end was so near at hand. His death which came in the midst of talk with his friends was in perfect keeping with his social character.

The funeral service, which was conducted by Mr. Stokes in Battell Chapel on April 13, got nationwide publicity owing to the presence of ex-Presidents Taft and Roosevelt as honorary pallbearers. The two men had not met since September 19, 1910, when their friend Henry C. White (Yale '81) brought them together at his house in New Haven for a heart-to-heart talk in the hope of closing the breach between them. Success was only partial. In the meantime, during the campaign of 1912 their quarrel had grown more bitter than ever. Their friends now wondered what their greeting would be at the funeral of their mutual friend.

Theodore Roosevelt and William Taft's friendship turned to feud.
Photo ca. 1909.
Library of Congress, photography by Harris & Ewing

When Roosevelt arrived with Brander Matthews I was standing with other pallbearers in the outer vestibule of Battell Chapel, talking with Taft, who as soon as Roosevelt approached extended his hand to him with a "Hello, Teddy." Roosevelt straightened up, throwing back head and shoulders, took Taft's hand limply, and returned the informal greeting with "How do you do, Mr. Taft?" Then he turned away to greet the other pallbearers. A minute or two later Taft again got Roosevelt's attention and inquired after Mrs. Roosevelt's health. He was assured that she was "very well." In return Roosevelt learned that Mrs. Taft was very well also and hoped that Mr. Roosevelt would call at the house after the services. Roosevelt regretted that he must leave as soon as the funeral was over. Taft was deeply hurt, as one could see, but his face quickly regained its composure.

XI. Dean of the Graduate School

There is no Yale Graduate School," was a common remark when I assumed office as its Dean, July 1, 1916. "Why," some of my friends asked, "did you accept an empty title? Here you are, at fifty-four, with a professorship which carries that maximum salary; you are Editor of the *Yale Review,* and on the side you are writing a biography of Henry Fielding."

I could not tell my older colleagues that I had seen professors in the dangerous fifties fall into ruts of routine teaching and that I was determined to avoid the mischance by a switch over to a track running in a little different direction. So my reply to all who felt concern over my decision was that if there is no Graduate School let us all get together and build one at a time when the University Corporation is ready to supply a moderate amount of money for the purpose.

I could not deny that Yale had no Graduate School organized as a closely knit unit like the Undergraduate and Professional Schools. But I could dilate on Yale's great heritage in the realm of graduate studies. Provision for graduate instruction at Yale had been made nearly two centuries before by Dean, afterwards Bishop, George Berkeley, the foremost British philosopher of his age, who, while living in Newport, Rhode Island, became interested in Yale College after his failure to found a college in Bermuda. On his return to England in 1732 Berkeley conveyed his Newport farm to the Corporation of Yale College for the nominal sum of 5*s.* on the stipulation that the rents of the property should be applied to the maintenance of three resident students during the period of study between their first and second degrees; that is, between their B.A. and M.A. degrees. Subsequently Berkeley sent over to the Yale Library a large consignment of books, nearly a thousand volumes, among which were a number of duplicate copies of the best critical Latin and Greek texts for the special use of scholars on his foundation. With the aid of Berkeley books and scholarships, Yale in its earliest history established a course of graduate studies in the liberal arts to further a farseeing philosopher's aim of raising the standard of teaching in the colleges of the New World. "Westward," Berkeley already saw, "the course of empire takes its way."

Success was immediate. Berkeley was still living when one of his scholars became the first President of Dartmouth College and another the first President of the College of New Jersey, not yet renamed Princeton. Within a century as many as eleven Berkeley men were elected to college presidencies, of whom one was the first President Dwight of Yale. No count could easily be made of the long line of professors and tutors at Yale and elsewhere who began as Berkeley Scholars. Throughout the South and Middle West Yale became known as "the Mother of Colleges."

For a full century and a little more graduate instruction was conducted wholly by the faculty of Yale College. The curriculum consisted of advanced studies in Latin and Greek literature and ancient philosophy, with the addition of mathematics, moral and religious philosophy, and the discussion of educational and political questions. But towards the end of this period other subjects were beginning to demand recognition, particularly science under the influence of the elder Benjamin Silliman, who urged that graduate students be segregated from undergraduates in a building or college of their own. On the advent of President Woolsey the situation was met in a large way by the creation in 1847 of a new department of instruction called the Department of Philosophy and the Arts. In this was set up for the Graduate Division a program of studies in philosophy, language and literature, history, and the social and natural sciences, leading to the degree of Doctor of Philosophy. Yale was the first American university to confer this degree—in 1861. The establishment at Yale of the Ph.D. degree requiring two and later three years of resident study with the exploration of some specific field of knowledge marked an epoch in the history of higher learning. Yale set the clock to a new time for all our great universities.

To indicate the quality of the guidance which Yale was soon able to give students enrolled for the Ph.D. degree, one has only to name James Dwight Dana in geology, William Dwight Whitney in Sanskrit and comparative philology, and Josiah Willard Gibbs in mathematical physics,

whose investigations in thermodynamics were to gain for him, in the estimation of Einstein, a place in science by the side of Sir Isaac Newton.
These and other scholars of high rank, however, conducted their graduate
work under difficulties. They were nearly all attached to one of the undergraduate schools, in which they were under obligation to give the usual
amount of instruction for the major part of the salaries they received.
Such time and energy as were left over they were free to devote to graduate students. It was during this lean financial period that Daniel Coit
Gilman and William Rainey Harper, both of whom had taken a prominent part in graduate instruction at Yale, withdrew to become the first
presidents of universities where large endowments were being provided
for research. The Ph.D. degree and all it stood for they took with them to
Johns Hopkins University and the University of Chicago.

During the administration of President Dwight, towards the close of
the nineteenth century, the way of the college professor who desired to
give graduate instruction was made somewhat easier. A few professors
were in part relieved of undergraduate teaching and several new ones
were appointed on the understanding that they should have ample opportunity to conduct graduate courses. A number of fellowships were secured
for graduates of Yale College; and Professor Arthur T. Hadley was
appointed the first Dean of the Graduate Faculty, to be succeeded three
years later by Professor Andrew W. Phillips. Hitherto there had been no
central office for the chairman or secretary of the Graduate Faculty. Dean
Hadley, it used to be said, carried the records about in his hat. He was the
last of that race. For the use of his successor a small house was set aside
near where Harkness Memorial Tower now rises. Here an office and
consultation rooms were provided for Dean Phillips, although in their
rear, and separated only by a door not always locked, there was the
University paint shop with its store of paint, varnish, and turpentine. On
the advice of President Dwight, when Pierson Hall was built off the
College Campus, a number of rooms in it were made available for graduate students, who as a rule were not allowed to occupy undergraduate
dormitories except as proctors.

Wilbur Lucius Cross, PhD, Yale 1889, professor, Yale 1884-1948, dean of the Yale University Graduate School, 1916-1930, dean emeritus, 1930-1948. *Images of Yale Individuals, Manuscripts and Archives, Yale University Library*

As the years passed these improvements were partially offset by larger demands for graduate instruction occasioned by an increase in the number of students. Though excellent work was still done in most departments, the tendency was to establish courses of study differing very little from the more advanced courses in the Undergraduate Schools. And the number even of these amorphous courses, open equally to graduate students and to undergraduate Seniors, that could be given in any year was dependent upon the varying load of elementary teaching which the professors might be called upon to bear. The danger of lowering the quality of research was at times altogether too real for the comfort of the administrative officers.

In fact, there was no one body responsible for maintaining uniform standards for degrees. The M.A. degree was still, as it always had been, under the jurisdiction of the faculty of Yale College; the M.S. degree, with more strict requirements, was under the jurisdiction of the Sheffield Scientific School. The only degree within the sole jurisdiction of the Graduate Faculty was the Ph.D., which was administered by a committee whose chairman, called Dean, was an active member of the faculty of Yale College. Three different faculties administering closely related degrees could result only in confusion of standards, amusing as well as serious.

Hanns Oertel accepted the position of Dean of the Graduate Faculty in 1911 on the assurance that Yale College would transfer to the Graduate Faculty control over the M.A. degree. The requirements for this degree he raised considerably. No work done *in absentia* was now to be any longer accepted; and the period of study was to be extended from one to two years. But owing to many commitments made to students already enrolled for the degree, the new program could not go into full effect until 1916; the delay irked Dean Oertel. His great disappointment, however, was his unsuccessful attempt to bring the administration of the M.S. degree under the aegis of the Graduate Faculty. This proposal met the determined opposition of the Sheffield Scientific School.

Unfortunately Dean Oertel did not complete his term of office, which was to run for five years. On his annual visit to Germany in the summer of 1914 he was caught in the meshes of the World War and remained on in Munich where he was to have a distinguished university career. During the first two years of his absence while there was hope that he might return to Yale, the Corporation appointed in succession two Acting Deans—Charles Schuchert, Professor of Historical Geology (with other titles) in the Sheffield Scientific School, and Williston Walker, Professor of Ecclesiastical History in the Divinity School, both of whom at his request, I suggested in turn to President Hadley. In these recommendations there was, I daresay, a subconscious motive, which was to give the Graduate Faculty a more distinct university character by loosening the strings which had bound it rather closely to Yale College.

On March 22, 1916, the now defunct Department of Philosophy and the Arts met to hear the report of a committee of five who had been appointed to recommend a Dean. The chairman, who presented the report, was Henry W. Farnam, Professor of Political Economy, who had a keen interest in the welfare of the whole University from top to bottom. He was also one of the most public-spirited men in New Haven and in the State at large. Though we were very unlike in temperament we were the best of friends. He often tried to persuade me to quit smoking, as he had done years before, by giving me statistics on the nation's huge waste of capital on tobacco, millions upon millions of dollars every year, and on the tremendous losses by fires set going in cities and forests by that innocent-looking little cigarette stub. Against this awful destruction of property, public and private, I set up a sort of alibi by claiming that I never smoked cigarettes. But I kept on smoking a pipe and cigars. He kept on trying to break me of a bad habit. And we kept on liking each other.

Professor Farnam, I was told, cast his report in the form of a political nomination speech such as I have since heard many times. I was nominated by acclamation Dean of the Graduate School and my name was at once sent to the President and Fellows of the University for confirmation (April 5, 1916). I was granted a leave of absence for five years from the Sheffield Scientific School and in view of the extra work my annual salary was enhanced by $500!

Events, it is now clear also, made almost inevitable my appointment in1916 as Dean. Ever since I had gained a footing against obstacles for my graduate course in English fiction, I had kept it going. I had served on several important committees under Oertel's predecessor, Dean Phillips; with Dean Oertel I had been intimately associated, and as an active member of his Administrative Committee was always ready for consultation on any problem that might arise. As a graduate of Yale College and a Professor in the Sheffield Scientific School, I understood the educational points of view of the faculties in both institutions. Withal I mixed with the faculties of the Professional Schools. Because of my knowledge of the University as a whole President Hadley convinced me that it was my duty to accept the office of Dean of the Graduate Faculty. So I decided to let destiny do its work despite the warnings of friends.

One of my first concerns was for the preservation of such records of the Graduate Faculty as were to come into my custody, which had reposed for a quarter-century as near neighbors to paint, varnish, and turpentine. Some of these records, I observed, were in the handwriting of Yale's great professors of former times, of Gibbs and of Hubert A. Newton, on whom Gibbs used to try out his mathematical formulas in the first days of his revolutionary discoveries. The Corporation at once set aside for my use a suitable house on the corner of High and Wall Streets, which was easily made over into offices and conference rooms, with a vault for past and future records, where, it was deemed, they would be safe against fire unless the fire were too hot. All offices and other rooms were largely refurnished by Professor Farnam with mahogany desks and chairs. The new headquarters were named Gibbs Hall. In passing I may add that Yale has no memorial worthy of Josiah Willard Gibbs, whose name, I have heard it said, is not as euphonious as some others. Even Gibbs Hall is now gone.

Of immediate concern also was a reorganization of the Graduate Faculty, which comprised a large body of professors of various faculties having divergent and sometimes conflicting interests. The plan of reorganization approved by the Graduate Faculty on October 28, 1916, split the faculty into three divisions and created an Executive Board of eight members which was empowered to determine the requirements for admission, to appoint all committees, to pass upon departmental recommendations for fellowships, and scholarships, and nominate to the Corporation professors and other officers of instruction. These extraordinary powers I requested for quick action at the right moment in the process of building up a Graduate School coördinate with the Undergraduate and Professional Schools of the University. The Executive Board rarely if ever took action on any subject unless the members were in complete agreement. All of them were in their fields leaders of independent judgment. Paramount among us was President Hadley who often made the most important motions and presented our conclusions to the Corporation, of which he was the presiding officer, which, so far as I can recall, approved them in every instance. Of all boards and committees with which I have been connected, no other has equaled this Executive Board in efficiency and mature wisdom.

The first test of the reorganization came with the question of admitting women as candidates for the M.A. degree. They had been eligible for the Ph.D. since 1892, but not for the M.A., which was then administered by Yale College, an institution founded and maintained for the education of men "in church and state." Even after the M.A. had passed to the Graduate Faculty, the admission of women for it met with objections because many advanced courses in the College were open to graduate students; but when it was announced that these anomalous courses were to be eliminated as fast as possible, the objections lost their force. A resolution that candidacy for the M.A. degree be no longer based upon sex was approved by the divisions without dissent and by the Corporation on January 15, 1917. Thus a question which had long hung fire was settled within a few weeks.

For the time being further progress toward building up a Graduate School was impeded by our entrance into the European War. The enrollment of students fell by 50 per cent, and thirty or more professors who normally gave graduate instruction were on leave of absence for war work overseas or at home. But in this lean educational period there was time to formulate and to discuss what the next steps in the development of the Graduate School should be when the war was over.

It was clear that if Yale was going to have a Graduate School which would take a commanding place among research institutions, it could no longer depend for the most part upon professors attached to the Undergraduate Schools but must have a body of professors and investigators of its own, and specifically that there should be organized a graduate Department of Education for the benefit of that large majority of students who intended to become teachers in colleges and secondary schools. It was clear, too, that immediate efforts should be made to secure endowments for fellowships to be awarded not only to graduate students who had shown proficiency in their work but also to brilliant students who after receiving the Ph.D. degree at Yale or elsewhere desired to go on into advanced research in fields they had partially explored. It is hardly necessary to add that we hoped to see the day when the Graduate School might have dormitories for its students and, in place of a dwelling house made over, ample offices for the administration of its affairs and consultation and seminary rooms for professors. All this would have been but an unsubstantial dream had not Yale seen in the middle distance the magnificent bequest to the University by the late John W. Sterling, who in his will designated the "Graduate Department" as one of the beneficiaries.

Further moves toward consolidating the Graduate School followed hard upon the close of the war. Late in 1918 President Hadley obtained the transfer to it from Sheff of the M.S. and all the higher degrees in engineering. It was his purpose, he said, to place Yale College and the Sheffield Scientific School on an equal footing as Undergraduate Schools by discouraging graduate extensions in both of them. Hereafter, he added, Yale must have but one Graduate School. When the temporary Board of Permanent Officers was replaced by a permanent one by vote of the Corporation in March, 1920, the Graduate School came into legal existence as an organic part of the University. Thus the goal towards which I had set my face when appointed Dean was reached.

The Divisions as organized by the Graduate Faculty were also extended throughout the University with such changes in grouping of departments of study as might seem desirable; the requirements for the M.A. and M.S. degrees were adjusted to the studies of the Undergraduate Schools; and a plan was authorized by the Corporation to facilitate students' taking courses in Yale College or the Sheffield Scientific School, no matter in which school they might be registered.

This last proposal was made the subject of a cartoon in the *Yale Record*. Ac★ is depicted as a girl of inquiring look with eyeglasses and flowers and Sheff as a green and bewildered young man. They are being married by President Hadley, whose eyes and open mouth are turned toward the heavens, while Dean Jones and Director Chittenden stand soberly by near a flower girl in the foreground dressed as a boy. Underneath is the inscription:

Holy Matrimony.
Ac and Sheff become one.

★*Editor's note: "Ac" refers to the "Academical Department" or more familiarly, Yale College.*

XII. A Trip to Hawaii

In the meantime I saw Hawaii. Sometime early in February 1920, President Hadley came over to my office a good deal perplexed in mind. He said that in April the Islands were going to celebrate the centenary of the arrival of the first missionaries, among whom were two or three Yale men and that he had been requested by the committee in charge to send a representative of the University. He had just seen, he said, the Dean of the Divinity School, who was unable to take the trip because of other engagements; so he had decided to ask me to go. To President Hadley's invitation I replied that I could probably qualify for the mission since the Graduate School had a department of religion as flourishing as that of the Divinity School. It might be difficult for me to leave my office for two months; but I had a most competent Executive Secretary in Miss Margaret Corwin, and I felt certain that Professor Clive Day would supervise the business of the Graduate School during my absence. I brought up the question of having my wife as a companion on the voyage. To my surprise I found that there would be no question about that; I was then unaware that the expenses of the trip were to be borne not by the University but by the Yale alumni of Hawaii. It took no more than ten minutes to reach the conclusion that Helen and I were to go.

I was elated. The idea of the Sandwich Islands, as they were once called, had haunted my imagination since childhood. My father and later my uncle Franklin, who had visited the Islands on their whaling voyages to the Northern Pacific, used to tell me long stories about the paradise of the world. My college roommate, Walter Frear, had often described the manners and customs of the natives, who he understood and loved. Sometimes in those days I foregathered with groups of other students from Honolulu while they told stories of Hawaiians or danced the hula-hula with nothing left out of its primitive abandon. Now as a guest of the Frears I was to enter the land of my dreams, where Mark Twain had been and Robert Louis Stevenson.

Before setting out I read again an account of the missionary enterprise in whose centennial celebration I was delegated to take a part. It was not an uncommon thing more than a century ago for stray Hawaiian boys to find their way to the United States on trading vessels plying between Honolulu and Atlantic ports. Two such boys worked their passage to New York in 1809 in a ship commanded by a captain who brought them on to New Haven. According to the story one of the boys, Opukahaia, was discovered one day by Yale students sitting on the steps of the chapel or the President's house in the College Yard. The students were naturally interested in him and invited him to their rooms. A zealous Senior took him in hand and explained to him the Christian way of life, which he was eager to adopt. Presumably he was baptized under the name of Henry Obookiah, for he was afterwards called by that name.

With the intention of returning home as a missionary, Obookiah spent some time among the theological students at Andover, Massachusetts, and attended a mission school at Cornwall, Connecticut, established for Christian training of Indians and stranded boys from the South Seas. Never quite acclimated, he died at Cornwall and was buried there. The story of Obookiah's conversion and untimely death spread far and wide throughout New England, and no doubt helped to induce the American Board of Foreign Missions to send out a small group of missionaries to the Sandwich Islands to free the natives from the bondage of Satan.

Stalwart young men were chosen for leaders. First among the volunteers was Hiram Bingham (the grandfather of Senator Hiram Bingham), a graduate of Middlebury College, Vermont, who received an honorary M.A. degree from Yale in 1819. Second among them was Asa Thurston, Yale B.A. 1816. Both Bingham and Thurston had studied at Andover and were duly ordained as ministers of the gospel in the Congregational Church. Closely associated with them was another Yale man, Edwin Whitney, who had just completed his Freshman year. Thus, one may see, the influence of Yale predominated in the mission. In its inception it was essentially a Yale undertaking, now forgotten by most Yale men.

The little bank of missionaries sailed from Boston October 23, 1819, on a brig named *Thaddeus* after one of the Twelve Apostles. There were twenty-two of them, including wives and children and two native Hawaiians from the Cornwall school, of whom one was Hopu, the boy who ten years before had landed in New York with Obookiah. It was a perilous six months' voyage round Cape Horn, 18,000 miles in a ship good for no more than 8 knots an hour. Thurston, as one of a party of six, disembarked early in April, 1820, at Kailua off the Kona coast of the island of Hawaii to found a mission near the King, who wanted the two natives as servants for himself and his five wives in the royal household. He wanted to be a Christian too. Bingham and the rest went on to Honolulu on the island of Oahu, where on April 19 they all went ashore and were given shelter in a group of thatched cottages. There they organized their parish with church and schools after the manner of the Puritan pioneers in New England.

Helen and I began the journey near the middle of March and returned near the first of May. On leaving Chicago we met on the train an old acquaintance, Henry van Dyke and his daughter Paula. They were going, I think, to Japan with a stopover in Honolulu for the celebration to which Van Dyke had been appointed as Princeton's delegate. During the next days there was some rather big storytelling between Henry and myself while Helen and Paula listened and smiled as we exposed our blind spots to full view. In San Francisco we parted company to meet again in Honolulu. The Van Dykes embarked on a Japanese boat whose bar opened beyond the three-mile limit, while Helen and I were booked for a boat on the American Matson line whose bar in those days of national prohibition was kept closed. There were remarks about our different liquid habits as we went our ways.

Our boat was comfortable "and we weren esed atte beste." Most of the company were on the way to the celebration but there were some who were going to Honolulu for other reasons. An octogenarian with shaking hands and legs told me that in his youth he had lived for several years in the Islands and that now, his wife dead and his children dispersed, he was going back to die amid the old scenes at Hilo. The first day out I spoke to James Rolph, the popular Mayor of San Francisco, for whom claims were made of his descent from the only son of John Rolfe and Pocahontas through the Rolphs of Virginia. He was the most persistent amateur poker player on board. Once in a game he always at it through. Years later when we both became Governors I was to tour California with him as his guest.

On the evening of the same day as I was walking the deck I fell in with a surgeon from Salt Lake City. Our conversation drifted to medical science and the natural sciences in general, and I casually remarked that the racial origin of the native Hawaiians was still an enigma. His illuminating reply was: "To us there is no enigma about that. They are of the lost tribe of Israel." The secret was out. The surgeon was a Mormon. In semiprofane language I took him to task for believing "that damned rot." He seemed to be in no way offended by my explosion.

With him, he said, were his wife, who he said was one of the numerous granddaughters of that much-married Brigham Young, several children, and a nurse. The object of their trip was to bring back a son who had been in the Mormon mission of Oahu for a year and to leave in his place their eldest daughter, a girl of eighteen, as a propagandist for their sect among the native Hawaiians. Mormonism, he claimed, was spreading fast among the few full-blooded Hawaiians in the country districts. He invited me to visit a Mormon Temple in the heart of Oahu where, he assured me, I would be permitted to enter all its parts except the Holy of Holies. The next morning he introduced me to his large family. Never have I seen children under better and easier control. The nurse, not so devout as the rest, was, however, not restrained from flirting as much as she pleased.

One morning we passed Diamond Head and entered the harbor of Honolulu. On the dock were many Yale men with their families. As we went ashore to be greeted by our friends who threw leis round our necks, a brass band, which had been playing national airs, struck up "Boola Boola" and "Down the Field." Just before we stepped into a car with the Frears to be driven to their home my emotions were subjected to a severe nervous chill. Doremus Scudder (Yale '80) the master of ceremonies, who was standing by, handed me a card listing the addresses I was expected to give during the next fortnight, one, two, or three every day beginning the next noon. He even had me down for a sermon in the church of the oldest native Hawaiian parish in Honolulu. I protested against that assignment to a man who was not a clergyman and had never tried his hand at a lay sermon. It was impossible, he rejoined, to let me off on that account. So I was confronted with the problem of how to escape that sermon without offending anybody.

Scudder had announced that Van Dyke and I were to go out as a pair of spellbinders to make addresses. Van Dyke, who had acquired a master's technique in extemporary speaking, was always ready with a ten- or fifteen-minute speech of apt and beautiful phrasing, which he could easily spin out of half an hour if the occasion so demanded, by the further elaboration of his central ideas, which could be adapted, with minor changes, to any audience. Having at my command no such fund of semireligious ideas or experience in public speaking, I was forced to rely on the inspiration of the moment, if there was any, and on what incidental knowledge I could gain of prospective audiences and their special interests. We appeared together or singly before all those sorts of groups, large or small, that comprise the civilization of mankind—religious, social, educational, historical, scientific, commercial, and agricultural. I had a jolly time; it was educative also.

Two or three days I spent in visiting schools and other institutions of learning and in the discussion of educational problems with teachers and administrators, among whom I nearly always found Yale men with whom I was acquainted. Among them was John R. Galt, chairman or president of several committees and associations dealing with semi-educational and social problems which concerned the Islands as a whole. Naturally I was greatly interested in the University of Hawaii over which Arthur L. Dean presided, a former young colleague of mine in Sheffield, who was doing much to control, if not to cure, leprosy by the use of chaulmoogra oil. I was interested, too, in Oahu College, originally founded by the missionaries for the higher education of their children, where Frear prepared for Yale and afterwards taught for a year or two; as well as in the grade of common schools leading up to a good high school, where all through the system various races commingled as students and teachers.

I recall a morning spent in a primary school where a Japanese girl was teaching children, whites, native Hawaiians, and several other races, how to read and write English. She was doing a wonderful job. Her own speech, which she was passing on to the children, resembled our Yankee dialect in accent and intonation. I asked her whether she was born in Connecticut or in Massachusetts and learned to my amazement that she was born in Honolulu and had never been out of the Islands. She had been taught to speak English by a descendant of the missionaries who were mostly New Englanders.

Racial antagonism appeared to be nonexistent everywhere we went. Interracial marriages were so common that they seemed at first sight to be the rule. One day I met at luncheon a very cultivated woman of strange beauty, the wife of a man with whom I was acquainted. That afternoon several of the party drove up to Pali at the head of the Nuuanu Valley for an expansive view over coral beds and ocean. We returned to the gardens of the Royal Palace, no longer the residence of kings and queens, in the heart of Honolulu where I addressed a league or association of women over which this lady presided. In her introduction she told the company that I had driven the speech she intended to make out of her head by impertinent questions. Perhaps by indirections I had tried to find directions out. She was part white and part Hawaiian, with perhaps a tincture of Chinese blood. At any rate, she had inherited the best characteristics of the races to which she belonged.

Native Hawaiians of the older generation in whom not much other blood was infused we saw at one of their outdoor feasts under the shade of tall cocoanut trees. They displayed great deftness in twisting poi from large bowls round two fingers and conveying it to their mouths without dropping a particle of it. On this, their staple diet, they had grown fat. Rotundity seemed to be cultivated by women as a mark of beauty. They still wore loose Mother Hubbards similar to those with which their ancestral mothers were clothed by the first missionaries who were shocked by scanty attire.

For poi, a fermented paste of taro roots, I acquired no taste. But for breakfast I liked papaya and a cup of Kona coffee having a flavor like no other. Delicious ripe Hawaiian pineapples I ate without limit just as in my boyhood I had eaten muskmelons from my grandfather's garden, one after another, when nobody was around to molest me. I thrived then and thrived now at the age of fifty-eight. Rather taken by the sweetness of unrefined cane sugar, we went out to one of the best equipped sugar mills and watched the process of milling. For twenty years I had owned a few shares of stock in different Hawaiian sugar plantations. After inspecting this modern mill I bought a few more!

The young generation of native Hawaiians had broken away from the dress and habits of their parents and grandparents. We saw them all at play at Waikiki where they were riding the high waves on planks or in out-riggers. With the Frears Helen and I tried an outrigger and wanted to try it again.

An event with an amusing sequel occurred at a pageant depicting significant scenes in Hawaiian history since the advent of the missionaries, such as the breaking of pagan images before the adoption of Christianity. The panorama was unfolded on the slope of a rocky hill. A platform for special guests was built well down the hill where they could see and hear all. On the platform strong but roughly made chair were arranged in rows with an aisle down the center. I took a seat by the aisle three or four rows back. In the front row on my side the seats were marked "Reserved." I asked why and was told that His Royal Highness, the Prince of Wales, who came into the harbor the night before on a man-of-war which was taking him round the world, had been invited to attend the pageant and had graciously accepted the invitation. At length he appeared with his entourage of naval offices and was conducted to the front row of seats while the rest of us rose in his honor. After viewing several scenes of the pageant the handsome boy of light-brown hair (who looked eighteen though he was twenty-six) became restless and soon rose to go. Again we all rose while he walked down the aisle and stepped from the platform. As soon as we sat down everybody looked towards the vacant chairs, oblivious of the pageant. In order to relieve the tension I exclaimed so all could hear, "Aren't some of you ladies going to steal the chair in which Edward, Prince of Wales, has sat?" Thereupon there was a rush-and-scramble. A young woman near me first got a hand on the back of the chair, and so it was hers. The last I heard of that chair, she still kept it as a memento of her raid.

My sermon to a native Hawaiian congregation was destined never to come to pass. On Saturday, while I was meditating the sermon for the next morning, a committee of the Hawaiian Chamber of Commerce called on me in great distress. Mayor Rolph of San Francisco who, they said, had promised to give the main address before the Chamber at a luncheon on Monday in honor of the Admiral and other officers of the Pacific fleet had just informed them that he would be unable to keep the engagement because he was not feeling very well and his private secretary was not with him for assistance in the exigency. So they had to come to me to help them out. The address was to be on "Americanization," a subject with which I must be familiar. I told them that I hadn't enough time to prepare the kind of speech they wanted unless they could persuade Doremus Scudder to free me from the sermon in which I was then entangled. They easily persuaded Doremus to take a minister of the Gospel as a substitute. Thus I happily maintained my reputation of never preaching sermons, of which I had heard too many for my comfort.

It seemed strange that anybody should be asked to give an address on Americanism while standing by the most conspicuous racial melting pot in these modern times. But on inquiry I was informed that considerable fear had been awakened of the influence of a Buddhist Temple in Honolulu and a school connected with it in which, it was alleged, principles of government were being taught in direct conflict with Americanism. Out of curiosity I spent an hour or two in that school, where under the direction of a Buddhist teacher Japanese children were reciting in loud chorus something which I could not understand, though I thought that the instruction was wholly religious in character. At any rate, I decided not to try to dethrone the Buddha in his temple.

The meeting of Honolulu's Chamber of Commerce was a large open one. A thousand men and women sat at the tables. Henry van Dyke made a short speech with hits at me who hit him back. Mayor Rolph, who sat by my side, was in a happy mood over his escape from a speech by an excuse which was accepted at its face value. Before coming to my conclusions on the subject assigned to me, I could not refrain from burlesque comment on that emotional wave of "100 per cent Americanism" which swept over the mainland of the United States after the World War.

Hysterical sociological experts were still in the field who had plans for quick Americanization of polyglot races in industrial cities by the use of money in various quantities. In one small city it was estimated that the job could be done for $75,000, which businessmen were solicited in vain to contribute.

Money-shakers were likewise invading the field of foreign missions with schemes for quick conversion of all the world to the Christian faith. It was to be done country by country on a large financial scale. An American millionaire, for instance, on a visit to Constantinople inquired of the President of Robert College, an American endowed institution, how much money it would cost to bring into the Christian fold all the Turks of the Turkish Empire. More absurd still, an American missionary organization had a plan to raise a hundred million dollars for the wholesale conversion of China so that an end might be put for good to Christian endeavor in that vast country. A scout who was sent out to China to survey the field reported that the estimate of a hundred million dollars was a little low because large masses of Chinese were living on a social and economic plane from which they would have to be lifted several pegs before much could be done with them.

Speaking on the fringe of the United States, then bursting with spurious Americanism, I reminded my audience that their ancestral missionaries learned from experience that the only way to Americanize an alien race is through the slow process of child and adult education. Those pioneers, not afraid of innovations, established local schools, at once religious and secular, all over the Island as fast as they could train native teachers for them. And so I concluded we still needed good teachers with a notion of what "American ideals" really were.

At several functions I fell in with the Reverend William E. Clarke, head of the British Mission at Apia, Samoa, who gave me an intimate story of Robert Louis Stevenson in his island home. Parts of the story he afterwards wrote out for the *Yale Review*. It was a gorgeous tropical morning when Stevenson, his wife, and Lloyd Osbourne landed at Apia from a trading schooner. Mr. Clarke, who met them on the sandy street along the beach, not knowing who they were, thought that they might be a vaudeville troupe with banjo and mandolin on their way to Australia, so unconventional were they in dress and general appearance. An hour later he called on them as they were sitting on the veranda of the little Apia hotel. R. L. S. told him that his name was Stevenson, saying no more about himself except that he was traveling for his health. The next day Mr. Clarke had the three at the mission for dinner. In the evening Stevenson turned the conversation towards the fascination which tales of horror have for many readers. Mr. Clarke admitted that not long ago he felt that fascination when he sat up all night to read and ponder the psychology of a tale called *The Strange Case of Dr. Jekyll and Mr. Hyde.* "By the way, Mr. Stevenson," he casually remarked, "it was written by a namesake of yours. Have you ever read it?" Stevenson, who, I daresay, maneuvered the conversation up to this question, replied that he had not only read it but wrote it and dreamed it before he wrote it. That evening marked the beginning of a close friendship which never faltered.

When Stevenson settled at Vailima, the name he gave to the house which he built on the lower wooded slope of Mt. Vaea, Mr. Clarke helped him set up a household with the sons of native chiefs as a staff of servants on the understanding that there should be family prayers every evening. The day was rare when the two men did not meet either at Vailima or the Mission House. Whenever Stevenson wrote a prayer which he regarded as particularly eloquent, he would mount his gray horse "Jack" and ride down the rough road to Apia to read it to the missionary, concluding with a look upward as if asking the Lord God of Heaven if any of His servants could beat that supplication. Sometimes Stevenson went with Mr. Clarke on his visits to native churches. And once he wrote a story of the Samoans which Mr. Clarke translated for him into Samoan. It was "The Bottle Imp." Being unfamiliar with fiction, the natives at first thought that Stevenson had a bottle with an imp in it which brought untold riches to its possessor. Thereafter they called him Tusitala (The Teller or Tales).

As if I heard it but yesterday, I remember all that Mr. Clarke told me about the death and burial of Stevenson. Summoned one day towards evening by a native messenger who kept crying, "Tusitala has fallen and

is dying," Mr. Clarke hastened on horseback to Vailima. He found Stevenson lying on a couch in the great hall, and he knelt and prayed by his side
while his life slowly ebbed away. Few but native Samoans were able to
climb the steep and ragged path to the top of Mt. Vaea where they buried
Tusitala on a narrow plateau overlooking on one side the red roofs of Vailima and on another a boundless ocean. It was the place which Stevenson
had chosen for his burial. After reciting the Episcopal service for the dead,
the missionary read the noble prayer which Stevenson wrote and read to
his household the evening before his death. In conclusion Mr. Clarke
addressed the Samoans in their native language and then dismissed the
congregation with a benedictory prayer. For a few minutes they all stood
by the grave in the silence of that mountain aerie as their last tribute to
their friend, the teller of tales.

At length our days in Honolulu were drawing to an end. My wife and
I had been royally entertained by old and new friends. We had been
received as part of the Frear household. I had been a guest at a banquet
of the Hawaiian Yale alumni, who well represented the professional and
industrial interests of the Islands. We had laid away in our memories grand
and lovely scenes. It yet remained, however, for us to see the volcano of
Kilauea over on the Island of Hawaii, which in one of its periodic eruptions was putting on, reports said, an extraordinary show. Frear invited a
little group of us to take the trip with him. He had tramped over the volcanic area many times since childhood, once with Professor J. D. Dana,
Yale's distinguished volcanist. Besides Helen and me, there were in the
party Mrs. Aurelia H. Reinhardt, then President of Mills College in Oak-
land, California, her father (William W. Henry, then eighty-one years old),
and Paula van Dyke. At first Henry van Dyke intended to go with us; but
he changed his mind when the Bishop of the Protestant Episcopal Cathedral in Honolulu invited him, though a Presbyterian, to preach the sermon
on the Sunday we were to be away. I argued with Henry in favor of the
volcano as against the church but to no avail. The temptation to step into
a pulpit still associated with the Church of England was too great for a
Presbyterian divine to resist. In bidding me Godspeed he expressed the
hope that the sight of an active volcano emitting strong sulphur fumes,

which he called brimstone, would do me good as a warning of what awaited me unless I mended my ways.

A Saturday night on a steamer on whose deck natives lay sleeping brought us early the next morning into the palm-fringed harbor of Hilo on the east coast of the Island of Hawaii. Between sunset and sunrise, I was soon aware, we had passed into almost another world. From the boat we saw a long straggling town quite different from Honolulu. The sun seemed brighter, the air more moist and warm. It was a glorious morning when we started out on a long motor trip southward over the plain lying between mountains and ocean, as far as Puna, through the most tropical scenery, I was told, of the Islands. We passed from sugar plantations into deep forests, with here and there small clearings, where tall trees were trimmed high, out to the black sands of the wide beach of Kalapana. Black beaches, of which this was an extraordinary example, have their origin in old volcanic lava flows which spread out into the ocean, then crack and crumple into particles as small as the yellow sands of other seas. The view of the black lava beach was a good prelude to the sight of a volcano in eruption, whose lava streams might likewise run down to the sea.

That afternoon we retraced our journey to Hilo and thence up to the Volcano House for the night, the only time to see a live volcano in all its splendor. We waited for deep darkness before driving along the edge of a large dead lava field to the great pit of Kilauea. By Frear's orders the car came to a halt behind a tall pile of rock and lava which the volcano had thrown up on previous eruptions, so that in walking round an end of the pile we might come suddenly and unexpectedly upon the crater of fire. It was a dramatic stroke. I found myself saying "My God, Frear!" over and over, to the amusement of a group of men and women sitting on a rock near by. Moving along the rim of the volcano for different points of view, we looked down into that molten mass of lava flowing in rivers or rising like waves of the sea to throw red-hot rocks high into the air. Here and there a man or woman screamed as they took a glance into the crater. There was current the story of a man who once came a long distance over the waters to see the volcano in eruption and after one look into the fiery pit turned and ran away, apparently forever. But Kilauea in action was one of nature's grand spectacles of might and beauty. Nothing before, nothing since, has ever seemed so tremendous.

A river of lava had broken somewhere through the walls of Kilauea and was flowing down the mountain side, spreading out into a wide field along which, some nine miles away, we walked the next morning. The hot lava, moving slowly, cooled so quickly on the surface that within a few minutes it would bear the weight of a man's body if anyone dared to try the experiment, as I did under the supervision of a guide who understood his business. Afterwards we inspected one or more of many old lava tubes, incrusted channels, several feet in diameter, through which great streams of lava had once poured down mountain sides into the surrounding seas.

Before leaving Hilo that night I visited its industrial school which had a historical interest for me. This and similar schools were founded by the missionaries for the education of native Hawaiians long before there was anything of the kind in the United States. From them, particularly from the one at Hilo, Gen. Samuel C. Armstrong, the son of a Hawaiian missionary, derived the pattern of a great industrial school for the education of the Negroes coming up from slavery after the Civil War. He was the founder and first president of Hampton Normal and Agricultural Institute. The success of General Armstrong's experiment no doubt gave the cue for a revolution in our whole system of education—including the establishing of trade schools for the training of skilled workmen, now common throughout the United States. To stand on the ground where Armstrong had stood as a young man was for me a sentimental satisfaction. On that spot a great idea came to him, the full development of which is not yet in sight.

On returning to Honolulu I gave Henry van Dyke a more glowing than trustworthy account of my trip in order to bring home to him the mistake he had made in choosing the church instead of the volcano. I told him that, though most of the other visitors wore goggles to protect their eyes and covered mouth and nose with handkerchiefs to keep from coughing, my unprotected eyes easily withstood the hottest flames and my lungs breathed in and out sulphur gases as if they were built to inhale them. So I could see no reason for changing my way of life. On this decision I was going to take my chances.

The next Sunday the preacher in the Central Union Church at Honolulu was a clergyman from the mainland. He began his sermon, I was
informed, with the remark, "A visitor to the volcano a few days ago was
heard to exclaim on his first sight of it, 'My God.' His words were uttered
doubtless in great reverence while he stood face to face with the wonderful works of Almighty God." I did utter at least those words in admiration and in awe if not in reverence.

In accepting the mission to the Hawaiian Islands I had an ulterior
motive which I have not yet made manifest. Besides pleasure and an
extension of a knowledge of the world, I wanted to do something which
might enhance the prestige of Yale. The opportunity was at hand. Two
years before the trip Herbert E. Gregory, Silliman Professor of Geology
at Yale, had spent a few weeks in Honolulu while on his way back from
Australia. As a scientist he became tremendously impressed by the work
being done by the Bishop Museum of Natural History, of which Albert
F. Judd, a prominent Yale man, was a very active trustee. When he reached
home, Professor Gregory could talk about nothing except the Bishop
Museum at Honolulu. He asked for a leave of absence to accept for one
year the directorship of the Museum which had been offered to him. His
request was granted. He also asked that Yale enter into some sort of agreement with the Museum for joint scientific investigations in the Pacific
area. But his proposal was too vague for positive action for or against it.
To some of Gregory's colleagues who had never heard of the Bishop
Museum it seemed fantastic.

Before leaving New Haven for Hawaii I had a conference with President Hadley who requested me to make a survey of the activities of the
Museum and report to him on the advisability of proceeding further with
Professor Gregory's proposal. Not only was my report most favorable but
I had Walter Frear draw up a preliminary agreement between Yale University and the Trustees of the Bishop Museum for coöperative research
on scientific problems covering Polynesia. According to its terms the
Director of the Museum was to be a member of the Yale faculty and one
or more members of the Museum's staff were to come into residence at

Yale for periods of one or two years. There were other provisions which opened the way for an exchange of research assistants and research fellows. With this agreement in my pocket I set out for home via San Francisco and the Grand Canyon.

The agreement, which the authorities of the Bishop Museum had already approved, was ratified by the Yale Corporation the following October. By this act Yale acquired an outpost in the Pacific for scientific exploration in association with similar institutions in Japan, China, Australia, and New Zealand.

Mory's Association, a private club for Yale associated members is now housed at 306 York Street, New Haven, once the home of Wilbur Cross. Purchased in 1912. Photograph prior to 1930.
Yale University buildings and grounds photographs, Manuscripts and Archives, Yale University Library

XIII. Provost

By one of those peculiar ways of Providence in dealing with the affairs of men, I was to serve as Provost at Yale for a year and a month. After the death of Professor Williston Walker, the first incumbent of the office, in March, 1922, spring and summer passed without a Provost. In the middle of September President Angell wrote to me saying that he was "at his wit's end" and could see no way out of the woods unless I would accept an appointment as Acting Provost for a year. He had no desire, he said, to have me resign as Dean of the Graduate School or Editor of the *Yale Review*, but thought I might make the provostship a half-time job by concentrating my attention on departmental budgets and leaving questions of educational policy largely to the Schools of the University. In the circumstances I regarded his request as a command and accepted the position, content that it was only for a year, as no Provost amid the stir of University reorganization could expect to last longer than that. For ease in doing business and for keeping a broad hand spread over three jobs, I brought the offices of the Provost under the roof of Gibbs Hall. In passing from the Graduate School or the *Yale Review*, both on the first floor, to the Provost's office I had only to climb a stairway—which is just about enough exercise for a man with a reasonably sound heart.

The functions of a Provost were not at first very precisely defined. He was to be an aide to the President, a sort of liaison officer between the chief executive and the Schools and University departments of study. Doubt as to what he should be had been evident in discussions over the title which this new officer should bear. Some thought he should be called Assistant to the President, but that title, it was finally agreed, lacked dignity. Others would have him called Chancellor, but that implied executive powers which it was not intended to grant him. Finally Provost was selected, as a title midway in dignity, which might be pronounced in any one of three different ways: Prōvō, Prōvōst, or Prŏvŏst. I preferred, when the time came for it, to be addressed as Prōvōst, though I answered to all three names.

Immediately I began to receive inquiries from the graduates of my time about this strange office which the Corporation had created and to which I had been elevated. They became so numerous that in an address I gave on the next Alumni Day, February 22, 1923, I attempted to relate the duties I had undertaken. In abbreviated form this is what I told my fellow alumni:

"The Provost is *ex officio* a member of all the ten Faculties of the University and he sits with the Corporation and the Prudential Committee *without* the right to a vote, and he is secretary to the Corporation's Committee on Educational Policy *with* the right to a vote. He is also chairman of the University Council. And besides, he is *ex officio* a member of the Library Committee and of all the committees of all the Faculties so that he may see with both his eyes all that is going on. He is a sort of watch dog—not unlike that Cerberus that lay by the threshold of the underworld. He is the Ko-Ko of Gilbert and Sullivan's "Mikado"—the Lord High Executioner of this comic opera; or Pooh-Bah, the Lord High Everything Else. It is unnecessary to tell you that he must bluff a good deal. All the recommendations for appointments from all the Departments and all the Faculties go through his office to the Corporation—professors, associate professors, assistant professors, and instructors. All the budgets of all the Departments also travel the same primrose path to the University Comptroller."

When I looked full in the face what President Angell intimated would be a half-time job, I wondered what he regarded as a full-time job. It was, I soon saw, my province to reduce a medley of activities to a simple system of procedure. This I had really accomplished in large measure before I tried to explain to the alumni the miscellaneous functions of a Provost.

My most conspicuous scene of action was the Corporation room in Woodbridge Hall where, as chairman of the University Council, I saw at the head of a long table facing two rows of administrative officers and representatives of ten faculties, with Elihu Yale looking down upon us out of a large portrait. Near the outset of university reorganization of the Council sent to the Corporation a resolution requesting authority to consider means for letting down the bars between Yale College and Sheffield

Scientific School so that students might pass easily from one to the other in choosing their elective studies. This resolution, duly approved by the Corporation, had lain dormant for nearly three years. At the first meeting of the Council, a fortnight after I assumed office, I asked that this resolution be taken from the table. The Council thereupon appointed a special committee to canvass the problem of coördination in its many phrases. Buttressed by the report of this committee three months later, I proceeded at once with a proposal that there be established a Faculty of Arts and Sciences which should include the Permanent Officers of the three Undergraduate Schools, with the President as chairman. That is, three faculties were to be merged into one, with the President over all, to act upon all questions in which the three had, in his opinion, a common interest. A general aim was to promote harmony in procedures and development.

No sooner was this proposal made than hornets rushed from their nests and swarmed about my head. They came mostly from the eaves of Yale College, whose ancient prerogatives as the Mother of Yale, it was feared, would be doomed to death by the creation of an all-inclusive undergraduate faculty. Such a faculty, whatever might be its initial purpose, would gradually usurp, it was asserted further, the functions of the existing separate faculties. In the end Yale College would go; the Sheffield Scientific School would go; the Freshman Year, recently organized by the Corporation as a new School with its own faculty, would go. There ensued a dramatic controversy so hot that it would not be expedient to describe it in all its details. I was the villain of the piece. I was acting outside my province as Provost. I was a meddler. I was the worst enemy Yale College had ever had. I was a traitor to my Alma Mater. I was advised to quit.

After a while the hornets quieted down for the time being. The plan for an Undergraduate Faculty of Arts and Sciences was adopted by the Corporation as soon as it reached that body (February 10, 1923). The Council, so authorized by the Corporation, issued for the use of students a combined catalogue of the three Undergraduate Schools and a pamphlet giving the time and place of all courses of student therein. In this way the fence which had been built high between Yale College and the Sheffield Scientific School fell to the ground. Hereafter students were to be free in the choice of such electives as they and their advisers deemed best for them in preparing for the profession or occupation they had in mind. Of this privilege students are, or were up to the war, making increasingly larger use.

Next I proceeded with another proposal. The Sheffield Scientific School readily accepted the recommendation that it substitute the B.S. for the Ph.B. degree inasmuch as science was not to predominate in its curriculum. Yale College in taking over the Select Course in which the humanities predominated, decided at first to take over the Ph.B. degree also to be administered along with the time-honored B.A. Subsequently, however, to meet the recommendation of the Council, the Permanent Officers of Yale College passed a vote recommending to the Corporation that the Ph.B. (a degree for those with little or no Latin) be abolished on the understanding that Latin be dropped as an entrance requirement for the B.A. degree and be made an elective study in the College.

Immediately an alarm was sounded over this imperfectly concealed threat, it was declared, to dethrone Latin from the high place it had held for more than two centuries as a prime essential for the B.A. degree. Greek had gone; now Latin was to go. Again the hornets swarmed out. Everybody who had anything to do with the educational policies of the University was pelted with letters in protest against so disastrous an educational calamity. It was a well-organized opposition into which were brought Headmasters of large preparatory schools and a number of prominent alumni of the older generation. The militant minority of the Permanent Officers of Yale College, who had been outvoted two to one, submitted a brief to prove that Latin should be left untouched; and a poll was taken of the Assistant Professors in the general faculty of the College, which showed an overwhelming majority of those voting not only in favor of retaining the Latin requirement for the B.A. degree but also against the abolition of the Ph.B. degree.

When the original recommendation of the Permanent Officers of Yale College reached the Corporation in company with a volume of protest, there ensued a long and able debate which ended in laying the main issue on the table. While the debate was becoming rather warm, I remarked in a short informal speech that all subjects of study ought to be put on a competitive basis and left to take their chances; that in a college there was no place for a protective tariff, however good an issue it might be for the Republicans in a political campaign. With this impromptu climax I sat down, and Chief Justice Taft, a member of the Corporation, who had a seat by my side, jumped up and, slapping me hard on the shoulder, exclaimed: "Young man if you live long enough, you will see the light on what protective tariffs have done for our country." I broke in to thank him for his compliment to my youthful appearance. I was then a full sixty years old.

A few weeks afterwards President Angell put an end to the hullabaloo over Latin by exercising his right to a pocket veto. In taking this action he knew that time would settle the question. Yale College went on with its two degrees with no important changes until 1931, when the Corporation on its own motion abolished the Ph.B. degree and made Latin an elective for entrance and an elective in the College. There was left but one restriction. Candidates for the B.A. degree were still required to take the Freshman course in Latin if they were qualified for it, or a course in Classical Civilization, either Greek or Roman, such as the University Council had recommended in the days of my provostship.

The sting of defeat I bore lightly. I seem to have found an "escape" (I was then reading Freud) by means of a little byplay with Latin among my friends. It so happened that at the next annual initiation banquet of the Phi Beta Kappa Society (March 28, 1924) I was toastmaster. A traditional feature of this occasion at Yale is a Latin address, usually read, to the initiates by a member of the Latin faculty. This year the orator was the man who commanded the phalanx which marched against those of us who would repeal the protective tariff which Latin had long enjoyed in the College curriculum. With his consent I introduced the orator in Latin. Apparently he expected from me, "an enemy of the classics," only a few words; but that was not my design. With some difficulty I wrote out a Latin speech in a simple style, avoiding unusual words, and then committed it to memory. Without manuscript, I spoke the rather long speech slowly as if I were making it up as I went along. I threw in references to intelligence tests, then first becoming common, to the Teapot Dome scandals, and to prohibition which had turned the United States into a desert. I paid the orator some questionable tributes, for example, as *homo sapiens* and, to mitigate any offense I may have given, I concluded with a high-flown eulogy of a man *qui in tenebris nostri temporis, incerti, inculti, atque insani, lampada antiquae doctrinae et optimarum atrium sustulit—ad suum honorem ac gloriam universitatis Yalensis*. He smiled as one who liked that splurge of oratory, in part purloined from Cicero.

The appointed orator of the occasion then read to the happy young men who were being admitted into Phi Beta Kappa an address in classical Latin, which few seemed to understand. As we were breaking up, a colleague asked me how I dared perpetrate so cruel a jest. It was, however, only good-natured banter. And another colleague remarked that he never knew I could talk Latin like that.

A few months later there was a second Latin episode. In former times the B.A. degree had been conferred in a Latin formula. One day when our talk reverted to the Phi Beta Kappa episode, I asked President Angell how he would like to have the old custom revived for the Ph.D. degree at the approaching Commencement. He replied that he would like it. We kept our intention a close secret except that Clare Mendell was called in to check up on our Latin. No other member of the Corporation or of the faculty nor any candidate for this degree was told what was to happen on that Commencement day. When I rose and began my presentation address to the President with *Praeses Clarissime*, I observed a look of wonder on the faces of dignitaries sitting near me on the platform, and when I turned toward the rows of candidates for the Ph.D. degree down the hall as a signal for them to stand while the President conferred the degree upon them, they came to their feet. They knew the primitive language of gesture better than Latin, which was, for all their study of it, a dead language. Several of my friends scattered through the large audience reported to me the behavior of graduates back for their reunions. Many bent forward to listen and inquired of their neighbors what language I was speaking. One asked, "What in hell is Cross trying to say?"

But by the time Mr. Angell started to confer the degree in beautiful

Latin phrases, some of the alumni, I daresay, recognized the language he was speaking as one they once learned to read and rip to pieces in school and college as if it were an old corpse from which the spirit of eternal ideas departed nearly two millenniums ago. For a score of years I had endeavored to no avail to persuade instructors to teach Latin as a living tongue, for its liquid consonants and open vowels make it the most eloquent language ever uttered by man. I am happy that one may still hear Latin at Yale Commencements spoken by the President and the Dean of the Graduate School.

XIV. The Invisible University

As Provost I was the recipient of flashes of notice in educational quarters outside of Yale. Schools and colleges and teachers' associations invited me to address them. Two universities—Columbia and Michigan—conferred upon me honorary degrees, which I prized highly. The presidents of two other universities quizzed me on my attitude towards proposals to leave Yale and come to them. Another university picked me out for its customary address to the students at the opening of the academic year so that faculty and trustees might look me over at a time when the president of that institution was about to retire. I gave the address and accepted the liberal fee. All suggestions that I desert Yale I attributed to the wiles of Satan.

At the close of my term as Provost in 1923, I settled down to give all my time, outside the *Yale Review*, to completing under President Angell the work I had undertaken as Dean of the Graduate School during the consulship of Hadley. The first stage in University reorganization under President Hadley did not go far beyond providing a mechanism which was yet to be made to work smoothly. This was one of the problems which awaited President Angell, another fine mind, who was destined to rebuild Yale's superstructure without greatly disturbing the old foundations. His plan, as I apprehended it while acting as Provost, was to build evenly, making one department of study as strong as the rest, with perhaps a predilection for the social and natural sciences. He was well aware that the Graduate School, though older in its inception than all others, had not kept pace with some of them in the coördinated research which was assumed to be a function of a great university. With President Angell as my superior I undertook the development of instruction and research in the Graduate School along lines on which there was never any material disagreement. It was a labor of seven years. Then I retired from the scene.

The Board of Permanent Officers grew within a few years to a body of more than forty professors of the first rank, of whom twenty-eight were new men. This group of investigators, supplemented by staffs of associate and assistant professors, finally freed the Graduate School from its long dependence on the undergraduate faculties. At the same time the faculty was greatly augmented by a plan soon put into effect for cooperation with the Professional Schools in studies having a common nonprofessional interest.

First of all there was organized in the Graduate School a Department of Religion for the benefit of Divinity students who, with or without a preliminary B.D. degree, wished to proceed in due course to the M.A. or the Ph.D. degree. They belonged to an increasing class of students who as a rule came to Yale to qualify not so much for the Christian ministry as for teachers and investigators in some division of the extensive field of theology and religious education. At that time I had in mind several of my once young contemporaries who had had difficulty in gaining the knowledge they desired because of the rather sharp separation between the Divinity and Graduate Schools as distinct University units. One of my friends who squeezed through the barriers was James H. Tufts, who eventually became the head of the Department of Philosophy in the University of Chicago. Another was Marion L. Burton, sometime President of the University of Michigan. A Department of Religion removed all the old barriers and so made the road clear for the new generation. Soon nearly fifty Divinity students enrolled in the Graduate School.

On a larger scale articulation quickly followed with the School of Medicine. Dean Winternitz often reiterated that a medical school has two functions: first and foremost, the education of doctors of medicine, and second, the training of investigators in medical science all the way up to clinical problems. Though admitting that these two functions do not run along in strictly parallel lines, he made the general distinction between them apparent by providing that students midway in their medical course might choose which of two roads they would take. Prospective doctors of medicine were to proceed to the M.D. degree, and investigators were to enroll in the Graduate School for the Ph.D. degree. Dean Winternitz organized various divisions in the biological sciences into "study units" for joint attack upon difficult problems, much as was being done in the

University departments of chemistry and physics. The final accomplish-
ment of this human dynamo, which ran at full speed through light and
darkness, is now a part of the University's history.

One day in March, 1928, on the advice of President Angell, Dean
Winternitz and Dean Hutchins of the School of Law let me into a project,
as yet divulged to only a few, for an Institute of Human Relations, in
which they had awakened the interest of the Rockefeller Foundation.
They asked me to join with them in the undertaking. They would do all
the work, they promised, if I would act as advisory chairman. I consented.
While their plans were developing, always changing day by day, or
between morning and night, those two young men (Hutchins was only
twenty-nine years old) gave me, a man of sixty-six, a lively merry-go-
round. Sometimes in moments of excitement I felt as if I were a snowball
between two balls of fire which in an instant would consume me. But the
balls of fire cooled and the snowball remained, though somewhat damaged. It was a great experience to play the part of adviser to two young
men of boundless energy, who after loud and profane protests would
usually heed my advice to slow down a bit.

Two years after they disclosed their secret we saw rising a large and
dignified building for the sole use of the Institute of Human Relations.
For construction, endowment, equipment, and maintenance, the University received munificent grants in which the Rockefeller Foundation took
the lead. Pope as a poet had said, "The proper study of mankind is man."
In modern scientific phrasing, the founds of the Institute defined its purpose roughly as the study of man as a mental and physical being in his
social environment. The original aim of those two young men, as I understood it, was a synthesis of the biological and social sciences. One a doctor
of medicine, the other a lawyer, they started out with the declaration that
both medicine and law are social sciences. In a sense the assumption was
of course true. But law and medicine have so many different ramifications
that only a genius could bring them into a system of coördination. Had
Hutchins remained at Yale instead of running away to Chicago, more
might have been accomplished in a bold attempt to integrate related

sciences. As it was, the Institute of Human Relations undertook notable investigations in the social background of the biological sciences. For graduate students the Institute, with its well-equipped laboratory of psychology, opened areas of original research hitherto unexplored at Yale.

In addition, those who desired to specialize in comparative psychology or psychobiology now had available for the first time an anthropoid station in New Haven and another in Florida, which were established at this time. Out of curiosity I used to visit occasionally the first New Haven colony of chimpanzees. I looked on while the staff on a morning weighed and measured them for records of their growth. I saw chimpanzees pile boxes to proper heights for successful jumps to get between their teeth bananas hanging from a ceiling. I watched them at breakfast. Their table manners were dreadful. At last I stood by while they were at play, cashing one another from room to room, quietly lifting latches of closed doors. From experience, not from books, they learned the adage "Look before you leap!" At first the chimpanzees seemed a little afraid of me. That was only shyness which wore down. I got along with them almost as well as with young men. When chimpanzees spit at me, I understood what they meant by it.

The process of coordinating the Professional Schools with the Graduate Faculty as a central administrative body continued until the major divisions of the University were included: Law, Forestry, Engineering, Nursing, Music, the Fine Arts, and the Theater and Dramatic Criticism. The pattern for each was essentially the same, though there were differences in details. This large program of integration was carried through by successive steps with the greatest caution so as to avoid professionalizing the degrees within the jurisdiction of the Graduate School.

The policy of promoting scholarship in Professional Schools by affiliating them with Graduate Schools was a unique experiment which met with considerable objection outside of Yale. Well I remember a strenuous encounter with members of the Association of American Universities who were then considering ways and means for raising the standards of education in Professional Schools. Undue attention to medicine as a science, they argued, would tend to smother the real purpose of a medical school, which is to train doctors of medicine. Similarly, the real purpose of a law school is to train lawyers, and so forth. Where, I inquired in reply, is there any better place to advance the science of medicine or of law than in schools devoted to these spheres of knowledge? The conclusion was that the interesting Yale experiment would be watched in the hope that it would succeed. I think it has succeeded; the Professional Schools have maintained a balance between scholarship and training, much as in the Graduate School itself original research and the education of teachers have gone hand in hand without the impairment of either.

Whereas in 1916 the funds annually available for fellowships and scholarships in the Graduate School amounted only to $23,000, they rose by 1930 to $166,000 and, owing to large endowments and special grants, Yale was then expending on research projects more than $600,000 a year. Preëminent were the immense grants of Sterling Trustees, amounting to several million dollars, for professorships carrying stipends for research in unrestricted fields of study, and a supplementary grant of a million dollars for fellowships to be awarded to high-ranking scholars. Numerous, too, were gifts of educational foundations and industrial corporations for specified investigations in the social and natural sciences. It was not so easy to obtain outside assistance wholly for the promotion of humanistic studies which have no direct application to current life. To this prevailing attitude there was a notable exception which was naturally stimulating to those who were pursuing knowledge with no ulterior motive except for the light it throws on the history of civilization. In 1927 the General Education Board of the Rockefeller Foundation made a grant of $195,000, to be prorated over a period of five years, for advanced studies in ancient and modern languages and literatures, on the understanding that the University would match the gifts. In all, that grant provided financial assistance to forty projects, individual and coöperative. It was worth while to be Dean of the Graduate School in those days. The seas were calm and bright. The halcyons were brooding on the waves.

Soon after the death of John W. Sterling (1918), whose bequest provided for a large building program, it was generally understood that first in order of construction should come a new University Library, and in close proximity to it a Graduate School quadrangle, with administrative offices, seminar rooms, and dormitories for students. The Library with all its other purposes was to serve as a laboratory for faculty and students engaged in advanced humanistic studies. To carry out this preliminary plan the University engaged Bertram G. Goodhue, one of America's leading architects, who submitted designs for a Library on its present site and a Graduate School just across the narrow Wall Street. The two groups of buildings were to be connected by a graceful bridge. But the Yale Corporation decided to eliminate the Graduate School from the Goodhue plan and to treat the Library as a separate unit. It soon became apparent that the site first selected for the Graduate School was to be reserved for the School of Law. Naturally I took alarm, fearing that the quadrangle for the Graduate School might drop out of the picture. It was this anxiety more than anything else that led me to resign the provostship. At any rate I requested of President Angell permission to plead the cause of the Graduate School before the alumni at their next annual meeting in New Haven on Washington's Birthday (1924).

On that occasion I undertook to answer three questions of my own about the Graduate School. They were: "Where is it? What is it? And why is it?" As I now reread the words I can still feel the old undercurrent of concern, if not fear. I will quote, beginning and ending with the first question:

"Where is the Graduate School? We all know where Yale College is, where the Sheffield Scientific School is, where the Law School, or the Divinity School, or the School of Medicine is. But where is the Graduate School? Who of you has ever seen that institution? What collection of buildings is known as the Graduate School? What towers mark it? What vaulted cloisters? Or broad quadrangles with umbrageous walks and green velvet lawns? A casual visitor would conclude that Yale has no Graduate School unless he happened to see a dwelling on the corner of High and Wall streets made over into offices for the Dean and named Gibbs Hall in memory of a very great scientist, once a member of the Faculty. . . . So much on the site on the Graduate School, on its existence in the realm of visible fact. At best it is a case of 'low visibility,' to repeat the now famous phrase of admiral Jellicoe when he let the German fleet escape him in the evening twilight of the North Sea.

"Not having made out very well with the first question, I will now proceed to the second: What is the Graduate School? Saint Paul once said that
there are things seen and things not seen, and added by way of comment
that things seen or temporal, while things not seen are eternal. An unseen
spirit, the Graduate School permeates the University. It is the spirit of learning, of knowledge, of investigation, pursued not as a professional aim or
professional art, but for its own sake mainly. It lives and thrives in the minds
of instructors and students wherever they may be. As the University
expands, the spirit expands also. A new laboratory in physics or chemistry
or biology or engineering, and, last though not least, a new library—each
in turn gives the spirit of learning an enlarged dwelling place.... So much
for the Graduate School in the realm of metaphysics....

"I will close by returning to the point where I set out. There is a very
fine sermon by Cardinal Newman, in which the great preacher draws for
the imagination a picture of the Invisible Church—the immense company
of prophets, apostles, saints, and martyrs—the unnumbered men and
women who have ordered their lives in an abiding faith in an Unseen
Power making for the good of the world. But that sermon Newman followed immediately with another no less eloquent on the Visible Church
as 'an encouragement to faith,' wherein he showed how faith would faint
and die were it not for the Visible Church where men and women may
gather together for worship in the midst of figures and symbols of things
unseen. Even the Quakers have their meetinghouses.

"The time must come when graduate students, a majority of them in
residence for three years, shall no longer live on the fringe of the town,
apart from the life and traditions of this historic University, but shall be
brought together in dormitories within the circle of comfort and beauty;
when, too, the professors in the humanistic studies shall be brought
together in their midst, just as the professors in science now have their
laboratories. The new Sterling Memorial Library will be an immense step
forward to this end. It is likely to be a building unsurpassed in architectural
beauty. The books that it will contain form one of the great collections of
the world. Facilities for study and investigation will be on a scale hitherto

unknown at Yale. Here instructor and student in the humanities will meet for their common work much as do now the scientist and his young investigator in any one of the laboratories. It will still remain to provide, as indicated by the architectural designs recently published, offices and lecture rooms for certain departments near the library and to give the students a dwelling place in a quadrangle close at hand. No one, of course, knows what is in the minds of the gods, but so far as one can see into the future, Yale, while maintaining the great traditions of the Undergraduate and Professional Schools, is destined to take, in the next generation, a conspicuous place in all those advanced studies and investigations now associated with the Graduate School. This is the vision; this is the gleam."

It seemed a long time before that vision materialized. The year I saw the sign of a distant star Goodhue died and soon afterwards the School of Law edged in on the first proposed site for the Graduate School. The question then arose as to where the Graduate School should stand if it were ever to be made visible. Eventually an irregular piece of land at the head of Wall Street was chosen, the best available site left near the new library. James Gamble Rogers, who had designed Harkness Memorial Quadrangle, was appointed as architect. On a morning sometimes in 1928 President Angell asked me to appear two days later before the Corporation's Committee on Architectural Plans with preliminary sketches for a Hall of Graduate Studies, for which the Sterling Trustees were ready to make an appropriation of $3,000,000. Within those two days and two nights I was able to transfer from head to paper ideas for offices, seminar and lecture rooms, professors' studies, and dormitories, with lounge and dining hall and kitchen, which I had long carried under my hat.

At that and subsequent meetings I was the victim of some heckling, particularly by President Angell who asked me why I needed so large an office for myself and why a man who belonged to "an unwashed age" insisted on so many bathrooms for students. Angell was a delightful companion and a master builder. One day he expressed regret that the Hall of Graduate Studies could not be completed while I was Dean as a climax to my career. I countered by vowing to petition the Corporations to keep me on after my age of retirement unless the architect's designs

were adopted before that day. Under this threat, he promised to get immediate action.

Gamble Rogers designed a group of buildings after the heart's desire,
surrounding a court made very beautiful by its deviation from a standard-
ized quadrangle. But unexpected delays in construction intervened so that
I was out and away in Hartford as Governor of Connecticut before
the cornerstone was laid. I came down from Hartford to assist in that
ceremony.

XV. The *Yale Review*

Few, I daresay, know that there was behind the *Yale Review* a tradition nearly a century old, of a quarterly magazine conducted by Yale graduates and members of the Yale faculty though not as an official organ of the University. First in line was the *Christian Spectator* consisting mainly of "religious communications" supplemented by educational and scientific notes and a few items of special interest to Yale men. The *Christian Spectator*, beginning in 1819 with the blessing of President Jeremiah Day, closed its career in 1838. It was succeeded five years later by the *New Englander*, a magazine of wider scope, designed to promote "the New England way of thinking" in theology, morals, and education, and incidentally in science and literature. Within its pages appeared, as I have related, Lounsbury's revolutionary program for teaching English. Reasonably liberal in its theology, the *New Englander* won a high rank among the best American quarterlies when the *North American Review* was in its prime.

From 1857 to 1892 the Editor of the *New Englander* was William L. Kingsley (Yale 1843), a Congregational minister and a fine and cordial gentleman of the old school. For many years one of his co-editors was Timothy Dwight, soon to be elected President of Yale University. By 1880 the general interest in theology was fast waning; and the clergy were then finding more specialized avenues for publication. In this editorial crisis, Kingsley attempted in 1885 to transform the *New Englander* into a monthly "literary magazine," and enlarged the title to *New Englander and Yale Review*.

Kingsley was the first Editor to notice me. One day when I was a student in the Graduate School he invited me to call on him to talk over something I had written which interested him. It was, however, much too long for a magazine. But after I had migrated to Pittsburgh I sent him an account of an Ibsen play which he liked and published. A few months later he accepted a similar essay on a modern Icelandic novel.

While I was looking forward to its appearance, the manuscript was returned with the news that Kingsley had been stricken down by a sudden illness and that in consequence the *New Englander and Yale Review* must suspend publication.

On Kingsley's enforced retirement the magazine, with its title shortened to *Yale Review*, was passed on to his son-in-law, Henry W. Farnam, and other members of the Yale faculty as co-editors, who converted it into a quarterly devoted entirely to political science, history, and economics. So restricted a program, however, soon developed trouble similar to that which Kingsley had experienced with theology. First rose above the horizon the *American Historical Review*, to be followed by the *American Economic Review*, both national in character. Thereupon the *Yale Review* entered upon so rapid a decline that by 1910 it was on the way out. Professor Farnam decided to discontinue the magazine in its old form, and offered to convey all his rights in it to the Yale Publishing Association, of which Edwin Oviatt was President and Manager, with the understanding that I would undertake to reorganize it as Editor in Chief. I was urged by President Hadley, Secretary Stokes, and the University Council's Committee on Publications to agree to this proposal; and Mr. Farnam promised a generous subvention to the business management for a period of three years. A new adventure thus beckoned. I was naturally not a little intrigued by the prospect of having a magazine of my own in which I could publish anything I might write. No more of my manuscripts were to come back from other editors with keen regrets that my article, "though interesting, is not quite what we want for the immediate future."

My spirits, however, underwent a severe chill as soon as I discovered what kind of a renovated magazine most of its sponsors had in mind. The revelation came at an excellent dinner which Farnam gave to a representative group of the Yale faculties. It was proposed, not by me, that there be set up a rather large board of advisers to the Editor in Chief, each of whom should guarantee to supply two articles a year from his department of study. To supplement these there would probably be available for every number of the magazine at least one of the many lectures given annually by distinguished men on the various University foundations. Occasionally, too, it might be advisable to publish an abstract of a Ph.D. dissertation. At any rate scholarship should always be represented by one learned article, carefully documented. To lighten up any issue the Dean of one of the Schools might be invited to give an account of some of the "interesting things that his faculty were doing." Attention was particularly called to the famous Primitives in the Yale Gallery of the Fine Arts which the general public as well as Yale graduates would like to know something about. Contributors, as they would be mostly Yale men, would not expect any payment for their articles and book reviews beyond a free subscription to the magazine for a single year. And the Editor in Chief should be willing, for the present at least, to serve without remuneration inasmuch as he would probably be relieved of some of his teaching.

All these things were said to convince an editor that he would have little to do, in fact that the magazine would run itself, with nothing more than a directing hand. Though I had never edited a magazine, I was then the general editor of a series of forty textbooks and so knew something of the nerve-racking labor involved in correcting the bad English of carelessly written essays. I was at the same time amused and dumfounded by what I heard that evening.

A fatal weakness of the plan became apparent when several professors remarked that they could not be held responsible for any articles from their departments, though they themselves might now and then write one, because it was better, especially for young instructors, to contribute to periodicals which were founded for publishing the results of investigations in their own fields. I suggested that specialists might enhance their reputations by occasionally "humanizing" their knowledge for the benefit of the general public. It would be a waste of time, some replied, to draw men away from their researches to write "popular articles." Not all held to this view. Notable exceptions were William Lyon Phelps in literature, Albert G. Keller in the science of society, and Lafayette B. Mendel in physiological chemistry. Still, it was clear that a majority of the group sitting round the table were not very eager to continue the magazine, whatever might be its character, learned or popular. When we parted that evening I felt certain that if I assumed the editorship of the *Yale Review* under the proposed plan the magazine would soon come to an end from which there would be no recovery.

Happily the *Yale Review* was not yet prepared for a third death. A few days after the dinner conference I met President Hadley on the street under a drizzly sky. He was going to his tailor's two blocks away (on the corner of College and Chapel Streets). We walked along together under his large umbrella, and after he had been measured for a suit of clothes we walked back to his office. I gave him a summary of what had been said at the dinner and then proceeded to unfold my ideas of a magazine which might take an honorable place in a fast-moving world. The editor of the reorganized *Yale Review*, I told him, must be given a free hand if he is to succeed, for he will be engaged in a doubtful experiment. His policies should not be determined by a board of associates, and yet a group of advisers thoroughly interested in the project would be of great assistance to him at the start. Becoming more personal, I went on to say that if I were appointed editor my aim would be to make the magazine "a national quarterly" dealing with public questions, social and natural sciences, religion, history, literature, and the fine arts, all in so large a manner as to include sometimes foreign questions that might affect or interest the United States. A special feature should be independent, signed book reviews, cut loose from publishers' advertisements. In building up a magazine of this large scope, I concluded, many Yale graduates, within and without the University, who had come to the front as writers, could be drawn upon, but the Editor must have an open field for soliciting articles of the kind he wanted wherever he was able to find them. And they must be paid for.

This "interesting program" President Hadley promised to support despite many dangers of its failure. In reply to a direct question, I said that with this understanding I would accept the editorship of the *Yale Review* and take a chance with the grave dangers which he foresaw.

The revivified *Yale Review* made its début in October, 1911. Associated with me as Assistant Editors were two of my former students, Henry Seidel Canby and Edward Bliss Reed. The next year Helen McAfee, a graduate of Smith College, who had just returned from three years of teaching at the American Woman's College in Constantinople, joined the staff. The Business Manager was Edwin Oviatt, Editor of the *Yale Alumni Weekly*. Amateurs all, we had to work out our own salvation without the aid of experts, one of whom predicted the demise of our magazine when the Farnam subvention expired. There were indeed crises ahead of many kinds, but we learned to anticipate them soon enough to temper if not always to escape the force of hard blows whenever they might strike.

The leader of the first number was an essay on war, written by the late William Graham Sumner some eight years before but so far as I know never published. When this essay—or perhaps an undelivered address— was discovered after Sumner's death among his multifarious papers, I jumped at the chance of taking it as the first article in the hazardous enterprise of initiating a new magazine. The one word "War," which Sumner placed at the head of his manuscript, struck in a sense far wider than anyone could have apprehended the keynote of all our subsequent history. Our whole world since 1911 has been attuned to it.

It was while the world in 1903 seemed to be rolling on with no disturbing sounds that Sumner saw in prophetic vision the approaching catastrophe. He then wrote:

> Never, from the day of barbarism down to our own time, has every man in a society been a soldier until now. . . . There is only one limit possible to the war preparation of a modern European State; that is, the last man and the last dollar it can control. . . . There is only one thing rationally to be expected; and that is a frightful effusion of blood in revolution and war during the century now opening.

Some who read this prophecy in our pages regarded it as purely academic and were entertained by it as if it were no more than the imaginary "anticipations" of the future with which H. G. Wells was nourishing the public. Not until May, 1914, did a big war appear to anyone to be immediately imminent. Among my friends President Hadley, who knew German well, then said that war was near at hand.

The Editors awaited comment on the first and succeeding numbers of the *Yale Review* with considerable trepidation. Except for humorous thrusts here and there, the reception by press and subscribers was very favorable. An editorial in a metropolitan newspaper announced that "a star of the first magnitude had swum into the constellation of our magazines"; and a college president congratulated the *Yale Review* on its freedom "from cant, from pedantry, and from vaporous theorizing," in spite of its "many articles by university professors." A Harvard instructor defined a well-educated man as one who could read and understand all the articles in science and the humanities which the *Yale Review* was publishing.

Remarks in a lighter vein helped to keep me from taking my editorship too seriously. There was the tired businessman who canceled his subscription because the *Yale Review* carried few or no illustrated advertisements to rest his mind after a long day in his office. James Ford Rhodes commended it because when he wanted to rest his legs he could lie outstretched on his back on a couch and read the large type without hurt to his eyes. Robert Frost, on inquiring at a desk in the Congressional Library for the current issue of the *Yale Review*, was directed to go upstairs—where he found a copy already placed in cold storage with the back numbers of other periodicals. A Boston woman, it was reported to me, remarked that she had to read every word, covers and all, as the magazine cost so much. To begin with, we accepted no short stories, though I myself wrote many articles on contemporary fiction. The soundness of this policy I felt was confirmed when I heard of a colored cook in a girls' school who said that she liked the *Yale Review* because there was no "friction" in it.

Not all appraisals were so pleasant as these. One day when I was aboard a train from New Haven to Boston, a young man at the Hartford station conducted a young woman, his wife no doubt, into the Pullman where I was sitting meditation over a speech I was to give that evening. She took a chair next to mine and opened a copy of the *Yale Review* to an article on Masefield, I think by Henry Canby. The husband, exclaiming, "Oh hell, can't you find anything better than that to read?" abruptly left the car without even saying good-by.

In the spring of 1917 I met one of those emergencies familiar to editors

that rise from the necessity of preparing material some time in advance
of publication. Early in February ex-President Taft dictated in my presence
an admirable leader for the April *Review* on the crisis that had developed
between the United States and Germany. The next day he was to start on
a tour through the West, leaving a typewritten copy with me to put into
final shape. War seemed not far away; but just when it would come was
uncertain and the next number of the *Yale Review* was due to appear late
in March or early in April. There were indications that President Wilson
might appear before Congress any day and ask that war be declared. From
an editor's point of view here was apparently a first-class dilemma. I suggested setting up the article nearly as dictated, without a forecast of immediate war, but so phrased at crucial points that in case war were declared
in March the article might be timed to it by making a few alterations here
and there. With a chuckle, the ex-President of the United States agreed
to this procedure. Taking the lesser of two risks, I issued the April number
of the *Yale Review* with the Taft leader earlier than usual, ten days or more
before the fateful declaration of war against Germany. In other similar
instances I was not always so lucky as this. Occasionally I was caught with
an article so out of date that it had to be scrapped.

One day when Taft was in my office I placed on the table before him
the two-volume life of John Marshall by Senator Beveridge who had been
chairman of the Bull-Moose convention which in 1912 nominated
Roosevelt for the presidency. I told him that I was keeping the volumes
for him to review. He asked if I intended the request as an insult and
laughed aloud. He was not interested, he added, in anything that Beveridge
might write about the great Chief Justice. A few days later I met Taft on
the street. He had read a copy of the book which the author or the publisher had sent him. "I want to take back," he said, "the remarks I made
the other day about that life of John Marshall. It is the best thing I have
ever read on Marshall, and I have just written a letter to Beveridge telling
him so." This endeavor to be just to all men, whether friends or foes, was
one of the prime characteristics of Taft's mind.

Both Taft and I belonged to a faculty club organized early in the
eighteenth century when the first Timothy Dwight was President of Yale

University. It is still known as the Old Men's Club because until recently only the older professors were eligible for election. I was taken into the club at the age of forty-nine as "a young man," thus breaking the tradition. Mr. Taft was elected soon after his appointment as Professor of Law. There I met him at fortnightly "suppers" during the academic year when we were all on our dignity. He and Simeon E. Baldwin, ex-Governor of Connecticut, differing in their political philosophy, usually took the lead in the discussion of public questions to which I was beginning to pay attention. The debates were educative for me at just the right time in my career.

Even before the World War I began in an uncertain way to carry out my initial design of a magazine which should not be narrowly American. Its theme was to be the United States in relation to all nations of the earth. In the very first number it reached out into Canada. In the next it invaded Ireland where it obtained from Lady Gregory an account of the Irish literary renaissance. In the fourth number it was in England with a criticism of pragmatism by Vernon Lee. A year later it captured Gilbert Murray. Afterwards, for four anxious years, questions bearing some relation to the World War were in the ascendant.

The war over, John Galsworthy came into the *Yale Review* with several remarkable essays, among which was the beautiful "Castles in Spain." There was H. G. Wells, too, assailing critics of his *Outline in History*, and later Virginia Woolf with a bundle of charming essays. Came, too, "the gloomy Dean Inge" of Saint Paul's, who, though not an optimist, was anything but mournful. Once I sat next to him at a dinner when he was in so genial a mood that I remarked he must be amused by being called gloomy. "On the contrary," he replied, "nothing in my life has more annoyed me." In course of time the *Review* had contributors in France, Germany, Italy, Spain, Russia, Japan, China, and Australia.

Scouring Britain and other countries in search of material for the *Yale Review* greatly enlarged my acquaintance with men of letters and men of affairs, even though the relationship might be restricted to intercourse through the mails. Replies to inquiries for manuscripts from persons I had never met were as interesting as any others. None were better than those from writers who gave reasons why they could not comply with

my requests. Lytton Strachey, whom I asked for a portrait of Queen Elizabeth, put me off until he could finish one of his books and then went
abroad for rest. No word more. But eight years later appeared his *Elizabeth
and Essex*, the most brilliant of his biographies. In one of his letters Strachey confessed that he always found it "unpleasantly difficult to write at
all"—something many other great writers have said of themselves, like
Rousseau, for instance. "Easy writing," remarked Sheridan, "makes
damned hard reading."

Sir Walter Raleigh, Professor English Literature at Oxford, on being
asked for an article wrote back, "I fear I can't. My promises are like a train
I have missed, and I am running after it along the line. Sometimes, in
despair, I sit down and take a nap." Raleigh, when he was afterwards
in New Haven, told a story about his name being associated with the
name and title of the other Sir Walter Raleigh, the chivalrous favorite of
Queen Elizabeth, who introduced tobacco into England. On landing in
New York Raleigh was met by a Canadian who was to conduct him
directly to Toronto. The Canadian, never having seen him, knew him only
by description as a man of broad shoulders, 6½ feet tall. He stepped up to
the first man of that breadth and height who left the ship and inquired:
"Are you Sir Walter Raleigh?" "No, sir," the stranger replied with a quiz-
zical glance, "I am Christopher Columbus from Missouri."

A very fine letter from Kipling, which I lent to a friend to copy, never
came back. When I asked him for its return, I was informed that one of
his children had probably torn it to pieces and eaten it up. I accepted the
explanation without making any fuss. I am hoping, however, that a fac-
simile of the letter will sometime find its way into a book, for it is too
good a letter to be irretrievably lost in a child's stomach.

Our editorial relations with France were less intimate than with Britain
except in a few instances. Of all contemporary French writers I knew best
André Maurois. All his books which appeared in English, he told me, were
first written in French and then translated into English, not by another
but by himself. Just for the fun of it, I persuaded him to write his next
essay for the *Yale Review* directly in English. It was only an experiment
for it was easier for him no doubt to develop his ideas first in his native

language. Besides that, he wished, I think, to do nothing that would impair his mastery of French which possesses nuances of style alien to English.

For several years Edith Wharton, while living in France, acted as an outpost of the *Yale Review* by sending in the names of men among her wide acquaintance in France who might be willing to write on current public questions. Once she took me severely to task for reproducing a group of Max Beerbohm's cartoons of the participants in the World War which she denounced as "abominable caricatures" against France and England by a pro-German artist. She was so piqued by my editorial conduct that she threatened to withhold an article on Marcel Proust which she had nearly completed for the *Yale Review*. On the advice of one more expert than myself in feminine psychology, I ignored the umbrage she had taken against these caricatures, saying nothing about it, when a few weeks later I asked her to send along her Proust. The shadow passed. The article came. It was a very fine analysis of Proust's literary art; I have never read a better.

The year before this emotional outburst, Mrs. Wharton came to New Haven on a sultry afternoon in June to receive the next day an honorary degree at the Yale Commencement. I asked her what she wanted most to see that afternoon. Without hesitation she replied the Italian Primitives in the Art Gallery. As I watched her examining those early paintings one by one I began to surmise that she might have had them and the experiences of their collector, James Jarves, in mind while she was writing *False Dawn*, just published, which is the story of a young New Yorker who a hundred years ago was disinherited by his father as a fool and spendthrift for paying "the vast sum" of $5,000 for a collection of "worthless" Italian Primitives which eventually sold for $5,000,000. So I put the question to her directly. She smiled but did not shake her head.

It reminded me that, fifty years before her, Thomas Huxley, who had argued that there must have been a five-toed horse in the evolution of that animal, also visited Yale for one sole purpose. It was to examine, in fulfillment of his prophecy, fossils of American horses having three, four, and five toes, recently discovered by Professor Marsh, a collector not of Italian paintings but of fossil vertebrates.

My experiences with American writers at home, whom I might meet any day, were no less interesting at the time. In search of a light article on feminism and hunger strikes, I wrote to Mary Wilkins Freeman, a popular novelist, who pleaded a lack of knowledge for so difficult an undertaking: "Women are now flying about so rapidly that I do not understand, until they keep still, how one can get an unbiased point of view. Please allow me to wait until they are settled down." Mrs. Freeman out, I turned to Mrs. Gertrude Atherton, who after my first letter requested me never to address her again as Mrs. A career woman like herself, she held, should marry early if she so desires but have it all over by the age of thirty, and no longer be compelled to see across the breakfast table every morning the same old face, year in, year out. Bah! When she sent in her essay, she remarked that if I thought it "too strong" for readers of the *Yale Review*, she would substitute for it an article to prove that the metallic substance which Plato in his *Atlantis* called orichalcum was not a beautiful white metal as usually assumed, but copper which was the basis of the so-called Bronze Age. I chose "The Woman of To-morrow" (April, 1913), a capital, if rather sensational, survey of the part women are laying and are to play in the twentieth century.

To give distinction to the first number of the *Yale Review*, I had tried hard for an article from Elihu Root, then a United States Senator from the State of New York. In reply to my request he said that his official position required him to express himself so often on national affairs without adequate preparation that he feared he was unable to talk good sense when he had to talk. An article was out of the question. He did, however, consent some years later to act as judge on the award of an annual prize which the *Yale Review* was offering for its best articles on public questions. And at meetings of the American Academy of Arts and Letters after the business sessions were over he was always ready to give to a private group of the members his views on the state of the nation. His was one of the most original minds with which I ever came in contact, for whatever his conclusions he always came to them in his own peculiar way, independent of the ways of other men. In my last conversation with him, I inquired not too seriously: "Mr. Root, are you still a Republican?" His reply was in like vein: "Mrs. Cross, I still vote the Republican ticket."

At the outset, too, I endeavored to engage Justice Oliver Wendell Holmes as an occasional contributor but met with slight success. When a boy of eighteen I saw him at Marion, Massachusetts, where he had a summer residence on the shore of Buzzards Bay. I stood by while he and my uncle Franklin Cross greeted each other at the beginning of the season. Holmes was then a young man not quite forty years of age, "a promising Boston lawyer." When that young man had risen to become an Associate Justice of the Supreme Court, I at once discovered in correspondence with him that he could not write on a subject which, though not at the time controversial, might be regarded as controversial in his historical implications. Thus when I asked him to review the *Arguments and Speeches* of William M. Evarts who had defended President Johnson in the famous impeachment proceedings, he said that he could not comply with my request. But later he wrote that it would be safe enough for him to deal with a book like Professor Woodbine's edition of Bracton's *De Legibus* which was centuries old.

In my first years as Editor, the three distinguished brothers of the Adams family were still living. When I was introduced to Charles Francis Adams at an annual joint dinner of the American Academy and the National Institute of Arts and Letters, I thought his hand the most frosty I had ever touched. But when he sat down to dinner with men near his own age the frost quickly disappeared. Winter was gone and summer had come with the free and witty talk between him and his friends: Hopkinson Smith, Ford Rhodes, Owen Wister, Professor Lounsbury, and several others. By chance I sat near the group and listened to the cross fire of repartee.

Much as I enjoyed the articles of Brooks Adams, the youngest of the three brothers, I was more entertained by the sardonic humor of his personal letters in which he spared no one, not even his brother Henry whom he loved and admired. My acquaintance with Henry Adams, though it never reached beyond a few short letters which I received form him in his old age when he was almost blind, seems now to have been closer than that with his brothers. When I inquired whether he had any unpublished manuscripts which we might have the honor of publishing in the *Yale Review*, he wrote in reply from Washington under date of December 15, 1913:

> You have all been so kind and helpful to me, at Yale, that I would very much like to do anything that you ask, but my active days are past, and I can no longer write or read. I am quite out of the world, as far as present activities go. I have nothing in my drawers to show, having cleaned out all my old manuscripts long ago; unless indeed you are for poetry, which is an old plaything, and might perhaps yield something that would fill a few pages. I will give you anything I've got that you will indicate, but I am very near bankrupt since Mr. Cram has run away with my Virgin of Chartres.

Before December was over he sent me a copy of "Buddha and Brahma," a long poem which, never published, had circulated in manuscript among his friends. It had been written in 1891 while he was on a trip around the world with John LaFarge via the South Sea Islands and India. On the journey, Adams wrote to John Hay, they "stopped for an hour to meditate under the sacred Bo-tree of Buddha in the ruined and deserted city of Anuradjapura in the jungle of Ceylon." Resuming their course on the Indian Ocean, Adams, bored by the calm of a tropical sea and the greater calm of Buddha, amused himself by writing in his notebook a poem in which he attempted to reconcile two conflicting ways of life glorified in two mystic philosophies. Though one way begins with Buddha in contemplation and the other with Brahma in activity and suffering, both end at last in nirvana, a state of quiet content free from all concerns of the world. He seems to speak of himself in the lines:

> But we, who cannot fly the world, must seek
> To live two separate lives; one in the world
> Which we must ever seem to treat as real;
> The other in ourselves, behind a veil
> Not to be raised without disturbing both.

Through all the trials and tribulations of the *Yale Review* I received loyal assistance from my associates. In the formative years Edwin Oviatt, as I have related, was the enthusiastic promoter and business manager of the magazine which he conducted along with the *Yale Alumni Weekly*. In 1926 the Yale University Press took over the *Review*, which has since owed much to the keen interest of George Parmly Day, the President of the Press. Two breaks in the editorial staff I regretted exceedingly. Henry Seidel Canby withdrew in 1920 to accept the editorship of the *Saturday Review* of New York, and Edward Bliss Reed followed him a few years afterwards to become the educational director in the administration of the Commonwealth Fund. For a short time Stanley Williams helped us out. Amid these and other mutations, Helen McAfee was appointed Managing Editor. To her breadth of knowledge and fine literary sense the *Yale Review* was immensely indebted during my editorship. To paraphrase a famous sentence of Terence, nothing pertaining to human culture seemed to be alien to her mind. Without her devoted aid, I should have been compelled to forego many other enterprises to which circumstance or inclination called me. Through its long career, the *Yale Review* has also been fortunate in having the active cooperation of three Presidents of the University—Hadley, Angell, and Seymour—all of whom have contributed largely to its pages.

On January 1, 1940, I resigned as active Editor of the *Yale Review*, and accepted the chairmanship of an Advisory Council comprising besides myself, four men outside Yale who by virtue of their positions were in close touch with thought and opinion on public questions of the immediate present. At the same time an Editorial Board of four members was set up, consisting of Dean DeVane of Yale College, Dean Furniss of the Graduate School, and Professor Wolfers, Master of Pierson College, with Miss McAfee at the helm as Managing Editor. As an indication of how well this Editorial Board has functioned I may cite the authority of a friend who, by way of congratulation and supposing that I was still the Editor in Chief, remarked a year afterwards that the last number of the *Yale Review* was "the best ever."

Nevertheless in looking back over the history of the magazine I can console myself with what President Hadley said on stepping out of office in 1921: "I believe that when the history of Yale during the twentieth century comes to be written the establishment of the *Yale Review* will be regarded as one of the two or three outstanding events of my administration." I am not likely to see that history. But I naturally hope that President Hadley will be accorded a place among the Major Prophets!

XVI. Three Books

The English Novel

The children of my brain mostly bore the stamp of studies in prose fiction. First to come was a brief survey of the English novel within the space of three hundred pages. This book was followed by large biographies of two great masters of their art and by many independent essays on the novel which were only partially collected. Altogether there were at last seven volumes.

These books and essays formed a part of my most intimate life. They were nearly all written at home in the midst of a happy family, in the early years while the children of the household at times were running from room to room playing their games. There was no command for silence, for I had trained my mind to concentrate upon the work in hand. Helen typed the penciled manuscripts, paragraph by paragraph, as I went along, leaving spaces for revision. No one else ever saw a book or an essay until it was in proof. One manuscript remained unfinished, when, on January 19, 1928, death suddenly took away a devoted wife and mother and left me desolate. That was the darkest day in my long life.

Always a novel reader, my professional interest in fiction dated from my graduate student days when I made a comparative study of English and other European fiction in the eighteenth century. A few years later, while teaching in Pittsburgh, I gave a series of twenty lectures on the English Novel, in which I showed incidentally the historical relations between one writer and another. The manuscripts of these lectures, hastily written, one a week, I brought with me to Yale when I was appointed an instructor of English in the Sheffield Scientific School (1894).

Around this time I fell in with Ferdinand Brunetière's *L'Evolution des genres* (1890), in which this most original French critic set forth the theory that literary forms develop in ways similar to the evolution of species in the natural world. This theory he illustrated in books on the French lyric, drama, and novel, all of which I read.

I was not wholly convinced of the soundness of this theory, for science and literature are two different things. Darwinian evolution, as then interpreted, implies progress or a movement forward to some definite end; whereas in the history of a literary form there are innumerable changes, but no one can say that there is progress as in the evolution of species. No one, for example, can say that *Vanity Fair* is a better novel than *Tom Jones* because it came a century after. I saw at once that I must satisfied to show why the art of these two realistic novels was in many respects quite different because Scott, romancer and realist, came in between them and for other reasons. Discarding this theory of evolution, except for some analogies, I devised a simple formula (hardly a law) of development which, it seemed to me, would make clear the course of English fiction from the Arthurian romances down to Kipling or to Henry James on this side of the Atlantic. By trying out my formula here and there I concluded that by keeping rather close to the masters who had really made the English novel what it was, I could present the essentials in the history of the most popular of all literary forms within the compass of a single volume. Others had published books dealing with various periods or phases of the English novel. But oddly enough no one had yet attempted to indicate in a cohesive narrative a development which had been going on for centuries. This was the novelty. I named the book *The Development of the English Novel*, and dedicated it by permission to M. Ferdinand Brunetière.

The manuscript was duly submitted to a publisher. Three months later I received the following cooling-card:

> We have taken longer than we expected to in our search for a market for your "Development of the English Novel." The most trustworthy demand for books of this sort is a demand from college classes, and we fear that because of its size and certain features of its structure, this book could not hope to serve the purposes of a class text-book. At any rate, the chances of such use appear to us so small and the general market so dubious that we must reluctantly ask your instructions for the return of the MS.

I liked the phrasing of this letter so well as a model for rejecting an unwanted manuscript that I committed the whole thing to memory.

Taking the criticism seriously, I cut down the first chapter by half, making it almost unintelligible, and checked the tone of the humor, wherever any occurred, of all the rest. This action I now look back upon as one of my prime literary mistakes. Thus revised by wasteful months of labor, the manuscript went to George P. Brett, President of the Macmillan Company, who within a fortnight informed me that he would publish it on certain conditions, the most important of which was that I should have a sponsor for the book since so far as he could discover I had never published anything. Perhaps, it was suggested, some well-known member of the Yale English faculty would contribute an introduction for me. I appealed to Professor Beers who read the manuscript. At first he was a little perplexed by the pattern on which I had organized the book and quizzed me on the style, which was comparatively free from conjunctions, such as "however," qualifying general statements. We discussed the structure of the book, and on the question of style I told him that my generalizations were so carefully considered that there was no need of hedging on anything I had written as fact or opinion. I reached the height of youthful egotism by remarking that the style was direct, that one sentence ran straight on into another as in Greek prose, as in Thucydides for example. He smiled. Though he declined to write an introduction, he wrote a few paragraphs for a circular which the Macmillan Company might distribute.

I was anxious that the book should be free of obscure sentences and awkward phrases, so I persuaded a man who had written a rhetoric to read a set of the galley proofs. They were duly returned, blue-penciled all over. Nearly everything was wrong down to the paragraphing. I asked my critic if he intended to advise me to rewrite the book. "Oh, no," he replied. "I am simply showing you how you can improve your style if the book is ever reset."

The index also worried me. There kept humming in my ears a remark of Lyman Bagg, the author of *Four Years at Yale*: "Any fool can write a book but it takes a genius to make an index." That mine might pass muster, I sought the aid of a young librarian to check me up and comment on my job as a whole. He did not check me up, for that seemed unimportant from his point of view, but he reduced to lower case the initial letters of most of the words. That, he said, was the latest style. As I viewed the result I felt the approach of a nightmare. The index maker was cast into limbo along with the rhetorician.

From the day my first book was accepted for publication until reviews began to come in I was under the spell of continuous excitement. While I read the proofs at night by dull gaslight the words I had written sometimes seemed to be magic formulas, and I a magician sitting in dim light, smoking a corncob pipe. When the excitement reached its height at eleven o'clock, I often went out into the cool air, mounted my bicycle, and rode over to the Graduates Club for a hot scotch, then a popular mild drink, to quiet my nerves.

The Development of the English Novel came out in September, 1899. It had a better press than I had ever dreamed of, and its formula of development was generally accepted, at "least as serving well for practical purposes," to quote the London *Spectator*.

The most thorough damnation of it appeared in a provincial newspaper of good standing in a university town. Everything about the book, beginning with the title, was wrong; there had been no development of the English novel "since the days of Fielding," nothing more than a few minor changes. My characterization of individual novelists always missed the mark and in some instances showed "phenomenal stupidity." "Mr. Cross is an assistant professor of English at the Sheffield Scientific School. We wish those whom he instructs joy of him." This was the only review of the book that I ever read to my students.

Despite the failure of a certain publishing house to find a market for the book, it went into a second printing very soon and within a year was taken up by colleges from which it has not yet disappeared. One young woman, one of my former students, remarked several years ago that she once saw the book on the table of an American or English official somewhere in the heart of China. She just looked at it and burst into tears, "sick for home," like Ruth, in an alien land. Such are the flashes of fame.

Like other young writers I subscribed to clipping agencies so that I might follow the reception of the book day by day. Whenever I heard the click of a metal flap as the postman dropped letters through the door I rushed to pick them up. With clippings from newspapers came congratulatory letters from friends and others. A strange thing happened. My first letter of congratulation fell to the floor a full week before the book was actually published! At first I was puzzled by this. That the writer had read the book was evident. But how, I wondered, did he get hold of a copy before any were placed on sale or even sent out to the newspapers for review? Here was a nice problem and my mind began to work on it. The book had been announced for publication on September 10. The letter of congratulation was dated September 11. But owing to a delay at the bindery, of which my admirer was unaware, no copies were received by the publisher until the middle of the month. Taking all things into consideration I concluded that the man who was so eager to congratulate me must have read the book in manuscript. He was not the person who read it for the Macmillan Company, whose name I knew. The obvious inference was that he was the man on whose advice the other publisher turned down the book.

I was not quite certain of my circumstantial line of reasoning until, ten years later, when *The Development of the English Novel* had gone through ten printings, I met the president of that company at a metropolitan club. He expressed regret that his house had failed to take the book. As for himself, he set up an alibi: the manuscript had never been referred to him as it should have been. He could not tell me on whose unfavorable report the book was rejected without violating the confidential relations between publishers and their advisers. All he could say was that the man was one of my friends. Thereupon I made this casuistical proposal: "I will name the man and read the answer in your face." I named him, and was met with, "How did you know that? Did he tell you?" I gave the publisher the story as I have related it. We had a good laugh and a good dinner and became fast friends.

Laurence Sterne

Next after the book on the novel came Laurence Sterne, who was to stay with me, off and on, for a quarter century. One Sunday morning sometime late in the autumn of 1903 I received an unexpected visit from Rutger B. Jewett, a member of a New York publishing house, J. F. Taylor and Company. Among their projects for 1904, he informed me, was a complete edition of the works of Laurence Sterne. On a previous visit to New Haven he had asked in turn, he said, two other members of the Yale English faculty to take the editorship. Both declined the honor. One of them denounced Sterne as a scoundrel and an indecent country parson whom he did not care to touch. Both referred Jewett to me. Since then he had read what I said about Sterne in *The Development of the English Novel* and thought it looked like my job.

We passed the day together discussing the project. Jewett was a delightful companion, several years younger than myself. It came out in our conversation that he had been a professor of Greek and had traveled extensively. Though his immediate interest in Sterne may have been commercial, it was at bottom literary. Most of the recent so-called complete editions of various authors, I told him, were only reprints of old collected editions, sometimes with the addition of an unimportant essay, story, or letter. Such, for example, was *The Complete Works of Henry Fielding, Esq.*, just published by a New York firm. There were, however, interesting unpublished manuscripts of Sterne's in the British Museum, a few scattered little things, and many stray letters, published and unpublished, some of which could be brought together. We agreed on a program and an honorarium. Jewett would have copies made of the British Museum manuscripts and such others as were available; and he would arrange for the proofreading of Sterne's major works. I would look after all the new materials and write an introductory essay on Sterne. Thus began the most pleasant and yet the most difficult piece of editing I have ever undertaken. As I proceeded, Jewett kept pace with me, step by step, as much interested in the work as I.

When I made the bargain I did not know what I would be up against.

In particular I was to have a difficult time with Sterne's letters, the main published collection of which was brought out by his daughter, Mrs. Lydia Sterne de Medalle, seven years after Sterne's death. These letters, some of them undated, were thrown together without much reference to time or place of composition, and I soon discovered by comparing them with the British Museum manuscripts that some had been altered.

The *pièce de résistance* in the British Museum collection was Sterne's "Journal to Eliza," written in 1767 when Sterne was fifty-four years old. It had been seen by several writers on Sterne but never published. Thackeray, for instance, had it by him when he was preparing an onslaught on Sterne in *The English Humourists* and *Roundabout Papers*; and Percy Fitzgerald quoted from it in his *Life of Sterne*. I decided to publish it entire.

The Eliza of the Journal was the young Mrs. Elizabeth Draper who at the age of fourteen was married to Daniel Draper, twenty years her senior, an official of the East India Company at Bombay. This child wife had two children, one born when she was fifteen years old and the other when she was seventeen. In 1765 the Drapers brought their children to England and placed them in a school near London. The husband soon returned to India, leaving his wife behind under the protection of a rich retired commodore named William James and his charming wife Anne. Sterne began dining with the Jameses on Sundays in January 1767. There he met Mrs. Draper, then in her twenty-third year, and fell in love with her.

Their intimacy, which grew rapidly, was broken within three months when Draper summoned his wife home by the first boat. At the news Eliza fell ill and Sterne feared that he was going to die. For consolation they passed much of their time in each other's apartments. Mrs. Draper sailed for Bombay in April and the next month Sterne set out for Coxwould, his favorite Yorkshire parish, so ill that most of the way he had to lie on his back in his chaise as if he were but "a bale of cadaverous goods consigned to Pluto and Company." There, in intervals between recurring hemorrhages, he set about completing his last literary legacy to the world.

All summer long, when he was able, Sterne sat at his desk in Shandy Hall writing *A Sentimental Journey* or recording incidents and emotions in the Journal which he hoped would some time be read by Eliza. On his desk he placed her miniature to inspire him and encouraged a cat to lie near his elbow whose purring kept his emotions at an even temper. In imagination he fitted up and decorated an apartment and built a pavilion in the garden for Eliza in anticipation of the day when she would become mistress of Shandy Hall. Sometimes he had the hallucination that Eliza walked into the room, looked over his shoulder at what he was writing, and vanished before he could speak to her. It was, however, no hallucination when one day his wife and daughter, who had been living abroad, returned to Coxwould. This was for Sterne "the last trial of conjugal mistery." All visions of Eliza were dissipated, and the Journal was laid aside forever.

But Eliza lives on. Her gift to Sterne was that subdued emotional mood and delicate humor which permeate *A Sentimental Journey*. Without the memory of that girl his last book would have been something different. Under various names Eliza sat for the portraits of the brown lady, the grisette, the *fille de chamber*, Nanette, and even "poor luckless Maria." Something of Eliza is in all of them.

Now Thackeray, relying upon a letter of which the year was not given, in Mrs. Medalle's collection, claimed that Sterne was making love to Lady Percy in April, 1767, while his heart was "breaking" over the loss of Eliza. The superscription of this famous letter was only "Mount Coffee-house, Tuesday 3 o'clock." Sterne, professedly sitting there in dejection, wrote on gilt-edged paper to Lady Percy, whose "eyes and lips" had turned him into a fool, to ask her if she would be alone at seven and suffer him to spend the evening with her. Otherwise he would take a sorry hack and jog on to the theatre to Miss *******'s benefit. On looking through the lists of benefit performances in Genest's *History of the Stage* I had to go back to April 23, 1765, before I could find a benefit for an unmarried actress on a Tuesday night, that is, nearly two years before Sterne first set eyes on Eliza. The benefit was for Miss Wilford, a beautiful dancer, who made her debut as an actress on that evening. Her name was disguised, I daresay, by Mrs. Medalle, in the seven stars, each standing for a letter in the name of Wilford.

This was one of the more successful pieces of scouting that went into the making of *The Works and Letters of Laurence Sterne*, which appeared in twelve volumes in January, 1905. There was a York Edition, a Sutton Edition, each limited, I think, to 750 sets, and a superb Stonegate Edition of 150 sets printed on Japanese vellum. All three editions were generously illustrated by photogravures from paintings, sketches, and photographs. Yorick leaning over the gold bars of paradise, if he ever got there, must have been pleased with the honor paid him.

The stint was done. But I was not satisfied with my editorial work, which had had to move too fast in order to meet the demand for quick publication. I had no opportunity to check for mistakes copies made by another hand than mine of manuscripts in the British Museum and elsewhere, though of minor misreadings I was reasonably certain. Moreover, the edition of Sterne's works was hardly off the press before I heard of unpublished letters here and there in the hands of collectors and rare-book dealers. Above all there was a part of a Letter Book in which Sterne kept the first drafts or the copies of letters which he wrote to his friends. Some of the letters had never been published; others had appeared in a little book published twenty years after Sterne's death, but had been regarded by critics as forgeries. These and other Sterne manuscripts had been recently acquired by the first J. Pierpont Morgan. My publishers were very glad to add a supplementary volume of letters. With all this fresh material at my disposal, I decided to write a new life of Laurence Sterne. So I at once started in.

The summer of 1906, three months of it, I spent in England, with one excursion into France to go over the main part of the route of Sterne's travels as described in *A Sentimental Journey*. I first settled in York, the heart of the Sterne country, where I boarded with two Quaker spinsters who introduced me to Dr. George A. Auden, a local antiquary and physician to the cathedral clergy. I called on him and we hit it off perfectly. He knew more about Sterne than anyone else in York. Two or three years before he had acted as guide to Dr. Osler in trips to Sterne's three parishes in the neighborhood. They had a common professional interest in Dr. Slop of *Tristram Shandy*, the man midwife who broke Tristram's nose when he brought him into the world with forceps. Those very forceps Dr. Osler found and presented to the York Museum. Taking them in his hands, Dr. Auden showed me just how a fine nose might easily be flattened out almost level with the face.

In York I was made the victim of a good-natured practical joke. There were two offices near the cathedral, a little distance apart, where I hoped to discover something new of Sterne. One was presided over by A. H. Hudson, registrar of the Diocese of York, and the other by T. B. Whytehead, clerk of the Dean and Chapter. When I asked Dr. Auden to introduce me to these two officials so as to smooth my way, he abruptly turned the request aside with the remark that there was no need of that, for he had already spoken to both of them about me. He went on to say casually that though I might find Mr. Hudson rather brusque, Mr. Whytehead was "a man after my own heart." I thanked Dr. Auden for letting me in a little on the character of these two men with whom I was to do business.

The next morning I called on Mr. Hudson. He received me not brusquely but with a courtesy as fine as any I have ever met with. Without my asking it, he promised to bring together for my use everything in the Diocesan Records concerning Sterne. Happy over my success with a man called brusque in the Yorkshire dialect, I thanked him for his promise and walked on to the office of Mr. Whytehead who, as I entered, was sitting at a table facing the door, smoking a pipe. He did not rise to greet me nor did he invite me to sit down. He simply stared and asked me what my business was. I stepped forward, took a chair on the other side of the table, and began my story. While I was telling him that I wanted to examine the records of the Dean and Chapter for all the years that Sterne was a member of that body as a prebendary of York, he stopped me with the exclamation, "Young man, you don't know what you are asking for. They are big books locked up in the cathedral. No one can see them without special permission."

Undisturbed by this outbreak, I lighted, with his consent, a large cigar, one of many that had sailed the seas with me. He watched me closely and looked as if he would like a cigar too. So I dipped into my pocket for a handful and asked him if he would like to try one. He took them all and spread them out on the table, felt of each one, and remarked, "I don't see how you Americans can smoke green cigars like these." He rose and placed them on the mantel where, he said, they would dry out in a day or two enough to smoke.

Both of us a little more at ease by this time, I remarked that if he did not object I should like to ask Canon Watson, who, below the Dean, was the ranking member of the Chapter, if I might go through the records. "What! Do you know Canon Watson?" he exclaimed in surprise. "Oh, yes," I replied, "he has granted me the unusual privilege of taking books out of the Library of the Dean and Chapter." At once the Tartar civilized: "It will not be necessary for you to see Canon Watson. As you are one of his friends, I will have one of the volumes brought over here tomorrow afternoon. Which one do you want first?" He informed me that the book must be read under his supervision, and he could be disturbed for no more than two hours, from two o'clock to four—adding with a grain of humor that there would be a fee of a shilling an hour.

I appeared the next afternoon precisely at two o'clock, began reading in the volume which covered Sterne's first years at York and Sutton, and was soon taking notes. Mr. Whytehead, who assigned me to a seat at a table near his, was in no better humor than the day before. When I came upon a Battersea lease, which I remembered that Sterne somewhere referred to, I inquired what that was and got a thunderous answer: "A Battersea lease! Don't you know what a Battersea lease is? Don't you know that the Church of York owns land in Battersea, London, which it leases?" A little farther on there was a long entry on the Reverend John Blake, Master of the Royal Grammar School near York. When I saw that name I could not help telling him that I had discovered the man, never before identified, to whom Sterne at one time wrote a number of confidential letters. Mr. Whytehead glared at me with fierce eyes and requested me in no uncertain words to break in on him no more.

On the third afternoon he ordered me to go into an adjoining room with the book and to shut the door. I asked him whether he wasn't afraid that I might cut out a page or two, say on Blake, if left alone. As to that, he said, he would have to take his chances. From that time onward I was entrusted with volume after volume without supervision. And I heard no more about the fee of a shilling an hour, or about restricting my visits to two hours in the afternoon.

In the meantime I had asked Dr. Auden why he had tricked me by reversing the manners of Mr. Hudson and Mr. Whytehead. He said it was because he wanted to hear the story I would tell of an unexpected encounter with a man like Mr. Whytehead. "By the way," he added, "a small club of the young clergy of York—ten or twelve of them—have a nine o'clock supper together every Sunday night. They have invited me for the next Sunday and asked me to fetch you along too. Will you go?" I went. They were a very interesting group of men somewhat different in outlook from any I had ever associated with at home. No vile gin cocktails, but just enough of the finest Scotch to keep the storytelling in full swing till midnight. Being a little obtuse, it did not then occur to me that this was the audience Dr. Auden had selected to hear the tale of my dealings with the Clerk of their Dean and Chapter. I did not flinch when the request for the tale came as if by chance, not by malice prepense. When the laughter was over I was questioned on American slang and colloquialisms, such as were just reaching these people, like "nothing doing," "what is there in it for me?" and "it's up to you." "That's the limit," or "he's the limit," no one of the company had ever heard of. They looked blank at the expression until I illustrated its meaning by a pertinent example which they could all understand. Across the water, I said, a practical joke such as Dr. Auden played on me would be called the limit, and the man who perpetrated it would be the limit also.

There was, however, a sequel so sad that I wished I had never told that story in York. Only a few days after that Sunday night, when I entered Mr. Whytehead's office he was not there. In his chair sat a young man who said, "My father had a paralytic stroke last night. I am to take his place until he is able to return." Mr. Whytehead was never to return. The son in temperament seemed to be just the reverse of his father. Much as I had interrupted the father with questions about this and that, so that son interrupted me with questions about Sterne and Yale. As I became better acquainted with him I remarked that I did not understand his father's ways. This led to his saying that his father's irritable temper, which had grown with age, was really the outcome of a nervous breakdown of some years before. As a matter of fact he was very much interested in what I was doing. "He was really fond of you and talked of you evenings. He talked particularly about the conversations with you before and after your day's work." I asked him about the "green cigars." He said that his father smoked one of them every night until they were all gone, complaining that he could not get such good cigars in England.

From York my way led to the scenes of Sterne's boyhood at Halifax, and then to London where I walked through streets and parks that Sterne had walked in keeping this or that engagement, so that I might form in my mind a composite picture of him moving about among his friends.

Sterne preached but one sermon in London. It was a charity sermon which in his first fame he was invited to give into the chapel connected with the Foundling Hospital in Guilford Street. Knowing that he would have a large audience of politicians, wits, and men of fashion, he entertained them with a Shandean performance in which he asked God directly why He let some men grown rich and kept other men poor. His eloquent appeal for aid to the orphans sitting in the gallery was eminently successful. The collection taken while the choir was singing the anthem amounted to more than £55. Remembering this dramatic occasion, I went out to the Foundling Hospital for the service on a Sunday morning. The gallery running round the lower end of the chapel and up each side was still there. The children were in their seats with their teachers and nurses among them. I took a seat in the gallery where I could look into the faces of the boys and girls. No one else was there; the fashionable men and women of Sterne's time had long since departed. That morning the old pulpit was deserted too. A high improvised pulpit had been erected to the level of the gallery, near where the children sat. A young man mounted the high pulpit, smiled towards the boys and girls, glanced at me in surprise, and began his sermon, choosing for his text the old nursery rhyme of "Jack and Jill" which he moralized to the good, I think, as well as to the amusement of the children.

My explorations came to an abrupt close while I was still in France. After a strenuous summer of extreme heat I fell an easy victim to ptomaine poisoning and was forced to give up my researches and go home before I had planned. For three months I laid Sterne aside. I could do no more than carry my routine teaching with the extra burden of a slight fever.

Suddenly one morning I awoke feeling perfectly well. That very day I began the first chapter of a life of Sterne, which was to take me three years to complete, for the writing of books could be for me, as for every other college professor, only an avocation. Outside week ends and vacations, my work on the book was confined to evenings, usually the four hours from eight to twelve o'clock.

The Life and Times of Laurence Sterne was published by the Macmillan Company in May, 1909. As a compliment to the land of Sterne's birth, I adopted certain English spellings which differ from American usage. To some Englishmen of that time "honor" had no meaning unless it were spelled "honour." A man out of Chicago, who regarded Sterne as "the foremost philosopher of the world as well as the greatest wit," was so offended when he opened the book and saw me "toadying" to the British that he closed it again. He was affected, he wrote to me, in the same way as he would be if he saw the British flag flying above the Capitol at Washington. I assuaged his temper by promising never to do it again and he read the book. Indicative of the part Sterne has played in my life for forty years is the nickname I still bear—"My Uncle Toby"—the whimsical character in *Tristram Shandy* who would not harm a fly and whose light oaths the Recording Angel blotted out forever. The name was first transferred to me by Dean Oertel while we sat talking with friends on an evening in the Graduates Club.

Henry Fielding

On that eventful Sunday morning when I agreed to edit Sterne's works, I told Mr. Jewett that I must finish with Sterne by the end of the next year because I was preparing to write a life of "the father of the English novel." But since I was myself unable to let Sterne go, five years slipped away before I returned to Henry Fielding. This interval turned out to be a piece of good luck because within it or immediately afterwards while I was engaged on Fielding many new facts about him came to light.

I was drawn to Fielding by an eager desire to relate the true story of his life so far as it could be ascertained, and to match my interpretation against the man his biographers depicted—a dissipated fellow, libertine, and spendthrift, always in debt, who bilked tradesmen and came down on his friends now and then for a dinner or a guinea or two which he never repaid. To this shabby picture were often added, as if his own, the darker vices of the most disreputable characters in his novels and plays.

While reading the biographies of Fielding, one after another, I used to stop at times and look towards my bookshelves, where I kept in full sight the latest sixteen-volume edition of Fielding's works, and wonder how they could have been written within the space of twenty-five years by a Bohemian who spent his nights in taverns with noisy companions until three or four o'clock in the morning and then went home to begin his day's work of writing with a wet towel round his head, as Thackeray imagined. As I read those volumes I could find nothing there to suggest "a hangover" in the score or more of plays, many essays, and four novels, each a masterpiece in its kind. At the head of the line was *Tom Jones*, in Fielding's own phrase "the labour of some thousands of hours." The more I pondered, the more the wonder grew at the sharp line which as a rule was drawn between the man and his books. Where and why, I asked myself, did the traditional Fielding originate and by whom was he built up? What, I asked, were the facts? The stories told of Fielding were mainly disproved by their absurdities.

The task which lay before me was clear. It was to ascertain and correlate, if possible, the facts of Fielding's career and to present and interpret them honestly and justly whatever might be the consequences. I embarked for England near June 1, 1911, for the summer, made several tours of the Fielding country, and sat in the British Museum, day after day, week after week, searching for the facts of his career. There was little help to be had from Fielding's first biographer, Arthur Murphy, who instead of ascertaining the facts of his subject's life contented himself with interesting but apocryphal stories. He claimed that when Fielding had contracted for a play or a farce he would go home late from a tavern and deliver to the players in the morning a scene "written upon the papers which had wrapped the tobacco, in which he so much delighted." Three mornings, Murphy added, were sufficient for a farce. This feat would require, according to my arithmetic, fifty papers a morning for Fielding's shortest farce, and for the largest five times that number; or for a farce of average length 150 pipes. Twenty-five pipes of English tobacco on a morning would be, I should think, all that a hard smoker could stand! As with his plays, so with his novels. Murphy would have it that Fielding wrote *Tom Jones* merely for relief and amusement while he was Justice of the Peace at the London Bow Street Court; whereas he was in fact engaged for three years on that masterpiece and had it all completed before he assumed his judicial office.

It appeared that by the irony of fate the Fielding legend was set going by Fielding himself. His portrait of down-and-out Harry Luckless in *the Author's Farce* was taken for a portrait of its author, though Fielding at the time was very likely living not in Grub Street but in Piccadilly.

All through his career—as editor, pamphleteer, novelist, lawyer, and Justice of the Peace in England's most important municipal court—Fielding was engaged in innumerable literary and political controversies. When he was attacked in hostile newspapers he replied with devastating ridicule and irony, which aroused to a white heat enemies who had no way of retaliation except to endow him with all the vices they could discover in books he had written and in vile anonymous pamphlets which he had neither written nor read. "A heavier load of scandal," he once said, "hath been cast upon me than I believe ever fell to the share of a single man."

Fielding died in Portugal, and was buried in a cemetery on a hillside which British merchants doing business in Lisbon had long ago chosen for their dead. In 1920 news reached me that the massive marble tomb erected to his memory in 1830 was in need of major repairs. I undertook to help collect the funds necessary for its restoration. Our appeal to admirers of Fielding met with quick response, and within a short time checks were received amounting to $750. It required only $150 to relay the foundations of the tomb, clean it, and recut its inscriptions. The unexpended balance was turned over to the officials of the English Church at Lisbon as trustees, who were to invest it in British consols with the stipulation that the income be used for maintaining the tomb in perpetuity.

The chaplain of the church sent me large photographs of the renovated tomb from various points of view, and with them careful copies of three Latin inscriptions. The longest ascribed to Fielding the highest qualities of head and heart; he was a genius who sought in his writings to improve the conduct and character of men, though he himself was sometimes involved in vices and follies from which he should have kept free. When I read that qualification of excessive praise, I felt at first that no words of mine printed on paper could ever compete with words cut into marble. I soon regained my composure, however, on the reflection that words writ in marble cannot withstand wind and rain forever and that in the meantime few of the numberless visitors to the tomb of Fielding will be able to read any inscription written in Latin. So I concluded that I had not wasted my time in writing a new life of Fielding, which appeared in the autumn of 1918 in three volumes under the title, *The History of Henry Fielding*. On its composition I expended more thousands of hours than Fielding expended on *The History of Tom Jones* after which it was named, but there the comparison ends.

Part III

XVII. Nomination for Governor

As I trust has been made clear in earlier chapters, my interest in politics dates from childhood, perhaps from the time when, held tight between the knees of a black Republican farmer of Mansfield, I shouted out, to his astonishment, the name of the newly elected Democratic Governor of Connecticut. But even earlier than that, when I was hardly out of the cradle, I had to tell my father, whenever he asked for it, who was the Governor of Connecticut, whether he was a Democrat or a Republican. In my imagination a Governor was a very exalted person, a sort of superman, who ranked very little below God and the angels.

In my boyhood there settled near our house in Gurleyville a man who had actually seen a Governor of Connecticut. More than that, he had had the honor in his youth of driving Gov. Chauncey F. Cleveland of Hampton (1842–44) into Hartford or New Haven for meetings of the General Assembly. (There were then two capitals of Connecticut.) As I watched him at work in his shop—he was a harness maker—he often described to me the dignified Governor's luxurious coach drawn by four horses, black I think, over the rough roads of Connecticut hills. "You bet, when I set on that high seat with all them reins in my hands I had something to do with them hosses." I saw and listened as if in fairyland. I had read, or my mother had read to me, the tale of Cinderella, of her coach gilded all over, six gray horses, and her coachman, his face covered with whiskers like the coachman who drove Governor Cleveland.

The first Governor of Connecticut I ever saw was no slight airy being out of fairyland. He was a rather tall, substantial, fine-looking man, whose silk hat and long Prince Albert coat, "buttoned all down before," made him appear taller and bigger than he was. He was dressed exactly like the minister of the little Methodist Church in Gurleyville on Sundays, only his clothes looked fresher, as if they were new. He rose, thrust one hand in the lapel of his coat and, after an ahem, let his voice go in sonorous speech. He spoke as one convinced of the truth of every word he uttered.

He was, I thought, the greatest man in the universe of God and men. Later I was to associate with many Governors within and without Connecticut. I was to observe that there were limitations to their knowledge and that God had endowed them with a good share of the imperfections of human nature. Still my childhood feeling about a Governor of Connecticut remained with me for a long time.

Of course it never occurred to me that I was destined to join so august a company of immortals. That end was reached along a curious way, which I will describe. Back in the days of President Wilson's second administration a group of New Haven citizens, mostly Yale men, ten or twelve of us, began meeting at the Graduates Club on Thursday evenings. We used to stroll in an hour or more before dinner for drinks and a free and reckless discussion of state and national affairs. No politician, however high he climbed, was spared in the talk about him. Someone dubbed us "the Sunday School Class" of the Graduates Club. Our leader was Nod Osborn, the distinguished Editor of the *New Haven Journal Courier*. Next to him in our regard was Dr. Carmalt, an eminent surgeon, very brusque in speech and manner. Of the first days of the club there now remain in 1943 only Bob Corwin, Professor of German, and myself. Among later members of the Sunday School Class were Professor Daniels, who had long been a member of the Interstate Commerce Commission, and Professor Vance of the Law School, by birth a Kentucky Democrat. There was an outer circle including President Hadley, who took part in all the talk. Some stayed on for dinner but most of them went home to dine with their families.

During the campaign of 1920 the spirit moved me to make the Sunday School Class a speech in burlesque of Candidate Harding's address to a company of theatrical people who visited him at Marion, Ohio, in order to see face to face and hear the voice of a man who professed unbounded interest in the drama. His memory at fault, Harding made Shakespeare the author of a non-existent play, *Charles the Fifth*, and transformed a novelist, Richard Harding Davis, into an actor. The play he had in mind was doubtless *Henry the Fifth* in which Richard Mansfield played the leading rôle. My burlesque ran somewhat as follows:

"This is one of the happiest days of my life. I extend to you all my most cordial greetings, Republicans and Democrats alike, if there are perchance any Democrats among you. You are performing a great public service in holding the mirror up to nature. Perhaps you are unaware that when a young man I took an active part in amateur theatricals here in Marion, and was praised for the manner in which I performed leading rôles. One play, as I remember, was in French, and I had to learn to speak French in order to play my part. Perhaps, if I had gone on, I might have become a great actor instead of a great statesman.

"I once saw that great actor, Richard Harding Davis, if I remember correctly, in a great play of Shakespeare's *Charles the Fifth*, if I remember correctly. He may have been related to me, for his middle name was Harding. *Charles the Fifth,* you know, is known in history as Charlemagne. That, you know, is a French name which, being translated into English, means Charles the Great.

"There was in that great play one great scene which I shall never forget. It is the night before a great battle. The King and his generals and aides are encamped on the side or the top of a hill. It is not yet quite dark. Rather, it is evening twilight. The earth will soon become enveloped in darkness. The King looks down into the wide valley where his men have pitched their tents. Lights flicker by the tents all over that wide valley. They are preparing their evening meal. The King turns to his generals and says he is going down among his men, nothing but common soldiers. He wants to talk to them, he says, as if he were one of them. His generals try to persuade him not to undertake so dangerous a journey, but in vain. All alone, he walks from tent to tent chatting with his men and comes back unharmed.

"That great scene in that great play taught me a great lesson. It is that we should never look down upon people who have been less fortunate in life than ourselves as inferior beings; for as my friend Harry Daugherty, who is sitting here by my side, has often remarked, 'Warren, we are all created in God's image.'

"Now I must bid you all a happy good-by as I have to receive this afternoon a delegation of a Christian temperance society who are coming to ask me how I stand on prohibition. I need a little time to think out a courteous address which will please the reformers and assure me of their votes without, however, committing myself to any definite policy. As I look into your faces I can see that you at least are all patriots on whom I can depend for your votes in this great crisis now confronting the very existence of the Republic founded by George Washington and Alexander Hamilton. 'Back to normalcy' is my slogan."

This, my first political speech, I gave every Thursday evening through the campaign with such variations as seemed necessary. Dr. Carmalt, an octogenarian Republican who was always there, kept interrupting my oration with, "Shut up there, Cross. We've had enough of that damned rot."

The election over, the conclave met on the next Thursday to anatomize the corpse of the Democratic party. President Hadley and others were sitting on the sidelines. After a lively debate on the ills which had killed the Democratic party, Nod Osborn brought forward a proposal for the resurrection of the dead here in Connecticut. He would run, he said, for the United States Senate if I would run for the Governor's chair. "What about that, Cross?" I replied that Barkis was willin' provided we could frame a platform which would straddle every important question in Harding's adroit way so as to get the votes on both sides of the fence. Nod asked for specifications. "Well," I began, "there is the question of national prohibition. We are both agin that." "No problem there," said Nod. "You can pose as 'a moderate dry' and I will be 'a moderate wet.' That's easy." What is to be our attitude, I next inquired, towards the Ku Klux Klan, who were then, it was said, burning their fiery crosses on hillside pastures. "Don't worry, Cross, about Ku Kluxers in the State. You can go ahead and rip them up the back. I will say nothing for or against them publicly. All I have to do is tell their leaders privately that they have nothing to fear from Cross is he is elected. They will understand. They will line up for you." When at last we reached the question of protective tariffs we had to stop and think hard. As political descendants of Thomas Jefferson we were bitterly opposed to all forms of special privilege. But as Connecticut politicians out to win, we knew that we must give the impression that we are "protectionists" without quite saying so. The formula we finally agreed upon as having a good squint each way was: "We are strongly in favor of a revision of the tariff for the benefit of Connecticut industries and the protection of our workers against the sweated labor of Europe and Asia." Then, satisfied with our deliberations, we went out to dinner.

Nonsense may be but an ebullition of good sense. Harlequin, remarked Thackeray, is a sober man at heart. That is sound psychology. No doubt Colonel Osborn and I had a submerged desire to sit for a term in the chair of a Governor or a United States Senator. But there was then not even a remote chance to gain that distinction. During the next years the Democratic state and national tickets went down to disastrous defeat. The skies brightened for a while in 1928 when the battle was fought under the banner of Alfred E. Smith. Still it was defeat as usual. During the campaign of 1928 many new young men became politically active and soon afterwards one of them, Archibald McNeil of Bridgeport, was elected Connecticut's member of the Democratic National Committee. He and his associates became known as the New Guard in distinction to the older leaders of the Democratic party who naturally were called the Old Guard. Between the groups there arose considerable antagonism in a struggle for control of the Democratic State Central Committee.

In the spring of 1930 both Guards were hard up for a candidate for a Governor willing to sacrifice himself on the altar of his party. McNeil called on Colonel Osborn, the patron saint of Connecticut Democracy, and asked him if he would accept the nomination if it were offered to him. The Colonel, who was forced to decline because of ill health, told him that Cross was his man. Near the same time while I was lunching at the Graduates Club with a tableful of friends, Professor Vance, who was among them, suggested that Cross ought to quit his political banter and seriously consider running for Governor, now that he was retiring from the deanship of the Graduate School. The upshot of the talk was that Vance was delegated to present my name as an available candidate to the Democratic Town Committee of New Haven, which was under the control of the Old Guard. I consented to the proposal, more in jest than in earnest. My time had arrived.

McNeil now called on me to see whether I was of the right political caliber and character for a candidate for Governor. And after receiving Vance's letter and making some further inquiries about my qualifications for high office, the secretary of the local Democratic Town Committee invited me to attend a banquet in honor of the Democratic State Central Committee late in June at Wilcox's Restaurant over the waters of Savin Rock. I accepted the invitation. Arriving late, I was greeted in front of the restaurant by a group of politicians, reporters, and cameramen. On that spot my first photograph surrounded by politicians was taken, to the amusement of my friends who saw it reproduced in the newspapers the next morning. But events were moving rather too fast for me. I quizzed a reporter, who said that the State Central Committee had just held a meeting in a private room and had agreed to send up a trial balloon on my candidacy. I asked him how he knew that. He replied that someone had forgotten to close the transom over the door leading into the public dining room.

Patrick B. O'Sullivan presided as toastmaster over the banquet. There were two or three eloquent speeches on the past achievements of the Democratic party in State and nation, interspersed with a damnation of the Republican misdeeds. They were of that fervent kind that bring orators to their toes and sweat to their brows. Last on the program came an hour's dreary speech read slowly by a Congressman imported from the Middle West, on the iniquities of the Hawley-Smoot Tariff Bill then awaiting President Hoover's signature. By that time the clock registered 11.30. Despite the hour, the toastmaster remarked that the audience expected a few words from me, and he facetiously introduced me as a novice in Connecticut politics. The gist of my reply was this:

"The people of Connecticut would like to know how our party stands on several important questions of today. Half a dozen issues lie at our feet to be picked up. I observe, for instance, that no one this evening has said a word for or against national prohibition. Is there any truth in the rumor that both of the leading political parties are being urged to duck this issue in the coming campaign? Don't do that. It is a stratagem of Republicans to deprive us of an issue which they fear to meet. It is my opinion that a clear majority of our fellow citizens want to see the control of the manufacture and sale of alcoholic liquors returned to the State. You want to see it returned. I want to see it returned. We are all sick of bootleggers who are breaking the law and inducing others to break the law. Why are we silent?"

I could get no further because of the commotion. After a shaking of hands I went home to sleep and dream.

News was at once flashed across the country that at a Democratic rally in New Haven, Connecticut, Dean Cross of the Yale Graduate School and Editor of the *Yale Review* had come out strongly against national prohibition. Though a teetotaler himself, he declared that prohibition has no place in the Federal Constitution, that the control over alcoholic liquors properly belongs to the States. In an interview he said that he had no objection to being considered as a candidate for Governor of Connecticut on the Democratic ticket. Pressed by reporters afterwards, I rectified the state in regard to my private habits. "I can't say," I told them, "that I don't know the smell or taste of whisky. But I am not a habitual user. I never take a drink unless I want one."

Members of the Sunday School Class were pleased with the outcome of the rally. Colonel Osborn began to line up the newspapers of the State in favor of my candidacy. A group of young Yale professors, representing various faculties of the University, met and urged me to seek the nomination. On the other hand, a few of my friends advised me to drop the idea of becoming a Governor, which in this State was only an empty title. They were Republicans. Likewise two Republican doctors, whom I had at times consulted, volunteered the opinion that I would likely break down under the stress of a campaign which would certainly end in defeat and disappointment. To check up on their opinion, I asked a Yale physiologist whether the strain of a political campaign or the strenuous labors of a Governor, if I were elected, would end in physical and mental disaster. He asked whether I still had the habit of breaking the day's work with an hour's sleep. I told him that I did. His reply was, "Nothing can kill a man of your temperament."

As usual I went to Burkehaven, overlooking Lake Sunapee, New Hampshire, for the summer, canoeing, fishing, writing, picking a few bushels of blueberries, and swapping stories on the veranda of the post office with natives much like the members of the old House of Commons who in my boyhood gathered at the village store in Gurleyville; the main difference was that nail kegs and cracker barrels had long since given way to rickety armchairs. Through July I received many clippings from Connecticut newspapers announcing that this or that town committee had declared for Cross. In August a majority of the delegates to the Democratic State Convention were reported to have taken final action in favor of my candidacy. It was predicted that Bridgeport would go Democratic by a plurality of more than 5,000, and that I would probably carry by good majorities Norwalk and Stamford, normally Republican strongholds. Two candidates for the nomination for Governor had withdrawn in my favor. There was nothing for me to do now, I was assured, except to write an acceptance speech. This information I took with a grain of allowance, for I yet had to reckon with leaders of the Old Guard who, though not hostile to me, were generally holding aloof from outward activity in my behalf.

The Democratic State Convention on nominations was held on Wednesday and Thursday, September 10-11, at the Fort Griswold House at Eastern Point by the sea, across the Thames from New London. At the evening session Homer S. Cummings, an old Democratic war horse who had fought many battles in state and national politics, gave the keynote speech in which Cross was extolled as a providential candidate. It was clear from the first that a large majority of the delegates were for Cross for Governor and were ready to accept such associates as he desired on the state ticket. But a bitter fight immediately developed between the Old Guard and the New Guard over control of the party organization. The Old Guard would listen to no proposals for change in the officers of the Democratic State Central Committee. The New Guard supported me in a demand that the present officers, who had served for several years, resign and give place to others whose names I submitted for consideration.

The crisis came at three or four o'clock on Thursday morning, when McNeil pounded on my bedroom door and told me to get up quick. In slippers and pajamas ("wrinkled blue," said the newspapers), I jumped out of bed, ran into my sitting room, and opened the hall door where McNeil stood at the head of a line of men and women who had come in distress to make me an early morning call. They told me that the game was up, for a poll of the State Central Committee showed that the Old Guard was still on top. Now, if ever, was the time for me to speak up.

As they filed out a smaller number of Old Guard leaders filed in. greeted them cordially. I feared, I told them, that they misunderstood me: I had no animus against any one of them, but if I were to head the ticket I must be permitted to choose the managers of my campaign. They hotly replied that it was a prerogative of the Committee to elect its own officers without any dictation from the outside and that they intended to follow the usual procedure now. I remarked that I was merely asking something which they could easily do if they so desired.

At this point a member told me to go to hell. I retaliated with equally strong words. The storm rose higher when I was charged with being not a Democrat but a Republican in disguise. The storm quieting down a little, I told them to go their own way and count me out, for I could not trust the fate of my campaign to defeatists who had never won a state election for reasons I could only guess. They left the room abruptly. I crawled back into bed and slept without a break until the breakfast hour. The heading of one news item read: "Delegates meet Dean Cross in his pajamas and lose their shirts."

When I entered the dining room, tables were buzzing with stories of what had occurred in my apartment just before the birds of morning began to sing. The Convention was to meet for business an hour later. I let it be known that I would be on hand and explain why I could not accept the nomination for Governor, and then formally withdraw my name from consideration in favor of a compromise candidate who would be satisfactory to both wings of the party, for no bird can fly if deprived of one wing.

Fearing a blowup of the Convention, the leaders of both factions of the party asked me to meet them in a general conference. They were all there. A night without sleep was conducive to quick action. It was agreed that ex-Congressman Patrick B. O'Sullivan, who was willing, should be recommended for election to the chairmanship of the State Central Committee and in this capacity manage the campaign. I was delighted with the prospect of working with him, a Yale man, able, and broad minded. It was then suggested that in the spirit of harmony the next highest place on the ticket should go to Daniel J. Leary, a young Old-Guarder, who as Comptroller of the City of Waterbury had already shown extraordinary financial ability. After an interview with Leary I assented to his nomination as Lieutenant Governor in order to come to conclusions while the Convention was waiting for us. In view of Leary's subsequent financial career it should be said that he then bore an excellent reputation. His nomination, according to an editorial in the *Waterbury Republican*, was "gratifying to Waterbury."

In the absence of Colonel Osborn, who was too ill to leave home, I was put in nomination for Governor in an eloquent speech by Philip Troup, one of my former students, distinguished even in his undergraduate days as a debater and spellbinder. He described Cross as a man in whom were united the political philosophy of Thomas Jefferson and the humanitarianism of Abraham Lincoln. Like Homer Cummings, he could see God in the heavens coming to the rescue of the Democratic party. After several speeches for me and two passionately against me, I was nominated by acclamation as the Democratic candidate for Governor of the State of Connecticut. I was another Joshua destined to lead the Democratic party into a promised land, flowing not with water but with wine and milk and honey. I was surprised by the intimate knowledge of Holy Writ shown by my new Democratic friends.

My acceptance speech was devoted largely to my ideas of the function and duties of a Governor in contrast with the views held by John Henry Roraback, the supreme ruler over the Republican cohorts of the State. I began by saying:

"You have nominated me for Governor of the State of Connecticut. I accept the honor and the responsibility. I have not been a militant candidate for the nomination. But I owe my career to the social and educational institutions of the State, up from the red schoolhouse on the country hillside, through the public high school, and on to a university founded by the colonists far back of the first days of the Republic. As a poor return for these benefits I stand ready in the present crisis to give to my fellow citizens such services as they may ask of me provided nothing is asked beyond my abilities. Whether these services, freely offered, are wanted will be determined in November. Already I have been warned from the camp of the enemy that they will not be wanted. It is a solemn warning that no one bearing the Democratic badge can be elected Governor of Connecticut. In the conviction that the independence of the citizens of the State has been vastly underrated, I accept the challenge. . . .

"If half of what has been alleged is true, the elections in this State have become a farce. Whoever is elected Governor or to any other office, state or national, on the Republican ticket is only the shadow of another man. Under whatever name Governors may come and go, the man who is really elected is another man who sits behind the screen. Public office in Connecticut is no longer a public trust. It is a private business. There is no hope for change in a situation disgraceful to democratic government except by a political upheaval, smashing all party barriers. Put other men to the front in the state Republican organization, and the screen will still be there and the same man will be dictating through the screen. When did the State of Connecticut last have a Governor free to act on his own best judgment? Has there been any real Governor since Simeon Baldwin? He was the last Governor in the tradition of James E. English and Marshall Jewell—the one a great Democrat and the other a great Republican. Do the citizens of Connecticut want another Governor? Or are they ready to let the great office lapse? This is the main question in the campaign."

Other issues I discussed briefly. On prohibition I said:

"Prohibition under the Eighteenth Amendment and this law enacted by Congress for its enforcement has collapsed. You cannot reform a nation by sending respectable citizens as fast as the courts can act to jail or prison for doing what they and their ancestors for generations have regarded as a matter of private concern. President Wilson vetoed the Volstead Act, and Congress passed it over his veto. The Democratic party of Connecticut stands for the repeal of this law and for the repeal of the Eighteenth Amendment, that the control of distilled and fermented liquors may be restored under the most rigid regulations to the States where it belongs. Action is imperative if the people of the United States are to be kept from degenerating into a nation of gin drinkers with all those biologic, social, and economic disasters which are certain to come in the wake."

Immediately after the adjournment of the Convention, I addressed, by invitation, the Democratic State Central Committee. The old officers having resigned, I drew from a vest pocket a slip of paper bearing the names of three persons whom I wished to take their places as managers of the strenuous campaign which awaited us. The names were Patrick O'Sullivan, chairman; Fannie Dixon Welch, vice-chairman; and Joseph Tone, secretary. My request was at once granted. Nearly everyone present took me by the hand and promised full support for the ticket. A day which broke in a political storm ended with the heavens serene and clear. There are some old rhymes which my father who had been at sea used to repeat to his children:

> Rainbow in the morning, sailors take warning,
> Rainbow at night, sailors' delight.

XVIII. The Campaign

The committee of three who with the nominee for Governor were to plan and conduct the campaign chose New Haven for headquarters, a bare apartment of only three rooms on Court Street, which we equipped with a few old chairs and desks, a telephone with a single extension, and a screen for confidential dealings with political visitors. The subordinate staff consisted of one stenographer, one clerk (John B. Doughan, well acquainted with Connecticut politics), and "Big Boy" (John A. Donlan) to drive me over the State for conferences and speeches in an antiquated Buick, good for about thirty miles an hour. It was the setup of a political party submerged in poverty.

Soon the little company was augmented by Kenneth Wynne who, when a young man just out of the Yale Law School, took an active part in the state campaign of 1910 when Simeon Baldwin was nominated for Governor. He could tell us how a state election was won by an expenditure of only $7,000. In several other respects there were resemblances between that campaign and the one we were about to wage. For fifteen years before the days of Simeon no Democrat had sat in the Governor's chair. One Democratic nominee for Governor after another had been smothered in the ashes of defeat. In 1910 Baldwin, having reached the age of seventy, automatically retired as Chief Justice of the Supreme Court of Connecticut. With his consent a group of young Democrats, some of whom had studied under him in the Law School, brought him forward as a candidate for Governor and without much of a contest he received the nomination. Among the prime movers was Samuel Fisher, who was afterwards to perform distinguished services for the State. Of them, too, was Norris Osborn, who gave him aggressive support in the *New Haven Register*, of which he was then Editor. In a still younger set associated with them were Philip Troup, of the eloquent tongue, and Kenneth Wynne, who served through the campaign as head of the publicity and speakers' bureau.

These and other men, young and old, working in harmony with the regular Democratic organization, were out to make a supreme test of the vitality of the Democratic party in Connecticut. Democrats as well as Republicans shook their heads as they watched enthusiastic neophytes trying to run a campaign in the vain expectation of victory. But the so-called neophytes knew what they were about. Baldwin was elected Governor by a small margin. Two years later, when the Republican party split into two camps, the regulars under President Taft and the progressives under Theodore Roosevelt, he was reëlected by a large majority, bringing in with him the rest of the state ticket, a Democratic Senate, and a House almost evenly divided between the two parties, though the Republicans held on to the edge. Five of Connecticut's six Representatives in Congress were also Democratic that year.

After Baldwin left the Governor's chair, the shadow of another fifteen years of almost complete defeat fell upon the Democratic party. Within that period no Democratic candidate for Governor came near election. In 1925 the State Senate was adorned with only two Democrats, and in 1927 the two shrank to one. The next year when Al Smith ran for the presidency, the Democratic party in the State began to crawl out of the shadow. In 1930 it seemed that the time had arrived for the remnant of the group who had stood behind Baldwin to unite with another group which had sprung up in the meantime to make the supreme test once more for a return to power. When I now look back upon the desperate situation into which I stepped, I am astounded that I ever dared to enter a game in which the cards were all stacked against me. I was confronted with a hard, ruthless, closely integrated Republican organization, obedient to the will of one man, J. Henry Roraback. I could not count upon the full support of my own party, certain leaders of which, it was alleged, had been kept quiet for years by retaining fees and other emoluments dropped from the Great Man's table. It was often asserted that Connecticut was cursed with a double machine. As a rule, all officeholders were Republicans, with the exception of small groups here and there who, it was charged, were given jobs in various departments on the recommendation of a few members of the Democratic party who were on friendly terms with the Republican leader. Whatever their political complexion,

officeholders, no one denied, could be shaken down for such contributions as were deemed necessary to assure a Republican victory.

Such was the opposition, somewhat exaggerated in the public mind,
which a Democratic candidate for Governor had to face in 1930, with
funds barely sufficient for the running expenses of a central office and for
slight assistance to the towns in bringing out the Democratic vote. For
these purposes some $15,000 was collected, most of it coming from men
and women who rarely or never contributed to political campaigns. It
was clear that the election could be won only in the outmoded way: upon
issues to be presented and argued throughout the State. These issues were
embodied in a straight and clean-cut platform which any reader could
understand. Republican newspapers for the most part made sport of it.
Except for the stand taken against prohibition which, they said, was a
moral, not a political issue, the platform was only a series of promises con-
cocted to flimflam voters. When the campaign got into full swing,
however, they had to open their eyes to the appeal which flimflams were
making to the electorate. The *Hartford Courant* stood almost alone among
Republican newspapers in warning their party at once that they were to
have a real campaign on their hands.

On examining the outcome of the election of 1928 when the Democrats made a good showing under the banner of Al Smith, I concluded
that neither of the two political parties could really claim as certain a
majority of the voters of the State, that in the present circumstances there
were thousands of voters, so-called independents, who notwithstanding
party preferences would likely cast their ballots in accordance with their
honest views on the questions submitted for their determination. If I were
able, with the aid of other speakers, to present these questions clearly and
persuade the voters that the Democratic platform was right on all or most
of them, the election might be won. My estimate was that 50,000 votes
outside the Democratic party would be sufficient for a close victory.

On this assumption I went to work. I set out immediately to visit as
many towns in the State as there was time for. Usually I made three half-
hour speeches every night including Sundays. Sometimes the number ran
up to four or five. Occasionally, too, I worked in four o'clock rallies in

small villages. Several times a week I also attended political luncheons of the Federation of Democratic Women's Clubs presided over by Fannie Dixon Welch, who with a little company of young women traversed the State, adding largely to their membership everywhere. Rarely was I home for bed before one or two o'clock in the morning. Altogether I made during the campaign as many as 170 speeches, all but a dozen, perhaps, purely extempore. This method of speaking, without manuscript or even notes, enabled me to fit my words to the temper of my audience whatever it might be. Reporters who followed me were kind enough to keep out of the newspapers such indiscreet remarks as I sometimes made in a spirit of fun.

I did not hit the trail at once. A wise friend, who had read reports of some of my first speeches, criticized them as too impersonal I must bring in, he said, more humorous incidents of my career to lighten up sober discussion of the issues at stake in the campaign. An occasion came for trying out this advice when I made the principal address at a Democratic rally in the town hall of Tolland, the county seat of my boyhood. I stepped to the front of the platform and began with "Mr. Chairman, fellow Democrats, and lost Republicans who have come in here to inquire the way home." This greeting put the audience in the proper frame of mind for a familiar cracker-barrel talk seasoned with the native dialect which they all liked to hear.

I related for them stories of my boyhood and youth which made them laugh. I gave them an account of the county celebration at Tolland marking the hundredth anniversary of the signing of the Declaration of Independence, which, I reminded them, came from the brain of Thomas Jefferson, the founder of the Democratic party. With other children and their parents, I told them, I came over the hills to Tolland from Mansfield on the day before the celebration, sitting on a floor of straw in a cart drawn by two yoke of oxen gaily decorated with small flags and bunting. The next day I marked by visiting the county jail to see the cells where two young Mansfield fellows had slept for a month for stealing a hive of bees, too severe a punishment, I thought, just for a love of honey.

The greater part of my talk was capped with political allusions.

I lamented, for instance, the loss to education in the passing of "mental arithmetic" such as was once practiced in the old red schoolhouse, whereby boys and girls became adepts in numerical processes without the aid of slate or paper and pencil, just letting the head to the work in the way God intended. This art, I claimed, had been of great use to me during the Hoover Depression; for every night I could calculate my losses of the day by merely looking at the figures which my mind projected into the air.

The Republicans had held their state Convention, a cut and dried affair of two or three hours, and their nominee for Governor, Ernest Elias Rogers, then Lieutenant Governor, had begun to read campaign speeches on what his party had done for Connecticut, evading or ignoring at first the issue I was raising. I showed my audience a newspaper with a front-page photograph of the towering Republican chief standing between the then Governor and Lieutenant Governor Rogers, who were looking upwards into the face of their master, as one of whose political genius they admired. How long, I inquired, are the citizens of this State going to lie under the incubus of a man who every two years makes and unmakes a Governor who will be subservient to his will?

A little perplexed over how to answer this rhetorical question, I observed in the audience Henry Hanks of Mansfield, nearly ninety years old, the last surviving grandson of the man who set up the first silk mill in the United States. In my youth he was a breeder of "fancy fowls." From the platform I asked him if he remembered that when a boy I paid him $5 for a gamecock. He replied that he well remembered the sale and that I got my money's worth. This conversation led to the trouble I had with settin' hens. "Take the eggs out from under one," I said, "and throw her out of the nest, and she will come back as soon as she is left alone. Put chestnut burrs into her nest in place of eggs, and she will still come back. The only way to get rid of a settin' hen is to kick her out of the coop. Likewise the Republican organization and its leader have been settin' on rotten eggs for fifteen years without hatching out any chickens. The only way you can get rid of this old hen is to throw her out into the snows or cold rains of next November."

Another story I told at Tolland was of my experiences with obstinate cows which kicked and would not give down their milk. My political opponents did not take me up on the settin' hen, but one of them remarked in a speech that my only qualification for the office of Governor, so far as he could see, was that I still knew how to milk a cow.

National prohibition lent itself to a display of fireworks. In spite of the fact that a large and influential section of the Republican party was clamoring against prohibition, Roraback decided that the safer way was to straddle the question, with a leaning towards the political drys. He hammered through the Republican Convention a candidate for Governor whose lips, the press said, never touched liquor and yet who had no conscientious scruples against permitting others to drink as much as they pleased. In harmony with the views of his candidate, Roraback insisted upon a verbose prohibition statement in a vague platform which, appropriating an animal that Theodore Roosevelt introduced into politics, I described as weasel words. Each sentence was a weasel to kill the sentence immediately preceding, until a reader reached the last sentence which I myself dispatched. All the words then lay dead, void of meaning.

To manipulate the straddle required three kinds of speeches. There were the bone-dry Republican spellbinders who toured country towns under the hallucination that farmers were red hot for national prohibition. They said that Dean Cross would never live to see the Volstead Act repealed. In following them I sometimes asked my audience if they were advised to cut out buttermilk as a beverage and feed it to the pigs who love it for its exhilarating effect if mixed with cornmeal; or to cut out the root beer they made from a secret receipt handed down by their grandmothers; for both buttermilk and that delicious beer which sparkled and trickled pleasantly down the throat sometimes contained more than half of 1 per cent alcohol, which was all that the Volstead Act allowed within the law.

A second set of spellbinders were the very moderate wets, sent into special communities, who thought that the alcoholic content of beer might be raised without harm to 2, 3, or even 4 per cent. The third, those assigned to large cities, were cautiously in favor of a repeal of the Eighteenth Amendment if a safe way could be found to do it. But calling a general convention of all the States, as Dean Cross suggested, would be a dangerous procedure, for such a body, once in session, might throw overboard the whole Constitution of the United States. We must wait and be patient a little while until the demand for repeal became irresistible.

In the meantime I was discussing prohibition from all points of view that occurred to me, enlivened by three-minute burlesques of the three types of speeches which I have described. But when the Republican candidate for Governor was persistently asked whether he was in favor of returning to the States the control over alcoholic liquors, he merely replied that as a member of a Republican General Assembly he once voted against ratification of the Eighteenth Amendment. There was very little more for me to say. This evasion left the question at issue to be determined by the electorate without further ado on my part. Thereafter in my speeches I used to take a step forward to the edge of the stage and say, "Now we come to the subject of national prohibition. Perhaps up in this part of the State you are all in favor of national prohibition. But I am in favor of a repeal of the Volstead Act and the Eighteenth Amendment as quickly as possible." Then amid laughter I took up other pertinent issues of the campaign.

I inquired why the delay in the proceeding with plans for the construction of the Merritt Parkway, a project which was already authorized by the General Assembly to provide, in addition to the Post Road, an ample outlet for automobile traffic through Fairfield County to New York and points farther south and west. I inquired also why politicians treated humorously the slogan, "Take the farmers out of the mud," for many rural roads were almost if not quite impassable during the rains and break-up of the front in March and April. The farmers, I submitted, needed good roads at all times for taking their dairy and other products to market. It so happened that in the previous April while I was being driven through the ruts of a Mansfield dirt road at the rate of ten miles an hour, I asked the man at the wheel to speed up to fifteen miles an hour. Almost immediately a spring snapped. I walked the next mile or two as the surer way to keep an appointment at a village store, where I told the story to a group of farmers and others. In my speeches I advised farmers to unite in an effort to persuade the next General Assembly to make an allocation from the

Highway Funds sufficient to initiate improvements in rural roads throughout the State. Going Further, I described to general audiences a rough
plan for an ultimate system of coördinated highways, then regarded as but
an idle dream.

I could joke about habitual wets who voted dry for political reasons or
about shoveling farmers out of the mud, but there was at least one subject
which was not suited to jesting. The State's sanatoria for the treatment of
tubercular patients had become alarmingly inadequate. The chairman
of the Tuberculosis Commission informed me that the growing waiting
list for admission to these sanatoria had already reached four hundred; and
many letters came to me from poor families saying that they were unable
to care properly for their members suffering from the disease, in some
instances that a wife or husband, a song or daughter, had died for want to
hospitalization. Steps for relieving this situation, I promised, would be
taken immediately if I were elected Governor. My political opponent
came back at me in his usual way. Ignoring the need of larger facilities for
the treatment of tuberculosis, he read at an Italian rally statistics purporting
to show that Connecticut under Republican administrations had long
stood "in the forefront . . . in humane work." He threw in a few ironic
remarks on my awakened "interest in the women and children of the
State" and in "humanitarian measures" as a means of corralling votes for
myself. His thrusts at my concern for the sick and dying were not well
taken by the public.

Greater harm was done to the Republican cause by Roraback, who
made me the subject of heavy humor. I was "Dean Somebody" whose
name he couldn't remember. We were not personally acquainted. In fact,
I had never seen him and knew him only by report and by some of his
works which lay unconcealed. My main quarrel with him was that he was
the president of a large public utilities corporation and at the same time
head of the dominant political party, which controlled both branches of
the Legislature. "Ye cannot serve God and Mammon." In that experiment,
I said, God is the one who is likely to be left in the lurch.

In previous campaigns Roraback had rarely come out in the open as a
spellbinder. His function had been to direct the storm, when there was

any, from behind the scenes. But this year things were not going very well for him on the stump. The Republican campaign lacked fire. Cross was getting altogether too much publicity in the press which he supposed he owned. So he decided to enter the lists as the superspokesman of his party. His aim was to break down any imaginary appeal I might be making to the electorate as a man qualified for public office. In a speech at Red Top (Harvard's rowing headquarters on the Thames) he declared that I was a pedagogue without any experience in public affairs. God save Connecticut from a pedagogue in the Governor's chair. In another speech at the Hartford Club he described me in pitying language as "the dear old gentleman down at Yale who, I understand, is for old-age pensions, and if I were in his place, I'd be too." A system of old-age pensions, he estimated, would cost the State a hundred million dollars. How, he inquired, can that vast sum be raised? (As it happened, the kind of pension system I had in mind could probably be financed by a $3 poll tax.) He predicted that the Republican candidate would be elected by a vote of 2 to 1, that is, by a plurality of 135,000!

Roraback's Hartford speech came as a thunderbolt to his own party, for there was a growing sentiment, irrespective of political considerations, in favor of old-age pensions as a substitute, so far as possible, for the poorhouse over the hills of this fair State. He was denounced by the press as a callous politician of a bygone age and advised to make no more speeches. He took the advice and retired to his former seat behind the screen to perfect a political organization already unsurpassed by any other State in the country.

At once I became known as "the dear old gentleman down at Yale," and was often so introduced at political rallies. I admitted that I was eight years older than Roraback and four years older than Rogers, adding that they would catch up with me in time if they lived the good life. Age, I contended, is a biological question. There is, for example, Schuyler Merritt down in Stamford, hale and hearty at seventy-seven, whom Roraback is letting run for Congress on the Republican ticket, without criticism on the score of age. The trouble is that there are a lot of Republicans in the State who, drinking wet and voting dry and as a result breaking down, cannot understand how a man like myself who has reached the age of fifty and upwards can still be in sound health with no indication of a congested liver or ulcers on the walls of his stomach. The only hope for them is to come over into the Democratic party where they will be permitted to drink dry even though they vote wet.

Though Roraback quit electioneering, the Republican High Command, taking a leaf out of his Red Top attack on me, proceeded to deflate my claims to qualifications for the governorship in comparison with my rival's enviable record in business and statecraft. For this purpose use was made of the "deadly parallel" in a full-page advertisement published in newspapers all over the State. Under *Rogers* was a long list of activities rising higher and higher in importance as one read down the column. Under *Cross* were blank spaces everywhere, except for an item here and there such as "Edited Stevenson's *Travels with a Donkey*." Rogers was still doing things while I had been retired by Yale on reaching the age of uselessness.

This political abuse, too overdone to have much effect upon the electorate, supplied me with good material for the rest of the campaign. During the last days of speechmaking I carried that advertisement along with me and substituted in place of my own name those of Washington and Lincoln to show how badly they would fare when contrasted with the achievements of the Republican candidate for Governor. Unlike him neither of these heroes of the Republic began his career in the silk business. Washington's first job was as a surveyor of land beyond the Blue Ridge. Lincoln's first job was as a rail splitter. Unlike Rogers, neither of them was ever a dealer in grain, though they both liked to watch corn and wheat ripen; neither of them became the president of a trust company; neither of them received his first training in statesmanship as alderman and Mayer. And so on, to the conclusion that neither George Washington nor Abraham Lincoln would have met the high standards for public office set by J. Henry Roraback and his first lieutenant, Harry Mackenzie.

There was another onslaught from the same source which was intended to finish me for good. Under Republican auspices one John J. Splain, a political officeholder, a friend of Eamon DeValera, and Vice-President of an organization known as the Friends of Irish Freedom, addressed to me a scurrilous circular letter. It charged me with being Ireland's "implacable enemy" because back in 1920 I signed a petition urging members of Congress to vote against a resolution to recognize the then nonexistent Irish Republic, on the ground that any interference with the domestic policy of a friendly foreign nation like Great Britain was clearly against international law as interpreted throughout the history of the United States.

Several days before the open letter appeared it was whispered about that the Republican organization had something up its sleeve which would be a knockout blow from which Cross could never recover. Having a good intelligence service, I got hold of an advance copy of the Splain letter and so was ready with a reply the moment it appeared in the press. I did not deny that I had signed the petition with sixty-odd others, most of whom were Republicans, and that under the same circumstances I would do the same thing again. I asked any Republican politician who differed from me to recall to his memory that foreign powers had sometimes tried to intervene in American affairs and our ancestors had told them where to go. In particular I asked Ernest Rogers how he stood on the question raised by Splain. Silence reigned.

Soon after this Al Smith passed through the State on his way to Boston to make a speech in behalf of Joe Ely, who was running for Governor of Massachusetts. It was arranged for him to say a few words in favor of the Connecticut ticket at stations where his train was scheduled to stop. Immense crowds greeted him in Stamford, Bridgeport, New Haven, and New London. In New Haven the throng was so dense that several policemen were required to conduct me to the rear platform where Al stood waving his brown derby while the train slowly pulled in. We shook hands amid cheers. Al made a ripping speech of five minutes. Then as a climax to the scene he presented me with a hat, in size and fashion like his own. At once two brown derbies exactly alike began waving high. (In an autobiography nothing should be concealed. The hat which Al crushed down on my had had been bought for the purpose by Joe Tone.)

On the long midnight drive home from Thompsonville, where I made my last speech the night before election, I mused, half awake, half asleep, on my chances. My audiences, I reflected, have generally been large.

Among them have been scattered Republicans. The speeches have been regarded by the press as good copy. On the other hand, they say that Republicans listen to me only for the stories I tell and that very few of them will vote for me. Is that so? There will certainly be some defection among the Democrats. I remembered a town where only a dozen Democrats attended a rally instead of the two hundred I expected. But an independent Republican of that town who is going to vote for me claims that more than four hundred other Republicans will vote the same way. If so, the town is safe. Then there is another and larger town where no more than fifty greeted me, though the hall was large enough to seat eight hundred or a thousand. This means defeat for the Democratic ticket there.

My mind wandered into more auspicious incidents of the campaign. A group of thirty-three staunch Republicans down in Greenwich, bankers, lawyers, and merchants doing business in New York, have issued a large broadside declaring that they intend to vote for Dean Cross this year and wishing others to do so, for "we believe in the man and the principles he stands for." A leading citizen of Darien, an Independent in politics, has published in a newspaper a page advertisement urging Republicans to oust "a boss-ridden party" by voting for Dean Cross. In New Haven and elsewhere Republicans and Independents have come out in statements advocating my election. So, too, have the Crusaders, a large organization opposed to the Eighteenth Amendment.

Then I thought of a memorable day which I passed in the northern towns of Litchfield County. After making two speeches in the afternoon to old-time Democrats, I drove to the Knickerbocker Hotel in Canaan, J. Henry's "home town," for dinner and another speech. While sitting on the veranda, I saw coming up the walk a large man whom I had not seen for several years. He was Michael Idvorsky Pupin, one of the eminent scientists of his time, then living more or less in retirement in Norfolk. He had come over, he said at once, to tell me that he and ten or twelve Republican leaders in the neighborhood were going to vote for me. The others, he added, would have liked to come also, but they did not quite dare; he had, however, permission to give me their names. It was a roster that amazed me. While reliving this scene in memory, I could say to myself that I had stormed and damaged J. Henry's fortress, but whether I had taken it, nobody yet knew.

The next morning I voted early, in jest asking an officer as I entered the booth how to split a Republican ticket. Hand on lever, I stood smiling at the cameras and then hastened home to take up the revision of *The Development of the English Novel* at the point where I had left off in September. This did not mean that I had no hopes of election. Far from it. But as I well knew, a candidate for office who talks mainly to people who are in friendly accord with his own political principles is likely to forget that there is a large body of citizens who are in complete disagreement with him. Whether it was defeat or victory, I resolved to keep the hair on my head.

I went to the Graduates Club for luncheon. The talk was all about the prospects of my election. As I was leaving I greeted two Republican friends who were sitting at a small table. Stepping aside to speak to another, I overheard one of them say to the other something like, "Cross won't be so happy when he gets the news tonight. It's too bad. He doesn't seem to know that he can't possibly win. I wonder how he will take his defeat." I went down to Democratic headquarters to inquire how things were going. The vote being cast, I learned, was heavy for an off year. This news I regarded as a good omen. I then returned home for a good rest—two hours' sleep—so as to be in condition to watch, if necessary, till morning.

By eight o'clock I received an urgent summons to headquarters, where a crowd was gathering. New Haven's report was already in. In quick succession came reports from the other large cities, Hartford, Bridgeport, and Waterbury, and the smaller cities, showing with only two exceptions, overwhelming pluralities for the Democratic ticket. Norwich, Norwalk, and Stamford were safely Democratic. Then came reports from smaller towns, some of which went Democratic for the first time in many years while others still remained in the Republican column though with reduced pluralities. At ten o'clock something rather queer occurred. Suddenly many small towns became silent. Towards midnight reports which apparently had been held up by concerted action rolled in over the telephones thick and fast. At 12.30, all but four towns having been heard from, the Associated Press announced my election. The State was clearly slipping from Roraback's pocket.

It was a wild night everywhere in Democratic circles. When I reached home fifty or more neighbors, as many Republicans as Democrats, were there with congratulations. Photographers, of course, were on hand to take pictures in all sorts of poses. On the way to salute me were a thousand paraders carrying red torches and headed by a brass band. I addressed the crowd from the front porch, while some of them were climbing through the windows of the house. They overran it but found nothing worth taking, for I was a poor man. The party did not break up until Aurora began to open her golden gates.

By good luck all members of my family were in that happy company: my first son Wilbur with his wife Alice and their children, Wilbur, twelve years old, and his brother Robert, four years behind him; and my second son Avery with his wife Ella and her intimate friends. All of them were asked by reporters to relate such anecdotes about me as they remembered, particularly when we were on long summer vacations at Burkehaven. My sons and their wives were rather careful not to give me away. Not so my grandson Wilbur the third, who remarked: "If you could see my grandfather . . . out getting blueberries with an old pair of pants, an old shirt, and a farmer's straw hat, you wouldn't think he was Governor-elect of Connecticut." When asked whether he did not regard his grandfather as really a great man, he replied, "Oh, yes, he is a great man. He gives me a lot of Christmas and birthday presents and puts a lot of money in the bank for me."

Bob, who was already developing a sense of humor, listened to his brother and smiled.

Morning newspapers shone with the headlines of "A Democratic Sweep." It was not, however, a "clean sweep." Cross was elected Governor by a plurality, according to later official returns, of 5,465. But the rest of the Democratic state ticket lost by almost 7,000 votes; and both branches of the General Assembly remained under Republican control, though with a greatly reduced number of seats. Of the five Democratic candidates

for Members of Congress two were elected—Augustine Lonergan for the first district and William Tierney of the fourth district. Not then knowing the value of sheriffs in political organizations I did not understand why the Republicans took special pride in the election of their candidates in "all the counties save one." Had the Democratic party exerted its full strength, it could have carried its entire state ticket and elected four Members of Congress instead of two. Still, it was so notable a victory that it dumfounded Republicans. The political reporter of the *Hartford Courant*, who had proved by an elastic use of statistics that my election was impossible, apparently failed to provide himself with an up-to-date photograph of "the dear old gentleman down at Yale" in case of a miscalculation in his prophecy. So he had to display a photograph taken back in the days when I wore a walrus mustache of the kind which scared children.

XIX. An International Jest

The election over, there remained the victory dinner at the Hotel Bond in Hartford. It was expected that I would take the occasion to announce what big things I was going to do as soon as I was seated in the Governor's chair. As I did not know what I could do with a Republican General Assembly, I thought it the better part of valor to keep silent on political questions until my Inaugural Address, when I could lay directly before the Legislature a program for their consideration. Accordingly I left politics, state and national, to be discussed by Congressman-elect Lonergan, and by Governor-elect Ely of Massachusetts, who had been invited to make one of the principal addresses, and contented myself with relating some of the incidents of the campaign, keeping clear of controversial questions except by innuendo.

I can come through the ordeal of the campaign, I said, in better physical condition than when I entered it, while my aides broke down at frequent intervals. Joe Tone, for example, who was at the telephone most of the day and made speeches as soon as darkness came on, lost his voice; and Patrick O'Sullivan was always having colds which at last terminated in a bad case of grippe that put him to bed. On the other hand, I emerged from the campaign without a trace of a cold, with never a scratch in the throat and my voice as clear as a bell. How do I account, I asked, for my escape from the plight of my aides? Well, for one thing, I rarely got home from speech-making until an hour or two after midnight and that was too late for a bath. Nights out like that meant that I must sleep till ten or eleven o'clock in the morning, again an hour altogether too late for a bath before breakfast. In the thick of a fight it is dangerous to stop for a bath.

I went on to tell of my experience in boyhood and youth with the washbasin and the washtub in the great unwashed age of the countryside, when, it was sometimes said, farmers got safely through the summer with one good washup in the millpond after the haying season. Later on, when I entered college, I formed the habit, on a doctor's advice, of taking a tepid bath once a week and a cold sponge bath out of the washbowl every morning. Still later, as soon as I could afford a bathtub of my own, I always ducked myself in cold water on rising. The shower bath, except for athletes, had not yet come into fashion. All went well with me as I lay in a bathtub with the cold water flowing over me from the faucet until about 1920, when I began to have serious trouble with my sinuses. I was sneezing all day long. A doctor tried a number of usual remedies. He even gassed me. Nothing availed. I was desperate.

One day I sat down alone to diagnose my case, if I could, without the aid of doctors. Why is it, I wondered, that for a long series of years a cold bath had an exhilarating effect and then suddenly a cold bath put me out of commission? In a moment I had the secret. It was the Volstead Act. Before enactment of that famous law, I used to complete my cold ablutions with a grain alcohol rubdown. After that unfortunate day I could get no pure grain alcohol without a doctor's prescription which cost $3. So I resorted to so-called alcohol rubs, polluted with formaldehyde, which apart from its nauseous smell irritated my thin skin terribly. As a short way out, I threw aside all alcohol, defiled and undefiled, and took my cold baths straight. It was then, as I remembered, that my sinuses fell into evil ways. To test out my diagnosis I resolved to go three weeks without touching water except for drinking. At the end of that period of abstinence I was cured of sneezing.

No man really knows why he holds to this or that opinion. My hostility to national prohibition, I daresay, had its inception in my experience with formaldehyde.

As my fellow Democrats seemed to be interested in what I was saying, I gave them a short historical sketch of bathing among various nations, which I improvised from half-remembered notes I had once taken down in cursory reading. I could find, I asserted, no statement in the Bible that Moses, who talked with God, ever took a bath; and it is well known that the children of Israel, God's chosen people, were so afraid of wetting their feet, except in religious ceremonies, that they preferred to remain captive in Egypt until the waters of the Red Sea were opened to give them a passage through over dry land. On the other hand, the Romans, once a hardy race who built an empire, degenerated under the influence of public baths into a people so effete and dissolute that they became an easy pretty to the barbarians who overran Italy and sacked and burned Rome. Remembering the fall of the Roman Empire, England looked askance upon bathing down to a century ago. The Reverend Laurence Sterne often spoke of himself as "a lousy parson." The Earl of Essex I can still hear calling loudly for a clean shirt at the court of Queen Elizabeth. This is an indication that he was nothing more than a lousy courtier. Apparently at that time Queen Elizabeth was quite alone in the habit of taking a periodic bath. Of her I find it written by a contemporary: "She hath built herself a bath, wherein she doth bathe herself once a month whether she require it or no."

Not until the administration of President Fillmore, less than a hundred years ago, was a bath installed in the White House with running water, both cold and hot. The President's request of Congress for an appropriation for a bathtub in the executive mansion awoke a storm of criticism which shook the nation. He was denounced in the press for a desire to indulge in a luxury quite out of keeping with democratic America.

Physicians declared that it was dangerous to bathe in the latitude of Washington during the winter months except under medical advice. For the protection of her people, white and black, Virginia laid a special tax of $30 a year on every bathtub brought into the State, and for a similar reason Massachusetts forbade the introduction of any bathtubs into that State under the penalty of a fine. And Hartford and many other cities quadrupled water charges to all their inhabitants who had bathtubs in their houses.

Certainly President Fillmore stirred up the hornets. And who was he? He was one of our so-called "dough-faced" Presidents, a Whig, who lined up with the "Know-Nothings" and finally went over to the Republican party where he met his fate. In ability he in no way compared with the great men of the Republic—Webster, Clay, Calhoun, Hamilton, Jefferson, and Washington—who, if they ever bathed, said nothing publicly about it.

And if, as some may infer, I shy at bathtubs, I have with me several great predecessors in the Governor's chairs—John Winthrop for instance, who obtained from Charles II a charter uniting all the Connecticut settlements, or Jonathan Trumbull whom Washington called "Brother Jonathan," neither of whom ever saw anything resembling a modern bathtub. I should feel honored by the comparison between them and me if it were made by someone other than myself. I advised my brother Democrats to be careful when they stepped into bathtubs where more accidents occur than in flights through the air.

This address was taken to heart by many who did not hear it. Newspapers had headlines reading something like: "Governor Cross of Connecticut says he never takes a bath." The president of a bathtub concern protested against my attack on a business by which he made his living; and the secretary of another concern informed me that she could show me how a bath need consume no more than three minutes of my valuable time. Less seriously, a friend in South Africa sent me from that distant clime a beautifully carved scraper of the kind used by the natives of Zululand instead of water for removing the sweat of their bodies.

Best of all, a friend in Italy sent me a copy of *Guerin Meschino*, a comic weekly something like *Punch*, published at Milan. It contained two

cartoons. Over one was the inscription: "The new Governor of Connecticut, who is seventy years old and in the best of health, declares that he
owes his excellent condition to the fact that he has never taken a bath."
The other inscription modified this extreme statement by saying that I
owed my youthful energy to the habit "of going months without a bath."
One cartoon represents a man wiping his neck as he stands bent over a
washbowl and crying to a maid-servant to bring him a stimulant for he
feels exhausted. In the other a mother is scolding her small son for refusing
to get into a bathtub. Facing her in a defiant attitude, legs far apart and
hands behind his back, the boy is saying, "Mamma, I want to grow up to
be the sort of man Dr. Cross is."

XX. The Art of Hamstringing a Governor

When it was said that I had no qualifications for political office except that I knew how to milk a cow or "break up" a settin' hen, I used to quote to myself a remark of Henry Adams who wrote, "Knowledge of human nature is the beginning and end of political education." Thereon I reflected that I had been unconsciously learning a good deal about the ways of mankind ever since my boyhood days when I was clerk in a village store. Someone who was acquainted with stories of that cracker-barrel age predicted that when I was promoted to the chair under the gilded dome I would turn out to be another "Connecticut Yankee in King Arthur's Court." That was a good jest. But before writing his story, Mark Twain had to find out what was going on in King Arthur's Court.

So I had to find out what special functions would fall to my lot as a Governor of my native State. I spent the two months between my election and inauguration in a study of the administrative structure of the State government. I was amazed at its heterogeneous character and its dispersion of powers among elective officers, commissions, and boards acting more or less independently instead of being strictly responsible to the Governor in whom, says the Constitution, shall be vested "the supreme executive power of the State." In this survey I came to some definite conclusions as to who among the major Commissioners, supposed to be the direct arms of the Chief Executive, were doing their work well and who were easy-going politicians. Their annual reports told the story. They were all, I observed, Republicans.

I called on Governor Trumbull, who greeted me cordially, and we were photographed together on the steps of the Capitol. He reported to his friends, one of them told me, that I was not a bad sort of chap. He invited me to a conference to consider the appointment of a committee to study questions connected with unemployment, which was increasing at an alarming pace; and to sit in with the Board of Finance and Control through December so that I might see how the business of the State was being conducted. To this body of ten members, which included the state elective officers from the Governor downward, the General Assembly had granted, for the long periods when it was not in session, vast powers, executive and semilegislative. Though the Governor was ex-officio chairman of the Board, it was so constituted, it seemed to me, as to act as a partial check on the exercise of his executive authority under the Constitution. The members of this powerful Board, supreme above all other departments of State, were all Republicans with the exception of one Democrat of doubtful authenticity. I wondered how I should get along as chairman of a group of men of this political complexion, who could give me a run-around whenever they dared. Would my "knowledge of human nature" be sufficient to prevent that spectacle? I did not exactly worry. But I scratched my head.

In the meantime I began a round of visits to the educational, humane, and penal institutions of the State, about which there had been much wild talk during the campaign. My guide was Edward F. Hall, Commissioner of the Board of Finance and Control, who had an intimate knowledge of them all. Reporters often followed us to listen to questions and comments for a story. The chairmen of Boards and Trustees, with two exceptions, and all the superintendents of humane and penal institutions, with one possible exception, were Republicans. I talked with patients, prisoners, and wayward boys and girls wherever I went. In the hospital for the insane at Middletown the superintendent led us into a ward of noisy women who were, he said, on the road to recovery. As we stepped into the hall the superintendent announced "Governor Cross" and I at once extended my right hand towards a woman standing near the door. She straightened up, drew back, and shouted, "I am a Republican. I do not care to shake hands with a Democrat." According to the story I read in the newspapers the next morning, I remarked to the little company of Republicans with me, "Now you see where the Republican majority in Connecticut has gone." Similarly at a later date an inmate of the State Prison at Wethersfield appealed to me, in an open session of the Board of Pardons, of which I was chairman, for a mitigation of his severe sentence on the ground that he was the only Democrat in that institution.

Of the nineteen judges of the Supreme and Superior Courts, every one an able and upright man, only three were Democrats. Among the judges of the Court of Common Pleas, there was no Democrat. All the judges of the city, borough, and town courts were an integral part of the Republican political organization. If here and there a Democratic judge or prosecutor was admitted to this inner circle, he was a man who would "listen to reason" and create no disturbance in the usual administration of justice in the minor courts.

The Republican leaders looked upon my election as a fluke which they would never let happen again. What worried them most was a fear that a Democratic Governor might disrupt their beautiful system for the control of all offices in the state government. To prevent this political catastrophe, it was announced in the press two days after the election that the General Assembly would be advised among its first acts to curtail the Governor's appointive power so far as this could be done without violating the Constitution of the State. By skillful use of legislative machinery the Republican organization, it was argued, might gain rather than lose prestige during a Democratic administration. There was, too, a hint that the Governor could be discredited by the disapproval of such measures as he might advocate. It seemed incredible that any political party could adopt so stupid a policy; more incredible still that it was willing to show its hand before playing the game.

Ready for the game, win or lose, I was inaugurated Governor of Connecticut, January 7, 1931. For the first time I met with my staff and Executive Secretary, Kenneth Wynne, for luncheon at the Hartford Club which I made my headquarters. Gene Tunney, a member of my excellent staff whom I appointed major, I jocosely designated as my special bodyguard. That afternoon in a gorgeous procession led by cavalry and the Governor's Foot Guards and the Putnam Phalanx, all resplendent in the British uniforms of colonial days, Governor Trumbull and I were driven to the Capitol where an immense throng greeted with an uproar two men in silk hats who walked side by side over the esplanade up steps to wide-swung open doors. A Yale classmate, standing by, smiled to see me dressed in that style as I lifted my hat to him.

The oath was solemnly administered by Chief Justice William M. Malt-bie. I had addressed many audiences under strange circumstances, but never under any so strange as this; for the white light of a photographic set-up beat upon the throne and blinded my eyes, rendering invisible everything before me except the bald head of my friend, Freddy Baker, the Republican clerk of the Senate, who was sitting on the secretary's platform just below me. Keeping my eyes upon my manuscript, now and then glancing down for relief upon a head which resembled a cherub's I read my Inaugural Address to an unseen audience in front of me and to that wider unseen audience which heard my words as they came over the air.

The temper of the address and the legislation I recommended were generally approved by the press and the public irrespective of party. Many editorials declared that I described precisely the kind of nonpartisan government which the citizens of the State had long been looking for in vain. Some amusement was created by my references to or quotations from Darwin, Dickens, and Chaucer, which were too far afield, it was thought, from the subject in hand. There was indeed a story afloat that when I mentioned the name of Chaucer in a passage on prohibition a member of the House inquired of his neighbor in the next seat who Chaucer was and received the reply: "Why, don't you know? He is a minister over in Wethersfield." Naturally Republican leaders who were interviewed by reporters were chary of comment. The "boys" had not had time to get together and talk it over.

In dealing with men who differ with you the only way to accomplish anything is to find some common ground, wherever possible, to start out from. After the inauguration ceremonies the General Assembly recessed until January 15. On the very day of reconvening I requested an appropriation of $10,000 to defray the current expenses of the commission to investigate the unemployment situation, which had been organized by Governor Trumbull in consultation with me. Favorable action on this recommendation was immediately taken under a suspension of the rules in both Houses. This was my first act under the principle of partnership in legislation solely for public welfare. An appropriation of $100,000 was also approved for clearing certain state forests of brush and dead wood and improving state parks, on the stipulation that the funds be used to relieve unemployment by giving work during the winter and early spring to several hundred idle men who knew how to swing an axe. This project which succeeded beyond the most sanguine expectations anticipated in a small way the Federal Civilian Conservation Corps camps.

I was in no wise deceived by these gestures of friendly coöperation. There was no occasion for believing that the Republican organization had abandoned its announced purpose of hamstringing a Democratic Governor by some sort of jugglery with the Constitution and the laws defining his functions. The only doubt I had was just what the procedure would be. I did not have to wait long for an answer. On January 30 Raymond Baldwin of Stratford, a member of the Judiciary Committee, introduced into the House of Representatives a bill, "providing that each nomination by the governor for appointment, by and with the advice and consent of the Senate, of any commissioner or other state officer, shall be transmitted to the Senate on or before the first day of April of the year in which the term of office of such commissioner or other state officer is to expire. If any such nomination so transmitted shall not have been confirmed by the Senate within fifteen days after such transmission, the office shall be filled by concurrent vote of both Houses." The general aim of this bill was to strip the Governor of his most important appointive powers. Its immediate design was to make certain the reappointment of all Republican Commissioners whose terms of office were approaching their end.

It was said in justification for the Baldwin bill that the November election was really a Republican victory in that the Republicans came into control of both Houses of the General Assembly and carried their entire state ticket except their candidate for Governor. Cross crept in by a relatively small plurality, "almost insignificant in comparison with the total vote." In the circumstances, "the Democratic Governor ought to consider himself as hardly more than a guest in the state government" and "if he conducts himself in any other way he should be suppressed by whatever legal measures can be created for his suppression." My reply, whenever it was asked for, was that the Republicans on their state ticket who were

President Roosevelt and Governor Cross

elected likewise crept in by small pluralities and so might be regarded as guests to be held in check by the Republican organization, as they undoubtedly would be. As for myself, I made it clear that I was nobody's guest. For good measure I added that the number of Democratic Representatives had doubled since the election of 1928 and that of the thirty-five members of the Senate fourteen were Democrats.

The Baldwin bill never got beyond a first hearing. It was overwhelmed with denunciation and ridicule by the press of both political parties. The most influential Republican newspaper in the State declared in a leading editorial that Cross "should be a full Governor just as much as though he had had a majority of 50,000 and a full ticket of elective officials with him." J. Henry Roraback, I was told, met with several Republican editors and scolded them for their treatment of a measure of which he approved as just the thing to keep a Democratic Governor under proper restraint.

There was nothing for me to do but to go about my business as Governor in King Arthur's Court. As I sat in my office I now and then looked across the room to a fine portrait of Mark Twain hanging on the wall, or stopped to read his advice to a group of young men and women, which rested in a frame on my desk: "Always do right. This will gratify some people, and astonish the rest."

Weeks before the deadline set by the proposed Baldwin bill I submitted to the Senate all my nominations which required confirmation by that body or by the General Assembly as a whole. To emphasize the principle of partnership in government, I occasionally sent in names in pairs, one Democrat and one Republican at a time—a policy that lent some color to the sobriquet which Al Lavery, the Republican President pro tem of the Senate, gave me of Trader Horn. With one exception, all my nominations to commissionerships were promptly confirmed. Richard Joyce Smith, a brilliant young Assistant Professor in the Yale Law School, whom I nominated as a member of the Public Utilities Commission, was at once rejected. He was altogether too wise and too progressive a young man to be satisfied with a formal administration of antiquated laws governing the public utilities of the State. Naturally my nominations for the reappointment of judges of the Superior Court, mostly Republicans, met with immediate approval.

The attempt to annul the Governor's appointive powers by circumventing the Constitution having failed, Republican leadership tried to usurp the function of the Supreme Court of the State by claiming that certain statutes conferring upon the Chief Executive the right to nominate to the General Assembly judges of the Court of Common Pleas and of the City Court of New Haven were unconstitutional. The Assembly passed bills repealing the statutes; and I vetoed them, inquiring why constitutional doubts disturbed no one until the election of a Democratic

Governor. The Republican leader of the House moved the passage of the bills, "the Governor's veto to the contrary, notwithstanding." Only a majority of votes was necessary to do the business for him. But his party had an adverse public opinion to reckon with. All my judgeship appointments were eventually confirmed.

Near the time of my election the Judicial Council of Connecticut recommended to the General Assembly that in place of the present city, borough, and town courts there be established a District Court system in which the judges should be appointed by the Governor, subject to confirmation by the Senate and the House. In my Inaugural Address and in two special messages to the General Assembly I urged this recommendation as a means of mitigating the influence of politics on our minor courts and of integrating them into a coherent whole with common ideals and procedures. But though the draft of a bill was introduced, it never stood a chance. It was rejected by a party vote, ostensibly in part on the ground that it would be unconstitutional but really because it would eliminate a host of jobs.

All the jobs in the lower courts thus made safe, from the judges down through deputy judges, prosecutors, and other officers, in some instances as many as ten or twelve to a court, there was no further interference with the Governor's appointive function. I was now free to go ahead with more than a hundred appointments, major and minor, which could not be transferred to the jurisdiction of the General Assembly without amendments to a score of statutes, a political undertaking altogether too conspicuous to attempt without evoking public condemnation. I reappointed the Republican Commissioner of Public Health, and replaced the Republican Commissioner of the State Police, over whom hung a cloud, with able Anthony Sunderland, who was an officer in the National Guard. The political hotbeds of certain state institutions could be cooled by splitting the trustees between the two parties. I began the policy of appointing to important boards and commissions outstanding lawyers and businessmen who, though they would never submit to the abuse heaped upon candidates for office, were always ready to serve the State in any other capacity desired.

Meanwhile I saw cast aside measures which I regarded as of vital importance. A bill introduced at my request for the appointment of a nonpartisan committee to report on a plan for the reorganization of the state government in the interest of economy, efficiency, and centralized responsibility, though it made considerable appeal to business members of the Legislature, was at last killed by the intervention of the outside Republican organization. The request that a committee be appointed to canvass state and municipal tax systems "with the aim of a more equitable distribution of the tax burden and the relief of our industries, our rent-payers, and our real estate owners" also fell by the way, as did a bill to give the Public Utilities Commission adequate jurisdiction over rates and service of light and power companies and the issue of new securities.

Several ideas, it was apparent, lay behind a do-nothing policy. One was that the Governor was overreaching his constitutional function in rec-ommending specific measures to the General Assembly instead of leaving it to that body to determine for itself what legislation was necessary to meet this or that situation. He must be kept where he belonged. Another was that the Governor must be restrained from appointing committees to report to the next General Assembly as if he expected to be reëlected. He seemed also to assume in his recommendations that the industrial depres-sion would not be over by 1933. This was true only in so far as I regarded the immediate future as uncertain and wanted the state government to be forearmed with plans to deal with any crisis which might arise, first of all by reducing expenditures and leveling off inequalities in taxation.

It did not occur to me that there could be any objection to such proce-dure until I learned by chance one day that the Appropriations Commit-tee of the House had denied my request for a renewal of a grant of $100,000 for continuing work on the woodlands the next winter, on the ground that favorable action would have a bad psychological effect upon the State because of the inference that in the opinion of the Legislature the industrial depression might last for another year. At that time Calvin Coolidge was writing for the newspapers short syndicated articles on "the retardation in business," in one of which he ventured the prophecy that business would soon strike its old pace partly through new enterprises springing up, such as Tom Thumb golf. In this unreal atmosphere of wishful thinking I was trying in vain to take precautions against the future. When the crisis came two years afterwards, it had to be met in part by a drastic cut in the salaries of all employees in the service of the State.

Although many measures near my heart miscarried, all were not lost. As soon as jobs had been mostly distributed in a way fairly satisfactory to both political parties, opposition to the legislation I desired became less active. Republicans and Democrats joined hands in an act authorizing the Governor to appoint a commission to investigate the subject of old-age pensions and to report its findings and recommendations at the next session of the General Assembly. And the Senate confirmed without opposition my nomination of Joseph Tone, a member of the A.F.L., to be commissioner of Labor and Factory Inspection. With his assistance Connecticut was to become a leader in progressive legislation for improving the condition of industrial workers. At the same time the first effort was made to take the farmers out of the mud by an allotment of $3,000,000 a year from the highway fund for rural roads. Looking towards the completion of the Merritt Parkway, for which surveys were being made and land purchased, the General Assembly authorized the Governor to appoint a commission of nine members to coöperate with the Highway Commissioner in making the Parkway, when constructed, a thing of beauty and safety. The project was charged with life by an appropriation of $1,000,000.

The General Assembly approved a building program of some $8,000,000 for humane, educational, and penal institutions, with emphasis on sanatoria for tubercular patients, to be expended during the next two or three years. So large an undertaking was made feasible by a surplus in the treasury of nearly this amount, which was accumulated during prosperous years, then, alas, at an end. I was particularly pleased when the long-drawn-out controversy over the site of a new home for children suffering from bone and glandular tuberculosis was finally settled by the purchase of a large tract of land fronting on the sea. On my request Cass Gilbert designed the main building. Fortunate, too, was the site chosen for a Veterans' Home at Rocky Hill overlooking the Connecticut River. Provision was also made for the most enlightened treatment of first offenders among the inmates of the State Prison at Wethersfield by the purchase of 1,600 acres of land in Enfield with the buildings thereon for a prison farm, to be named after Norris G. Osborn, long chairman of the Board of Directors of the State Prison.

My first experience with a Legislature has long since become a pleasant memory. Too much, I now feel, was said about my being lonesome. My dearest political enemy, Maurice Sherman, Editor of the *Hartford Courant*, wrote in lofty language: "Governor Cross stands out as a solitary figure on Capitol Hill. He is a sort of Olympic Jove, but he seeks no encounter with the giant crew, who, let us hope, will not seek to pull him from his regal state." Never before nor since have I come into comparison with the omnipotent and immortal Greek god, who had a devil of a time with the giants when they climbed Mt. Olympus to drive him from his throne. More picturesquely, a stalwart visitor from Missouri, descending for his imagery from Mt. Olympus to the lower world, remarked that a man in my situation reminded him of "a celluloid rabbit chased through hell by a pack of asbestos hounds."

The fact is I was supported by large minorities in the legislature under the skillful leadership of Frank Bergin in the Senate and William Citron in the House, who on important bills demanded yea or nay votes. The Lieutenant Governor, Samuel Spencer, and the Republican leader of the Senate, William Leete, were both Yale men; and as often as once a fortnight Chief Justice W. M. Maltbie, another Yale man, came into my office for a talk on things in general. And when I went over to the Hartford Club for luncheon I sat at a round table in a company which included my classmate Lucius Robinson, Bill Corson, Ed Day, Andy Gates, and other Yale men. With us too was Maurice Sherman, a graduate of Dartmouth, and M. Lewis Hewes, a Maryland Democrat by birth, who could quote Scripture to corroborate any opinion he held, however fantastic. I was never alone anywhere.

The first of the Republicans on Capitol Hill to call on me was Albert Lavery. He usually greeted me at the beginning of the legislative week to inquire how I was getting along. Because of his wit he was a very popular toastmaster, and he once introduced me as Trader Horn at a banquet of the Connecticut Chamber of Commerce. "Though I may be Trader Horn in the disguise of a Governor," I replied, "I have never been able to do business with Al Lavery, he is so different from my Democratic friends who always spread their cards out on the table. With them the trade is quickly over, whoever wins. But Al, he always puts on a poker face when I try to find out what he will give me in exchange for the tusks of a dead elephant. . . .

"Last month Al laid aside his poker face for a face of another hue, which alarmed me when I first saw it. As President pro tem of the Senate, you know, he would automatically become Governor of the State if both the Governor and the Lieutenant Governor should step out for any reason. Sam Spencer became so ill in March that the Senate had to pass a resolution for his quick recovery. A few weeks later I fell sick with the grippe, which kept me in bed for ten days, longer than usual, I suppose, because neither the Senate nor the House sent me resolutions to help me on the road to recovery. On the very morning of my return to my office Al walked in to inquire how I was feeling. I told him that I was perfectly fit again. As he looked me over while I was sitting at my desk and smoking a Connecticut seedleaf, his face grew pale and troubled. I have seen many sad faces in my life, but none so unutterably sad as Al Lavery's on that dismal morning. The tusks of the dead elephant I still have with me. They are no longer available for barter in view of the election next year."

The General Assembly recessed for a week in May in order to give me time before final adjournment to consider a last group of bills submitted for my approval or disapproval and thus to prevent me from exercising the Governor's right to pocket vetoes. When they met on May 27 to adjourn *sine die* I duly reported to them that I had signed all the bills which came to me during the recess except two or three "for restoring the civil rights of certain Republicans in different parts of the State who had been convicted of crime." These I could not sign, I explained, because no one of the beneficiaries had by him the necessary fee of $5, the standard price in Connecticut for regaining civil rights once lost through indiscreet conduct. I further expressed the hope that the two hundred or more members of the General Assembly would come to the rescue of these poor devils and make up a purse of $15 for their benefit so that three good votes might be recovered for the next election. This was the first opportunity I had to condemn a racket which the best men in both parties still deplore.

"And now, as I bid you good-by with best wishes for the future, I hope that I may see some of you back here two years hence."

XXI. Connecticut and the Washington Bicentennial

Time was when a Connecticut Governor had little to do except when the General Assembly was in session. During the intervals of his absence the routine of his office was entrusted to a clerk who might be kept on for a half century, whichever political party were in power. But years before I ascended the throne the work of the Governor and the social demands made upon him had so increased that it became necessary for him to have a well-equipped office of assistants and to be at the Capitol for consultation on several days of the week. Owing partly to the problems rising out of the industrial depression, I soon saw that in order to perform the heavy and exacting duties I had undertaken I must devote my undivided attention to the people of the State. I made the governorship a full-time job. This was an innovation.

An important part of the State's business was conducted through the Board of Finance and Control, over which the Governor presided. The Board had, for instance, power to add, at its discretion, to the appropriation of the General Assembly for any department or institution of the State, and upon it devolved supervision of the large building program. For many years it had delegated some of its powers to an Executive Committee comprising the Governor and a few others of its members. The times were so serious that I asked the Board to discontinue its Executive Committee and to meet as a whole, usually once a week. Hereafter also all the members present at any meeting were required to sign the minutes; and no increase in an original appropriation by the General Assembly was to be made except over the signatures of every member of the Board.

There was rarely any intrusion of politics in our deliberations except by one member, who was easily squelched. I even ventured on the reappointment of a Republican, Edward F. Hall, as Commissioner of the Board, being well enough acquainted with him to know that he would put the public interest far above partisanship in carrying out my policies. One day an old-time politician greeted Commissioner Hall: "You're a hell of a Republican, Ed. Why don't you now and then trip up the old man? You have plenty of chances." If I was ever tripped up by Ed Hall, I was unaware of it.

My recreation was confined mostly to tours over the State, occasionally across the border, to address by invitation various groups and organizations. On the assumption that I had not wholly given up the intellectual life on becoming Governor, I was frequently invited to appear before college and university faculties and students for talks on subjects half literary, half political. In the list were two formal Phi Beta Kappa addresses and four lectures on fiction at Amherst College. Students were so persistent in their inquiries about the chances of success in a political career that I wrote an article on "Young Men in Politics" for the April, 1932, *Forum*.

One particular pleasure was association with the many racial groups within the State, among all of whom I made lasting friendships. Their folkways interested me; and at the same time I was impressed by the quick

PLAYING HIS OLD ROLE
IN DIXIE CONFERENCE—

ease with which they fell into old Yankee traditions. Despite racial differences it was plain we were all fast becoming one people in this State. The
new knowledge of Connecticut I was gaining was a light of hope for the
future shining through the darkness of the depression.

One morning I received, and immediately accepted, a formal invitation
to attend the annual convention of the Connecticut branch of the A.F.L.,
to be held in Bridgeport. When I stepped upon the platform, I was greeted
with a stare by a large audience of men, many of whom were smoking
pipes. I did not know what that stare meant until the chairman introduced
me as the first Governor of Connecticut who had ever accepted an invitation to address the A.F.L. Having already come out for organized labor
by appointing an A.F.L. man Commissioner of Labor, I now said that I
stood squarely for collective bargaining. The hysterical reception of that
announcement made it difficult to go on.

The climax of the many patriotic celebrations of 1931 was the sesqui-
centennial of the surrender of Cornwallis at Yorktown on October 19,
1781. On the request of Governor John Garland Pollard of Virginia and
the Richmond Blues, I attended, accompanied not only by my staff but
by the Connecticut Governor's Foot Guards and the Putnam Phalanx.
Never was I more proud of my State than when I saw everybody near
me stand and applaud as the Connecticut troops passed the reviewing
stand. President Hoover, the guest of honor, was among the first to rise to
his feet.

On my return to Hartford I installed in my office a bust of Washington.
Yorktown was a prelude to state and local celebrations, the next year, of
the Bicentenary of Washington's birth, for which Connecticut and her
municipalities were already making elaborate preparations. Sometime in
November while I was sitting by the plaster of Paris bust of Washington,
I received a visit from the Reverend Richard Arden Morford who had
come to invite me to give the usual annual patriotic address on Washington's birthday before the Washington Association of New Jersey at
Morristown. At first I declined the honor because of many engagements,
a list of which I read to him from my appointment book. Still he persisted.

I weakened a little when he ran over the names of the statesmen, scholars, and orators who had addressed the Association during the last half-century. When he saw that I was wilting he played his trump card. "You know, Governor, that there is an honorarium of $300." He smiled. I smiled, too, and said, "I will be with you and my subject will be 'The Character of George Washington.'"

February 22, 1932, was a memorable day in my life. In the morning I addressed the returning alumni of Princeton University in old Nassau Hall on the edge of the battlefield where Washington won a notable victory over the British when the American cause was waning. In that hall, too, the Continental Congress sometimes met after it was forced to leave Philadelphia. President Hibben introduced me. As I looked down the long narrow room flanked with cheering Princeton men I saw hanging on the wall to my right Peale's portrait of Washington and I fixed in my imagination the very spot where Washington once stood when the President of the Continental Congress congratulated him on his "brilliant military exploits" and "the late glorious peace."

Washington's historical associations with old Nassau so filled my mind that I forgot to take from my pocket the address I had prepared for the occasion and spoke extemporaneously on the private life of Washington, mainly in his youth: on the boy who never told a lie and at the age of six proved the existence of God to the satisfaction of his father; the boy who like other Virginia boys could never learn to spell words correctly and yet was admitted to William and Mary College to study surveying; on his love of the ladies before he was subdued by Martha Custis, his love of music and amateur acting, of noisy companions and racy stories, and the whistle of bullets on his first military expedition into western Pennsylvania when commissioned as lieutenant colonel by Governor Dinwiddie of Virginia. And so on to later years when he entertained Lafayette and other intimate friends at Mount Vernon and lighted them to bed at midnight. I claimed Washington as a Yale man as well as a Princeton man because both of these famous colleges conferred upon him the degree of LL.D. I had a good time with those Princeton men.

After the battle of Princeton, Washington went into winter quarters at

Morristown. So after my informal speech at Princeton I drove to Mor-ristown for my "$300 address" in which I drew a full-length portrait of Washington, man of unconquerable will. And that evening I returned to New Haven in time for a dinner with the Second Company of the Gov-ernor's Foot Guards to whom I recounted the incidents of a long eventful day. Three speeches in one day was a token of what was to come after.

I was in New York by invitation to take part in the representation of two great scenes in Washington's career. With me as aide was Maj. Gene Tunney of my official staff. In the morning we drove down to the Battery to greet a George Washington on his arrival to bid farewell to his Generals at Fraunces Tavern. We were guests of Jimmy Walker, then Mayor of New York, and Grover Whalen, master of ceremonies. In a little company we stood on the landing at the foot of Wall Street to welcome the hero of the Revolution as he stepped ashore from his scarlet-covered barge equipped with oars and oarsmen in white uniforms, and an outboard motor which had helped them row across the bay from Jersey. On first sight of Washington the boys sitting on the wharf, their legs dangling over the water, shouted "Hello, George." Washington smiled and waved a hand towards them.

A platoon of mounted police led the way to Fraunces Tavern. The improvised Washington rode in the old coach which conveyed his name-sake in 1789 to his first inauguration as President of the United States, followed by another coach full of notables of his day, among them his generals and Governor Clinton of New York. The rest of us marched to the tune of the "Washington Post March" played by the New York Police Band. The step was a trifle quick for our legs, encumbered as we were with the top hats and cutaways. Arriving at Fraunces Tavern, Washington was left at the foot of the stairway while his generals and a few of us mounted to the "long room" with a long table. Near one end of the table assembled some of Washington's companions in arms, among them Knox, Gates, Wayne, Steuben, Kosciusko, and Connecticut's Israel Putnam. At the other end of the table stood Jimmy Walker, Grover Whalen, Gene Tunney, and myself. The contrast between the two groups struck me as very funny. At a signal the Commander in Chief entered the room and

took a position among his generals. Raising a glass of wine to his lips, he
drank to their future happiness, grasped their hands, one by one, and bade
them a solemn farewell.

When the salutations were over the impersonator of George Washington, who had not been thoroughly trained in the rôle he was to play,
seemed uncertain what else he should do. He began a genial talk with his
generals and took a drink or two of hard stuff with them. I whispered to
Grover Whalen to tell him to quit all that and to walk out, as the real
George Washington had done, silent and alone, ahead of his generals. They
could come back afterwards and drink all they liked at lunch.

Washington made six trips into or through Connecticut, which was loyal
to him to the core. His last visit was on his triumphant tour of southern
New England in the autumn after his inauguration. He came back to meet
his old friends and to acquaint himself with the common people of the
northeast, their habits, the yield of their soil along the valleys, their pioneer
industries in the larger villages, and their ways of life in general. It was a
leisurely trip, this time not on horseback but in a coach drawn by four
horses over his old route from New Haven to Springfield and Boston via
Middletown and Hartford, where he purchased cloth for a suite of clothes
at the first woolen mill built in the State. He often put up at an inn and
after breakfast or before dinner walked about the village to view the prospect from surrounding hills. In his diary he wrote: "There is a great equal-
ity in the people of this State. Few or no opulent men—and no poor." But
he was irked by the Connecticut law which prevented traveling on the
Sabbath Day and made it expedient for him to pass a Sunday at a poor inn
and listen to "two very lame discourses" in a village meetinghouse.

Of high international import were three special trips which Washington
made in 1780–81 from his headquarters on the Hudson over to Hartford
and beyond to confer with Rochambeau and other French officers in command of several thousand soldiers in Newport, Rhode Island, who had
been sent across the seas by France to coöperate with him against the British in the hope of bringing the war to a speedy close. The main question
at issue was the best disposition of the French troops. Neither of the first

two conferences settled the matter. The third was a triumph for Washington's strategy. At noon on September 21, 1781, Washington and General Knox, who had arrived at Hartford two days earlier, met Rochambeau and his officers in gay uniforms and conducted them in a full-dress military parade to Wethersfield where the conference was to be held. With Washington were Governor Trumbull and Colonel Wadsworth as advisers. The next morning Rochambeau accepted Washington's plan for the campaign. The French troops at Newport were to join Washington's army on the Hudson. Army and Navy were to threaten New York, then in the hands of the British, and move southward as circumstances might permit to attack Cornwallis, wherever he might be. The outcome was the victory at Yorktown where they found him.

The three days of entertainment at the conference cost the State £291, of which more than half went into wines, punch, toddy, grog, brand-slings, and broken glass. In addition to so large a sum in good Connecticut currency, Washington entered in his account book a personal expenditure of £35 10s. High drinking which gave a wide range of choice to different palates no doubt contributed to a quick decision on the strategy destined to win the war.

Because of Washington's intimate associations with Connecticut many celebrations were planned throughout the State, which were in a general way under the supervision of a commission appointed by the Governor with the approval of the General Assembly. By general agreement Lebanon was selected for the last of these—Lebanon where time had stood still for a century and a half, leaving the village nearly as it was when Washington first saw it. In all ways the scene was reminiscent of the Revolution. The platform on which I stood was in the rear of the beautiful church designed by Col. John Trumbull, the great portrait painter, who was the second aide-de-camp to General Washington. Before me was a large Yankee audience of my own lineage in which were represented all the patriotic organizations founded to keep in memory from generation to generation our War of Independence. From my point of vantage I could look some distance down the mile-long Lebanon Green where Washington had reviewed Connecticut militia and Rochambeau had encamped with five regiments of French troops on his way from Newport to Washington's army on the Hudson. Facing the Green in full sight were the house of Governor Trumbull and his War Office, where he had conferred not only with Washington and Rochambeau and Lafayette but with Franklin, Jefferson, and John and Samuel Adams. There William Williams and other freemen met in 1770, after the Boston Massacre, and drafted a declaration of rights and liberties, six years before the Declaration of Independence.

As I was then midway in a political campaign it was quite natural for me to congratulate Lebanon on being the birthplace of six Connecticut Governors and to express a wish that I had lived in the good old times of Jonathan Trumbull who was elected unanimously to the high office for fifteen consecutive years without the trouble of stumping the State. The remark seems to have had some effect, for in the following November election Republican Lebanon gave me 141 votes against 61 in 1930!

XXII. The Campaign of 1932

Early in 1932 the political cauldron began to boil and bubble. One day in March a stalwart and fine-looking man was ushered into my office at the Capitol. He announced that he was a Republican from Missouri on the way from Boston to Washington for a conference with President Hoover. He remarked that he had heard in Boston that I was seeking the nomination for Vice-President on the Democratic ticket. I sketched out for him the true story, which was about like this: The proposal that I try for the nomination for this high office really originated with a group of Connecticut Democratic politicians who were endeavoring to shove me out of the Governor's chair in favor of another man "who would listen to reason." Once in the air, it was taken up by the press along the Atlantic seaboard. Now and then a newspaper even came out for me as President on the ground that it would be an interesting experiment to have in the White House "a man who tells right out what he thinks about things . . . in ordinary words such as you use around your own house." On mature consideration, however, most newspapers came to the conclusion that my age was rather too advanced for a President's job, though I might be able to endure the light labors of a Vice-President. As a precedent was cited Senator Henry Gassaway Davis of Maryland, whom the Democrats once nominated for Vice-President at the age of eighty-one. True, he wasn't elected, but he would have been good for two terms and for several years of rest thereafter before passing on into paradise at the ripe age of ninety-three. Still, though I was comparatively a young man, I told the Missourian that he need have no fear that I would enter the lists against his friend, Vice-President Charles Curtis.

Again, as two years before, the Democratic party in Connecticut approached the campaign, this time national as well as state, with a cupboard which was bare. In the emergency I came forward with a cheque large enough to pay the rental of Bushnell Memorial Hall, across the street from the Capitol, for the May Convention called to elect delegates to the

Democratic National Convention to be held in Chicago six weeks later. For months a storm had been brewing between the two bitter factions in the party which I had tried in vain to mitigate. When all hope was lost I withdrew and let the rain fall and the wind blow wherever they might list.

Pandemonium reigned (this is a pun) for two days at the Convention in the Bushnell Memorial. It was a noisy contest of applause, boos, and catcalls between the Old Guard, augmented by a newcomer, Mayor Hayes of Waterbury, and the New Guard who had lost some prestige since 1930. Each faction was after full control of the Democratic organization—specifically of the National Committeeman and Committeewoman and the delegates to the National Convention. The Old Guard, who were in a small but safe majority, wanted the delegates instructed to vote for Al Smith, and the New Guard, who were for Franklin Roosevelt, wanted them to go to Chicago without instructions on the presidential nominee. In the maneuvers of the Old Guard there was a covert intent to chuck me out as candidate for Governor. Any move, however, in that direction was for the present rendered inexpedient by the loud reception of my opening address to the Convention.

Except for this address, I kept away from the Convention hall and made it clear that I would take neither side in the acrimonious disputes which were certain to arise. I had pleaded for cooperation and had been unheeded. Now it was up to the delegates to work out their own salvation and save the party from disruption and disaster. But I had on the floor of the Convention two able representatives, Kenneth Wynne and my friend Dick Smith of the Yale Law School, to report to me from time to time what was going on and to urge harmonious action whenever there was a chance.

With a whoop and a yell the Convention quickly passed a resolution instructing the delegates to the National Democratic Convention to vote as a unit for nomination of Alfred E. Smith for President and to keep it up until released by him. This resolution, suddenly sprung on the Convention by the Old Guard and put through by a *viva-voce* vote, flabbergasted the friends of Roosevelt, of whom there was a large minority. In turn the New Guard introduced a resolution endorsing Archibald McNeil for reëlection as National Chairman, which on a roll call was defeated by a comparatively few votes. Needless to say, no resolution concerning myself either for Governor or for a place on the national ticket showed its head. The Old Guard was technically in command. Its position never-theless was perilous for itself and for the party.

In the crisis, both Guards being a little nervous over the situation, Pro-fessor Smith stepped forward with a resolution, seconded by Kenneth Wynne, to the effect that the election of a National Committeeman and Committeewoman be left to the delegates to the Chicago Convention on the understanding that they should seek the advice of the Governor and adhere to it. After considerable debate this action, which squinted two ways, was taken. I interpreted it to mean that the two Connecticut members of the National Committee were really to be appointed by myself. In spite of all maneuvering by the two Guards I had come out on top by keeping quiet.

The Connecticut delegation was borne to Chicago on a special train named "The Charter Oak," which pulled out of New Haven on a Sat-urday in June. Just before leaving the station a snapshot was taken of me in the engineer's seat, hands on the wheel, as a symbol of leadership! The Charter Oak halted for several hours in Detroit, time enough for the admirers of Father Coughlin to derive out to his Shrine of the Little Flower. I went along with them. To their disappointment, the radio priest was not there. He was already in Chicago promoting the political interests of Roosevelt. Near an ugly tower, denominated a shrine, was Father Coughlin's plain church, where most of us attended Mass. Two young priests with beautifully trained voices officiated at the altar. I had a pleasant talk with them before leaving. The next morning we all arrived in Chicago and put up at the Hotel Sherman for a week of bedlam at the Stadium where the Democratic Convention was held. In miscellaneous ways I performed meticulously the duties of a leader of the Connecticut delegation, which included a short speech seconding the nomination of the Happy Warrior and the honor of carrying at the head of a noisy pro-cession a banner bearing his name written in large letters.

At length came the memorable session of Friday evening, July 1, when

on the fourth ballot Governor Roosevelt was nominated as the Democratic candidate for President of the United States. Not being in the secret,
I went over to the Stadium expecting that this ballot would be inconclu-
sive like the previous three. But when in alphabetical call of States California, whose delegates had been pledged for John Garner, the favorite
son of Texas, went over to Roosevelt, it was reasonably certain that the
Democratic ticket would be Roosevelt and Garner. In rapid succession,
State after State jumped on the band wagon. Connecticut was the first
not to be stampeded. As Al Smith had not yet released the Connecticut
delegation, I quietly cast her sixteen votes for him and was loudly
applauded by his friends in well-packed galleries. Really, however, I was
like the boy who stood on the burning deck whence all but him had fled.

There were lively scenes at the Hotel Sherman and elsewhere that
night. The "unholy deal" between Roosevelt and Garner was denounced.
Portrait posters of Roosevelt were ripped to pieces and insane rumors
were afloat as to what was going to happen in the Convention hall the
next day. Two hours after midnight Roosevelt called me over the telephone from Albany for a little talk. I promised my full and ardent support
and told him that I had already arranged for a meeting of the Connecticut
delegation in the morning to elect the State's representatives on the
National Committee.

At that meeting I recommended the reëlection of Archibald McNeil
as National Committeeman. Debate on the question was forestalled by a
request from Roosevelt himself, presented by Homer Cummings, that we
take this action. The vote for McNeil was unanimous. Trouble arose when
on my own request Fannie Dixon Welch was nominated for National
Committeewoman. A hot debate ensued. I argued that, though I had no
personal objection to a rival candidate whom certain delegates had in
mind, Roosevelt was entitled to have in this position a woman devoted
without any doubt to his cause. Then I put the question on a *viva-voce*
vote and declared Mrs. Welch elected. At once irreconcilable members of
the Old Guard jumped up and walked out of the room in a huff, as if by
concerted action.

The tussle between the two factions was renewed at the Convention for the nomination for state ticket, held in September, as two years before at the Hotel Griswold on the rocks of Eastern Point. Without formally announcing my candidacy for renomination as Governor, I let it be known that I was in a receptive mood. In the meantime I sought to smooth out all factional differences.

The stumbling block to agreement was Daniel J. Leary whom the Old Guard wanted renominated for second place on the ticket. My opposition to Leary was based on my experience with him during the campaign of 1930. A pleasant fellow enough, his ten-minute speeches were nothing more than an appeal to his audiences to vote the Democratic ticket because of the multitude of jobs which would fall into the laps of the faithful as soon as the Democrats came into power. As a dealer in beverages during the prohibition era, he evoked considerable mirth just before the campaign was closing by issuing a circular letter to his fellow bottlers of the State urging them to vote for him on the ground that it would be a good thing to have a bottler at the Capitol to fill quick orders.

The political situation was apparent on my arrival at Eastern Point towards evening on Wednesday, September 7, to listen to the eloquent keynote speech of Robert Butler. The rank and file of the delegates, as shown by the applause, expected my nomination for Governor without a contest. The leaders of the New Guard submitted to me for approval a partial list of nominees for the entire ticket. The Old Guard likewise had their partial list, which they did not divulge beyond the name of Leary for Lieutenant Governor, on whose nomination they were to insist to the bitter end. If I would accept him, it was intimated, nominees for the rest of the ticket would be left for negotiations with me. Otherwise, they would ignore my opposition to Leary and proceed in their own way, which was rather cleverly devised. It was clearly their intent to move my nomination for Governor by acclamation and then move that the same action be taken for Leary as Lieutenant Governor, and so on down through the rest of their ticket. The weak point in this program was the assumption that my desire to go on as Governor was so strong that, however much I might squirm, I would be forced to take the punishment they had in store for me. There they were mistaken.

That night I slept soundly while others were conferring, for I had thought out with Kenneth Wynne a plan to outmaneuver my political enemies. On waking in an elated mood, I began to hum the famous lines of the Earl of Montrose:

> He either fears his fate too much,
>   Or his deserts are small,
> Who dares not put it to the touch
>   To win or lose it all.

Primed for a fight, I drew up a ticket in the morning with the aid of a few friends. In place of Leary we put Thomas Hewes or Michael Connor, the choice between them to be determined by the general situation as it might develop.

The Convention, call for ten o'clock, did not convene until nearly noon. It was three o'clock when Kenneth Wynne, whom I had chosen to put my name in nomination, took the platform and, in accordance with my request, asked Chairman Butler that the nomination of Governor be held in abeyance until after the nomination of a Lieutenant Governor. The proposal was greeted by Leary's followers with boos, hoots, and cries of "shut up" and "put him out," which were, however, soon drowned by the wild cheering of the rank and file of the delegates. The Convention was in an uproar. Quiet partially restored, there followed a series of events more dramatic than I anticipated. Against the protests and yells of Leary's friends, the Convention voted a recess, which lasted for an hour, for con- ferences between the leaders of the two factions, in which I maintained an immovable stand against Leary, though I was willing to consider another Waterbury man instead of him. Almost equally objectionable were certain nominees proposed for other places on the state ticket, whose names were then first made known to me. With them and Leary as running mates, I could see nothing but defeat for us all on election day. I surmised that this was the intent of a double-headed machine.

The recess over, the Convention was informed that no agreement had been reached. Thereupon, on the motion of Wynne, the delegates voted amid more yells and applause that the rules of the Convention be suspended and the nomination of Governor be deferred until all the other nominations were made. When the fury awakened among Leary's friends by this action had subsided, the men on the ticket I had drawn up in the morning were nominated, one by one, without contest. Thomas Hewes was the nominee for Lieutenant Governor. For better or for worse we had put the fate of the Democratic party in Connecticut as well as my own fate to the test and had won. As I walked through one door into the Convention hall to deliver my acceptance speech, Leary's followers were walking out by another door into the lobby.

The Republicans nominated as their candidate for Governor my three-term predecessor, John H. Trumbull, who after my inauguration in 1931, remarked, according to a report from the golf links of St. Petersburg, Florida: "I believe that I could have defeated an opponent had I wanted a fourth term, but carrying out traditions of the family I told party leaders I did not choose to run."

The campaign was late in starting. Time was required for bringing the two Democratic factions to an understanding; and the Republican leaders were concealing the hand they intended to play. The interim was mine to find out, so far as I was able, how I stood with various groups of citizens irrespective of party divisions, first of all with the farmers. I visited all the country fairs to which I was invited, inspecting the exhibits, discussing with the farmers their problems, of which the most acute was the sad case of milk producers who were receiving from distributors no more on the average than 3¢ a quart for their fluid milk. My advice, which met with approval, was that an appeal for remedial legislation be made to the next General Assembly and the Governor whoever he might be. That was the closest I came to politics. As a result of my canvass of country districts and industrial centers, I concluded that I was likely to receive enough rural and labor votes, taken together, to offset any losses because of factional quarrels within the Democratic ranks.

To appease these quarrels the Democratic High Command brought into the State several prominent men of the party who, after strenuously opposing nomination of Roosevelt, had come out for his election in no

uncertain language. Conspicuous among them were Governor Ritchie of
Maryland and Governor Ely of Massachusetts, who was a favorite of the
Connecticut Democracy. They both urged complete support of the
national and state tickets and predicted victory. The climax of this appeasement effort was a trip of Al Smith through the State along the shore to
Providence and Boston. Wearing a brown derby which matched his,
I boarded his train at Stamford. As I entered his private car I saw seated
together in the rear leaders of the Old and New Guards, neither of whom,
as I read their looks correctly, seemed quite at ease. I rode on as far as
New London, where I left the train for Hartford. All the way heavy
autumnal rains poured down. Great crowds nevertheless greeted Al at all
stations where the train was scheduled to stop, the largest being in New
Haven. His voice already husky, he did not dare to speak in the wet air.
So he gesticulated and threw cigars into the crowd and give reporters
copies of the speech he would have liked to make, telling everybody to
cast a ballot for a straight Democratic ticket, state and national.

This pantomime journey was followed by big rallies throughout the
State, in nearly all of which both factions took part. On the surface reconciliation seemed complete, except in Waterbury where an attempt was
made to stage mainly an Old Guard rally, to which I was not to be invited.
I announced, however, that I would be there and have something to say.
Then the invitation came and I was loudly acclaimed by the rank and file
for my nerve. What I most missed when the campaign got into full swing
was the presence of Roosevelt himself. Early in September Mr. and Mrs.
Roosevelt had indeed been given an enthusiastic reception in Bridgeport
as the guests of Mr. and Mrs. McNeil, but that was a social affair. And a
few days before the election he drove into Connecticut from Massachusetts but he had to cut short his tour because of a very hard rain. In neither
instance was he visible to the great mass of voters who determine elections. Still, it seemed reasonably certain that he would carry the State.

It was well on in October before the Republicans showed their hand
on the state campaign. I was then basing my claims for reelection on my
record, and tried to enliven the details by describing the ways in which
political opponents frustrated some of my plans for the promotion of the

public welfare. It was all rather good-natured ridicule which audiences greeted with laughter. To my surprise there were few or no retorts from Republican orators. At the same time Mr. Trumbull, making little or no attempt to justify the behavior of the leaders of his party in the General Assembly of 1931, was extolling his three administrations during which he pursued a pay-as-you-go policy and created a large surplus in the general funds of the State. I replied that I, too, advocated the same fiscal policy in my first Inaugural Message but was prevented from putting it into effect by Republicans who denied me the legislation necessary in a period of depression which they regarded as only psychological.

There was one light passage of arms between us. Mr. Trumbull intimated that I was showing a lack of devotion to my State by smoking Sumatra cigars. This was a good opening for the retort that the wrapper of my favorite cigar was shade-grown, native tobacco, which, though it looked like the product of a rich tropical valley, really came from the rich valley of the Connecticut River. The binder, I admitted, was grown in Ohio and the filler in Pennsylvania, States which were now going over into the Democratic column.

By this time it was clear that the Republican High Command had adopted the policy of ignoring what I might say. Let Cross go on talking until he talks himself out. Pay no attention to him. Give him no chance for comebacks. Organization, not talk, will eliminate a Democratic Governor for good. Get the full Republican vote out on election day. That is all there is to it. Such, I imagined, was the advice which Roraback received from his lieutenants, who were this year managing the Republican campaign for him.

"The boys" were more brazen in their methods than they were two years before. They openly organized all the departments of the State, except those under Democratic control, for the collection of campaign funds and for work on election day. They appointed a chairman, a secretary, and a treasurer of their organization, who in turn appointed one or more agents in each department to "shake down" employees and to distribute cards inquiring of them what automobiles they would have available for taking voters to the polls. For the faithful, election day was to be a grand holiday. Several employees asked me if they should sign the cards. My advice was to wait awhile and see what would happen. Reporters got hold of these cards and inquired of various Republican heads of departments whether they were distributed with their knowledge and approval. Some heads were silent. Others approved and added that they could see nothing wrong in the procedure. The whole story was played up in newspapers and was savagely condemned by Republican and Democratic editors alike. After exposure, the organization went on with the job under cover, and in order to raise sufficient funds Commissioners or their deputies, I was told, were compelled to take a hand in the shaking-down process.

It was believed by rank partisans that they had got me this time. Within the Capitol, in the very anteroom of my office, it was asserted that I could not possibly be reëlected.

I came out with a five-point program, combining the old and the new, looking forward, I hoped, rather than backward. The five points were headlined in the newspapers and ably discussed by editors, for the most part favorably. The contest was clear-cut. It was a contest between a party which had a progressive program and a party which had an organization strong enough, it was thought, to whip into line all its members. The issue was doubtful.

The morning of the day arrived when the issue was to be settled by the electorate. I voted early and was in my office at the Capitol at the usual hour. Disturbing rumors immediately began to come in. I was being heavily cut, it was said, in Waterbury. On the heels of this story an independent Hartford Republican, greatly excited, came into my office with the news that the Democrats in his ward had no automobiles to bring voters to the polls, while the Republicans had automobiles without number. On inquiry over the telephone I learned that the situation was the same in other wards of the city. I learned, too, that the reason given for the lack of Democratic automobiles was lack of funds. Was it true, I wondered, that certain Democratic leaders were working in collusion with the Republican organization for my defeat? If so, the only hope was that the number of Republican votes for me would balance any Democratic loss. Before the day was over I corralled a score of automobiles with the aid of a few friends. New hope also came when I was told that Hartford Democrats in large numbers were walking to the polls.

That evening I sat with friends at the Hartford Club listening to election returns. In another room at the end of the hall were ex-Governor Trumbull and his family, and we had a pleasant conversation. In a long room between, the chef and his waiters were making preparations for an elaborate victory supper for the ex-Governor and his political friends to be served at midnight. The situation caused some humorous comment. By ten-thirty when the votes for me were piling up in cities, boroughs, and many country towns I felt certain that I was elected Governor again. On a dare of a member of the Hartford Club I ate three sandwiches from a table intended for others, drank a Manhattan, went over to the *Hartford Times* building for a tabulation of the votes, and started for home to receive the greetings of my family and neighbors (among whom there were as many Republicans as Democrats), and to make porch speeches to delegates who came to bid me good morning and good luck.

The full election returns, as they came in the next morning, seemed peculiar. I was elected by a plurality nearly twice as large as in 1930, but the other nominees on the Democratic state ticket failed of election by a few hundred to a few thousand votes. Lonergan, the Democratic candidate for Senator, was elected, while Citron, the Democratic candidate for Congressman-at-Large, was beaten by over 2,000 votes. Of the 6 candidates for Congress the Republicans elected 4, all but 1 on a close vote. Roosevelt, who stood on a platform for repeal of the Eighteenth Amendment, lost in Connecticut to Hoover, still advocating prohibition, by a plurality of nearly 7,000, though a referendum on a petition to Congress to submit to the States a virtual repeal of the Eighteenth Amendment was carried by a vote of 6 to 1.

This illogical outcome of the election indicated that there had been much cutting by members of both parties, by several thousand Democrats, presumably irreconcilable Al Smith supporters who voted for Hoover, and a still larger number of Republicans who voted for me. The Democrats who cut me appear to have been of the faction whose leaders tried to play hide-and-seek with me in the State Convention that nominated me for Governor. A leader of this faction told me face to face that he was sorry I had been elected. I asked the reason. He replied that as a lawyer he was receiving from the State less professional business under my administration than under my predecessor's.

On the whole, the election showed that the Democratic party, despite its divisions, was working its way to the front line in Connecticut. Republican candidates who won came through on slight margins compared with previous years. My plurality was so large that I could no longer be called "a guest" at the Capitol. Augustine Lonergan was to be the first Democratic Senator from Connecticut for more than a half century and the State Senate was to have a majority of one after eighteen years of waiting.

To have one House of the General Assembly Democratic gave me particular satisfaction. How that happened is an untold story. That one Senator necessary for a majority came from a rock-ribbed Republican state senatorial district, largely rural. A friend over there remarked to me one day that he wished he could vote for me, but he couldn't do that, for he was a Republican; but "I can tell you 'bout a Democrat over here who if he was nominated for the Senate he'd be 'lected. Everybody knows him and everybody likes him. I'd have to vote for *him*." "I s'pose you'd have to vote for me, too, if I'm nomnated," I remarked, "for we all three was born in the same town." "I dunno. Might, but get him nomnated fust," he replied. Edwin Dimock, the man to whom he referred, was nominated and elected then and twice afterwards with increasing pluralities.

Democratic control of the Senate was disquieting to those Republican Commissioners who, though they were to come up for reappointment, acquiesced in having their departments made the centers of intense political activity in the hope of ousting me out of office. A fortnight after the election one of these Commissioners called on me to say that he had been offered a big job outside the public service and that it would help him to come to a decision in regard to it if he knew whether I intended to send his name to the Senate for reappointment. I advised him to take the big job if he wanted to play safe. Of course I could not initiate the appointment of any commissioner who had taken, in what he regarded as his own interest, a flier on my defeat.

If a man loses a bet, he has nothing to complain of, however serious the consequences may be. The moral is that otherwise one should never bet. I have sometimes bet, but always well within my means so that if the other fellow won I should not be financially embarrassed (a word I learned with difficulty to spell correctly when a boy). Ten days after the election I made my last public bet, which was the smallest since childhood. It happened in this way: I was attending the annual conference of the New England Council in Boston, where in a financial discussion I explained the difference between a bank that is 100 per cent liquid and a prohibitionist who in his habits is 100 per cent liquid. The treasurer of the Council, John S. Lawrence, remarked that Harvard was going to wallop Yale in the forthcoming football game at New Haven. I asked him how much he was ready to risk on his foreknowledge. "One cent," he replied. I took the bet which was recorded by a representative of the Associated Press who spread the news over the length and breadth of the land.

Yale won by a score of 19 to 0. The Harvard man was slow to ante up. Hence arose the problem of how to get from him that 1¢. I could not bring suit against him because gambling debts are uncollectible in both Massachusetts and Connecticut. Nor could Lawrence, he was told by a legal friend, send 1¢ by post without violating a Federal law which prohibits the use of the mails in connection with games of chance. So to avoid committing a crime he eventually sent me the red coin as a gift. For its safe arrival he enclosed it, glued to a visiting card, in the smallest of a series of eight envelopes, one within another, with registry and special delivery stamps amounting to 24¢. He claimed, however, when interviewed by the press, that he made a quarter out of a one-cent bet by selling my signature for a half dollar. When a man is foolish enough to bet he may technically win and yet really lose. This lesson I pass on to all who hazard their money or their jobs on the unpredictable outcome of a game or an election.

XXIII. The General Assembly of 1933

Banks, Labor, and Alcohol

The General Assembly convened on January 4, 1933. The Democrats of the Senate, with their majority of one, chose as their floor leader Frank Bergin, who had brilliantly served in this office under my first administration and as their President pro tempore David Goldstein. The Democrats in the House, where they were in an aggressive minority, elected as their floor leader John A. Markham. The Republican leader of the Senate was Howard W. Alcorn, and of the House Raymond Baldwin, who in 1931 had joined with others in an attempt to shear the locks of the Governor, whose had was not yet bald. The Speaker was William Hanna of Bethel, a neighbor of Harry Mackenzie. The three were able young men, socially agreeable, representing, however, the Republican organization rather than the rank and file of their party. Their function, it was anticipated, would be not merely to harass a Democratic Governor but to kill the legislation he might advocate in so far as that could be done without arousing a hostile public opinion to the danger point. For the Republicans a fly in the ointment was the election to the Senate of that Democrat in a hitherto Republican district, Dimock of Mansfield. On the first returns Dimock's plurality was announced as only one vote. Another count of all the votes of the district, it was then hoped, might give the election to his Republican opponent. But while this question of a recount was in the air, it transpired that, owing to a mistake in the tabulation of votes, Dimock's plurality was not one but a hundred and one, altogether too many to overcome. The fly remained in the ointment. At the same time many Democrats, among them the Governor, feared that danger lay in wait for them in a Senate where the Democratic majority was but one. Already there was an ugly rumor that a Democratic Senator might line up with Republicans in an attempt to cripple the Governor.

Nevertheless, as if only serene days lay ahead, I urged in my Inaugural Message that both political parties, working together, keep an eye single upon the public welfare; for it is written "When thy eye is single thy whole body is full of light." "Nothing can be accomplished," I commented, "whenever the mind moves in the darkness or in the twilight of partisanship." To the best of my ability I argued for the enactment of legislation which had failed in the last General Assembly and for the immediate consideration of financial and social legislation made necessary by the continuing depression which was producing a crisis in the affairs of the Commonwealth.

By February 1 it became evident that a deal was forming between a small group of Democratic Senators and Republican leaders, within and without the Assembly, for a division of the spoils of city, borough, and town courts. Three Democratic Senators who were under the influence of a leader of the Old Guard bolted, and on Washington's Birthday, according to reports, met with two lieutenants of the Republican organization to determine who were to be judges of the courts of Hartford and vicinity. Subsequently they settled the judgeships for all the minor courts of the State, except one or two which for lack of agreement they had to leave to the mercy of the Governor. In general, if not in all cases, the recommendations of five politicians were approved by the Assembly on joint resolutions. Fifteen of the eighteen Democratic Senators kept out of the deal. On roll calls they voted as a rule nay.

In an interview with reporters I described the men who put through the deal as maggots on the body politic, like the maggots I used as a boy to watch break out of huckleberries, crawl over them for a while and feed, and then grow sluggish and perhaps drop dead. The disquisition, which was regarded as a humorous exaggeration, caused but slight offense. Editorial comment was very savage on the judgeship deal, which, it was feared, might be the first step towards a general coalition in the Senate to scrap the Governor's legislative program. The fear proved ungrounded. After the three bolting Democratic Senators had split up the minor courts to the satisfaction of the Old Guard, they fell into line, with now and then an exception, in formal support of the measures advocated in the Democratic platform and in my Inaugural Message.

With Senator Cooney, a very astute and likable young man then associated with the Old Guard, I had many informal talks over prospective
legislation, one of which neither of us can ever forget. Early in the session
a member of the House introduced, by request of the tax collector of
West Haven, a bill providing in its main intent for the taxation of all real
estate owned by Yale University outside New Haven if used for athletic
purposes. Yale was already paying taxes on its ball fields where a fee was
charged for admission to public games, but claimed, under its charter and
subsequent legislation, exemption of taxation on a large tract of land in
West Haven which was being developed as a recreational center with

Portrait of Wilbur L. Cross by Underwood &
Underwood NYC, n.d.
Courtesy, Mansfield Historical Society

tennis courts and golf links solely for the use of students and faculty. A special bill aiming openly at the taxation of this recreational center stood no chance of favorable action by the General Assembly. So its proponents looked about for some way to make the bill appear more general in character though serving the same purpose. With the aid of the State Tax Department, they undertook a survey of all the athletic fields of educational institutions within the State and discovered, so they thought, that among them all Yale was the only one which owned athletic property outside the town wherein a school or college had its local habitation. In the light of this discovery the original bill was amended by substituting "educational institutions" in place of Yale University. By this clever device the way seemed to be cleared for taxing Yale's athletic development in West Haven without raising a rumpus elsewhere. Towards the close of the session the amended bill was rushed through both branches of the General Assembly without a public hearing. I returned it to the General Assembly with a veto message in which I took the position that physical training as a means of preserving the health of students was a part of the educational process. The House immediately repassed the bill over my veto.

Action by the Senate on my veto was scheduled to be taken the next day. I thus had but a few hours for preventing if possible my veto being overridden by the Senate. In a search for another educational institution besides Yale which might be affected by the bill, I picked up the telephone and asked Monsignor Flynn, the Chancellor of the Catholic diocese of Hartford, whether St. Thomas Seminary, a divinity school for the training of Catholic clergy, and its athletic field were in the same town. He replied that its main buildings were in Bloomfield but that if an athletic field were developed it would run over the boundary line into West Hartford. Thereupon I told him why I had asked. He was greatly disturbed. As it was too late for a public hearing, one or the other of us suggested that a conference be held in the Governor's office during the afternoon with the Catholic Bishop of Hartford and himself and such others as I might think it well to invite. I immediately called into my office Senator Cooney, a sponsor of the bill, for one of our little talks. He informed me that my veto would certainly be overridden in the Senate the next morning and then

launched out on some severe criticism of Yale's attempt to escape just
taxation on its real estate. While he was proceeding at a good speed I interrupted him to remark that as a good Catholic he ought to know that St.
Thomas Seminary would be hard hit by the bill as the boundary line
between Bloomfield and West Hartford ran straight through its property,
perhaps cutting off the athletic field. "Bishop McAuliffe and Monsignor
Flynn," I informed him, "are coming in for a conference with me at four
o'clock and I am sure that they would like to hear you expound your
views on the taxation of educational institutions." He stared, then smiled,
and said a conference was not necessary for he would have the bill tabled
when it came up for passage in the morning. In this manner the bill was
quietly put to death.

A series of measures which failed in the General Assembly of 1931 now
failed again, partially or completely, because of Republican opposition.
Proposals for amendments to the Constitution for giving the Governor
larger veto power over legislation and for establishing a District Court
system in place of local minor courts went down to quick defeat. So, too,
fared old-age assistance and jury service for women and several other
measures. The Republican leader of the House feared that if women were
permitted to sit in the jury box, they would lose "that sweet femininity
that makes the sex so blessed." I was amused as well as startled by the fact
that the Democrats in the Senate voted solidly for the District Court bill
on the very day when three of them were in the midst of the court deal
against which the press was thundering. Rather more consideration was
accorded a recommendation that the Governor be authorized to appoint
a commission to make an exhaustive study of our public service statutes
with a view to their complete revision, and their extension, where deemed
necessary. I did not get that authority. Perhaps I was premature in suggesting that the time was arriving when the State would be faced with
the problem of rural electrification at low cost to consumers. I soon saw
that I had merely hoisted a red flag which frightened electric light and
power companies.

The fiscal condition of the State was then a cause of great concern.
During the last twelve months the income from taxation had been falling

off heavily. Without drastic remedial legislation, the deficit promised to amount to $12,000,000 or more by June, 1935. I suggested temporary expedients for ameliorating the desperate situation, such as the abolition of the office of coroner, whose investigations of former times were already being largely conducted by the State Police, and of the traffic court of Danbury, which had no value, so far as I could see, except as one court more for judgeship deals.

All these recommendations were anathema to politicians whose interest was first in jobs. A bill authorizing the Governor to appoint a commission to report on a plan for the reorganization of the State Government two years hence was overwhelmingly defeated in the House; and when it came up for action in the Senate, one Democrat being absent, the result was a tie vote which was broken by Lieutenant Governor Wilcox who cast his vote against the measure. Nothing was left on which there was agreement for the reduction of expenditures except a cut in the salaries of state employees and officers, the details of which were to be worked out on a graduated scale of percentage by the Board of Finance and Control. Generous as was the cut it came nowhere near balancing the books. The drop in the Governor's annual salary was from $5,000 to $4,300. In my Farewell Address to the General Assembly I asked the members why they did not cut their own compensation to the same tune, by which, according to my mental arithmetic $100,000 might have been prevented from going down the river. They laughed.

On taxation the same policy of delay was adopted. The Governor was granted authority, under pressure of the Connecticut Chamber of Commerce, to appoint a commission of seven experts and businessmen to submit to the next General Assembly a plan for a comprehensive revision of the existing structure of state and municipal taxation. But no legislation besides the salary cut was enacted for the immediate ease of the fiscal situation. The State was to go on piling up during the next two years a deficit against which there was no check except such as might be devised by the Board of Finance and Control, to whom the buck was passed.

In sharp contrast was the nonpolitical manner in which the General Assembly dealt with the banking and insurance crisis. On my arrival in Washington very early in the morning of Saturday, March 4, to attend the inauguration of President Roosevelt, I was informed by reporters that the President intended to proclaim a bank holiday after taking the oath of office. That night I hurried back to Connecticut to take such action in behalf of the State as might be necessary in connection with the President's proclamation. I found that Lieutenant Governor Wilcox, acting as Governor in my absence, had unearthed an old statute which enabled him to designate Saturday and the ensuing Monday as "days of fasting" and as such he declared them to be "legal holidays." On Monday I extended the proclamation to Tuesday and Wednesday. This was the best that could be done, for there was no Connecticut statute empowering the Governor to proclaim specifically bank holidays.

I immediately called a conference of the leaders of both political parties and representative bankers in different parts of the State to meet with me on Tuesday morning, the first legislative day of the week, to consider a program which might safeguard all the State's banking institutions, whatever their character. On that very day the General Assembly passed a bill under a suspension of the rules, conferring upon the Governor the power to declare "legal holidays to be known as bank holidays" during which all banking transactions were required to be suspended except that the Bank Commissioner, with the approval of the Governor, might prescribe for any or all state bank regulations in conformity with the regulations "prescribed by the Secretary of the Treasury with the approval of the President of the United States." At once I signed the bill and issued a proclamation which I had already written.

This was the first of seven acts which, taken together, gave ample protection to Connecticut banks of every description. The time was also auspicious for new measures providing for the merger of two or more banks and for a restricted system of branch banking. For all this legislation, usually originating in the Senate, credit was due to the leadership of Senator Wadhams, himself a banker, whose sound judgment, based upon long experience, carried great weight with both political parties.

Some hesitancy over insurance legislation was quickly overcome when the tired president of a life insurance company, at my request, appeared before a conference of legislators to tell the story of the demand of policy holders, large and small, for the immediate cash surrender values of their policies or for loans upon them. The next day Senator Blackall, Chairman of the Insurance Committee, introduced a bill which gave the Insurance Commissioner, subject to the approval of the Governor, almost dictatorial control of the State's life insurance companies during the bank-holiday period. Without debate the bill passed both Houses under a suspension of the rules. By this act loans and surrenders were carefully regulated in the interest of insurance companies and policy holders equally.

Meanwhile the unemployment situation was becoming more serious. A procession of "Hunger Marchers" who were tramping the State halted at Hartford and surrounded the Capitol. They brought a petition demanding of the Assembly an appropriation of $10,000,000 for the relief of men and women out of work. Police kept them out of the Capitol while five of them came in to see me. I received their petition to be passed on to the Assembly and held out hopes to them for help either from the State or the Federal Government. They left in good cheer. I sat for a long time at my desk to think over what could be done for all in their situation.

A delegation of Mayors also come to urge that the State take over all welfare work. The Connecticut Unemployment Commission, it was conceded, had been of great help to municipal committees in an advisory capacity. But more than advice was now needed. The Mayors suggested that the General Assembly lay a special sales tax, or issue serial bonds, or divert a part of the income from the existing gasoline tax for aid to the unemployed.

No relief program such as was submitted by the Mayors and hungry men and women, I soon discovered, was in immediate sight. Nothing more could be expected from legislation than wider leeway for municipalities to issue bonds. The 169 cities and towns of the State were to be left to bear individually the fast-increasing burdens of unemployment which were causing distress in industrial centers such as Connecticut had never known before. Suddenly the face of the picture changed when in May, 1933, Congress passed the National Industrial Recovery Act for giving financial assistance to the States, many of which could no longer cope with the rising tide of cost for relief. I immediately requested the four floor leaders of the Assembly to draft a bill to set up machinery for receiving and allotting, under state supervision, Federal grants to municipalities for relief purposes. The result was an act creating for the State a Municipal Finance and Unemployment Relief Commission for five members besides the Governor who was to serve in an ex-officio capacity. On June 7, the day the Assembly adjourned, I put my signature to a measure for the control of municipal finance so drastic as to make my hair stand on end like Macbeth's after he had murdered Duncan. The Commission, for instance, was empowered to authorize during the emergency a municipality to issue serial bonds for unemployment relief under the State's guarantee for their payment. In case of default on the payment of interest thereon, the Commission might apply to a judge of the Superior Court for the appointment of a receiver for that municipality. In face of these dangerous provisions I approved the bill because it placed municipal relief under state supervision and permitted the Commission to apply to the Federal Government for such financial aid as Congress might make available "for emergency, industrial, or unemployment relief purposes."

The story of what was accomplished is too big and too intricate to relate here. It is a marvelous story. I recall the excitement occasioned by the first Federal grant which was engineered by Mr. Hook, chairman of the old Connecticut Unemployment Commission. With Newton Brainard, chairman of the new Commission, he went to Washington on June 15 and obtained within ten minutes a promise from Harry Hopkins, the Federal Administrator, of a large grant for reimbursing the towns to the extent of one third of their relief expenditures during the first three months of 1933. The check, made out to the Governor of the State of Connecticut, arrived ten days later. It read $858,526. This was but the beginning of monthly grants running at times from one to two million dollars. In the course of a year and a half the municipalities received more than $30,000,000, a sum almost equivalent at that time to the entire annual revenue of the State from taxation, including the tax on gasoline. Towns which had been fearing bankruptcy came through safe and sound. Very few of them were forced to issue bonds for relief. None went into the hands of a receiver.

Along with the industrial depression, Connecticut was invaded by sweatshops which were the wings of garment concerns located in New York City. Like a plague they spread out through Fairfield and New Haven Counties, on to New London, and up river valleys. It was estimated that by the end of 1932 there were as many as two hundred of them in the State, of which some fifty could be counted in New Haven alone. The managers of these New York outposts, who were really contractors, usually set up their shops in a loft or abandoned factory which they equipped with a few sewing machines for finishing shirts, underwear, and dresses, the material for which, cut into patterns, was shipped to them from New York manufacturers. Another type of contractor farmed out work to be done at home; and the worst type of the lot took on girls as apprentices for a three months' trial at 5¢ an hour, or in some instances without any wage at all, firing most or all of them at the end of the period as "incompetent."

Commissioner Tone, with the aid of other members of the Department of Labor and Factory Inspection, made a survey of these contemptible sweatshops and aroused public indignation against them by numerous addresses before audiences of all sorts throughout the State. He raided some of the worst of them and drove them out of the State. But existing laws were inadequate for coping with "fly-by-nights." He appealed to the General Assembly for new and drastic legislation which I supported with all my might. Here was a question of the welfare of workers, of fair wages and sanitary conditions of labor, which far transcended party politics. Both Republicans and Democrats united in enactments which, in their judgment, would enable Commissioner Tone to remove a dark blot on the body politic.

The legislation adopted for this purpose was at once simple and effective. It made mandatory that all "manufacturing and mechanical establish-

ments" be registered with the Commissioner of Labor and Factory Inspection by persons conducting them, and that no new establishment of this
kind be opened or permitted to change the location of its business without his written approval. Incidental to the enforcement of the law, the
Commissioner and his deputies were given freedom of ingress, without
obstruction, into any place of business described in the statute. Sweatshops were no longer to be allowed to flourish behind locked doors in
a loft or in dwelling houses and apartments. In dealing with cunning and
unscrupulous employers of labor, Commissioner Tone had a hard time
of it, but he made such rapid progress in ridding Connecticut of sweatshops that within a year only one here and there escaped discovery and
extermination.

The Commissioner was also authorized to appoint a woman, under
the title of Industrial Investigator, to inspect various occupations relative
to wages paid women and minors, their hours of labor, and their health
as affected by their special employment. He selected as his first Industrial
Inspector Helen Wood, later succeeded by Edna Purtell, wide-awake
young women who by strenuous efforts immensely improved the labor
conditions of their sex in factories and miscellaneous occupations. And
beyond expectation new legislation was enacted for the benefit of women
and minors of both sexes. Early in the session a bill was introduced in the
Senate for the creation of a Wage Board in the Department of Labor and
Factory Inspection, with power to determine and enforce in any industry
a scale of fair minimum wages. Nobody thought there was a ghost of a
chance for its passage. As the weeks wore on it seemed to be slowly dying.
But on the day before adjournment, it suddenly rose from the dead and
after being amended in some respects easily passed both Houses of the
General Assembly. Such legislative action in the State was revolutionary.
Nothing like it, I think, had occurred in Connecticut since colonial days.

Harmonious action on labor was a lull in a fierce political storm which
shook Connecticut's Capitoline Hill over legislation for controlling the
manufacture and sale of alcoholic liquors in the event that the Volstead Act
were liberalized or the Eighteenth Amendment repealed. A Commission

THE TOMAHAWK REPLACES THE GAVEL
AT THE RIGHT TIME

of seven members which was approved by the press generally prepared a
liquor bill. It was received by the Assembly in ominous silence. Then talking
in low voice s was heard around the lobby of the Capitol. There were conferences between outside politicians and members of the Assembly in small
dark rooms under the eaves. Rumors were soon afloat that the Commission's liquor bill was to receive its quietus, first in the House where the
Republican majority was overwhelming and then in the Senate by a coalition between the Republican minority and those Democratic members
who had taken part in the minor court deal. It leaked out that another bill
was to be substituted which would decentralize liquor control, presumably
by turning it over to the counties where it was in the old times before
national prohibition came in, when the issuance of licenses by county commissioners was a weapon of tremendous political power.

As soon as I became convinced of the essential truth of these rumors
which were becoming more explicit every day, I went over the radio on
the evening of my birthday, April 10, in a sober address to the people of

the State on the crisis in liquor control which was near at hand. In broad outline I described to them the Commission's bill which aimed to prevent the manufacture and sale of alcoholic liquors from falling back into the old arena of political manipulation. I told them that though I stood unalterably for the bill I must have their immediate active support in order to win the battle against the relentless opposition of politicians who put patronage above the public welfare. I appealed to them, if they agreed with me, to make their views known, by letter and telephone, to the members of the General Assembly, whose leaders I named.

The response to my appeal was instant and beyond my fondest expectations. Nearly all the newspapers of the State came out vigorously for centralized control under the Commission's bill. Likewise the clergy of every communion, Catholic, Protestant and Jew. Likewise men of all professions and occupations, educators and civic and welfare orders and associations, without distinction, whether they were for or against an emasculated Volstead Act and the repeal of the Eighteenth Amendment. At no time in my long memory had there ever been so widespread an awakening of public opinion in the State. Telegrams, letters, resolutions, and telephone messages bombarded my office and members of the General Assembly. It was one loud voice in support of the Governor, reverberating over the hills and through the valleys of Connecticut.

Nevertheless, in defiance of public opinion, the Republican organization moved forward with its secret plan and on April 13 the House received from the Judiciary Committee a report recommending the rejection of the Commission's bill and the passage of a substitute, not for the control of all kinds of alcoholic liquors, but merely for the control of the manufacture and sale of beer up to 4 per cent alcoholic content, as had been made legal by the Congress of the United States. The reason given by the leader of the House for the exclusion of spirituous liquors was that, while the demand for beer regulation was urgent, legislation in regard to liquor of high alcoholic voltage could wait for further consideration until after the State had ratified an amendment to the Federal Constitution repealing the Eighteenth Amendment; perhaps, a political prophet predicted, some two years hence, if ever.

Members of the House who had not been let into the secret conclaves were amazed by the extreme decentralization of wine and beer control which in its downward course did not stop at the counties but sank to the low level of the towns, any one of which might regulate the manufacture and sale of legal beer and wine in almost any way it desired. Town clerks were designated as the agents for the issue of permits, for which any citizen twenty-one years of age or over, whoever he might be, an Al Capone for example, was eligible if he had $25 in his pocket. There were no restrictions on the days of sale except Sundays and none whatever on hours of day or night. If a town so ordained, it might have a chain of saloons, centers of political intrigue, running the length of every street. As a cool-headed Republican remarked, "the bill contained the best method in the world for putting beer and politics together." The proposed act was popularly named the "Baldwin-Alcorn Beer Bill," for the reputed authors were Raymond Baldwin and Howard Alcorn, the respective Republican leaders of the House and Senate.

When Mr. Baldwin presented the new bill and moved that it be made the order of the day for April 18, the House was thrown into an uproar. He was asked if the Judiciary Committee had arranged for a public hearing on so important a measure. He replied that there was no time for that. Then the fun began. A Republican member protested against this haste, flourishing his arms and pounding his desk. Others followed suit. From time to time in the confusion of debate motions were made that the House adjourn, none of which prevailed. A facetious member proposed adjournment until January, 1935. In the end April 18 was set for action.

On the evening of April 14 I went on the air again to explain the provisions of the beer bill which I denounced as a subterfuge to kill the Commission's bill. I asked that the fight be kept up relentlessly. Lieutenant Governor Wilcox as the high-ranking Republican of the Assembly was delegated to reply to my onslaught. He evaded the main question, state *vs.* town control, confining his speech to mild abuse of an emotional Governor and to the inquisitional character of the Commission's bill because it provided for inspectors who were free to nose around in any place where alcoholic liquors were sold. I countered by recalling that the State also had bank, factory, and milk inspectors to see to it that the law was enforced.

By noon of April 18 gallery and lobby were filled with visitors who came to listen to what proved to be an acrimonious four-hour debate, in the midst of which Representative Goodman, as prearranged, quietly moved that the Baldwin-Alcorn bill be amended by striking out all after the enacting clause and inserting in lieu thereof the Commission's bill. This action was taken, after a prolonged hot debate during which the leader of the House failed in an attempt to force an adjournment. The bill was passed by a majority of 4 votes, 63 Republicans voting for it in defiance of their leader. Two days later the amended bill passed the Senate by a vote of 27 to 7, and on my quick signature the Commission's bill became a law, having lost in the progress through the General Assembly nothing but its title. Mobilized public opinion had won a notable victory over a political organization.

It soon became clear to everyone that the act needed several amendments, but all attempts at revision met with the loud opposition of the young Republican masters, who said that the Governor had got the act he wanted and now let him take the responsibility for the consequences. I determined, on the day before the General Assembly must adjourn, to shift the failure of necessary amendments upon the shoulders where it belonged. At the opening of the session that morning I sent in to that honorable body a special message expressing disappointment that no consideration had been given to certain proposed amendments to the Liquor Control Act, generally regarded as essential, and particularly to one for rectifying an oversight in the bill which would work injustice to hotels in the sale of wine and beer. At that late date no action could be taken except on a suspension of the rules, a motion for which failed of passage in both Houses. And the Senate refused to receive my draft of a bill for the benefit of hotels, on the pretext that the Governor was overstepping his constitutional powers in suggesting legislation in so definite a form. I took the rebuff in good humor and left the next card to be played by three prominent Republicans of Hartford who called on J. Henry

Roraback with the request that he give the word to his lieutenants to let "the Governor's" amendments go through—or Cross would sweep the State in the next election. One of the three told me that Roraback was really in favor of the Commission's bill but had opposed it and its amendments because I had not reappointed two Republican Commissioners of large departments whom, above all others, he wished to have retained. He had waited, he said, a long time to see what I would do. In other words, he was waiting for me to let him have those two Commissioners in exchange for Republican support of a liquor control act on which he knew my heart was set. I was in no mood for a trade of this kind. I preferred a fight to the finish.

What happened that night I never knew except by inference. The next morning a series of amendments was introduced and all quickly passed the Senate without debate. An hour or two later the House took concurrent action. Evidently Roraback had given new commands by which he saved the Republican party from complete disaster. As for me, I had won, with the aid of the public, centralized control of the manufacture and sale of alcoholic liquors under a Commission of three members to be appointed by the Governor.

Before the General Assembly adjourned I set a date, under the authority of a special Act of that honorable body, for the election of delegates to a Convention for the purpose of ratifying or rejecting an Amendment to the Constitution of the United States, as proposed by Congress, for the repeal of the Eighteenth Amendment. On Tuesday, July 11, at ten o'clock in the forenoon the delegates met in the Hall of the House of Representatives for that historic Convention. As I sat on the sidelines watching the procedure, the fifty delegates one by one answered yea on the question of repeal of the Eighteenth Amendment. There was no debate.

Connecticut was the twelfth State to ratify the amendment for repeal. In a short speech the president of the convention, Lucius Robinson, predicted that national prohibition would soon be at an end. In a longer speech, in which I emphasized "the stupendous task" which awaited us in the enforcement of the State's Liquor Control Act, I enlarged rhetorically on Robinson's prediction, saying: "The Eighteenth Amendment seems to be going rather fast. I look forward to the time, not far off, when it shall be completely gone, leaving only the memory of it behind. When that time comes, you men and women who have fought the good fight . . . may furl your banners and lay them aside among memorabilia for the edification as well as the entertainment of your descendants." That time came in December.

Portrait of Governor Cross by Kayhart, New York, 1933.
Courtesy of Connecticut State Library, State Archives

XXIV. Rest from Labor

After the adjournment of the General Assembly I enjoyed several weeks of comparative rest from daily labor under the Capitol dome reverberating with voices. On Monday of Harvard's Commencement week (June 19), I gave in Sanders Theater the annual Phi Beta Kappa oration under the auspices of the Harvard Chapter. It was in my estimation the most signal honor in my literary career to be invited to take a place in the long line of scholars and men of letters who since colonial days had addressed Harvard members of America's oldest and most distinguished academic society. I ventured to take a cue for my address from that famous Phi Beta oration which Emerson delivered at Harvard in 1837, reminding my audience that 1837 and 1933 were alike in that they were both years of "economic confusion and public upheaval," and yet Emerson had no word about hard times, which must have been in the minds of all his hearers. "Looking beyond turmoil and distress, he did not let his gaze wander, for more than a moment, from the ultimate triumph of the human spirit over material things." He believed that "the day is always his who works in it with serenity and great aim."

By a coincidence Archibald MacLeish, another Yale man, gave the Phi Beta Kappa poem in which he retold the last incidents in the story of Ulysses' ten years of wanderings back to his Ithacan home which he had left peaceful and prosperous, only to find the land now in the throes of war and distress. The poem was a happy application of an ancient myth to the wide world in 1933. Both of us had essentially the same theme.

The next Thursday I was in Cambridge again, with Maj. Gene Tunney, to attend the Harvard Commencement, which was held under an immense tent erected in the historic Sever Quadrangle. It was the last time that A. Lawrence Lowell was to preside over the ceremonies of Commencement Day, for he was then retiring as President of Harvard after twenty-five years of distinguished service not only to Harvard but to university education throughout the country. From him I received on that memorable day the honorary degree of LL.D. along with Alfred E. Smith and the British and French Ambassadors to the United States. I was now both a Yale man and a Harvard man.

The midsummer Governors' Conference was held this year in California, for the discussion of problems which are supposed to concern all the States of the Union. Kenneth Wynne, a perfect traveling companion, went out with me. On the way we stopped over in Chicago, where with other Governors from the East and South we visited the World's Fair as guests of the officials. Towards evening the whole party, Governors, aides, wives, and other members of their families, boarded the Governors' Special for the Golden Gate.

Just across the California border near Truckee the train came to a sudden stop at midnight and the whistle blew. Some of us thought it was a holdup. Women screamed and all of us were a bit frightened. But it was only the end of our railway journey. Soon Governor Rolph, state and municipal officials, and Will Rogers were jumping aboard. They had crossed the mountains in a cavalcade of automobiles to greet us in a fake holdup, conceived and executed, I daresay, by the humorist of the movies. They had an old cannon drawn up to give us a nineteen-gun salute. But as it had to be reloaded for each shot it was slow shooting. So to keep us awake huge roman candles were shot off between times. Meanwhile, our special cars were safely sidetracked. Most of us decided to remain aboard until daybreak, some sleeping, some refreshing themselves in the observation car.

Early the next morning we were all taken by automobile to beautiful Lake Tahoe. On a slope above it was a very fine stand of tall and graceful fir trees, which was being christened Governors' Grove. Each Governor in the party was asked to dedicate a tree in his own name to his State. For Connecticut I chose a perfect fir which rose high above many others and was, according to a forester, about my own age.

After luncheon we drove to Truckee, a small ramshackle town frequented by lumberjacks and cowpunchers who put on a rodeo for our entertainment, under Will Rogers as commander in chief. For two hours we sat on a platform watching that exhibition of horsemanship, under heat so terrific that now and then we had to step down on the thin grass to keep the soles of our feet from blistering. Then we took our seats in a long train of automobiles for a three-hour trip over the Sierras to Sacramento, halting only at the Donner Monument near the site of the cabin where in covered wagon days forty of eighty Illinois men and women and children, overtaken by blizzards and deep snows on their way to the El Dorado of the West, perished from hunger and cold. That dreadful tragedy my father used to tell me about when I was a boy.

The dark cloud which hung over our spirits there lifted as we went on and began to climb the mountains along the edge of deep wooded canyons, magnificent in their changing colors under the light of a brilliant sun. In the distance the Sierras looked like long thin knives which needed sharpening. Then we went over the top and made the long descent into the broad California plains. The day, from one midnight to another, closed with a dinner given to the Governors by the city of Sacramento and a reception by Governor and Mrs. Rolph at the Executive Mansion.

The next morning, the Governors met for the first session of their Conference in the Chamber of the House of Representatives at Sacramento with the members of the legislature, then in session, as spectators. It was a formal affair. Governor Rolph bid us welcome in an eloquent speech, and silver-tongued Governor Blackwood of South Carolina responded in still higher-sounding phrases. The Secretary of War, George H. Dern, was there also, to bring the greetings of President Roosevelt and, at his request, to urge coöperation of the States with the Federal Government in the industrial emergency. Thereupon Governor McNutt of Indiana moved that the Governors pledge "their full-hearted active support of the President's recovery program." As prearranged, I made a short speech seconding the motion, which was unanimously carried. Thus ended the preliminary session of the Conference.

A few hours later we moved on to San Francisco in a special train, were met by a military guard, and later repaired to the Memorial Opera House (I think) where we were seated on the stage with the Mayor and other city and state officials. I sat between the chairman and Will Rogers, facing an immense audience. At last Will was called on for a speech. In burlesque of preceding orators, who had extolled San Francisco above the highest heavens, he praised some of the less admirable characteristics of "Frisco," and went on to say something about Los Angeles, which no one had yet mentioned. As soon as he uttered the word "Frisco," the chairman nudged him in the back and in a sharp whisper asked him to cut out all that, for it would offend San Franciscans. But Will kept on saying "Frisco" in nearly every sentence, offering as his apology that as everybody down his way always called the city "Frisco," he supposed "Frisco" was the right name.

The Conference got down to business the next morning in the Supreme Court Chambers at San Francisco and put in the day discussing tax exemptions and the sales tax. One day we spent visiting the Yosemite. As we came down into the park after viewing the valley from Glacier Point, I was a little startled by the sight of a big black bear sitting by the roadside while deer were feeding near him. A harmless fellow, we were told, just sitting there as a beggar for a morsel of sweetmeat from passersby. We were warned if we gave him a pittance to drop it on the ground and let him pick it up, or he would grab both pittance and hand, making no distinction between the one and the other. Like the race of men, he would take everything within his reach.

We dined sumptuously at a hotel facing Glacier Point and waited on until darkness settled down on the valley to see the famous firefall down the great height. The first sight of it was a bright light on the edge of Glacier Point rising, it was said, from a burning mass of fir bark which in a few minutes was pushed over the precipice, falling in a cataract of red-hot coals down the sheer mountainside. The spectacle was a bumptious stunt of man to outrival nature.

After a full day and the night before in Yosemite we left on a midnight train for Los Angeles. The slight business of the Conference over, everything was now to be play. I kept close to Will Rogers whose comment on the Governors I liked. He wondered why "Cross of Connecticut, a pleasant fellow who has a bunch of degrees after his name till it sounds like a radio station . . . was slumming in politics."

One evening Will presided as toastmaster at a banquet given at the Ambassador Hotel by the city of Los Angeles. At the head table were the visiting Governors, Governor Rolph, and local officials. He addressed us not as distinguished guests but as "distinguished guys." One by one he asked the Governors to rise as he presented them to the diners with wise-cracks, giving them no chance to come back at him until he reached me. I had been talking about "Bacon and Shakespeare and Winchell," he claimed, until he had all he could take of it. He described me as "an old barking prairie dog" and, after a little hesitation, remarked, "I think I had better let him bark for a few minutes."

I had to accept the challenge. In turn I described Will as a prairie dog who with a rougher voice than mine was trying to climb into a Governor's chair, who had been Mayor of Beverly Hills but, for reasons everybody knew, had not been reëlected, who was now afflicted with the delusion that he was Governor of Oklahoma because he was born there. While running on in this way, I observed for the first time that no woman at the tables was smoking a cigarette. I paused to congratulate them on never having acquired a habit common among the ladies of the Atlantic coast of smoking two or three cigarettes between the courses of dinner. This praise of California ladies broke their icy-cold behavior. They had refrained, it appeared, from smoking out of respect to a dignified bench of Governors, who, they assumed, had no human frailties. I had hardly ceased speaking before the smoke of a hundred cigarettes began curling up from all parts of the large dining hall.

Will or somebody else arranged for a grand entertainment of the Governors' party at Hollywood, which began with a noon reception and luncheon at which Jean Harlow acted as hostess for the studios. At the luncheon I was assigned a chair between her and Marie Dressler. It was a difficult seat, for I had to adjust my conversation to two different tunes, alternating one with the other. Marie Dressler liked to talk about her art and the rôles she had taken, and insisted that she was going on to the end in spite of the fact she was suffering from a mortal disease. I admired her more and more as she went on from incident to incident in her career.

Jean Harlow, the first of the platinum blondes, also talked about herself when encouraged to do so by several questions I asked. She, too, was devoted to her art; but she was less independent in character. When I offered her a cigarette she turned to Marie Dressler and asked her if she might take a few whiffs. Marie replied, "I think, my dear, that you had better not smoke in this company." But when I lighted a cigar, Marie changed her mind and told Jean that she might have just one cigarette. Before the luncheon was over Jean Harlow told me the story of her famous platinum gown, which she wore on that occasion.

When I next visited Hollywood both Jean Harlow and Marie Dressler were no longer living.

One day I broke away from the rest of the party to visit the University of California at Los Angeles for a more normal day with my friends there, President Ernest Moore, a former colleague on the Yale faculty, and Professor Frederic Blanchard, who had been one of my students in the Graduate School. A few years before, President Moore had driven me out to look over the new site of the University—acres of wild land on the lower slope of the Santa Monica Mountains, overlooking Hollywood with a distant glimpse of the Pacific Ocean. Since then great and beautiful groups of buildings had risen. It was a remarkable achievement and I almost wished that instead of "slumming in politics" I had joined the faculty three years before as a lecturer after my retirement from Yale. As it was, I accepted an invitation to give one lecture the next March before faculty and students.

The day of rest with old friends put me in prime trim for the next morning, which was Sunday, July 30, when Will Rogers was to have a roundup of Governors on his ranch at Beverly Hills. On the way there, I stopped with Kenneth Wynne at the Los Angeles Breakfast Club for my farewell address to California. Breakfast was over. Members and guests filled an auditorium. Secretary Dern, Governor Rolph, several visiting Governors, and a group of business and professional men were there. As usual, extravagant praises were being heaped upon California without reservation. No one, for instance, since we came into the State, had yet dared to utter the word "earthquake." No Governor from the East or South had a good word for his own State in comparison with California. When it came to my little speech, I decided to bring in Connecticut. As scraps of what I said got into the newspapers, I can now recall with their help the gist of my farewell:

"I am going back to Connecticut. I shall be glad to go, for it is my home. Connecticut cannot compare with California in grand scenery. It has no Sierras, no Yosemite Valley. Our mountains, 10,000 feet high in prehistoric times, have been worn down to grass-covered hills. We have no trees thousands of years old, rising three hundred feet in defiance of heaven like the Tower of Babel, which Jehovah destroyed for the Children of Israel. Our elms, oaks, and maples rarely live beyond a century but they are beautiful while they live. We can boast of no palm trees like yours, which have no roots in the soil and so feed on hot air for a brief time and then topple over in a gust of wind. Some of you say that your huge sequoia date from the Reptilian Age. We have no reptiles in Connecticut except harmless garden snakes, which children play with. Perhaps a rattler or a copperhead is now and then encountered in the cliffs of those hills which were once mountains. The earthquakes which threw up those mountains all belong to prehistoric times. The upheavals ceased with the coming of the Pilgrim Fathers. I suppose that the eye can get accustomed to your stretches of brown grass. But I like better the green grass of Connecticut hills and valleys. I have viewed your broad sandy river-beds with little streams trickling down through their centers, which, I am told, become in rainy seasons mad rushing masses of water which jump banks and devastate your low-lying towns. In Connecticut everything like everybody is moderately wet or moderately dry. The river after which my State is named is usually filled nearly to the brim and yet rarely breaks over its banks to damage the fertile meadows through which it flows. . . .

"Governor Rolph now has on his desk two bills just passed by the California legislature. One of them provides for a general sales tax and the other for a personal income tax. He does not know just what to do with them, whether to sign or veto them, or whether to sign one and veto the other. He is in a quandary. In Connecticut we have neither of these inconvenient kinds of taxation. I invite you to come to Connecticut to avoid them. But if you come, stay on until death overtakes you so that we can get your heirs on a stiff inheritance tax. That, however, shouldn't worry you as you will then be basking in paradise or in some other place equally warm."

When we reached Will Rogers' roundup, he was roping yearlings in a meadow below his house. I looked on for an hour. He never missed throwing his calves, one after another, however wild. While his herd of Governors was waiting for him to come up to the house, Mrs. Rogers, a charming woman, sometime a schoolteacher, I think, invited me into his library where he kept near his desk encyclopedias and miscellaneous reference books. She had just typed his short paragraphs which were to appear the next morning in a syndicate of newspapers. She showed me the original and her clear copy, which she was to take to the telegraph office to see that every word, as he had written it, went over the wire without a mistake.

After luncheon Will took us over the ranch. One of his guests for a visit of a fortnight was a man in the eighties who grew up with Will's father. They were cowboys together and afterwards each had his own ranch. I sat fascinated for a long time while this fine old rancher told of the old days when cowboys rode and drank all day and drank and gambled all night. He had many hairbreadth escapes but came through in good shape and saved money enough to buy a ranch which he had recently sold at a good price. He remarked casually that he supposed he must give up his gold as demanded by the Federal Government, and inquired what I was going to do. I replied that I had no gold to give up. He seemed surprised. He thought that a Governor must be a rich man. Though nothing but a rancher he had saved, he said, $135,000, all in gold, packed away in strong boxes of several banks. I asked him why he didn't deposit his dollars in banks where they would draw interest. He replied that he never had a bank account, that he always paid his bills in cash and got gold for what was left over, and put it where it would be safe. "Banks bust up," he said. "Iron boxes in a steel vault never bust." I mentioned burglars and dynamite. He admitted that danger, which he had, however, guarded against by distributing his gold in boxes of several banks, so as not to lose all if one or two of the banks were blow up.

This was the last time I saw Will Rogers. He was a true man through and through. To be with him even for a little while was to love and admire him. About his humor there was nothing artificial. It was a part of himself. He is among my most pleasant memories of a long life.

That evening Wynne and I started for home by a roundabout way through the Canadian Rockies. With us were Governor and Mrs. McNutt and their friend Miss Lucy Taggart, an artist, a daughter of Tom Taggart, the well-known politician. It was the right sort of party for a good time, and we had it, though the heat on that train became barely endurable. In the absence of thermometers which we searched for in vain, we guessed that the temperature must have stood still at 110° for two days. I longed for cool Connecticut hills.

College President Charles C. McCracken (l) observes Governor Cross sign the bill changing Connecticut Agricultural College's name to Connecticut State College, 1933. The name would be changed to the University of Connecticut in 1939.
University of Connecticut Photograph Collection, Archives & Special Collections, University of Connecticut Library

Governor Cross with Mr. and Mrs. Albert N. Jorgensen after the inauguration of Mr. Jorgensen as president of Connecticut State College, 1935
University of Connecticut Photograph Collection, Archives & Special Collections, University of Connecticut Library

XXV. Labor without Rest

After an absence of three weeks, I was again in my office at the Capitol. Evidence was at hand to indicate that there was spreading over Connecticut a spirit of restlessness, occasioned in part by recent national and state legislation, which, being out of the usual order, perplexed the people. It was the business of the Governor to explain the intent of the new legislation in conferences and in radio and other addresses and so allay unjustified fears. All this and much more I undertook as a task which permitted no rest for many months.

More than ever I went about among the people of the State. It was the year when Windsor and Wethersfield celebrated the tercentenary of their first week settlements. I greeted President Roosevelt when he attended the Yale Commencement in June, 1934; and on a private understanding with President Angell I interrupted the ceremonies by presenting William Lyon Phelps, the public orator himself, for an honorary degree. Neither Billy Phelps nor the audience was in on the secret. The surprise of both was followed by loud cheers for Yale's great and popular teacher. I gave addresses on public affairs at the Universities of Rochester and Oklahoma, and at the University of California at Los Angeles. At Hollywood again I had a chance to study the making of pictures, undisturbed by social engagements. But with these exceptions I kept close to Connecticut.

Not long after my return from California several delegations of citizens from Fairfield County, headed by their Planning Association, urged the immediate construction of the Merritt Parkway. Their request was reinforced by a petition bearing a thousand names. The proposal of the majority was a special session of the General Assembly to reconsider a bill which, after a public hearing, had been rejected by both Houses at the regular session only a few months before. The bill, which provided for a local authority to build and maintain the Parkway, with funds to be obtained by the issue of bonds and the imposition of tolls, I told them frankly, would, in my opinion, still stand no chance of passage. The Parkway, when completed, would become a section of an integrated system of state highways which should be built and kept within the jurisdiction of the Highway Commissioner. Connecticut had got rid of toll roads and toll bridges and would not be disposed to revert to the old practice unless it were absolutely necessary. For these reasons I declined to call a special session of the General Assembly. Instead of that I promised to call a conference in my office with the Highway Commissioner whom they might prod with questions to their hearts' content.

I recall the amazed look in the eyes of members of the Fairfield County Planning Association when Commissioner MacDonald informed them at that conference that, after overcoming many difficulties, he was no nearly ready to let contracts for the construction of the first nine miles of the Parkway from the border of New York State, for which he had, in prospect, ample funds, State and Federal, without resort to tolls to pay the interest on bonds. There followed an animated, a bit acrimonious, discussion of details, which came to a head in a subsequent mass meeting in Greenwich. The Commissioner was for a well-graded, fairly straight road. The spokesmen for Fairfield County were for a winding road, following the natural contour of the land, with less grading. Such a road, they thought, would be not only more picturesque but an incentive to slow driving. Agitation over the Commissioner's layout of the Parkway did not cease until the next spring when dirt began to fly. Inasmuch as commissioner MacDonald could now proceed to construct a full quarter of the entire mileage of the Parkway, I could see no good reason why it should not be left to the next General Assembly to provide means for its completion. In the meantime I hoped to obtain financial assistance from the Federal Government.

In the summer of 1933 the N.R.A. was just coming into full force. I rather liked the dynamic and temperamental Federal Administrator of the act, General Johnson, because I could never foretell what he might do. There was just enough opposition in Connecticut to any outside interference with economic forces to awaken his ire. One of his aides was reported as saying: "We have done all we can in Connecticut. The State can now go to hell." I protested against these defamatory remarks about "the land of steady habits" and received from General Johnson a nice letter in apology. Afterwards I reviewed with him, Governor Lehman, and others the mammoth N.R.A. parade in New York City. We laughed over the passage at arms. I could tell him that manufacturers and businessmen in Connecticut were cooperating to make the N.R.A. a success, that the Blue Eagle was hanging in windows all over the State, and that Hartford was to have an N.R.A. parade, too.

The labor unrest which gave me grave concern arose from a rather general misunderstanding of the codes in various industries, and in some instances, I am sorry to say, from attempts by employers of labor to evade by devious ways their obligations under the codes. Whether justified or not, complaints were common from labor groups that they were being gypped by manufacturers. Unfortunately, Connecticut had no industrial board competent to deal effectively with labor disputes. There was, it is true, a so-called Board of Mediation and Arbitration which had been created back in 1895 during the business depression of that time; but it had led an idle life of nearly forty years because it had no power to take action in a labor conflict except on the request of the parties concerned. My appointees to the Board all resigned. There was nothing, they said, for them to do. Efforts on my part, while the General Assembly of 1933 was in session, to persuade representatives of capital and labor to approve legislation for giving the Board initiative power in the settlements of disputes and strikes were met with indifference or with a decisive 'no.' So when trouble became acute over codes, I had to look elsewhere for means to enforce them.

On my request Washington appointed a State Advisory Committee of five members to handle all disputes relevant to codes to report for legal action any violations of them which were discovered. When the N.R.A. was superseded by other Federal agencies, the State Department of Labor was designated to carry on similar work, with additional authority to settle strikes by round-table conferences with representatives of both sides to a controversy. If this method failed, then the Governor stepped in with his own conference. If he also failed, it was his business to see that order was

maintained until the strike wore out. Fortunately there were comparatively few cases of this desperate kind. During the year 1934 the Labor
Department settled, with the coöperation of the Federal Government,
more than a hundred disputes, many of which would have culminated in
strikes except for skillful preventive measures. As a guard against the development of bitterness between employer and employee, disputes, even
those which bore the threat of strikes, were rarely reported to the newspapers. Business went on quietly without appreciable loss in production
and wages, despite rumblings beneath the surface.

However, the rumblings suddenly broke out in eruptions during the
autumn of 1934, beginning with a strike in a textile mill in Manchester,
and thence spreading to five or six other textile mills in the eastern part
of the State. The points of dispute were the wage scale and the stretch-
out system. Both parties in the conflict were determined to fight to a finish. Instead of listening to appeals for a peaceful settlement, the Manchester
workers, having nothing to do, roamed through industrial districts in "flying squadrons" fomenting sympathetic strikes in other textile plants, or, if
a strike was already on, joining picket lines. The situation became very
difficult to deal with when flying squadrons began to invade the State
from industrial towns in Massachusetts and Rhode Island.

Two considerable strikes which had been smoldering for some time
burst into flame when I was out of the State. The first was at Danielson,
the second at Putnam, a short distance away. After a talk with the State
Police Commissioner, whose men were on the scene to prevent disorder,
I had concluded that it would be perfectly safe for me to take a run up to
Sunapee, New Hampshire, on Sunday evening, September 9, to close my
cottage there. I advised my office that I would return not later than the
following Tuesday afternoon, and left orders that, in case of trouble anywhere, I be called back immediately. A three-hour journey would bring
me to the Capitol. On my arrival in Hartford at 6 P.M. that Tuesday, I was
dismayed by big headlines in the newspapers announcing that Lieutenant
Governor Wilcox, at the urgent request of the managers of two textile
plants, municipal and town officials, and the sheriff of the county, had
ordered the Adjutant General to call out several companies of the National

Guard and to disparch them at once to Danielson where there had been a serious clash between the State Police and strikers the night before, and to Putnam where there had been a less serious clash on Tuesday morning. More Foot Guard units were being mobilized for duty the next morning, among them a machine-gun company.

The Lieutenant Governor was not available for a little talk, but I managed to get word to him that I was back on the job and his public worries were over. The Adjutant General gave a full account of the situation as it had developed during the day. I expressed some surprise that I had not been informed of what was happening. Anyone of my office staff could have reached me over the telephone in five minutes or sent me a telegram which would have been delivered without delay. He replied that it was his function to obey the instructions of his superior without asking questions. I ordered him to demobilize the machine-gun company at once and to hold at the Hartford and New Haven armories the other National Guard units which he was mobilizing. Before proceeding further in this business I was going to make a tour of the strike area. He warned me against the danger of confronting an angry mob, but his warning gave me no fears.

I called up Kenneth Wynne who like me had just read in a newspaper the extraordinary news of the day. He promised to be in Hartford the next morning ready for a day's trip. Several newspapers were now to have some fun with a quixotic Governor who imagined that he could settle a strike by a joy ride.

Wednesday morning we set out for the Woodstock Fair, on the edge of the strike area, where I was to make an address. By arrangement we met there the sheriff of Windham County, who told us what he knew. Then we three began the tour through the strike centers, unheralded. At Putnam everybody—men, women, and children—seemed to be on the street watching the pickets as they strolled in pairs in front of the Belding-Heminway-Corticelli silk mills, while the militia stood by armed with guns and fixed bayonets ready for action. The crowd of spectators were armed with baskets of tomatoes. Instead of being pelted with rotten tomatoes, we were greeted with the shout, "That is the Governor's car," and a minute later with, "There is the Governor." At Putnam, as later at Danielson, I invited the strike leaders to send a delegation to the Capitol the next afternoon for a conference. The peaceful shouts continued until we left the scene.

At Danielson all was quiet. The President of the big Powdrell and Alexander curtain plant there had closed his mills with the intention, however, of resuming work as soon as might be feasible. I assured him and the first selectman of the town of ample protection when that time came. I visited the scene of the "riot" on Monday night and reviewed a Military Police Company, which, I was pleased to observe, was equipped, not with rifles and bayonets, but with clubs and side arms. I saw few strikers. At Willimantic, to which some troops were transferred that day from Danielson in fear of trouble at the American Thread Company, the same dead quiet prevailed. A half dozen troopers stood by the gate talking.

The delegations appeared in Hartford promptly at the appointed hour. We had a long talk, during which the strikers courteously urged me to withdraw the troops. With equal courtesy I promised to withdraw them as soon as all threats of further disturbance had subsided. Someone humorously suggested that I come over to Putnam as their adviser. I looked towards Joe Tone, who was present, and remarked "What's the matter with Joe Tone? He'll come over and try to keep you within the law and report to me every day on your behavior and act as mediator with the managers of the mills in the settlement of the strike." "He's all right!" they shouted in chorus.

Joe left for Putnam that night. Except for a flare-up on Monday, which seemed to require the presence of additional troops, order was restored at Putnam and Danielson by that evening, when the strikers sent me a pledge that there would be no more violence. The next morning, September 18, I ordered the gradual demobilization of the National Guard. Within two or three days the process was completed and the flying squadrons were being driven from the highways by the State Police. Strikers were going back to work not only in Putnam and Danielson but in other disturbed centers. Joe Tone was to be congratulated on his success in settling a widespread strike with a minimum of bad feeling. On Monday, September 24, more than 18,000 workers who had been on strike in eastern Connecticut were at their looms again.

XXVI. The Election of 1934

Amid these strikes the two leading political parties held their State Conventions to nominate their candidates for the November, 1934, election. Again the Democrats took possession of the Fort Griswold House at Eastern Point, a site of good omen, facing the blue waters. I arrived early on Wednesday afternoon, September 5, to take part in the preliminary organization of the Convention which was to convene at 8 P.M. As its chairman, I submitted to a committee a platform of principles which was unanimously approved after a few alternations in phrasing. All was as serene on the surface as the calm waters under a brilliant sun. I dined privately with a few friends. One of them was James A. Farley who, by request, had come on from Washington to address the Convention. That evening Jim Farley and Senator Lonergan made strong appeals for harmony. They were greeted with thunderous applause.

Noisy salutations over, I retired with advisers to my rooms for the shirtsleeve business of the night. In a larger apartment on the floor above were the headquarters of the captains of the Old Guard and their subalterns. One of the captains brought with him a complete ticket of nominations with which they all concurred. My name headed the list, then came Dan Leary's for Lieutenant Governor, "a loyal Democrat, who should be allowed to retrieve his defeat in 1930." When I was shown the ticket by an intermediary, I sent back word that under no circumstances could I accept Leary and some others they had agreed upon as my running mates. In place of Leary I suggested T. Frank Hayes, "the reform Mayor of Waterbury" who had miraculously reduced the tax rate of his city by some fifteen mills to the dollar, and proposed that other names on the ticket be left to a conference. This olive branch met with a blank refusal to make any change whatever in the ticket. My final word that night to the captains of the Old Guard was that they must count me out of their picture. I sent words that I was going to bed and must not be disturbed by anything unless it were a fire. There was to be, I made it plain, no second edition of that old four o'clock scene in pajamas.

At that moment the telephone bell rang. It was a call from a Hartford Club friend who had a summer cottage at Eastern Point. He was in the lobby and wanted to bid me good night, he said, before going home. He came up to my rooms with a niece and an entertaining young man, whose name I have forgotten. He proposed that we have a bottle of champagne together as a nightcap. Though I was on the water wagon for the duration of the Convention, I yielded to the temptation, for I was tired after a hard day. Just as I was about to order the champagne, the young man unbuttoned his coat and displayed two bottles of "Cliquot Club, Yellow Label." My troubles were soon washed away.

I was abed by midnight and asleep a few minutes after. When I rose, after six hours of unbroken sleep, and walked through the hallway, the only sound was the chorus of snorers. I descended by a back stairway to the lobby where nobody was in sight but a clerk behind his desk. I stepped out upon the broad front veranda and was enchanted by a sea rippling in the sunshine. It was an hour too early for breakfast, so I took a long stroll along the shore. When the time came, I was the first to have breakfast. No one else was in the dining room. I was alone, fancy-free. I took another stroll, sitting for a while on the rocks, smoking a cigar. When I returned to the hotel, delegates were at breakfast. I went into the dining room to look up Ken Wynne. There was considerable commotion through the hall. A rumor was spreading that I had positively refused to head a ticket framed by party leaders in a secret session. As no one had seen me that morning, and as my automobile was gone, delegates feared that I had run out on them. I told them how I had spent the morning and why they were unable to find an automobile which had been put up for the night at the Groton Police barracks along with my chauffeur, Tom Wilson. I assured the delegates that I intended to stay with them until the Convention adjourned; but that I would not head a ticket certain of defeat the moment it was nominated. My name, I said jocosely, was not big enough to give value to a row of political ciphers.

Reporters listened in. They had a story to tell of what happened in the rooms above me after I went to bed, through "the glamorous hours" till daybreak. This time the captains of the Old Guard were going to "call the Governor's bluff for good." One proposal of the defeatists was "to throw the election overboard by drafting a straw-man ticket for the Republicans to knock down." In this way the Governor and his appointees would be forever kicked out of politics with one fell swoop. The Old Guard, thus on top, would be able to nominate its own ticket, without interference, in 1936, and win the election under the banner of President Roosevelt who was sure to be renominated. To this desperate plan, it was understood, Frank Maloney, slated for nomination as candidate for the United States Senate, strenuously objected. He was no more willing than I to lead a forlorn hope.

Even the captains of the Old Guard were reluctant to sacrifice Maloney's chance of election on the altar of their dislike of the Governor. When they came down for a late breakfast they must have seen that any attempt to carry through their program would end in a riot. Tired and disenchanted, they asked for a conference. With very little debate, agreement was reached on a representative ticket which the Convention adopted by acclamation.

So harmonious was the final scene that a group of reporters asked me to tell them frankly whether it had all been a real battle or merely a sham which I had pulled off "to give color to the Convention and to dramatize what would otherwise have been a routine affair." I assured them that it was a real battle which began weeks ago and that I came to Eastern Point uncertain of the outcome, as they might see by reading the heading on their typewritten copies of the acceptance speech which they had in their pockets. "You will observe," I remarked, "that it is a speech described as being given by Governor Cross 'in case he is renominated for Governor.'" Not all of the reporters seemed to be convinced. "Why that twinkle in your eye, Governor, while you say this?"

The Republicans held their Convention in Hartford just a week later while I was on my "joy ride" through the textile area and negotiating with strikers and managers for peace. They nominated for Governor Hugh M. Alcorn, the able and courageous State's Attorney for Hartford County, to whom I had recently presented, in behalf of the National Flag

Association, a medal for his distinguished services in the enforcement of the law and in the prevention of crime. The orator who put his name in nomination said of him as a prosecutor, according to the newspapers: "His method of attack is relentless, piercing, rapier-like, until his opponent surrenders or flees. . . . The Democrat who challenges him to debate in this campaign will not do so again." I did not have to wait long for an exhibition of my rival's belligerent character. His aim, it became apparent, was to create in the campaign the atmosphere of a criminal court. The State of Connecticut was to be the court room. I was to be put on trial as a feckless Governor. He was to be the prosecutor. My fellow citizens were to be the jury to listen to a cross-examination on my conduct as Governor. There was no judge.

The most formal way of putting a question was essentially like this: "Is it not true, Governor, that on the day when you left for your summer home in New Hampshire, there were lying on your desk two and possibly three, telegrams indicating the probably necessity of calling troops? I do not expect an answer." In most instances the prosecutor demanded an unequivocal yes or no without any fencing on my part. But in some instances he evidently did not want an emphatic "no" to go to the jury. He held me responsible for all the strikes in Connecticut because I had failed to resurrect a dead Board of Mediation and Arbitration, ignoring the fact that a multitude of labor disputes and strikes growing out of some of them had been settled by a live Department of Labor. He scored delay in the building of the Merritt Parkway at a time when work was going on a full speed with funds partly supplied by the Federal Government; when, too, it was alleged, the Republican organization was shaking down contractors and foremen for contributions to the Republican campaign fund, $100 for a contractor and $10 for a foreman, while I was intervening to stop this sort of thing by both political parties. I was taken to task for using phrases like "shake down" and "cough up." I responded by quoting his invitation "to come up and see him some time when he became Governor."

One charge, that I was responsible for the deficit which might have been avoided if I had not launched in 1931 an $8,000,000 building program, was not often repeated, for it proved to be politically inexpedient to suggest that our humane institutions should have been left inadequate for the care and cure of patients afflicted with physical or mental disease.

At the very opening of the campaign the Republicans made a fatal blunder in their sweeping condemnation of the so-called New Deal. The keynoter at their State Convention gave them as slogan: "A Mendicant State cannot be a Sovereign State." Taking his cue from this, Alcorn declared that the New Deal was making "mendicants and beggars" of the people. This remark was a cruel insult to a hundred thousand workers in the State who had lost their jobs during the industrial depression through no fault of their own. In the crisis, mayors and town officials, as I have related, appealed in vain to the General Assembly for larger financial assistance in mitigating the condition of an accumulating horde of unemployed, many of whom were heads of families. The Federal Government then stepped in with grants to Connecticut and all the other States for relieving distress and for providing work on state and municipal projects. The aim of this policy was not to reduce the unemployed to the low level of mendicants but to prevent them from becoming such.

I often recall one unique occasion in this campaign. The headmaster of the Hotchkiss School, George Van Santvoord, a former colleague of mine at Yale, invited me to come over to Salisbury for a barbecue which the Democrats of the town were going to give a fortnight later in the near-by park. He asked me to come a full hour early for a visit with the trustees of the school after the meeting they were to hold that morning. I appeared at the appointed time and we all drove out to the park. The air was so damp and chill after a night of drizzling rain that the scene of the barbecue, which turned out to be an ordinary luncheon, was shifted from a grove to the large dining room of the clubhouse. As I took a seat by Van Santvoord I expressed surprise that there were so many Democrats in his Republican town. He cheerfully informed me that more than half of the audience before me were Republicans. "Down there in front," he said, "sit the entire Republican town committee. They had a meeting here this morning and I have invited them to stay on to hear what you have to say." "So this is a trick of yours," I commented, "to see me put over a speech which will satisfy the Democrats and not offend the Republicans. Watch me."

Van Santvoord introduced me as a statesman, not as a politician—which provoked laughter and here and there a shuffling of feet. There were to be no other speakers, he added, so the Governor may talk as long as he likes and say what he pleases. There was no laughter over the prospect of a long harangue, but when I rose to speak without manuscript or notes sobered faces began to light up with relief. Not knowing what I was going to say, I started in with something like this: "Sometimes I observe in Democratic rallies a few Republicans who, in the words of Shakespeare, seem to want to quit the primrose way leading to 'the everlasting bonfire' and are ready to climb with me and Bunyan the straight and narrow path which leads to the Celestial City. Almost always, also, I pick out a Republican spotter on a back seat who has been sent in to count and record the names of all the members of his party whom he sees there. I easily detect him for he has a way of getting up and going out with his list of disloyal Republicans who are in for punishment. But never before have I been called upon to address an audience, half salve and half free, to paraphrase Abraham Lincoln, who purloined his political philosophy from Thomas Jefferson, the founder of the Democratic Party.

Stumped for a moment on how to go on, I hesitated and looked towards the seat of my chair. In the pause I was struck by a flash of inspiration which enabled me to proceed. "That you may all go home contented, I am going to give you three short speeches, which may be rolled into one continuous whole. I will address you first as a Republican, then as a Democrat, and last as a statesman who looks upon all political issues with an impartial eye."

As a Republican I shot at the Governor, thick and fast, a score of questions of the "Is it not true?" character to confound him. As a Democrat I squirmed under some of the more personal questions involving the number of cigars I smoked a day and the number of drinks I took. As a statesman, who roams all round controversial issues before pulling out the conclusion which he already has up his sleeve, I got in a pretty good Democratic speech. As a statesman should, I relieved the mental strain of following a logical discourse by throwing in glittering generalities, praise of Connecticut, the home of constitutional government and three centuries of patriots, and, in particular, praise of Salisbury, her lakes and streams and mountains, the highest in the State, and the quality of the iron ore of her mines, from which were forged the cannon that won the independence of the United States of America.

Whether I gained or lost votes by this oratory I do not know for a certainty. But after the election, I saw that in Salisbury I ran ahead of my colleagues on the Democratic ticket by 26 votes! At the same time Joe Garner Estill, of the Hotchkiss School, was elected one of the Representatives of the town to the General Assembly by a majority of 10 over his Republican rival. On the whole, Salisbury, in the heart of the enemy's country, did rather well, whatever may have been the reason for it.

At another rally I was actually introduced under the name of a former Republican Governor, then no longer living. The chairman, who must have had several drinks, concluded his glowing eulogy with "I now give you His Excellency, Marcus H. Holcomb!" As if unaware of his mistake in nomenclature, the befuddled chairman looked perplexed when the audience broke out in loud laughter.

This year the best bomb was held back until the Thursday before the election so as to give scant time to get on one's feet after the explosion. It was a red-hot statement over the signature of a fiery labor leader of New London, whose occupation was to "pull off" strikes and prolong them as long as he was able. Somehow he contrived to get elected President of the Connecticut Federation of Labor, allegedly by packing the convention which named him. He charged me with leaving my post in the Capitol and going on a "fishing trip" while thousands of workers were striking for "bread-and-butter wages," with attempting to quell those thousands "with bullets, bayonets, and clubs," and with sending out airplanes to spy on flying squadrons. There was nothing new in these and other charges except the violent phrasing.

The story was "writ large" in the election. All the big industrial towns, outside Fairfield County, went Democratic, Hartford leading the procession with a plurality running far above 13,000. In Fairfield County the Democratic sweep was halted by Jasper McLevy, the Socialist candidate for Governor, who polled in that county more than 24,000 votes. He

carried Bridgeport, of which he was "the Reform Mayor," by a safe
plurality, bringing along with him three Socialist Senators of the Bridgeport
districts, and throwing Norwalk and Stamford into the Republican column
by the votes he received in those towns. In round number, 38,000 votes
were cast for McLevy throughout the State, quite enough to cut my plurality over the Republican candidate for Governor to 8,599, a few thousand
below the pluralities of other candidates on the Democratic state ticket.
Maloney was elected United States Senator and four of the six Democratic
candidates for the United States House of Representatives likewise came
through with flying colors. No Democratic victory in Connecticut com-
parable with this had occurred in the memory of men then living.

The path ahead, however, did not look lined with roses. The House of
Representatives remained Republican. In the Senate no party was to have
a majority. Of its 35 members, 17 were to be Democrats, 15 Republicans;
and the 3 Socialists would thus hold the balance of power. The question
which worried me was how, in a Senate so composed, I can could win
approval of the program of legislation which I intended to submit to the
General Assembly. That is a story for the next chapter.

XXVII. A Governor without a Party

Immediately after the election I started out on a general survey of the unprecedented situation. First of all, I assumed that Democratic, Republican, and Socialist leaders in the next General Assembly would stand by the legislative programs outlined in their respective platforms, which had much in common. Some of the questions yet at issue between the three parties I hoped might be settled on the basis of merit or present expediency. But whatever the fate of controversial questions, I could look forward to a large body of useful legislation concerning which the three parties were in substantial agreement.

Other questions were arising on which no party had yet taken a definite position. Chief of these was whether the State should at once resume a building program, suspended by the depression, for putting into prime condition our humane institutions which were proving quite inadequate to care for the growing number of patients. With a view to proceeding as soon as feasible, I visited Washington and readily received from the Public Works Administrator tentative approval of a series of building projects requiring a total expenditure of $18,000,000, to which or to any part of which the Federal Government would contribute 30 per cent of the cost. Such a program, which would involve the transfer of funds from the Highway Department, or new taxation, or the issuance of bonds by the State, I submitted to various party leaders for their meditation and to the press for editorial comment.

Both of the old political parties, as expressed in their platforms, were in favor of the "rapid development of humane institutions." (I quote from the Republican platform of 1934.) But neither party had yet presented a plan for the consideration of the incoming General Assembly. My object was to give them a plan. For a conference on this and other "social legislation" I asked Mayor Jasper McLevy, the head and shoulders of the Socialist party, to come up and see me. We had a good talk in my office at the Capitol, running all the way from hospitals and sanatoria to a state jail farm for the segregation of first offenders out of the reach of hardened criminals. As a result, certain political leaders and partisan newspapers proceeded to charge me with trying to make a deal with the Socialists. As a matter of fact, the substance of our conversation was all made public, and I had a similar talks with Republican and Democratic leaders.

Alan H. Olmstead, who conducted "The Wailing Wall" in the Bridgeport *Times-Star*, devoted a column to an imaginary account of the conversation between Mayor McLevy and myself. Here is a strip of it:

"I'm a common ordinary man," said McLevy. "I don't know anything about politics."

"Neither do I," said Uncle Toby.

"I'm just an honest man," said McLevy.

"That goes for me, too," said Uncle Toby, lighting a new cheroot.

"I understand," said Uncle Toby with a twinkle, "that you have been offered a Roraback plum."

"My doctor forbids fruit," said Jasper.

"It's fun to shake it down, though," the Governor commented.

"Will you tell my fortune?" asked the great Jasper eagerly.

"The present arrangement of the leaves seems to indicate that you and I are going a long way together," the Governor announced.

At the time of this episode a cloud of political mischief was hanging over proposals for the organization of the Senate, in which Democrats were short one vote of a majority. The hope, if there was any, of obtaining that one vote from the Socialists soon faded. They let it be known that they intended to act as an independent group outside of any deal with either of the other two parties. At first the Republicans were disposed to supply the Democrats with the one necessary vote, provided an agreement could be reached on a division of the spoils of office, such as county commissioners and judges of the minor courts. Rumors of deals filled the air.

Suddenly all plans for deals were upset by intrigues in the Democratic ranks. The two previous elections it was now conceded by the captains of the Old Guard might be regarded as Cross victories, inasmuch as he was the only candidate on the Democratic state ticket who came through. But the last election was not a Cross victory. It was a Democratic victory;

specifically it was an Old Guard victory. Cross was slipping. He was "the low man" this time—no account, of course, being taken of the act that I alone was up against McLevy with his 38,000 votes. The coming man, it was said, is Mayor Hayes, "one of us," who ran ahead of Cross by 4,000 votes. On the assumption that I was a back number the captains of the Old Guard proceeded with plans for an organization of the Senate against me. In order to do that it was necessary for them to have at their command a majority of the 17 Democratic Senators. They already had at their bidding 8 Senators from their own districts. Without too much difficulty they persuaded a Senator from another district to give himself in exchange for the promise of a judgeship in a city court worth perhaps $2,000 a year. A majority of one, however obtained, it was anticipated, would be just as good as a unanimous vote to put the Governor where he belonged.

Three weeks before the General Assembly was to convene the 17 Democratic Senators held their caucus to nominate their slate of candidates for the major officers of the Senate. Knowing in advance the names on that slate, all of them henchmen of the Old Guard, I protested against its adoption on the ground that it was not representative of the Democratic party as a whole. I asked for a general conference of Democratic leaders. I asked in vain. One Old Guarder, to whom I appealed over the telephone for a conference, bluntly informed me that the slate must stand as it was. "Everything has been settled," he said, adding, "I am sorry that you feel humiliated." I flared back, "There is nothing, sir, which you may say or do that will humiliate me." And I hung up.

The caucus proceeded according to instructions. Either then or later it adopted a unit rule which bound all the 17 Senators to the dictation of the Old Guard. The Governor was thus reduced to a figurehead by a controlled caucus which would meet from time to time when needed for this purpose, and by the officers of the Senate, equally subject to the same dictation. Senator Devlin, to be President pro tempore of the Senate, would preside over that body in the absence of the Lieutenant Governor, and be appointed to several important committees. The Old Guard expected to control him. Ex-Senator Cooney, as clerk of the Senate, would be able to keep the captains of the Old Guard well informed on all proposed legislation in which they had a particular interest. Senator Hagearty, as floor leader, would be the man through whom, if custom were followed, the Governor's measures would be introduced into the General Assembly. He would be chairman of the Judiciary Committee to which a majority of the Governor's bills would be referred. He would also be chairman of the Committee on Executive Nominations. In these various capacities he could hold up any or all of the Governor's bills and all his appointments which required confirmation by the Senate, none to be allowed free passage except on the advice of his masters. The plan thus devised for the organization of the Senate would largely usurp, if it were put into effect, the legislative and executive functions of the state government. Only the wobbly framework would be left.

The morning after the caucus (December 18) I issued a plain address to the citizens of Connecticut, warning them of the impending danger. Through three successive campaigns, I reminded them, the Democratic party has taken as its slogan the restoration of free constitutional government in this State. But no sooner has a clear Democratic victory been gained than the leaders of a faction have maneuvered themselves into power, sufficient, they think, to repudiate platforms and promises. I leave it to the press and to my fellow citizens to mete out to them proper punishment for the betrayal of what the Democratic party has stood for since I became Governor. As for myself, I shall still remain Governor of the State of Connecticut, whatever may be the personal consequences. This pledge received overwhelming approval from all parts of the State. Public anger was spiced with public humor. "We like the looks of the Governor," wrote an editor, "when he stands on his hind legs with his fighting clothes on." Others, not too seriously, liked the Governor to Leonidas at Thermopylae, Horatius at the Bridge, and the boy who "stood on the burning deck." These analogies were not so good as they appeared, for Leonidas was slain, the boy went up in flames, and Horatius had to swim across the Tiber to escape the arrows of Lars Porsena.

The next weeks it became clear to all but the politically blind that neither Republicans nor Socialists would give the Old Guard leaders the one vote they must have in order to put through their program. The test came on the meeting of the General Assembly, Wednesday, January 9, for organization, the first step towards which in the Senate was the election of a clerk. Each of the three parties had its own candidate for the office. Votes were cast all day on strictly party lines: 17 for the Old Guard Democratic candidate, 15 for the Republican, and 3 for the Socialist. Before the day ended there were 62 roll calls with the same result. After seven or eight hours of balloting with short intermissions for huddles behind the lines of battle, the Senate adjourned until the next morning, hopelessly deadlocked. The inauguration of the Governor and his associates had to go over until both Houses of the General Assembly were sufficiently organized to meet in joint convention and officially declare what everybody knew, the result of the recent state election.

Nevertheless, most of the ceremonies attendant upon an inauguration were enacted that Wednesday afternoon as if there were to be one. At noon I gave a staff luncheon at the Hartford Club in honor of my colleagues, after which we all rode in a grand parade to the Capitoline Hill through streets massed with crowds so large as to require the whole police force of the city to keep them in order. When we entered the Capitol we were greeted by shouts of another crowd of people from all parts of the State milling around and inquiring of one another about the latest roll call in the Senate. They stayed on until the Senate adjourned and the farce of roll calls was ended. That evening the Inaugural Ball was held according to schedule. We all received and acknowledged congratulations on our election to office for which we had not yet qualified by swearing to defend the Constitution of Connecticut. That was another face on a large scale.

And all went merry as a marriage bell.

On Thursday morning the three Socialist Senators called on me while Joe Tone was in my office for a little talk about what was going on in the Senate chamber. They deplored delay in the organization of the Senate which was preventing the consideration of urgent legislation for aid to the unemployed. They felt, however, that any intervention on their part to break the deadlock would be misunderstood. They neither asked of me nor received any advice. The object of their visit, it became apparent, was to inform me that they could not support the Democratic slate of nominations unless it were made over. The intimation was that they might reluctantly go along with the Republicans.

On reconvening that morning the Senate resumed the monotonous roll calls of the day before. Again the Capitol was jammed with spectators. Again there was no break in the political ranks until the 110th ballot was reached in the midafternoon. Then, while the galleries gasped with surprise, the three Socialist Senators in turn voted for the Republican nominees for clerk and President pro tempore, who, by virtue of his office, would appoint all Senate members of the General Assembly's committees. Thus ended, by the majority of one vote, the most scandalous battle for the control of the Senate in the history of the State. Victory might have gone to the Democrats had not the Old Guard insisted upon rule or ruin.

There was yet another sensation before the day was over. Senator Hagearty, as member of a committee to inform the House that the Senate had organized and was ready for business, burst out in his address to the Speaker: "It seems as if the Socialist party has sold out to the Republicans, at what price I don't know . . ." There was no all-out political deal between Republicans and Socialists. It was rather an understanding that the Socialists would give general support to the Republican legislative program, where it was not inconsistent with their own, in return for specific support of measures for the benefit of Bridgeport, whence they came. For example, the Socialists wanted the State to take over a highway running through the city, including a bridge out of repair, and authority to establish a merit system in municipal appointments and to refund serial bonds in the amount of some $2,200,000 which were becoming due within the next few years. Besides this and much more, they asked for certain labor legislation and larger aid from the State for the unemployed in industrial areas. Behind their program was a political motive to keep down the tax rate in Bridgeport. The Republicans fulfilled their promises. As I signed the necessary bills, I was accused of being in the "political deal" also. Color was also given to this inference because the three Socialists were often seen filing into my office on a morning. They came sometimes to explain a

bill of theirs which was coming up for action or to ask questions about a measure which I was advocating. When I gave formal approval of their refunding-bond bill I rallied them on this new way of paying old debts by leaving the debts still standing. I could not, however, be too hard on them because they were only following the practice of many corporations. They were three good men whom I liked to see coming through the doorway.

Except for one short break, I maintained cordial relations with the Republican floor leaders. Senator Bradley might be seen any morning, walking through anterooms to my office just before the Senate convened, to inform me of the attitude of his party towards bills in which I was especially interested. Whether we agreed or disagreed on this or that, neither of us ever displayed the usual hot temper of political opponents. Each of us was trying to understand the other.

My relationship with the Old Guard of the Democratic party after its defeat in the organization of the Senate was greatly improved. Senator

Hagearty was set aside as the Democratic leader of the Senate for Raymond J. Devlin; and John D. Thoms was appointed Democratic leader of the House. Neither of them was strong for the Old Guard. Both of them were young Yale men, who, though associated with the Old Guard, were not of the vindictive type. They were both assigned to the judiciary Committee where they could look after Democratic interests in important legislation. Senator John C. Blackall was assigned by the Republicans to the Committee on Executive Nominations as an assurance that my appointments requiring the assent of the Senate would be fairly considered. For all this, there loomed the danger of the Democratic caucus subject to the tight control of the Old Guard under the unit rule. Almost always the generalissimo of the Old Guard was on hand to whip the caucus into line for or against the Governor's bills as he might deem expedient. So uncertain was I of the outcome of his caucus which usually met every morning on legislative days that I sometimes hesitated to make a recommendation to the General Assembly unless I was reasonably sure that it would be approved by the other two parties. Several of the Old Guard Senators never entered my office during the long session. From their point of view they owed their allegiance not to the Governor but to an outside politician who could promise them judgeships or other positions in minor courts as soon as a court deal could be arranged to distribute the spoils. I was a Governor without a party.

XXVIII. A Lively Coalition Government

In my attempts to mould three parties to single objectives I had, as much be expected, only partial success. For consolation when I failed, I used to hum to myself a half-forgotten spiritual first heard in my boyhood:

> I'm sometimes up and sometimes down,
>   Oh, glory Hallelujah

Political experience, I argued with myself, is much like religious experience. Both have their ups and downs. In either case be ready to shout Hallelujah and move on to something else.

I had my first rising and sinking spell when on the very first legislative day of the General Assembly (January 17, 1935) I sent in a special message requesting the immediate passage, under a suspension of the rules, of an act continuing the Emergency Relief Commission, which would otherwise expire in February 1. Speed was necessary to enable the Governor to make application before it was too late for a Federal grant of $1,200,000 as Connecticut's quota of relief funds for the next month. Without debate both Houses took favorable action on the request by a unanimous vote.

But I was riding for a fall. The Judiciary Committee cut from the proposed act I submitted a provision for the creation of a Connecticut Rehabilitation Corporation to be administered by the Emergency Relief Commission with the addition of four members affiliated directly with the Federal Government. As far back as I can remember, many workers in manufacturing cities had been moving out into surrounding country districts where they built comfortable homes for their families on small parcels of land, sufficient for the cultivation of vegetables for their own use. The purpose of the Rehabilitation Corporation was to give impetus to this movement by Federal aid. Towards such a resettlement project I anticipated no objection whatever, for one reason because it involved no financial responsibility on the part of the State. But I was totally out on my reckoning. Owners of tenement houses in the cities feared a loss in their rentals; the State Grange feared that homesteads would have surplus products to sell in competition with regular farmers; and the Socialists were against the proposal as discriminatory in that it would benefit only a few families, no more than two hundred, not the whole army of industrial workers. After a week's vacillation the Republicans decided to make the Rehabilitation Act a party issue. The bill, with the aid of the Socialists, went down to defeat in the Senate, under the cry that a corporation such as was contemplated would be an encroachment upon the sovereign rights of the State of Connecticut.

This fine display of Yankee independence received high praise from Governor Talmadge of Georgia, who had ridiculed trivial N.R.A. projects like employing men to rake leaves back and forth from one pile to another at a wage of $3 a day as if this were work. Senator Huey Long of Louisiana likewise congratulated Yankees for unfurling the banner of States Rights and, in addition to that, inundated the businessmen of Connecticut with letters and pamphlets in the hope of converting them to his political philosophy whereby every man might become, like himself, a Kingfish.

As my guest, Governor Talmadge came into the State on the National Maritime Day of that year (Sunday, May 19) to plant a Georgia dogwood tree by the grave of Stevens Rogers in Cedar Grove Cemetery at New London. It was the 116th anniversary of the voyage of the S.S. *Savannah* from Savannah to Liverpool under command of Stevens Rogers and his brother-in-law with a New London crew, who were the first to cross the Atlantic in a ship propelled by steam. Governor Talmadge was a pleasant companion. I suggested that he quit raking leaves for a day or two and visit me in Hartford. I could assure him, I said, that the General Assembly would like to hear a speech as eloquent as the one he had just given. He appreciated the honor and expressed regret that he must get back home before the leaves of Georgia began to fall again.

Defeat of the Rehabilitation Act indicated an anti-New Deal atmosphere among Republicans and, strangely, among their Socialist affiliates which might spell death to important parts of my legislative program which I hoped to carry through in financial coöperation with the Federal Government. As I feared, the entire building program for humane institutions, after lingering debates, fell dead. There was, however, no disposition to abandon such Federal aid as the State was receiving through the Emergency Relief Commission, the Highway Department, and other agencies. Nor was there, it soon developed, any strong objection to Federal grants for several new projects which were to be set up for this or that purpose. But in the main the Republican policy preferred going it alone. The ghost of States Rights which the Republicans raised cost the State, I estimated, $10,000,000, which a different attitude might have elicited from Washington.

Enthusiasm over preserving the sovereign rights of Connecticut cooled to the freezing point when the General Assembly began to consider the report of the Tax Commission, appointed two years before, to revise the tax structure of the State and its subdivisions. The aim of the comprehensive report was to distribute the tax burden equitably between State and municipalities so as to make them, functioning together, sufficient unto themselves, without the uncertain assistance of Washington. Conspicuous among the recommendations were two emergency measures, one a personal income tax on interest and dividends to insure a balance of the State's budget, and the other a temporary sales tax, the income from which was to be allocated to towns and municipalities for relief of the unemployed and to lower the tax rate on real estate. I was in favor of the personal income tax provided the rate be reduced and of the sales tax provided food and clothing be excluded from its operation.

The two proposals of the Commission were long debated in both Houses. The socialists balked at both forms of tax and Republicans and Democrats feared that either would darken their prospects of victory in the next election. Except for a tax of one mill on every cigarette sold in the State (a bill saved in the Senate by a margin of one vote), and a revision of the tax on insurance companies and other corporations and on unincorporated business, the Tax Commission's recommendations were all thrown into the scrap heap. On the Governor's shoulders was cast the responsibility of balancing or unbalancing the State's budget; and Mayors and town officers were left to obtain from the Federal Government what they could to ease the burden of the unemployed, either through State agencies or by their own direct applications. Fortunately Washington was generous in grants in contrast with Connecticut, where political exigencies proved to be stronger than the desire to maintain "the sovereign rights of an independent State."

A report of the Judicial Council, signed by Chief Justice Maltbie and other eminent jurists, was submitted to the General Assembly, recommending a constitutional amendment calling for the establishment of a district court system and for the appointment of minor court judges by the General Assembly on nomination by the Governor. Bills incorporating these recommendations were rejected as usual. But on the question of negotiating a minor court deal with the Democrats there was some stalling by Republicans, who remembered too well the scandalous deal of 1933. To avoid a recurrence of anything like that, they discussed, I understood, a plan of ignoring the Democrats and of proceeding in their own way with the aid of the Socialists. This plan failed probably because the Socialists, loud in their cries against court deals, were reluctant to go along with them.

While the Republicans, near the end of the legislative session, were drifting towards the unsatisfactory conclusion that they must leave the appointment of minor court judges to the Governor, pandemonium broke loose among the Old Guard Democrats who, in order to organize the Democratic party in the Senate against the Governor, had made promises which they must keep. It had been agreed, they claimed, that they were to have their share of the minor court judges, and by God they were going to have it. Otherwise they would hold back in the Senate all further legislation by a filibuster down to the day of adjournment. All the Democratic Senators, it was announced jocosely, were to be supplied with Bibles. Every morning after the Chaplain's prayer, one after another was to be recognized by the Chair and to read aloud as long as his voice held out. So it was to go on, day after day, until a judgeship deal was consummated. Under no circumstances was a Republican Senator to be recognized, however loud his shout to the Chair. My reaction to this procedure was to remark that if the Senate would listen attentively to the reading of the

Holy Scriptures for a week or ten days I would willingly forego all further legislation by the present General Assembly.

Under threat of a filibuster Republicans yielded to a court deal as easily as frail human nature yields to sin. On the day of the consummation of the deal, May 28, 1935, a dramatic scene was enacted in the Senate. The Lieutenant Governor took his seat on the throne. A Republican leader and an Old Guard leader, neither of whom was a member of the Senate, took their places on the steps below him where they were to watch the proceedings and prompt him whenever he needed it. One by one the Republican chairman of the Judiciary Committee presented the names of the judges who had been agreed upon in the deal and moved the resolutions for their appointment. When his voice or his legs began to grow tired, another member of the Judiciary Committee took his place. It required not much more than an hour to distribute the jobs, as favorable action was taken in each instance without debate and under suspension of the rules.

But in spite of this unholy start, this General Assembly enacted more progressive legislation than either of its two predecessors in my administration. Some measures which had been ridiculed or played with or stubbornly opposed now gained easy passage. When in 1931 I advocated old-age pensions I was asked if I were looking for a pension for myself. Now, in 1935, a pension system was established with only one vote against the measure in the entire General Assembly. When I signed the bill my office was crowded with visitors. Again, in 1933, I could discover no representative of labor or capital who was in favor of making the old Board of Mediation and Arbitration a workable agency for the settlement of strikes and labor disputes. Now a bill for the purpose was passed in House and Senate without a roll call.

Along with this legislation, the maximum hours of labor for women and minors in factories were reduced from 55 to 48 a week; their employment in all kinds of night work was prohibited; and sweatshops were put under stricter control. There were also set up a Public Welfare Council, one of whose functions was the better care of young dependent children, and two Juvenile Courts, since increased in number to cover the whole State, to deal with delinquent boys and girls.

There was a sudden and unexpected collapse of long resistance against conferring upon the Public Utilities Commission larger power over the regulation of electric, gas, and water rates charged by public service corporations, over the issuance of new securities, over mergers of independent units, and over holding companies doing business within the State. Everything I had been working for was in the new statutes. Of all States, Connecticut was first in the field in requiring of all persons before marriage a favorable report on the Wassermann or a similar standard blood test.

A Planning Board which I had temporarily organized to cooperate with the Emergency Relief Commission on welfare projects was given legal standing. One of its first projects was an aerial map of the entire State, made from photographs taken by low-flying airplanes, on so large a scale as to show roads and streams. It proved to be of great value to the Highway Department and various commissions, such as those on Water Supply, Park and Forests, Wild Life, and in general on the geology and the natural resources of Connecticut. Sections of the map, studied closely revealed in several places privately owned unoccupied land which had long escaped taxation!

For my part in killing all hope of a pari-mutuel horse and dog racing by vetoing the innocent-sounding "Act Creating a Connecticut Racing Commission," I won the most opprobrious descriptive name in the English language. Henceforth to the end of the session I was called "an old son of a bitch," spoken in bitter accents by political enemies, nonchalantly by the indifferent, affectionately by my friends. I became so accustomed to the title that it lost its ignominy for me. I came to like it rather better than "the dear old gentleman down at Yale."

This session I had a novel experience. It was my custom from time to time to send to the General Assembly short messages on pending legislation, usually requesting haste on a particular measure. Such messages were referred to the proper legislative committees for consideration. This year the tables were turned by an open letter from Senator Bradley, who, as spokesman of the Judiciary Committee, asked me what was really in my mind concerning the reorganization of the state government which I had advocated in three Inaugural Messages. His letter was a challenge for a positive statement. It also had political implications; for during the recent campaign I was accused by Republican orators of ringing the bells for reorganization without playing any tune. Now, in accordance with the new Republican policy of quick action, Senator Bradley expressed the hope that a plan of reorganization might be worked out and put through the present session of the Legislature, perhaps without the aid of a special committee. At any rate, on this and other questions the Judiciary Committee would welcome recommendations from the Governor.

To his courteous letter I replied with equal courtesy, explaining why it would be necessary eventually to raise a committee to deal with many difficult problems of reorganization, though a beginning might be made with several mergers of departments and the passage of a few general acts, all of which I enumerated. Most of these recommendations became the basis of bills 1 drafted by the Judiciary Committee and reported to the General Assembly. Then began the fun.

The proposal that the functions being performed by the Departments of Domestic Animals and Food and Dairy be placed under the Commissioner of Agriculture was drowned in cries of opposition. Outweighing the estimated salvage of some $20,000 a year by this merger was the certainty that two Commissioners, their deputies, secretaries, and other members of their staffs would lose their jobs. One of the Commissioners who was in danger remarked to his friends, "The Governor don't love me no more." The attempt to unify the health services of the State by transferring a number of independent boards and commissions to the Department of Health also failed. This would have meant another loss of jobs, some of which, supported by liberal fees, were good for $4,000 or $5,000 a year. Again a bill embodying my recommendations that the office of county coroner be abolished, since the duties of coroners were being taken over by the State Police, was killed in both Houses. A saving of $50,000 in court expenses counted as nothing against the retention of twenty-odd jobs—eight coroners, eight deputy coroners, eight secretaries, and other assistants. Something, however, was salvaged by an act putting coroners on reasonable salaries and fixing the fees of their subordinates.

Against these failures House and Senate, on the day before final adjournment, passed unanimously a bill consolidating the two divisions of the Military Department. But on the discovery, after its passage, that the bill eliminated an office held by a popular colonel in the National Guard, it was recalled the next morning by a joint resolution of House and Senate from the engrossing clerk where it had spent the night. So the act was killed merely by not giving the Governor a chance to sign it. The Judiciary Committee met with better success in a bill centralizing the administration of state aid to veterans under one head. No loss of jobs was involved in that transaction.

My recommendation to the Judiciary Committee that two existing Welfare Departments be merged, after lying dormant for nearly four months, was favorably reported in a bill submitted to the General Assembly for action a week before adjournment. The bill passed both Houses in a rush, and I immediately signed it, unwilling to take a chance on its recall. When my appointment of Frederic C. Walcott for Welfare Commissioner was finally approved by the Senate, the way was opened for him to put upon its feet and set going one of the great departments of the State.

Finally, in schoolmaster fashion, I reminded my friend Senator Bradley that "no government can reach a high degree of efficiency and economy if the tenure of office in the various departments is subject to the whims of political leaders." This was the first clear call for a revival of the merit system of appointments, such as flourished in the time of Governor Simeon E. Baldwin but afterwards met with a violent death under the blows of its enemies. As a courteous gesture, I think, the act which Governor Baldwin sponsored and administered was revamped with some alterations and accorded a public hearing, at which the principle underlying the so-called merit system was fiercely assailed by concerted action. The superintendent of one state institution, who had had nine years' experience with civil service in Massachusetts, declared that it gave more protection to the inefficient than help to the efficient. Another said that he left New York State and came into Connecticut "to get away from the disgrace of civil service." These two men were followed by a miscellaneous crowd of politicians who sang to the same tune. A few voices spoke up in favor of the proposed bill, notably Mrs. Ruth Dadourian, President of the Connecticut League of Women Voters. Where, I wondered, were the professional civil service reformers of past years.

As a consolation for the failure of the General Assembly to establish a general merit system for the appointment of state employees, I was able on my own initiative to try out two experiments in competitive examinations in the Labor Department without special legislation. The first experiment was in the division which administered the State Employment Service in affiliation, under one Director, with the National Reëmployment Service as recently authorized by the General Assembly. In bringing these two services into harmonious action, I appointed an Advisory Council representing capital and labor with Dean Furniss of the Yale Graduate School as chairman. Examinations were conducted by a small committee. When I saw and talked with the young men and women who came through the ordeal with the highest ratings, I had no doubt concerning the efficiency of a merit system if administered by skillful hands. I felt what proved to be true, that the State's employment agencies were now placed upon a plane that would command the respect of our great manufacturing companies which soon began to make large use of them.

Subsequently in the more elaborate set-up for the administration of the Unemployment Compensation Act, the Governor was specifically directed to appoint a personnel committee of three, no one of whom should be a political office holder. President McConaughy of Wesleyan University I named as chairman. On my first meeting with the committee I told the members that as it was not written in the law how they should make appointments to this extensive service, they were free to take a long step forward by adopting the merit system of competitive examinations. They took the long step, with the coöperation of Miss Helen Wood, the Director of this division of the Labor Department. Their success was preëminent. Before they finished their work they made hundreds of appointments. In some of the States, among these the largest, where partisan politics was made the basis of appointments, the administration of the Unemployment Act broken down completely, while Connecticut's administration received very high praise from the Federal Government as a model of smooth-going efficiency. Officials from two or three other States were advised to come to Hartford to see how the law was working here.

Slight success in merging related departments of the State or in reorganizing others from within convinced everyone who was engaged in the experiment that little could be accomplished without thorough preliminary studies which would need months for their completion. It was a happy day for me (May 3, 1935) when I signed a bill which passed House and Senate without a dissenting vote, authorizing the Governor to appoint, with their "advice and consent," a commission of five to formulate a comprehensive plan for reorganization of the entire state government to be presented to the next General Assembly.

So representative was the commission which I was able to form that it also was approved unanimously. When a few months later I began to watch these men laying the foundations of the state government on the principles of a great business corporation, I was excited by the prospect that all the essential services which the State was then performing might be easily maintained, under proper management, at a reduction in cost of more than a million dollars a year. Such was the estimate of that mental arithmetic in which I claimed to be an expert! Like Bruce's spider, I could see not far above me the ceiling of one of my political ambitions.

A year after adjournment of the Assembly it was discovered that the date fixed by statute for the meeting of Connecticut's Presidential Electors to cast their ballots for President and Vice-President of the United States must be advanced from the traditional day in January following a national election to the first Monday after the second Wednesday in the preceding December. This change was made necessary by an Amendment to the Federal Constitution, ratified in 1933, declaring that the terms of President and Vice-President shall expire at noon on January 20, instead of at noon on March 4. Here was an emergency that necessitated a special session of the General Assembly to amend the state law; for if the Presidential Electors should cast their ballots on a day other than the one prescribed by Congress, the validity of Connecticut's electoral vote might be questioned. It surely would in the event of a close election.

After a conference with political leaders, I convened the General Assembly in special session on November 5, 1936, the second day after the election, when partisanship would be on a vacation. During the holidays besides taking proper action on the emergency and authorizing the city of Bridgeport to issue more refunding bonds, the Assembly passed two progressive measures of large significance.

In my Inaugural Message at the opening of the regular session in January, 1935, I had taken an unequivocal stand in favor of unemployment compensation, then less exactly called "insurance against unemployment," suggesting, however, that it might be well to wait for the outcome of national legislation on the subject, already under discussion in Congress. After the passage of the Social Security Act which provided for aid to States that enacted laws for unemployment compensation in harmony with the Federal Act, I appointed a committee to study the whole question and report a bill for emergency consideration, since action had to be taken before January 1, 1937, in order to secure all possible benefits accruing under the Federal law which went into effect on that day. With a few alterations the bill recommended by the committee was now quickly passed and approved by Washington.

For months I had been conferring with Father Panik, the pastor of a large Slovak parish in Bridgeport, over the creation of Housing Authorities for slum clearance in our cities. My inspection of slum areas in various places convinced me that this priest, who like his Master was devoted to the welfare of the poor, should be supported to the utmost of my influence in his endeavors to rid this city and the whole State of overcrowded and unsanitary tenement houses, the lurking holes of disease and crime, and to build, in cooperation with the Federal Government, on the old sites or elsewhere, groups of model tenements facing open spaces, for the health and comfort of families of low income. Though I was reserving consideration of a Housing Act, which had already been drawn, for the next General Assembly, I found to my delight that the present Assembly was ready to take favorable action upon it. The bill was readily passed and I signed it, notwithstanding that it was unsatisfactory to me in several particulars which I hoped might soon be modified.

The Housing Act was a worthy supplement to the Unemployment Compensation Act, on the passage of which in the House the Republican floor leader, Mr. Daniel F. B. Hickey, congratulated his colleagues in a little speech, beginning: "Today this legislative body has passed on of the most important as well as progressive pieces of legislation that any lawmaking body has ever been called upon to consider. You may indeed feel proud of your action, because you have laid the cornerstone of a far-reaching beneficial law which will aid and comfort hundreds of thousands in our State."

There was no irony in my address when I bade the General Assembly a second and last farewell.

After their meeting in Atlantic City, the 1937 state governors' convention travels to Washington, D.C. to meet with President Franklin D. Roosevelt. Governor Cross stands 2nd from left.

Left to right: Gov. George D. Aiken, Vermont; Gov. Wilbur L. Cross, Conn; Gov. M. Clifford Townsend, Indiana; Gov. Richard C. McMullen, Dela; Gov. Olin D. Johnson, So. Carolina; Pres. Roosevelt; Gov. James V. Allred, Tex; Captain Paul H. Bastedo, retiring White House Naval Aide; Gov. George C. Peery, Va; Gov. Harold G. Hoffman, N.J.; Gov. Bibb Graves, Ala; Gov. Henry H. Blood, Utah; Hon. Cary A. Hardee; Gov. Leslie A. Miller, Wyo; Gov. Homer A. Holt, W.Va.; Gov. Lloyd C. Stark, Mo; Gov. Blanton Winship, Puerto Rico; Gov. Fred P. Cone, Fla.)

Used by permission, Utah State Historical Society

XXIX. The Connecticut Tercentenary

Two highly celebrated events occurred during my terms as Governor. The first was the observance, which I have already described, of the 200th anniversary of the birth of Washington. The second was the commemoration of the 300th anniversary of the founding of the Connecticut Colony, which extended through the six middle months of 1935. The aim, as it developed in the minds of its promoters, was to present by word and scene the growth of three small plantations along the Connecticut River into the most independent State in the Union. Nothing as grand as that had ever been attempted in the history of Connecticut.

Five years were required to work out the details of a celebration on so large a scale. The initiators were representatives of various patriotic societies under the leadership of Dr. George Williams of Hartford, then President of the Connecticut Historical Society. On their request, Governor Trumbull was authorized by the General Assembly, in 1929, to appoint a Tercentenary Commission of seven members, of whom Dr. Williams was elected the chairman, and during my first term as Governor I was elected honorary chairman. Then began a delightful friendship with Dr. Williams, which was, however, cut short by his death towards the close of 1933.

In January, 1934, Col. Samuel H. Fisher of Litchfield was elected a member of the Commission and its chairman. It was my function through 1934 to assist Colonel Fisher in Addresses, some of them over the radio, foreshadowing coming events. I have reason to remember especially the Thanksgiving Proclamation of 1934, in which I paid tribute to the men and women, "the known and unknown, the dead and the living," who built the Commonwealth of Connecticut. For this purpose I took parts of an eloquent passage in Ecclesiastes in praise of famous men, arranging the quotation in the loose form of free verse, each line beginning with a capital letter. A Presbyterian divine came down heavily upon me in a sermon which he gave out to the press, because I nowhere mentioned the name of God, to whose wisdom and power were due all good that had ever happened in Connecticut, not to the personal achievements of a miserable lot of politicians, who deserve not thanks but utter condemnation. He admitted that I acknowledged "the many mercies of Providence," but claimed that I had intentionally used that phrase to avoid the word God. He seemed to assume that a Democrat must be an atheist. The real joker in his diatribe was that he apparently did not know that the Proclamation was based on words attributed to none other than Solomon.

An editor, though he could find no fault with the Proclamation, regretted that I did not give the source of my quotation, if indeed it was a quotation. "Thousands in Connecticut," he wrote with fair exaggeration, "have been trying vainly to ascertain the original, many searching libraries and reference books for it." He hinted that the Governor was perplexing "common scholars" with malice prepense.

The time came when I could hold no longer. The president of a Connecticut Press Association whose members were having a luncheon at the Hartford Club, caught me in the lobby and led me into a private dining room where fifty or more newspaper men were seated at a long table. "We have hauled you in here," he said, "to tell us where you got that quotation. None of us know." "If some of you will guess first," I replied, "and no one guesses right, I will tell you where I got it." A Dartmouth man guessed Shakespeare. A Yale man guessed Milton. Several guessed the Governor! I thanked them and expressed regret that they had all overlooked the eloquent passage in their casual perusal of the Holy Scriptures. Before we broke up I had to cite book and chapter for their own possible future use.

On the morning of April 26 members of the three great branches of the state government—legislative, executive, and judicial—marched from the Capitol to Bushnell Memorial Hall to commemorate at high noon the day when, 299 years ago, the General Court of the river towns—the first three Connecticut settlements, Hartford, Windsor, and Wethersfield—held its first meeting, the harbinger of constitutional government not only in Connecticut but in the United States. The long procession was led by the colors and music of the Governor's Foot guards in their red uniforms of the Revolution. The bell of the Old State House, designed by Bulfinch, was ringing, a dozen church bells chimed in, and whistles shrieked all over Hartford.

As I sat on the platform of the Bushnell Memorial and looked around and in front of me at the members of the General Assembly, numbering hundreds, at the judges of the high courts in their robes, and at the military display, and up at the galleries filled with spectators, I contrasted in my mind's eye that impressive scene with the first session of the General Court, centuries ago, comprising no more than eight freemen and a few town committees, who for a time performed all the functions of government, judicial and executive as well as legislative. They thrived very well for nearly three years without a Governor, and when they decided to have one, they took good care to bind him with so hard a knot that he could do no harm.

By invitation the Governors of the other New England States were present or sent their representatives. Most appropriately they chose for their spokesman Charles H. Smith, ex-Governor of Vermont, whom I introduced to the audience as coming from "New Connecticut," the earliest name of that colony in the north countree, where among the first settlers were young men with their wives from Connecticut in search of new lands which cost little or nothing. Ethan Allen of Litchfield was one of them. Some sixty places where they staked out homesteads they named from Connecticut towns whence they came. All this I put into my introduction of the ex-Governor, along with a story I once heard that when the Green Mountain boys met in a convention to frame a constitution they appointed a committee to draw one up and then adjourned after passing a resolution that in the meantime they would "abide by the laws of Connecticut and the laws of God until they could devise something better." As a matter of fact, Vermont came within an ace of being admitted into the Union under the name of "New Connecticut."

Prompted by Colonel Fisher, I had issued three months earlier a proclamation in behalf of the people of Connecticut, inviting "their fellow citizens throughout the Union and their friends over the border and beyond the seas" to join with them in the commemoration of the founding of a commonwealth where once dwelt the men and women from whom they descended. Whether the proclamation addressed to the whole world had any influence or not, I do not know. But visitors came and registered from every State of the Union except one, from Alaska and Hawaii also, from nearly all the provinces of Canada, and from a score of other foreign countries beyond the two great oceans. From Hertford, England, came an official delegation of citizens to greet the citizens of their Connecticut namesake.

The Tercentenary Commission arranged through local committees for church and other public celebrations in nearly all the communities of the State. And to accentuate Connecticut's religious history, I designated by proclamation both a Saturday and a Sunday in October for special services, which were attended by several hundred thousand people, Jews and Christians. Until that year I was unfamiliar with the ritual in the Eastern Church, as represented by the Greek, Armenian, and Russian Orthodox branches. I was in Easton, Connecticut, to assist in commemorating the organization of the first Methodist Society in New England by Jesse Lee, an itinerant preacher, who visited my native town when my great-grandfather, Ephraim Gurley, was a young man and near that time was converted to Methodism. I listened to a sermon on the history of the Baptist Church in America and made comments thereon. I gave informal talks to young people in two synagogues, in one instance as a part of the service.

I recall a field Mass celebrated at Danbury in memory of a field Mass celebrated in 1781 by the Count de Rochambeau who encamped there on the way with his French troops across Connecticut to join Washington's army on the Hudson. When I was conducted into the field with my military staff, I first caught sight of a beautiful extemporized altar on a high platform, over which floated the Stars and Stripes and the flags of Connecticut and the Roman Catholic Church. Altar and platform were flanked by various religious orders in full uniform, among whom I recognized the Knights of Columbus. It was to be, I could see, a civic as well as a religious memorial. Within a few minutes came the long procession of the clergy led by the Bishop of Hartford, who took their places by the high altar.

At the conclusion of the Mass, Bishop McAuliffe unexpectedly invited me to respond to the greetings I had received. When I stood upon the platform, I faced a multitude of men and women spread out in an immense fan, all standing except a large group of nuns in their white habits seated immediately in front. As the Bishop and Monsignor Finn of Norwalk had already said about all that could be said on the history of the Catholic Church in State and nation, I had to strike a new note. Near me was sitting a Syrian priest, then on a visit to the United States, to whom I had been introduced. I took him as my subject. That priest, I said, speaks a modern Aramaic language which in its oldest form was the language Jesus of Nazareth himself spoke. The presence of the man from Syria thus brings us near the Master whom we all worship, whether Catholics or Protestants.

As part of the celebrations, immense concerts were given at the Yale Bowl and the Music Shed in Norfolk with nationwide hookups. The Yale Art School and other art galleries displayed the work of portrait painters from colonial times down to the present day. There were several exhibitions of colonial arts and crafts; and numerous old houses, with their collections of colonial furniture and utensils, were opened for public inspection. Standing by the house of Governor Jonathan Trumbull in Lebanon, I greeted George Washington and his wife Martha, as they drove up in a coach, and Lafayette and Rochambeau who followed them in a tally-ho. The house had just been restored by the D.A.R. Over in Mansfield, on the beautiful grounds of Connecticut University, I impersonated one of my ancestors, that Wade Cross who was fond of blue stockings.

I opened with a short address the great exposition in the State Armory at Hartford, the aim of which was to present successive stages in the development at Connecticut's manufacturing industries from small beginnings to the ever-expanding industrial areas of the twentieth century. From memories of childhood in Mansfield village, where time moved slowly away from colonial days, I was able to go back to the survival of the woodshed and the adjoining forge, where farmers made their tools, on to the gristmill, the sawmill, and the first little silk mill which depended on a brook to make its wooden wheel go round. From there onwards a series of seventy-five murals, hung in the exhibition hall, represented the march of industry in the State through inventions and new procedures, and showed how Eli Whitney's ingenuity in devising a method of making interchangeable parts in the manufacture of guns revolutionized all mechanical industry and foreshadowed modern mass production in huge quantities. My grandfather's clock, still keeping perfect time after a century of labor, is a good representative of the transition period. The brass works were assembled from manufactured interchangeable parts, while its unique case was evidently made by the hands of one man.

The many spectacular scenes of the celebration culminated in October in the Hartford civic and military parade, a march of 20,000 through the length and breadth of the capital city. Prizes were offered for the best floats. In the competition Mark Twain was accorded special honors, as was fitting, for 1935 was the centenary of his birth. Prizes were awarded for three floats, in one of which Mark Twain was seen writing *A Connecticut Yankee;* in another was a miscellaneous group of his characters; and in the third Tom Sawyer was painting the fence. It was significant that among the purely historical floats the first prize was won by an Italian for "The First Thanksgiving Dinner at Plymouth," and the second prize by Swedish societies for the "Viking Ship," recalling the voyage of Leif Ericson of Iceland.

The year before, in my Thanksgiving Proclamation, I gave humble thanks to Providence for guiding the hands of innumerable men and women, long since at rest, most of them in unvisited tombs, who once, coming into a wilderness, laid the foundations of this fair and flourishing State of ours. Now, completing the circle of recent events, I praised, in another Thanksgiving Proclamation, "The Lord of Life, our source and our stay through long generations":

"Especially during this year in the festivals of our founding, we have felt beside us the presence of souls unseen who have rendered the story of Connecticut worthy of grateful honor, and have entrusted to us its children their patience, their courage, their faith, their charity, their work and the joy of their being. We have drawn closer the ties of blood and of neighborhood. We have been stirred afresh to love for this plot of earth that holds us as in the hollow of a hand; and to loyalty for the high aim, still hard beset, still strong and unyielding, to raise upon this earth a just, friendly, and enlightened community—the fairest of all our portions.

"As we keep and cherish these memories, with the remembrance of our many other blessings, it becomes us so to live out our lives by the truth of the past and the truth we see that our State may be in league with time, striving mightily forward, now and forever, towards the dawn of the Golden Age."

XXX. The Year of the Great Flood

In the spring of 1936 the river valleys of Connecticut were inundated by a disastrous flood, unprecedented in the State's history. Spring freshets have always been a common occurrence in New England, rivers, large and small, in that season of the year often breaking over their banks, carrying away here and there an old dam or an old bridge. Such scenes I have witnessed since childhood. The Connecticut River, all through historical times, has had the habit of occasionally rising some ten feet above the flood stage of sixteen feet at Hartford and spreading over wide areas of rich meadow land. When the great central river began its slow rise in March of 1936, no flood of more than usual proportions was anticipated; but when a few days later the river suddenly took a jump not of a foot but of several feet, we became alarmed.

Something was happening that had never happened in the last three hundred years. Warm rains which fell in torrents broke up the ice everywhere and melted the deep snows along the watersheds of the Connecticut's tributaries far to the north in Vermont and New Hampshire. In the first days of the flood a gigantic ice jam formed above the Bulkeley Bridge connecting Hartford and East Hartford, and there was another jam at the Middletown bridge, which engineers were preparing to dynamite. At the same time a small river winding through Bushnell Park below the State Capitol was choked up at the point where it enters the Connecticut River, creating by the backwash a lake which flooded neighboring streets. From the roof of the Hartford Club we watched day by day the great river as it spread out into an immense inland sea. Directly in front the congested east side of Hartford gradually became a part of this slow-moving sea. From other points of vantage we saw to the south waters rushing through broken dikes, and huge oil-storage tanks floating down the stream, bobbing up and down like corks.

The crisis came Wednesday, March 18. On that or the preceding day most of the families of the east side were evacuated. The next day the river rose to a level of 30 feet, higher by a foot than ever before. On Friday it leaped to 35.6 feet, and on Saturday the 21st to 37.5 feet. The river thus played recklessly with its history. On Sunday the level fell a foot, but the end of disastrous days, though then in sight, was not yet at hand.

The night of greatest fear was the night of Friday the 20th. That evening electric light, telephone, and city radio services, all three of them, went out of commission, and Hartford's municipal airport was a complete wreck. Save for here and there a kerosene lamp and candles shining in windows, the city was in utter darkness. By the light of a candle stub I went to bed towards morning. Rains, which now and then let up, were pouring down harder than ever. Rumors that later proved untrue were spread that the inmates of the State Prison at Wethersfield were in a wild insurrection. As a matter of fact, that Friday gang after gang of those inmates worked hard to save the prison walls next to the river. And they succeeded. One of the men who had had experience with floods acted as boss, and the Pardon Board later reduced his sentence. When the lights went out after supper the inmates went to their cells without disturbance. Their conduct was in all ways admirable.

From the beginning of the flood I kept in close touch with Mayor Spellacy of Hartford. As soon as danger threatened, state and municipal police worked in coöperation, the National Guard and the Naval Militia were called out and the local chapter of the Red Cross and the American Legion volunteered invaluable assistance. During the evacuation days these military and civic groups plied boats and canoes through the swirling waters of streets, rescuing from upper stories and roofs scores of families, who clung to their homes until all hope of retaining them was lost. Only one person drowned: a man caught in a little church, who was unable to make his escape through inrushing waters.

After the flood the State and municipalities were confronted with large and difficult problems of relief and rehabilitation, some of which demanded quick solution. In Hartford two thousand homeless people were at once housed and fed for weeks in the State Armory and in public schools where instruction of children had to be suspended. Diesel engines were used for lighting hospitals, hotels, and other public buildings. Haste was necessary in cleaning the Connecticut, Farmington, and Housatonic valleys of débris, refuse, and dead animals, which threatened an epidemic of typhoid fever. On the day when the waters began to recede I set up an Emergency Council for coordinating the work of all relief committees which could be reached throughout the State. Every morning they met in my office for a two-hour conference.

On the first morning I read telegrams from the chairmen of two national relief agencies freely offering their assistance. Three days later a committee of the Emergency Council–Attorney General Edward J. Daly, Welfare Commissioner Frederic Walcott, and I—started for Washington to confer with Henry Hopkins, head of the Federal Works Progress Administration. The afternoon before we left Congressman X called at the Capitol to inquire whether and when we were going. I told him that we intended to leave New Haven at midnight, breakfast at the Mayflower, confer with Mr. Hopkins at ten, and lunch at one with Senator Maloney. Having obtained this information, Congressman X abruptly left my office. When we arrived at the Mayflower, Congressman X with others was already in the lobby to greet us. How he got there before us I never knew. The weather was too bad for anyone to risk his life in a plane.

Precisely at ten o'clock we appeared in the anteroom of Henry Hopkins' sanctum. I informed a girl at the desk by the door that we had an appointment with Mr. Hopkins. She expressed regret that we would have to wait a little while, as he was in conference with Congressman X. When at length we were admitted to the inner office, I examined floor, corners, and ceiling but found no Congressman X. Mr. Hopkins said with a laugh, "He just went out that door." It was a private door. Someone gave it out to the press that Congressman X and another Congressman had been called in by Mr. Hopkins in advance of the Governor's party to give him a graphic account of the disaster at first hand, as they had spent the week end in boats on the swollen Connecticut River talking with victims of the flood. As it happened, the victims had already been rescued and were either being cared for in public buildings or walking dry streets.

Nor was much of the destruction yet visible, for the flood ladder still stood above 34 feet, only 3 feet below the top round. Still, it was a good tale to tell. I admired the art by which Congressman X jumped in ahead of everybody else. This is the way to get on in the world.

Harry Hopkins promised to allocate to Connecticut $3,000,000 if necessary, for work projects in the stricken areas. He appointed Co. Lawrence Westbrook as his personal representative in the State with instructions to proceed without delay. Admiral Grayson, national head of the Red Cross, assured me that his representative, Robert A. Shepard, would stay on in the State until all the poor people rendered homeless by the flood were fully restored to their previous ways of living. Their houses, if they had any, he said, would be repaired and refurnished for them.

The remnant of that strenuous day Walcott and I spent with the Admiral, whom I was meeting for the first time. Business over, we fell to storytelling. The Admiral had been the friend and medical adviser to three Presidents of the United States—Theodore Roosevelt, Taft, and Wilson, and on my prompting, he related anecdotes of all of them. When I mentioned President Harding he at first looked sober and was silent. After a moment's hesitation he said nearly in these words: "I had only slight acquaintance with Harding. Once he called me into his office on a trivial matter. As I was about to leave, he asked me not to go yet. I kept my seat while he bowed his head over his arms resting on his desk and muttered, wiping his eyes, 'They have betrayed me.'"

As soon as bridges and roads were made passable Admiral Grayson and Harry Hopkins visited Hartford. By that time the full extent of the wreckage along both sides of the Connecticut River was visible. Their representatives remained on as members of the Governor's Council, which continued to meet nearly every day for three weeks. On its dissolution the Governor dealt individually with its separate sections. By May 1 the Connecticut and other river valleys were cleared of the worst and most dangerous debris. All workers in the flood areas were inoculated against typhoid fever, with the result that not a case of this or any other infectious disease occurred. The C.C.C. boys had helped out admirably in their quick work in cleaning and disinfecting flooded houses so that their former occupants might return to them without undue delay. Just before they were to go back to camp, Mayor Spellacy, joining with the State, gave them a dinner at which each one of them was presented with a wrist watch along with other expressions of gratitude. A thousand new watches began to tick.

Nature restores and renews as well as destroys. By June all traces of the flood in Hartford, except in places along the banks of the great river, had nearly disappeared. Dwelling houses had been rebuilt or repaired. In that month Hartford was able to celebrate for three days the 300th anniversary of the arrival of Thomas Hooker and his congregation of men, women, and children, a hundred of them, driving their cattle before them. The historical pageant which opened the celebration was presented by 400 schoolchildren in Bushnell Park near replicas of Hooker's first house and first church in Hartford, both of which had been submerged by the flood. Rains and waters now gone, the deep green of lawns and slopes was revealed in the bright sunshine. Nature, proceeding in her own quiet way, had plucked beauty out of disaster.

At that time I was occupied with measures to mitigate, so far as possible, the ravages of periodic inundations of the Connecticut Valley. Mayor Spellacy was maturing plans for the protection of Hartford by a system of dikes and by diverting the Bushnell Park River through an underground tunnel to prevent it from ever again overflowing into the heart of the city. For the State there loomed the large problem of protecting lands and people on both sides of the Connecticut River all the way from the Massachusetts border to the Sound.

A geologist submitted a proposal that the course of the great river near Middletown be turned to the east into a prehistoric bed, which was still fairly well marked, so as to eliminate a narrow passage below the city which held back the natural flow of water for several miles to the north. This proposal appealed to my imagination. I liked the idea of going down in history as the Governor of the State who altered the course of the Connecticut. I looked over a part of that old bed. Though not an engineer, I could see enormous difficulties in such a project, enormous cost and doubtful success also. I recalled that there was once a wild scheme to give the river Rhône a wide sweep around the peninsular city of Lyons in France, which after a little consideration was abandoned. With this precedent in mind the vision of becoming the Governor who moved a river vanished into thin air. I was not to be a Moses who dried up a sea or a Joshua at whose command the sun stood still.

So, on the advice of engineers, I fell back on a less spectacular plan, which I had discussed with the Governors of Vermont, New Hampshire, and Massachusetts, for control of the wayward Connecticut River, whenever it went on an occasional fortnight's spree, by means of a series of reservoirs on its upper tributaries. After further study of the plan, the Governors decided to appoint a Joint Committee, three from each State, to draw up a compact under the terms of the Federal Omnibus Flood Control Act of 1936, then pending in Congress, whereby the cost of the flood projects was to be divided between the national government and the signatory States. Beginning on June 3 the Joint Committee held through the summer and autumn a number of meetings in Boston, which were usually attended by representatives of the Engineering Corps of the United States Army. Progress was rapid. A compact seemed to be in sight by the next year. What happened to the compact I shall presently relate.

XXXI. Political Landslide

Another political campaign was approaching, this time both state and national. Casual remarks of mine after the election of 1934 gave color to the inference that I would not seek a fourth term as Governor. But when the leaders of the Old Guard began to ignore me as if I were no longer to be reckoned with, I could not lie down and let them walk over me. I was not very uneasy because one of the Old Guard triumvirate was elected Democratic National Committeeman. I was ready to accept him for the sake of harmony. What irritated me was the attempt so to organize the Senate of 1935 that my major appointments would be subject to the dictatorship of the spearhead of the Old Guard, in the interest of Lieutenant Governor Hayes, who was to be my successor in the Governor's chair if all went well. How the tables were turned against these political maneuvers and how a large body of progressive legislation was enacted by the General Assembly of 1935 through the coöperation of the Republican and Socialist members, I have already related. On the day when a commission was created to revise the administrative structure of the state government, I could do nothing else but choose to run again, in the hope that a light which had led me on for six long years might be something more substantial than a will-o'-the-wisp.

For the present, however, nothing was said of this intention. Meanwhile the Lieutenant Governor, as a rival for first place on the Democratic ticket in 1936, began to criticize my policy of appointing Republicans to important positions. Let this go on a little longer, he declared, and there will be no Democratic party in Connecticut. At that time the slogan against me was "For every job there is a Democrat as good as any Republican."

Another Democratic rival for the Governor's chair was Mayor Alfred N. Phillips of Stamford, who summed up his opinion of me in the picturesque sentence: "The Governor is about as useful to the people of the State of Connecticut as last year's telephone book."

There was no need to announce my own candidacy for renomination.

Silence showed that I was in a receptive mood. An extraordinary incident occurred at a $25-subscription dinner at the Hotel Taft in New Haven as early as November 9, 1935, in honor of Homer Cummings, the Attorney General of the United States. Present were Jim Farley, National Chairman of the Democratic party, Connecticut's two Democratic Senators, four Democratic members of Congress, and state officials and leaders. I was honorary chairman. When I rose to make an introductory address I noticed a disturbance at a table in front of me. A young lawyer who was in a mellow mood was struggling to get to his feet out of the hands of friends who were trying to hold him down. He freed himself from their clutches and, straightening himself up to his full height, declared: "We are here tonight to honor Governor Cross whom we are going to elect again next year." Everybody was flabbergasted. The tense moment was relieved by loud applause. Jim Farley on his departure that night left instructions, I was told, "to let Governor Cross carry the ball as the best bet for a touch-down in 1936."

Farley came to Connecticut again to look over the political battlefield. It was well that he came; for since his previous visit there had set in a rising tide of fierce criticism of President Roosevelt and the New Deal. Democrats were worried. On the night of May 6, 1936, the chairman of the Democratic National Committee was greeted at the Hartford Club by an audience of eleven hundred, coming from all parts of the State, who filled the great assembly hall and the still larger adjoining dining rooms. He made a most telling and dramatic speech in vindication of President Roosevelt's policies. His appeal for harmony went far towards cementing all the Democratic factions in Connecticut for the duration of the campaign. When he finished there could be no doubt about who would head the State's Democratic ticket.

The matter was sealed on May 25 at an elaborate dinner given by Lieutenant Governor Hayes at the Waterbury Club in honor of the new Democratic National Committeeman. I was soon shaking hands with a hundred Democratic leaders from all parts of the State. On the surface it was a harmony feast. That night I heard men who had intrigued against my policies call me "the greatest Governor in the history of Connecticut" and express the ardent hope that I would accept a renomination—in one instance "unless I felt it imperative to be relieved of a heavy burden." I smelt the rat when my turn came to laud the new National Committeeman. The Lieutenant Governor, who as toastmaster introduced me, predicted that I would begin my fourth term as Governor next January. I replied that I was willing to run again provided he would accept a renomination as Lieutenant Governor. When I sat down, he said that he would go along with me if that was the desire of the Democratic Convention which was to meet in September. I hardly need to point out that there were hostile undercurrents in this exchange of courtesies.

The Republican Convention for the nomination of a state ticket opened a day in advance of the Democratic Convention with an incident which, like the flood, was unprecedented in Connecticut history. On coming into the Hartford Club on Tuesday, September 8, for a late dinner, I met in the lobby J. Henry Roraback and Harry Mackenzie. They had just dined together. We shook hands. Roraback remarked that they were going over to the Foot Guard Hall to hear the Republican keynote speech. He invited me to come along with them. I laughed at what I took to be a pleasant jest. When he began to urge me, assuring me of a grand reception, I declined the honor on the ground that my presence at a Republican Convention would be misunderstood by both political parties. Moreover, I added, "I know in advance what your keynoter will say. It will be a long continuous shriek of a party in despair." "Come along," he repeated, "you will hear some good things about yourself before we knock you out. This is your last chance." We parted with another shake of the hands.

That evening Roraback as leader of his party began his address before the Republican Convention with a eulogy of Governor Cross which in abbreviated form was something like this:

"I saw Governor Cross at the Hartford Club before coming over here and told him that the Republicans were about to nominate the next Governor. He seemed relieved. (Applause.) . . . We have been fortunate that during the last six years we have had an honest man who believed in law and order as the Governor of the State. It is no fault of his that we now have a deficit of $14,000,000. If the Governor had had his way, we would now be well on the way out of debt. Unlike the Republicans, the Democrats would not coöperate with him. But without his party's support, he has saved for the State millions of dollars."

In the course of his speech Roraback approved my plan for the reorganization of the state government. There was a good deal of consternation, until he forecast a Republican victory in Connecticut by a majority somewhere between 150,000 and 300,000. This news was greeted with thunderous applause. He concluded by announcing that he was going away for a short rest but would return in three weeks "with bells on and whistles blowing."

There was a sharp contest among the delegates over the question whether Hugh Alcorn, who was defeated in the last election, or Arthur Brown, the genial State's attorney for New London County, should be nominated for Governor to carry the Republican banner to the huge foreordained victory. The honor fell to Brown. The orator who put Alcorn's name in nomination predicted that Brown would be knocked out by Cross in the first round. He was booed.

The next evening the Democrats convened as usual at Eastern Point to nominate their state ticket. As I came down the stairway to Senator Maloney's keynote speech, the lobby, crowded with delegates, was in commotion. J. Henry Roraback was there looking for the Governor. He said that he had come down to see how the Democrats do business. "In the morning," he said, "I am going to start on a cruise in my yacht, *Heilander*, which is at anchor in the harbor. Before leaving I want to say good-by to you." I wished him "a fine trip." After advising delegates to renominate Cross, he departed with a friend.

Roraback's extreme courtesy, the Republican press generally held, was an assurance that the campaign would be conducted on decent lines. Some, however, thought that he was playing a shrewd political game. I surmised that he might be trying to kill me with kindness. Perhaps none of us was quite right.

The next day the entire Democratic ticket of 1934 was renominated by acclamation. The nominating speech for Governor was made by

Edward J. Daly, the Attorney General, who had been requested to indulge in no highfalutin talk. The platform, which was adopted unanimously, did not hesitate to recommend again measures that had previously failed of enactment, as introductory to a large body of new legislation looking toward the future. Every declaration was straightforward without a squint towards compromise.

The Republicans in their and political speeches sought to subordinate state issues to issues arising out of the New Deal, which they denounced as an attempt to overthrow constitutional government. Such state legislation as they advocated was more or less nullified by "escape clauses." Civil service reform ought to begin by rooting out the spoils system in the Federal Government. The report of the Commission on the reorganization of the state government should be carefully studied. The provisions of the Social Security Act should be considered in connection with the preservation of the sovereign rights of the State. The State budget should be balanced and our humane institutions should be maintained in accordance with Republican policies before the Democrats came into power. In all new legislation it should be remembered that problems like education, relations between employer and employee, care of the unfortunate, and old-age pensions are reserved by the Federal Constitution to the States.

In some of my speeches I attacked that plank in the Republican platform which decried "the use within Connecticut of Federal funds to purchase a surrender of the rights reserved to this State." "Am I to understand," I asked, "that if you Republicans come into power you intend to dam up this flow of Federal funds and to start a flow of your own by an enormous increase in state and local taxation to care for the unemployable and to provide work for the able-bodied unemployed? Just what is to be your policy? Have you considered that the citizens of Connecticut are paying Federal income taxes which nearly match the grants and loans of the national government? In the long run it will be an even break, whether or not you like the manner of it. In the emergency I am ready to lay the unsubstantial ghost of state sovereignty. I am ready to accept funds for the aged, the unemployed, dependent children, the blind and the crippled, for humane and educational institutions, for school and other buildings, for the extension of highways, and even for the extermination of mosquitoes in the marshes along the shore." Against this last proposal I received a protest from a sportsman who informed me that the extermination of mosquitoes would result in the extermination of ducks who feed on their larvae. This left me in the dilemma of deciding between the welfare of human beings and the welfare of ducks. I decided against the ducks.

The Republicans fell back on the question: who was responsible for the State deficit? It was as inane a question as "who killed Cock Robin?" The next year Connecticut was going to have, they said, a Governor who would balance the budget just as Governor Landon had done in Kansas. I remarked that the glory of Landon's feat was somewhat dimmed since the Constitution of Kansas compelled him to keep within the limits of a budget which he himself submitted to his legislature for approval, whereas the Connecticut budget was a log-rolling prerogative of the Appropriations Committee of the General Assembly. Bear in mind too, that several Kansas counties, in order to keep their budgets in balance, closed their schools for a time until President Roosevelt supplied Federal funds for reopening them. As for Connecticut, the deficit came nearly, if not quite, to an end on July 1, 1935. Expenditures no longer exceeded income though all the services of the State including education were being maintained as usual. This happy situation was due to increased income from taxation as a result of the improvement in business, supplemented by taxes imposed on cigarettes and alcoholic liquors by the Legislature in 1935.

On Saturday night immediately before the election J. Henry Roraback appeared on the stage in another surprising performance, during which he again declared that the deficit should not be laid at my door. The occasion was a Republican rally in West Hartford. The principal speaker was the Republican candidate for Governor who was very critical of my public record. On the orator's return to his seat Roraback as presiding officer rose and, waving a finger towards the candidate's head, chided him for his attack on me, saying, to put together scraps of his speech as quoted in the newspapers:

"Mr. Brown, I don't agree with you in what you have to say against Governor Cross.... Wait a minute until you hear what I have to say about

Governor Cross—that grand old gentleman. . . . He has made a good Governor . . . I have met him so often at the Hartford Club that I like him. . . . You shouldn't say all those things about him. . . . When I once referred to him as 'the dear old gentleman from Yale' I felt that a college man lowered himself when he went into politics and I meant to point that out to him."

For a short while the contest in Connecticut between Roosevelt and Landon (who had the better press) was nip and tuck. But Landon soon began to fall behind. He was now red hot against the New Deal, and yet for three years he had come down hard on the Federal Government for funds for relief projects in Kansas. He was charged with using troops to quell strikes and he wobbled over the Social Security Act which provided for unemployment compensation, thereby losing the labor vote in this State and almost everywhere else. He accepted the nomination for President on the condition that his party should support him in an effort to restore the gold standard and yet made no effective issue of the devaluation of the dollar, to the disappointment of hard-money advocates. He would abrogate all trade agreements with other nations, which were lifting Connecticut out of the slough of the depression. In the rear lurked another protective tariff act which Arthur Brown openly advocated as a means of curing the ills of the textile industry. Inconsistencies in Republican policies for which Landon was spokesman his manager attempted to submerge one way in the East and another way in the West. The effort was futile, for his words were carried into all parts of the country. It became clear that Republican policies in prime essentials aimed at "a return to normalcy," though that phrase could not be safely used, for normalcy now had come to mean Herbert Hoover.

There was one amusing incident just before the controversy died a natural death. I had been explaining to the farmers certain proposed amendments to the Milk Control Act. A Republican orator who was put on my trail told those same farmers that I was wasting my time on discussing milk, for if Roosevelt were elected there would be no cows to give milk. They would be unable to survive another four years of the New Deal. I went about much among the farmers. At a country fair a gentleman farmer tried to pin a Landon sunflower over my heart. "None of that, my friend," I said, drawing back. "It would be beneath the dignity of a Governor to wear a yellow flower which is grown mostly in clumps to conceal outhouses." "That's right," shouted a dirt farmer. "Give it to him hot. That's all sunflowers are good for."

While the Republican campaign was slipping, President Roosevelt made a tour through the central part of the State. Thursday, October 22, the day after they had toured Massachusetts, Mayor Spellacy and I met President and Mrs. Roosevelt in their private car at the railway station in Hartford. The President was revising his Hartford speech, deleting and adding phrases and sentences to his typed copy as the sheets were handed to him one by one by a stenographer. As soon as the speech was completed for reporters, we four headed a motorcade for the Music Shell in Bushnell Park where the speech was given. The streets were so thronged that it was difficult for the police to keep open a passageway. When the President stepped forward on the platform of the Shell and waved his left arm, he was greeted with "one of the greatest uproars in the history of Hartford tumults." It was estimated that 100,000 men, women, and children crowded into the park and surrounding streets. Avoiding all controversial questions, the President urged quick completion of the flood control compact between the New England States and gave a few precise statistics to show that prosperity was on the way back to Connecticut. When he finished his brief speech the people seemed unwilling to let him go.

By invitation of the President I rode with him and Mrs. Roosevelt over the journey southward to New Haven, Bridgeport, and Stamford. Senators, Congressmen, and local officials occupied by turns the seat facing us. Along the way out of Hartford streets were lined with people, and hands or flags waved from open windows. Wherever we passed a clump of houses, sometimes only a single house in country districts, the President was greeted with waving hands or shouts of families on the lawns. He made ten three-minute speeches that day. It was estimated that seven or eight hundred thousand people came out to greet him—almost half the population of the State.

After the President's tour there could be no doubt about which party would win the election in Connecticut. There was no more talk about a big Republican majority. Privately the Republicans hoped that Landon might come through with a small majority as Hoover had done in 1932. Cross they conceded might win but he would have a Legislature against him. I professed to have but one fear, which was that Landon might carry Kansas.

On the evening after the battle, I sat for a while at the Hartford Club with friends, Democrats and Republicans, listening to the returns. It was generally agreed that Connecticut might go Democratic by a good margin, but nobody anticipated a landslide. While we were speculating on the probable width of the margin, weighing this consideration against that, we were interrupted by a radio voice announcing at intervals that Hartford had gone Democratic by a plurality of 27,000, New Haven by 21,000, Waterbury by 14,000, and Bridgeport by 20,000 for Roosevelt and 16,000 for Cross. Greatly excited by the news, I went over to the receiving room of the *Hartford Times*, where the returns were being tabulated as they came in. The vote was proportionately much the same in other cities and industrial boroughs. Some of the small towns, too, were going Democratic and most of the rest were showing reduced Republican majorities. Assured of a tremendous victory, I visited the Democratic Headquarters to join in the pandemonium over "the sweep, landslide, and avalanche." Nothing like that wild scene had I ever witnessed before.

Thence I set out for New Haven, where a houseful of friends, mostly Republicans, were waiting to greet me. I telegraphed President Roosevelt: "Returns show that you have carried Connecticut by a majority so large as to strain my knowledge of arithmetic." At midnight I broadcast my thanks to citizens of the State for electing me a fourth time as their Governor. When I awoke in the morning and looked over the news, I had no further fears about Kansas. Only two states remained faithful to the Republican case: Vermont and Maine.

As officially determined, Roosevelt won over Landon in Connecticut by a majority of 103,444 votes. All state officers were reelected by varying majorities above 90,000. I led with a majority over Brown of 95,763, despite an active campaign against me as a back number by Mayor McLevy, the Socialist candidate for Governor, who polled 21,000 votes.

The 6 Democratic candidates for Congress easily won over their Republican opponents. Connecticut's representatives in Congress in both House and Senate now formed for the first time in my memory a solid Democratic body. The political complexion of the General Assembly was also materially changed. The 3 Socialist Senators who had held the balance of power were all defeated. The number of democratic Senators rose from 17 to 26, leaving the Republicans with a small minority of 9. The House, however, was still safely Republican, though chastened by a loss of 15 seats.

Happily both political parties were ostensibly with me on the legislative program I intended to submit to the General Assembly. Most courteously the Republican candidate for Governor issued a statement asking his party to "swing behind Governor Cross" on his progressive measures such as bills establishing a district court system and granting the right of jury service to women, which he himself had advocated during the campaign, though they were not in the Republican platform.

On the second day after the election the General Assembly of 1935 convened in special session to enact emergency legislation that could not wait for action by the new General Assembly which would not meet until January. On the emergency agenda was an Unemployment Compensation bill, which quickly passed both Houses without any display of political fireworks. In the atmosphere created by the election, partisanship seemed to be giving way to partnership in legislation for the public good, such as I had hoped for when I first took office six years before. How long, I wondered, would the new era last.

XXXII. "The Heel of Orion"

Time out of mind at this turn of the seasons when the hardy oak leaves rustle in the wind and the frost gives a tang to the air and the dusk falls early and the friendly evenings lengthen under the heel of Orion, it has seemed good to our people to join together in praising the Creator and Preserver, who has brought us by a way that we did not know to the end of another year. In observance of this custom, I appoint Thursday, the twenty-sixth of November, as a day of Public Thanksgiving for the blessings that have been our common lot and have placed our beloved State with the favored regions of earth—for all the creature comforts: the yield of the soil that has fed us and the richer yield from labor of every kind that has sustained our lives—and for all those things, as dear as breath to the body, that quicken man's faith in his manhood, that nourish and strengthen his spirit to do the great work still before him; for the brotherly word and act; for honor held above price; for steadfast courage and zeal in the long, long search after truth; for liberty and for justice freely granted by each to his fellow and so as freely enjoyed; and for the crowning glory and mercy of peace upon our land;—that we may humbly take heart of these blessings as we gather once again with solemn and festive rites to keep our Harvest Home."

In this Thanksgiving Proclamation, issued while the special session of the General Assembly was engaged in humane legislation, I felt justified in dwelling upon the good things which under a Divine Providence had come to our State during the year. As I left out the flood, labor disputes, and other disagreeable events, for which I could hardly give thanks, I received a severe drubbing from a Congregational minister who took the Proclamation as his text in a union Thanksgiving service. He was sorry that Connecticut had a Governor who could not face realities. He missed in the Proclamation, for instance, "a confession of sins on the part of the Governor, the legislators, and the people who form the constituency of the State and nation." It may be that he was disappointed in the outcome of the election.

For others the Proclamation struck a note in harmony with emotions prevailing at the close of the year. It was read in hundreds of churches within and without the State. It was read over the radio by Alexander Wollcott in a nationwide hookup, and published by him in his *Second Reader*.

About that one novel phrase it contained, the "heel of Orion," I received many inquiries. One day a college student called on me at the Capitol with a request that I settle for him two bets he had made about my Thanksgiving Proclamation, which he and his classmates had discussed with one of their professors of English literature. "Fire away," I said. "Did you," he first asked, "build up, as some of us think, your Proclamation around the phrase 'under the heel of Orion'?" I replied that Orion did not come into the Proclamation until the last revision. The boys could not find the phrase in either Milton or Shakespeare, he said, though they supposed one or the other to be the author. Nor was it in the Bible. "The bet is on whether you took it from some ancient writer or invented it yourself." I replied that credit for the "heel of Orion" belonged to Helen McAfee, my colleague on the *Yale Review*, who, so far as I knew, coined the phrase herself. He seemed perplexed. He had lost the first bet, he remarked, and was uncertain how the second should be decided inasmuch as the phrase, though not my own, had apparently first appeared in a Proclamation over my name. I recommended him to consult an expert in casuistry.

The origin of the phrase was thoroughly investigated by my learned friend, Dr. McGregor, pastor of a Congregational church in Norwalk, Connecticut, who held three Yale degrees. Assuming that "the heel of Orion" like "the heel of Achilles" had an ancient literary connotation with which he was unfamiliar, he started out in researches to determine what it was. He went through all sorts of reference books, in some of which he found Orion but never Orion's "heel." In his quandary he consulted the staff of the Hayden Planetarium in New York City, where an assistant curator found a quotation from Aratos, a Greek poet, physician, and astronomer of the third century B.C., which referred to "Orion's feet." Unable to pursue his investigations further, Dr. McGregor appealed to me for help.

Out of curiosity I looked up Aratos, whose astronomical poems, I discovered, so appealed to Cicero that he translated them from Greek into Latin. I learned also that Saint Paul quoted from one of them in his famous address to the Athenians on Mars' Hill, where he spoke of God "as one in whom we live, and move, and have our being, as certain also of your own poets have said." I looked again at an old drawing of Orion and saw on an exposed foot two other stars besides the one at the heel, all of which Aratos saw when he looked into the brilliant Grecian heavens more than two millenniums ago. Aratos and I have since become friends.

XXXIII. Sit-down and Other Strikes

S tar gazing came quickly to an end on rumors that a general strike in the metal industries of the State was brewing. During 1936 a large number of labor disputes and minor strikes, thirty-two of them in the summer, were easily settled by the Board of Mediation and Arbitration or by the Commissioner of Labor acting under the Board's authority. There were, however, two serious strikes which, other means failing, I tried to mediate as Governor.

My first attempt was with a walkout at the Lawton Mills, a large cotton textile plant which dominated the beautiful village of Plainfield in eastern Connecticut. As almost always, both sides were at fault. Every effort I made for a compromise on the wage scale, the question at issue, was spurned by a professional strike leader who was brought in from Providence. Hopeless of a settlement, the president of the Lawton corporation advised the stockholders to liquidate the concern. On March 3, the day when they met to decide the momentous question, I placed in their hands a personal letter requesting that they defer action until they had carefully considered a proposal to apply to the Reconstruction Finance Corporation for a loan to satisfy emergency obligations and to complete their equipment of modern looms so as to improve their position in a highly competitive business. They informed me that an application for such a loan had already been made and the loan had been denied on the protest of President Green of the A.F.L., who held it would be taking sides against the strikers. For lack of temporary financial assistance the Lawton Manufacturing Company went out of business, with irreparable damage to a hitherto flourishing mill community, leaving a body of skilled workmen to shift for themselves elsewhere. A similar walkout which was threatening in another village was prevented by quick action before a professional strike leader could get on the scene. But that is not in the public record.

My next experiment in direct action was in connection with a bitter strike at the Middletown plant of the Remington Rand company, a corporation organized under the laws of Delaware for the manufacture of all sorts of office equipment including noiseless typewriters. Besides the plant at Middletown the company had seven others located in the States of New York and Ohio. Apparently most of the workers in all the eight plants (6,000 of them) were on strike. As the company, with its plants thus scattered, was engaged in interstate business, it was a question whether any one State could legally intervene to force a settlement of the strike within its own borders. Nevertheless I decided to make a trial.

The strike in Middletown broke out on May 26, with disturbance approaching a riot. At the request of the Mayor, I sent to the scene a body of the State Police to assist the local police in maintaining order in the conduct of the strike. A week later the Connecticut Board of Mediation and Arbitration invited officials of the Remington Rand company and of the union to a conference to discuss all phases of the dispute with a view to a quick settlement. The President of the company, James H. Rand, Jr., ignored the "invitation" on the ground, as stated in the press, that the Board, being a state agency, had no jurisdiction in the case. Somewhat later, when he was summoned to appear before the National Labor Relations Board in Buffalo at a hearing to answer a complaint by strikers in his New York plants, he escaped that ordeal by obtaining an injunction against the prosecution of that complaint on the ground, it was said, that the strike was only a state affair. In this way Rand avoided for a long time any settlement of the strike, by playing state and national agencies against each other.

The strike in Middletown went on for weeks and months with no end in sight. For a short rest I took a run up to Lake Sunapee over the Fourth of July, leaving instructions with my Executive Secretary, Philip Hewes, to call me back on the first indication of a more serious turn in the strike. There was to be no recurrence, if I could help it, of the incident of 1934, when the Lieutenant Governor called out the National Guard without informing me of what he was doing. The summons came at noon on July 8. Four hours later I was at the Capitol. There had been the night before, I learned, a rather hot fight between strikers and strikebreakers. Rocks had been hurled through windows of the plant, and automobiles bearing strikebreakers had been stoned and overturned. The next day I conferred with my friends among manufacturers and Labor leaders. I visited Middletown. All was quiet. A hundred state policemen were on duty with nothing to do.

With the approval of advisers, I sent telegrams to Governor Lehman of New York, Governor Davey of Ohio, and James Rand asking for a conference with them in New York City. Rand refused to take part in any negotiations with Governor Davey, who, he feared, could not be relied upon to keep his word! For this and some other reasons the conference was never held. Instead Rand, on my invitation, met me at the Hartford Club for an hour's talk. He was in a genial mood, ready to do anything I asked of him. When we parted I thought that we were well on the way towards the end of the strike. I asked him to put in a concise statement what he was willing to do. Within a day or two came "the concise statement" in the form of a telegram which in substance reiterated his old position at the outset of the strike. As far as he was concerned the strike was over. Under certain conditions he would reemploy the strikers in so far as he needed them. But he would not enter into any negotiations with them or with leaders of their union for their return. So I understood him.

Still the strike went on. Near September 1 it reached a climax. Twice the State Police used tear gas to clear the main street of strikers, strikebreakers, and their sympathizers. I was between the devil and the deep sea. The Mayor of Middletown and other municipal officials urged me to call out the National Guard and to declare martial law. Officers of the Connecticut branch of the A.F.L. urged me to withdraw the State Police. I did neither. I asked the State Police Commissioner to do just two things: to replace the lieutenant who had resorted to the use of tear gas with another of better judgment; and to forbid his men to enter, except in an emergency, the yard of the Remington Rand company so as to make it clear that they were not in Middletown, as strikers alleged, to protect strikebreakers but to enforce generally law and order all over Middletown. The Police Commissioner was in full agreement with my proposals which we put into effect immediately.

The day after my renomination for Governor I address in Bridgeport the annual convention of the Connecticut branch of the A.F.L. It was predicted that there would be an uproar, that half the delegates would rise and walk out on my appearance in the hall. Nothing of the kind occurred. I was cordially greeted by the President, a friend who always voted for me, and the Secretary, another friend who never voted for me. I gave the convention a full account of my attempts to settle the strike with Rand whom I described as "a damned hard man to deal with." I allayed fears about my ordering out the National Guard. I told the convention about the progress being made in drafting an Unemployment Compensation Act, which I was to submit to a special session of the General Assembly. "I announced that I had appointed Joe Tone, the Commissioner of Labor, who was present, as my representative to take personal charge of the strike. Then came an uproar of approbation, amid which I could only try to say that he would advise me on the withdrawal of the State Police. I added that it was not the business of the national government to put an end to a scandalous interstate strike which Federal agents had already investigated and condemned.

Already the C.I.O. under John L. Lewis was attempting to corral under its banner employees of the State's metal industries, with what success it was difficult to discern. By February, 1937, it looked as if the first Connecticut plants on the C.I.O. docket would be branches or associates of General Motors and General Electric. Against any threat of tying up a large group of industries with sit-down strikes, the technique the C.I.O. was then using, I settled in my mind upon a procedure to enforce, whenever the emergency might arise, the laws of a State in which the right to strike does not carry with it the right to take possession of another's property and to hold it for some personal advantage in dealing with the owner. The test came unexpectedly at the Groton Electric Boat Company on the Thames across from New London, whose chief business was building submarines for the United States Navy. Its employees had their own union for collective bargaining about which there had been no serious trouble until a local of the Industrial Union of Marine and Shipbuilding Workers, a unit of the C.I.O., stepped in to get control of the company. Leaders of the Industrial Union, hailing from New York City, succeeded in bringing into their fold 108 of the 2,000 workers in the plant and towards the end of February, 1937, ordered a sit-down strike to force the company first to reinstate a discharged C.I.O. worker and then to recognize the local C.I.O. as the bargaining agency for all employees.

The sit-down strike lasted for only one day. Armed with bench warrants charging the strikers, after being discharged and receiving their pay, with trespassing on the company's property, the State Police evicted them all at midnight. Most of them walked out in obedience to police orders. A few were hustled out.

The next morning (Thursday, February 25) I received in my office at the Capitol a committee of the strike outfit comprising its organizer, treasurer, and secretary. With me were my Executive Secretary, Philip Hewes, Attorney General Daly, Police Commissioner Sunderland, Labor Commissioner Tone, and Morgan Mooney, who, as Secretary of the State Board of Mediation and Arbitration, had settled scores of labor disputes of which time has left no record. The state leaders were sitting on my right and left when the strike officials entered and were invited to take seats in front of me on the other side of my desk. Reporters brought up the rear. That the conference might start off in good humor I passed around a box of Connecticut seed-leaf cigars.

Few cigars were lighted before the organizer of the strike shouted at me across the desk: "Did you receive my telegram last night demanding that you remove them Cossacks you sent down to Groton? I demand that they be removed at once or there will be bloodshed." Considerably aroused, I jumped up and replied, with a slow emphasis on each word: "I want you to understand, sir, that there will be no sit-down strikes in Connecticut so long as I am Governor. State Police will stay on until the strike is over. They are down there to protect you strikers as well as everybody else. The workers outnumber you strikers twenty to one. Were the police withdrawn, you would all be thrown into the river." The three members of the strikers' committee complained further that the police "split" the picket line at the main gate of the plant. That action, I told them, was in accordance with Connecticut practice as a means of forestalling fights between ingoing and outcoming workers and strikers crowding around gates, which might lead, as you say, to bloodshed. "That there may be no misunderstanding in regard to the rules of picketing," I concluded, "Commissioners Sunderland and Tone will come down to Groton this afternoon to confer with you." So ended the conference. The way in which Connecticut dealt with its first sit-down strike was flashed across the country. It met with general approval except among groups of radical labor leaders and "progressive thinkers" who wanted to come to Hartford and convince me that the sit-down strike was legal in Connecticut as well as everywhere else. John L. Lewis warned the Governor to look out what he was doing. I accepted the challenge. I sent him word that Connecticut could manage its own affairs.

The Groton strike was of short duration. Its organizer was removed by the Industrial Union for some act, I forget what it was, which reflected on his character. He "skipped." The statewide strike in the metal industries involving General Motors and General Electric branches and associates never materialized. There were afterwards a few minor sit-down strikes, which were not permitted to continue into the night. Before asking strikers to leave their seats, on orders of the Governor, the police were instructed in all instances to arrange for a conference the next morning between a committee of the strikers and the managers of the company concerned. In this manner a number of disputes were amicably settled. In face of an aroused public opinion, the sit-down strike could not live in Connecticut.

XXXIV. Reorganization of the State Government

The General Assembly convened on January 6, 1937, and organized without a repetition of the long-drawn-out fight in the Senate two years before. True, there had been since the election a quarrel between the two factions of the Democratic party over who should enjoy the usufruct of great victory. But the triumvirate of the Old Guard, which was weakened by the defection of one member, could not hope to organize the Senate in their own interest, for of the 26 Democratic Senators 20 lined up in support of the Governor.

Had I myself picked the floor leaders of both parties, they could not have given me greater satisfaction. Raymond Devlin was reelected Democratic leader of the Senate and E. Gaynor Brennan Republican leader. The House chose Noah Swayne as Republican and John Thoms as Democratic leader. Joseph Lawlor, an old political war horse, was made President of the Democratic Senate, and J. Mortimer Bell, another political war horse, was made Speaker of the House. The setup in both Senate and House augured well for getting things done.

No one, I think, called attention to the fact that nearly all the official leaders of the Senate and House had some connection with Yale. Devlin and Brennan were graduates of the Yale Law School. Swayne was a graduate of Yale College, who at Commencement dinners used to lead the alumni in the national anthem and "Bright College Years," and Thoms was a graduate of both the College and the Law School. And the Chief Justice of the Supreme Court, W. M. Maltbie, was adorned with three Yale degrees: B.A., LL.B., and Honorary LL.D. Lack of hostile comment on this surplus of men trained at Yale surprised me; for when I first ran for Governor in 1930 I was advised to keep my New Haven connections in the dark if I wished to be elected.

I felt at home as one of this team, although I had not always been so fortunate in dealing with the party leadership of my first two administrations. After that, the reins began to flap loose. In 1937 the Democratic reins dropped from the old driver's hands. They fell, too, from the Republican dictator's hands. J. Henry Roraback, for months mentally ill, took his own life in May of that year. I attended his funeral and sat among his friends. For twenty-five years he had ruled his party as a benevolent despot and most of that time he had controlled the legislative and administrative policies of the State. His mantle fell upon the shoulders of lieutenants who did not command the respect of their party. Republican as well as Democratic members of the General Assembly were now relatively free to run through the mill a very large grist of legislation.

In my Inaugural Message and in conferences with members of the General Assembly, I let go of nothing which had failed in previous recommendations. Strangely enough, jury service for women, which had been advocated by the Republican candidate for Governor as well as the Democratic, was made a party issue in the House, where a sharp battle was fought over the question. As in 1933 and 1935, women were bluntly informed by Republican psychologists that they were too emotional for the sane consideration of criminal cases and wholly lacking in the knowledge of law and business necessary for dealing with civil actions. In retaliation, the psychologists received some hard hits from women members of the House, one of them a lawyer. On the final vote, 35 Republicans bolted their party and joined with the Democrats in the passage of the jury service bill by a small majority. In the Senate the majority was overwhelming, 29 to 5.

After a struggle of sixteen years, women won the right to sit in the jury box of Connecticut courts. The event was celebrated in my office when I signed the bill, surrounded by a large company of women facing a camera. I recited for them Clough's famous poem beginning:

Say not the struggle naught availeth.

I submitted a report from the Judicial Council, this time accompanied with a bill, for the establishment of thirty-three District Courts in place of some seventy city, borough, and town courts. The bill, which had behind it strong public support, stood no chance with the legislators who found all manner of fault with the lines on which the districts were drawn. In an endeavor to satisfy these faultfinders, chief Justice Maltbie redrew the district lines, only, however, to awaken as many other faultfinders. No one, of course, was deceived by this sort of criticism, which was a cover for the retention of several hundred political jobs connected with the seventy minor courts—judges, deputy-judges, prosecutors, clerks, stenographers, etc. To save something out of the original design the Chief Justice, at my request, drafted a third bill which made it permissive for two or more contiguous towns to establish, under certain conditions, judiciary districts. This bill passed the Senate but was defeated in the House by a vote of 2 to 1.

Public opinion was so incensed by the defeat of a modified District Court bill that neither political party, in view of the election next year, dared enter into another minor court deal. There were a few attempts at one, but none succeeded. As a result the General Assembly on the day of adjournment threw all but two of the minor court judges into the lap of the Governor for interim appointments. A political stalemate over the control of local courts presented an amusing spectacle. For one year at least I gained temporarily more than I had previously striven for in vain, which was that the judges of all courts, whether they be called major or minor, be appointed, not by the Governor, but by the General Assembly or the Senate on the nomination of the Governor.

The General Assembly was now developing and bringing to a conclusion a vast legislative program for which it will be distinguished in the annals of Connecticut history. First on the agenda was the consideration of the financial condition of the state government, which I summed up in my Inaugural Message. There had accumulated during the leanest years of the depression a deficit somewhat overestimated at $14,000,000 in the running expenses of the State. That it was no larger, I now informed the Assembly, was due to the policy of the Board of Finance and Control, whether Democratic or Republican, of making no addition to the existing services performed by the State, and confining capital outlays to the repairs of state buildings. It seemed to me that the time had come to put our financial house in order and to initiate a building program to meet the imperative needs of our educational, humane, and corrective institutions.

How far it might be necessary to broaden the base of our tax system to finance new activities was a question to be left for future consideration. The immediate proposal which I made with some trepidation, not knowing how it would be received, was that the State be authorized to issue serial funding and building bonds, running for twenty years, to an amount not exceeding $25,000,000, of which at least $11,000,000 would be available for the erection and equipment of a Veterans' Home for disabled soldiers and a new Training School for Defectives (for both of which land had been bought), for new buildings at the Fairfield Hospital for the mentally afflicted, at all the State's sanatoria for tubercular patients, and at the Connecticut State College. That this program, hardly more than indicated, might be greatly enlarged, I requested legislation which would permit Connecticut to avail itself of its share in such funds as might be allocated to States for building and other purposes by the Federal Government.

The proposal was greeted, not as I feared with cool silence, but with general applause which promised quick legislative action. A bill was passed under suspension of the rules, authorizing the issue of bonds in the amount I recommended and creating to supervise the issue a commission of five members, who elected the Governor as chairman. Under another suspension of the rules the Governor was designated administrative agent of the State to apply for and receive Federal funds for construction and other purposes. These two bills, passed by a Republican House, were immediately transmitted to a Democratic Senate which took favorable action upon them with equal dispatch. The Democrats were a little sore because the Republicans under the leadership of Noah Swayne got the edge on them.

At last, after six years of waiting, the day also arrived for repairing, if not rebuilding, the central administrative structure of the state government. The commission created by the General Assembly in 1935 for this purpose, known as the Reorganization Commission, placed in my hands a copy of its report on January 25, 1937.

The commission comprised Dean Clark of the Yale Law School, well known for his previous studies in government; Thomas Russell, who, as a member of the House some fifteen years before, had been chairman of a committee on a revision of the state government, which was ridiculed to death by political leaders of his own party who would have none of it; F. Goodwin Smith, who like Russell was a clearheaded businessman; Senator Kenneth Cramer, who was showing a keen interest in both the theoretical and practical aspects of government; and Tom Hewes of decided ideas, who, as the only Democrat among the five members was properly elected chairman. They chose as their secretary Benjamin Whitaker, afterwards Professor Economics at Union College.

These men had undertaken the heavy task of formulating a plan for the integration of the executive branch of the state government as I had often recommended in the interest of economy and efficiency, by the elimination of all duplicate services and efforts, by the abandonment, reconstruction, or mergers of existing departments and the creation of such new departments as might be deemed advisable. Investigation revealed in the executive group a mass of more or less independent commissions and boards, a few of which were appointed by the Governor directly, more by the Governor with the advice and consent of the Senate or the General Assembly as a whole, and several either by the Senate alone or conjointly with the House without nomination by the Governor. Over a number of executive agencies the Governor had no control whatever; in others it was difficult to determine where responsibility for any action lay because of scattered authority. As a matter of fact, in my first administration Commissioners of the large departments, critical of my policies, seemed to regard themselves as accountable not to the Governor but, as I have said, to the political organization of which they were a part, within and without the General Assembly.

That the Governor might keep in close touch with all executive agencies, the Commission proposed that the 116 administrative departments be reduced to 18 by grouping related activities, and that the Constitution be amended to make the State Treasurer, Comptroller, and Secretary of State appointive officers under the control of the Governor. Other proposed amendments were for an enlargement of the Governor's veto power and for the appointment of the Attorney General by the judges of the Superior Court. The only elective state officers left for the heats of a political campaign were to be the Governor and Lieutenant Governor.

This scheme of a simplified state government, recommended by a group of independent citizens, interested press and public as an ideal, but the question arose whether after all it would work out any better in practice than the present structure which had grown up through a natural evolutionary process. To prove that it would, the Governor and several members of the Commission took to the stump. I went on the radio three times and for two months I toured the State with addresses to large audiences. It was easy enough to evoke a laugh by a display of parallel diagrams, one representing 18 closely knit departments with the Governor in control at the head, and a hodgepodge of 116 departments, boards and minor agencies, many of them going their own way without supervision of anyone above them.

One always came back, however, to the main question, "How much will the cost of government be reduced under the drastic revision you are proposing?" I conservatively estimated the savings at $3,000,000 a year if the whole reorganization plan were carried through. When challenged to prove that, I could quote, for example, statistics to show that the price paid for specified foods in a selected group of state institutions varied during a normal month in 1935 on an average of 80 per cent. It was proposed to correct this situation by centralizing buying in the hands of a Supervisor of Purchases whose business would be to buy all materials and supplies for state departments and institutions through competitive bidding.

Strange things were now to happen. Though the General Assembly could not count on a majority to discontinue two small ferries across the Connecticut River, antedating bridges and railroads, it encountered but faint opposition to the abolition of the great Board of Finance and Control, which, as the maker of budgets, had financial supervision of all departments and other agencies of the State. In its place the Assembly created, as recommended by the Reorganization commission, a Department of Finance and Control with a Commissioner at its head as general manager. Its major functions were grouped in two divisions, respectively under a Director of the Budget and a Supervisor of Purchases, both appointed by the Commissioner with the approval of the Governor. Closely associated with this new department, almost one with it, was established a Personnel Department to administer under a Director a merit system of appointments to positions in the State Civil Service; and less closely associated with it was a Department of Public Works to put through the huge building program. Of all these departments the Governor was given direct oversight.

Legislation necessary for this organization was twice in real jeopardy, to say nothing of intermittent attacks by the Lieutenant Governor and others. First on the docket for action was the Civil Service Act which was passed by the House, where it originated, after a spirited discussion over a section which permitted employees in the classified service to play the political game much as usual, outside the hours when they were engaged in the State's business. The Senate, after holding up action on the bill for nearly a month, returned it to the House with two amendments. One prohibited employees in the classified service from participating in political activities at any time "on behalf of any political party or candidate for election." The other removed the Personnel Director from the proposed Department of Finance and Control, to which he had been properly assigned in the original bill, and created for him an independent department. The amended bill raised an uproar in the House. It was denounced by Republicans and by some Democrats, one of whom in his excitement declared that the bill was full of holes as "his wife's coriander," a slip of the tongue for "his wife's colander." After a long and acrimonious debate the House, not caring to assume the burden of killing the merit system of appointments, concurred in the Senate's amendments and then, through its Republican leader, challenged me to sign the bill. If I would veto it, he assured me, the House would raise another and better bill and send it on to the Senate. I had no desire to see the merit system, which the politicians of neither party really wanted, tossed back and forth between Senate and House, to be lost somewhere in the game. I had on my desk a very good bill, with fewer holes in it than a colander, and I signed it. That act was in major essentials among the very best civil service laws ever enacted in any State.

In connection with the Purchasing Act an incident occurred which still amuses me. The bill, originating in the Senate, was quickly passed by that body and transmitted to the House where, a canvass showed, there was a clear majority for it. At this point three leaders of the outside Republican organization, upon whose shoulders had dropped three pieces of J. Henry Roraback's torn mantle, intervened to retain the patronage of the old purchasing racket. They were assisted by a group of lobbyists representing a compact body of middlemen from whom the State bought most of its supplies. It was the business of these "corridor boys" to button-hole members of the House and whip them into line against the Purchasing Act, which, they claimed, was a Democratic measure to get control of all purchases for the State, then amounting to $8,000,000 a year.

On the morning of the day when the House was to take final action on the bill, the chairman of the Reorganization Committee, George L. Warncke, a fruit grower of Wilton, with whom I liked to do business because he was frank and aboveboard in the discussion of all questions at issue, appeared in my office with a downcast face to inform me that this was the last of the reorganization measures he would have anything to do with because of the insults he was receiving from the corridor boys, who, he feared, would be able to defeat the Purchasing Act. After a little talk during which I begged him not to give up the ship, I asked him to go and see Noah Swayne, the Republican leader of the House, with whom I had had breakfast at the Hartford Club an hour ago. He went at once.

The House usually convened at 11 o'clock or a little later. On that morning the Speaker called it to order at 10.15, the appointed hour. The Purchasing Act, after some other business, was taken from the table, explained by Chairman Warncke, and passed, in concurrence with the Senate, without debate. The three corridor chiefs were still in the Speaker's office conferring with a Republican friend of mine who, I daresay, was vainly arguing with them not to oppose the bill, when a messenger came running in, out of breath, with the announcement that the bill had gone through the House without a contest, even without any member asking for a yea-and-nay vote. In their excitement at the news the three corridor chiefs leaped up, one of them literally into the air, and rushed out, exclaiming that the house must reconsider its action. For once they were too late.

How far chance or aforethought entered into this sudden defeat of the corridor boys I never inquired. From smiles I observed on the faces of members of the House who afterwards came into my office on other business, I surmised that there was mischief somewhere. Perhaps I was mistaken. To this day I do not know whether it was the Lady or the Tiger.

Outside a few controversial issues, the General Assembly moved forward with great rapidity on measures recommended by the Reorganization Commission, revising and redefining the functions of executive and administrative departments, both elected and appointive, and adjusting related departments to one another so as to eliminate duplications which had grown with the years, conspicuously in the Treasury and Tax Departments. The breadth of this reorganization legislation is indicated by the fact that for its completion 107 separate acts were required, which I signed as they came to my desk, sometimes in bunches of a dozen or fifteen.

The one comprehensive aim of all reorganization legislation was to make the Governor the Chief Executive of the State within a frame of government which would work without undue friction and without waste. The Connecticut Constitution of 1818 declared that "the supreme executive power of the State shall be vested in a Governor." Few laws, however, had ever been enacted to open proper avenues for him to exercise this supreme authority. On the contrary, the trend of legislation for more than a century had been to limit the Governor's executive activities. Until I came in no Governor, so far as I could discover, had ever attempted to test out his general constitutional powers in an instance where there was no specific statue granting him authority to act. I made a threat so to act in the first days of the banking emergency of 1933, and I openly refused, in the public interest, a demand to appoint a certain medical board which I was directed to appoint under the Statutes. I was sustained in that case by the Superior Court. Of all means ever invented to shear the locks of a Chief Executive, none could surpass the Board of Finance and Control created under the Roraback regime. All the powers of this Board were now transferred directly to the Governor or to agencies over which he was to have proper control.

To these powers were added many others of prime importance. There was established for the first time in Connecticut history an executive budget to be prepared and administered by the Governor with the aid of a Budget Director. The Governor was enjoined to set up in advance for each department and institution of the State a quarterly instead of an annual allowance for expenditures, and to reduce or withhold appropriations for general purposes not necessary for maintaining the ordinary services being performed by the State. That no harm might come to these services, an emergency fund amounting to $100,000 a year was placed in his hands. When the General Assembly was not in session, he could buy, exchange, and sell land in the development of state institutions and for other purposes which he deemed advisable. He could, on the recommendation of the Attorney General, compromise disputed claims against and by the State or any of its departments. Hereafter no question could be raised against his authority to investigate and take proper action concerning any matter involving the enforcement of the laws of the State and the protection of its citizens. Henceforth, too, there could be no doubt as to whom the high officials of the Executive Department owe their faithful allegiance; for he was empowered to suspect or remove "any officer, commissioner, or deputy who has been or is guilty of misconduct, material neglect of duty or incompetence in the conduct of his office." To safeguard the rights of an official against whom any charge might be brought, the General Assembly was careful to prescribe an exact procedure for the Governor's action.

Something hitherto unheard of in Connecticut legislative history, the Governor was provided with a cabinet of eleven administrative heads of executive departments, to be appointed by himself, with whom he was instructed to confer on matters which especially concerned the smooth running of the state government under reorganization. Finally provision was made for a Legislative Council of five members comprising the four floor leaders of the House and Senate and the Governor ex-officio, to prepare a special legislative program for the next session of the General Assembly. The Council was in intent a substitution for the Reorganization commission, insofar as it was directed to study all the administrative departments of State with a view to a consolidation of activities wherever advisable.

For six years I had worn the empty title of Governor of Connecticut. Now I was to go on in an office, under the same name, with executive powers limited only by the Constitution of the State.

Side by side with reorganization legislation, the General Assembly took favorable action on a number of my recommendations besides jury service for women. All the Normal Schools were raised to the rank of Teachers' Colleges. The old question whether Sherwood Island in Fairfield County should be developed into a state part was settled by an appropriation of several hundred thousand dollars for the purchase of land and land-rights on the island and adjacent shore. The Publicity Commission under Willard Rogers as chairman was continued with a conditional appropriation for expenses. The Governor's Motor Vehicle Safety Council was supplanted by a Highway Safety Commission with Colonel Fisher at the head, and the law requiring semiannual inspection of motor vehicles was reënacted against an undercurrent of opposition.

My long agitation for a Connecticut Building at the Eastern States Exposition held every September at Springfield was quieted by a bargain whereby the Legislature appropriated $35,000 to become available to meet half the entire estimated cost of $70,000, provided the Governor were able to collect by private subscription another $35,000 before the first of January, 1938. In response to written requests for contributions and a few personal appeals in which I burlesqued the methods of black-mail, checks from manufacturers, merchants, and agricultural groups came rolling in up to $39,000 with promises of more. There I called a halt. The building was modeled after the beautiful old Hartford State House for the exhibit of Connecticut products of the soil and factory along with those of other New England States.

The long session came to an end late in the afternoon of June 9, 1937, following a week of legislative confusion. Months of strenuous work had worn nerves down to a frazzle. When on June 3 I informed the General Assembly in a special message that unless the State's income was increased by new taxation I should be compelled to veto nearly all appropriations which lay outside the budget as adopted, the Senate, as a gesture, passed a bill levying a 2 per cent tax on dividends in which it knew the House would not concur. Rather hot over this political byplay, the Republican leader of the House retorted, according to the newspapers: "There will be no more taxes from the House. If the budget is unbalanced, let the Governor balance it." Nevertheless my special message accomplished something. It balked the passage of appropriations for projects to please the old folks at home and it threw the onus of an unbalanced budget, if there should be one, on the General Assembly, where it belonged.

The tempers of its members restored by morning, the General Assembly completed an immense amount of work on its last day. And when, their strife, labor, and turmoil over, they gathered towards the approach of evening in the great hall of the House of Representatives to listen to the Governor's farewell address, they were all in a happy mood. I congratulated them on the passage of a series of acts reorganizing the central government, "which, considered as a whole, are more vital and more comprehensive in character than any group of acts passed by any General Assembly of the State since the adoption of our Constitution in 1818." In a wide sweep of praise, I now and then indulged in a bit of irony of the kind which does not hurt: "In no instance, I daresay, have you failed to relieve the dire distress of the communities in which you live. . . . As for me, I intend to sit for a while under the gilded dome and look myself over to see what damage I may have received during the last few months." These were destined to be the last words I was ever to the General Assembly in the rôle of Governor.

For his part in the legislative program now at an end, the Governor received curious and diverse honors. He was initiated into the Connecticut Pharmaceutical Association and granted the certificate of a registered pharmacist in reward for the stories he told of his boyhood days when as a clerk in a village store he dispensed strong medicines, against which no man born of woman could long stand up. He was also made an honorary life-member of the New Haven Advertising Club for his continuous praise of Connecticut's landscape along shores, streams, and wooded hillsides, whose beauty, he often said as Shakespeare had said of Cleopatra, "age cannot wither nor custom stale." A Democratic Senate passed a bill naming after the Governor a super-highway to run across the State to the Massachusetts border, and was ready to make an appropriation for the project which was ultimately to cost $100,000,000. A Republican House thought that an appropriation, however small, would be premature, but was quite willing that the Governor's name be given to a nonexistent highway.

The Commencement season at schools and colleges was at hand, during which I breathed the atmosphere of my former life away from political strife and toil. In June of 1936 I had addressed the graduating class at the Hotchkiss School, which included Henry Ford II who was going to Yale. I had a long talk with his grandfather during and after the lunch hour on the pleasures and hazards of a business career to which in my youth I was inclined. Henry Ford, the first of that name, was one of the most interesting men I ever encountered. Then absorbed in the cultivation of soy beans, he had a vision of the time when the automobile would be built out of farm products. As he put it, "The automobile would grow on the farm." The science of chemistry has begun to fulfill that dream.

This June I gave an address at the Kent School where Wilbur Cross, the third of that name, was graduating and going to Yale. Later he was destined to enter the Army and, after receiving his commission, to be first stationed on one of the Hawaiian Islands where in the mysterious chances of life his grandfather, great-grandfather, and great-uncle had all been. He now writes about the land and people much as his ancestors talked about them. His younger brother Robert, then at Kent, is now undergoing training for command in the Army Air Force. The family is thus maintaining its military tradition which dates from the earliest colonial wars.

XXXV. Reorganization at Work

On the approach of the day, July 1, 1937, when I was to function as Chief Executive in fact as well as in title, I called together my assistants to map out the work which must be done under the new mandatory legislation. They were an able group of men, each of them proficient in his calling. The act creating the Department of Finance and Control named Edward Hall as its first Commissioner. The Director of the Budget, Benjamin Whitaker, had served the State conspicuously well on both tax and reorganization commissions; the Supervisor of Purchases, Edward Geissler, had learned the art of shrewd purchasing as business Manager at the State Prison; and the Personnel Director, Harry Marsh, who was unanimously recommended for the position by an advisory committee, had had long experience in planning and administering State and municipal civil service merit systems in New York and elsewhere.

These four men sat down together several mornings a week to discuss their interrelated problems. It was my custom to join them towards the close of their conferences that we might pursue in unison the task of giving the State a more efficient and altogether better government. Efficiency implied economy, which in turn bears the hope of balanced budgets.

It was incumbent upon the Personnel Director to classify all new, and ultimately all old, positions in the civil service with the aid of his advisory committee and the approval of the Governor. Marsh performed his task with rare tact in the face of an inadequate appropriation for his staff and the necessity of making scores of temporary appointments in the Department of Public Works on the initiation of a huge building program. Under his hands the spoils system, wherever it existed, was progressively supplanted by the rule of merit.

Politicians took it for granted that as a favored class the merit law would not be too rigidly enforced against their organizations. One afternoon, so it was reported to me, a Republican leader appeared in the office of a state agency and demanded fourteen jobs for his Republican friends. A little later on the same day a Democratic leader likewise made a demand for seven jobs for his Democratic friends. The head of the agency told both men what vacancies were likely to occur in his department and promised to let them know when competitive examinations for them would be held by the Personnel Director. Both the Republican and the Democratic retorts were blasphemous, though they were not precisely the same in phrasing. It is a safe inference, of course, that the two political leaders had met and agreed upon their quota in the ratio of 2 to 1. The old way of dividing jobs between the two political parties did not work now.

Large savings immediately resulted from wholesale buying through open competitive bidding. The Supervisor of Purchases signed a contract for the State's stationery for the next two years at a cost of $100,000 below what was paid in the previous biennium. I asked him about the quality of the paper, and he replied that it was, on the average, much better than what we had been using. He was making use of the reports of the United States Bureau of Standards, particularly for food and clothing, and was conferring regularly with a State Standardization committee, comprising twenty heads of departments and institutions, which I had appointed on authority of the General Assembly. Subsequently, the superintendent of a state institution, claiming an emergency, wanted to purchase on his own hook a quantity of men's clothing from a middleman with whom he had long dealt. The request was denied. That clothing was quickly obtained under the rules of open competition at more than 20 per cent under the estimate submitted by the superintendent. At the end of the fiscal year the Supervisor of Purchases could say that he had saved the State $1,500,000.

The rules laid down in the law for the execution of an annual $50,000,000 budget progressively from one quarter to another were something entirely new in the State's history. Hitherto a department or an institution, for lack of foresight or poor business management, often came to the end of a fiscal year with a deficit which had to be taken care of by the old Board of Finance and Control and eventually by the next session of the General Assembly. Under the new regulations the State came through its first fiscal year, July 1, 1937 to July 1, 1938, with a surplus of $630,000; and when I closed my books as Governor of Connecticut on January 4, 1939, the maintenance budget was in balance, notwithstanding unreliable statements to the contrary.

Robert A. Hurley, a construction engineer, whom I appointed Commissioner of Public Works, was then Connecticut Administrator for the W.P.A., an office which he was conducting with uncommon ability. On April 29, the day after the Department of Public Works was created, I sent his appointment to the Senate for confirmation, with an oral request to the leaders of both political parties for action under a suspension of the rules, as there was a prospect of immediate grants by the Federal Government towards our building program. No vote was coast against the appointment. Hurley then set out for Washington with a list in his pocket of nine construction projects for the State's humane institutions. All were approved by the Federal W.P.A. Administrator under the proviso that the General Assembly appropriate $500,000 as its share in the cost. It was a sort of fifty-fifty proposal which Senate and House accepted on May 5, again under a suspension of the rules. Thereupon the new Commissioner organized his office with architects and draughtsmen and set moving an immense program of construction, reconstruction, and repairs. Three years of hard work lay before him.

During 1938 Federal grants came with a rush. In April W.P.A. funds amounting to $1,341,000 were received, which brought the total thus far from this source up to nearly $3,000,000. In July preliminary negotiations with Washington for an allotment of $9,000,000 in P.W.A. funds were taking so favorable a turn that I felt safe in approving a state building program rising from the original $11,000,000 to $25,000,000, half from the bond issue and other state appropriations, and half from grants by the Federal Government. By the time I left office all these grants were in hand or forthcoming, and contracts for all building projects had been signed. Moreover a special grant of $3,000,000 was made by Washington to the State Highway Department, primarily for completing the Merritt Parkway and building a bridge over the Housatonic River to connect with another new parkway which was to bear my name, running northward to the Massachusetts border.

A centralized building program over which the Governor had general supervision put an end, temporarily at least, to the erection of institutional buildings in the ugly and repellent style of old-time factories. At last what I had long striven for, with only partial success, came to pass. All buildings were carefully designed, in coöperation with superintendents and trustees, for the specific uses to which they were to be put, and in addition to be as attractive as possible. Architects and those associated with them were given a particularly free hand in planning entire groups of buildings for new institutions such as the Veterans' Home at Rocky Hill. Personally I had most to do with the new Southbury Training School for defective children, which was laid out as two villages of small houses, one for boys and one for girls. On the outskirts were schools, infirmary, and offices. With the trustees of this institution I met frequently during a long period, from the day when its site was selected, to the day when I left office. Their aim was to combine home and school and medical treatment for mentally handicapped children in a beautiful countryside. Within two years after the institution was opened, it was visited by more than 2,000 people, hundreds of them coming from other States to see how Connecticut was training subnormal children of all degrees for useful lives wherever possible.

All through the autumn of 1937 and the year 1938 the Legislative Council was hard at work, meeting once or twice a month, on reorganization and miscellaneous measures of large import to be submitted to the next General Assembly. The Council drafted an excellent act for combining in a single department all the agricultural activities of the State which were then loosely distributed among three departments and two boards; and an urgent act to place on the Adjutant General the responsibility for all military functions, which had long been divided between two more or less independent offices, an Armory Board, and an Armory Inspector, who for criminal irregularities was spending a year in the State Prison. Another proposed act would consolidate under an Executive Secretary twenty-one scattered professional and vocational examining boards which, being supported by fees, had never been put under strict financial control. Numerous complaints were received by the Council from motorists who alleged that they had been arrested by constables lurking in hidden places along highways to catch drivers passing red lights so obscured by bushes and trees as to be invisible to anyone who made a turn at an intersection. It was a racket, they said, for the collection of fees by constables and justices of the peace. At the request of the Council I appointed a committee to investigate fees and fines, with a view to mitigating the hardships of motorists (who were not always so innocent as they tried to make out) by giving state and local police entire control over traffic on the roads without the intrusion of constables in search of questionable fees for a living. The committee recommended that constables be relieved of further temptation by putting them on salaries. On my own initiative I instructed the Budget Director to make a study of the interrelated functions of the Comptroller, Treasurer, and auditors, having in mind the establishment of strict control over these departments such as large corporations deem essential. So ended my experience with Connecticut's first Legislative Council which amply justified its existence.

When I reviewed the vast reorganization program partly in effect, partly awaiting further legislation, I had no illusions about its permanency, so flexible were the discriminatory powers vested in the Governor. What of my successors? They might, with merely a formal approval of the acts of the Budget Director, throw on him the entire responsibility for a careful execution of the budget. They might, under the guise of emergencies, throw back into 116 separate agencies all purchases of goods and materials, provided no single purchase exceeded $1,000. They might order the Commissioner of Public Works to farm out all construction projects among their favorite architects—their political friends—and still keep within the letter of the law. They might, by an amendment to the law, substitute for a large nonpartisan advisory committee to the Personnel Director a small purely partisan committee of opponents to the Merit Act who would find a way to edge in a certain number of political appointments. And so forth. Even the Legislative Council might fall into "innocuous desuetude" by failure to make an appropriation necessary for its continuance. In short, the essentials of the whole reorganization program might be here and there weakened until it completely broken down. The state government would then revert to the spoils of Rorabackism, or Old Guardism, which is precisely the same thing. And termites were already at work.

XXXVI. New England

Early in my political career I began calling myself a New Englander as well as a Connecticut man. I always attended the Eastern States Exposition at Springfield and meetings of the New England Council in Boston. I made speeches, serious or humorous. I addressed New England societies in New York and Philadelphia, at the first of which I was informed by the chairman that Daniel Webster, whose patriotic speeches I had committed to memory in childhood and youth, had once been the orator of their association. I opened the New England exhibit at the Grand Central Terminal in New York. And so forth.

In driving northward from Connecticut, I used to say, I should never know that I was passing into another State except for a sign by the roadside. True, the great winding river shrinks within narrower banks, lakes spread out wider, and when we reach the north countree valleys deepen into ravines and hills rise into mountains. But these transitions are so gradual that one feels in whichever State he may be that he is still traveling through one beautiful land, separated only by the artificial barriers of state lines.

Why not, I asked, in an after-luncheon talk before my fellow New England Governors, break down these artificial barriers and merge our six States into one of respectable area as a means for stemming the rising tide of the cost of government about which we are hearing so much? The result would be a State only two-thirds as large as Kansas whence your friend Alf Landon hails. We have had from time to time mutual agreements, now called compacts, ever since 1643 when some of our ancestors formed a confederacy under the name of "The United Colonies of New England" for dealing with savage Indians. Lately we have entered into two agreements, one concerning labor laws and one concerning the pollution of interstate streams, which is killing fish in the lower Connecticut River. Just now we are fretting over a flood-control compact against which has arisen strong Federal opposition, which could not have developed had we been one State going our own way, building dams wherever we liked.

Compacts are good temporary contrivances adapted to special purposes. That is all. They make no money. They spend money. What is needed
now is a permanent union whereby the cost of supporting six state governments may be reduced to the cost of supporting one overall government. Just let your minds rest for a moment on the unjustifiable cost of
maintaining six Governors and six Lieutenant Governors and their aides,
their secretaries and stenographers to write and copy their speeches to be
read over the radio, and large allowances for their upkeep and for travel
all over the United States of America. And add to all this the enormous
cost of six annual sessions of Legislatures which never adjourn until they
are compelled to by law. What a racket! Millions of dollars which we now
waste every year might be saved merely by uniting under the banner of
one State and placing in the Governor's chair a man like Calvin Coolidge
who never let loose a nickel unless he had to. Such a man, if a bit superannuated, ought to be got for $5,000 a year. That is my salary. Finally, don't
forget that union and liberty are one and inseparable, as was said by Daniel
Webster, born in New Hampshire, died in Massachusetts, and yet still alive
in the hears of all New Englanders.

The editor of one newspaper said that Governor Cross had a good idea
worth careful consideration, though he doubted that the six States would
ever surrender their individual identities. Another editor wished that I
would sometimes treat important subjects seriously. Whether my speech
had anything to do with it I don't know; but a short time afterwards there
was formally organized a Governors' Conference for discussion and action
on affairs which especially concerned New England. The Governor of
Connecticut was elected chairman, probably because he would likely be
the first to become superannuated. Governor Murphy of New Hampshire
was elected secretary.

Questions came upon us thick and fast in those difficult days. We
met alternately in Boston, Providence, and Hartford. Once four of us
appeared before a committee of the Interstate Commerce Commission
in Buffalo to protest against a proposed revision of interterritorial railroad
freight rates which we feared would prove detrimental to New England

industries. Twice at least we were all in Washington. Uppermost in the minds of the public as well as in our own was the compact for flood control in the Connecticut River watershed.

By March, 1937, the Joint Commission on Flood Control representing New Hampshire, Vermont, Massachusetts, and Connecticut had completed its report. Nothing remained to do except to draft identical bills for submission to the Legislatures of these States. To make certain that the proposed compact conformed with the Federal Omnibus Control Act of 1936, I called a general conference between State and Federal officials which met in Hartford on March 8. There were present the Secretary of War, the Chief of Army Engineers, the four Governors of the States concerned, the Joint Flood Control Commission, and technical advisers. It was a friendly symposium, which reached harmonious conclusions. The Secretary of War, Harry Woodring, speaking for President Roosevelt, advised prompt action so as to secure Federal funds soon to become available for the project. For a different reason I also felt that action must be now while the great flood of 1936 was in everyone's memory, or action might never be taken. At that or a later meeting I suggested that the members of a subcommittee, of which Attorney General Daly of Connecticut was chairman, sit down at once and not get up until they had drafted the outline of the proposed compact.

They took my request more seriously than I intended. By five o'clock the next morning they completed the draft, which provided, as an initial experiment, for eight reservoirs in the Connecticut River basin: three in Vermont, three in New Hampshire, and two in Massachusetts on sites approved by the United States Army engineers. The Federal Government was to build the reservoirs on land leased by each of these three States to a Connecticut River Valley Flood Control Commission which was to maintain and operate them at the expense of the signatory States. The compact, after its approval by the Secretary of War, was ratified by the Legislatures of the four States and transmitted to Congress. A bill for its ratification by Congress was favorably reported by committees of both House and Senate.

The compact, however, got no further. It suffered a long, lingering death under the hatchets of a group of Congressmen, three of whom hailed from Connecticut, two of them from the Connecticut River Valley. These men seemed to be more interested in the development of hydro-electric power than in the control of waters in flood times; if I understood them correctly they wanted to create a Connecticut River Authority, an imitation of the Tennessee Valley Authority, for the production of electricity in competition with privately owned corporations. The time, however, was not opportune for serious consideration of so questionable an engineering project. The sites selected for the first reservoirs were the small tributaries in the upper basin of the Connecticut River which, in the opinion of engineers, had insufficient potential power for the profitable generation of electricity. And time was pressing for protection against another flood like the one of 1936, which was the first and last interest of the sponsors of the compact.

The hostile Congressmen formally requested an analysis of the compact by the Federal Power Commission whose chairman replied that, though it complied, except in immaterial respects, with the Federal Omnibus Flood Control Act, it represented an unsound national policy in that it did not convey to the Federal Government in fee simple all the land required for impounding waters for flood control and other purposes, such as the eventual development of hydro-electric power, that is, a regional T.V.A. With this opinion the President and the Attorney General of the United States were in essential accord. In one of his letters to me the President declared that in dealing with "the water resources of the Nation or their development . . . the National Government should preserve inviolate its plenary powers."

To meet the views of the Federal Government as thus expressed, the Congressmen who were unalterably opposed to the original compact sponsored a substitute measure, known as the Brown-Casey Act, under the general terms of which Massachusetts and Connecticut might enter into a compact of their own and, if reservoirs outside these two States were required for their protection against floods, the Secretary of War might take land and build reservoirs wherever he list in Vermont and New Hampshire. To this high-handed proposal I paid my respects in an address before the New England Council at their annual meeting in Boston, November 18, 1937. "It seems to have been forgotten," I said in closing, "That the people of New England are all kin in whichever State they may live. Neither the Governor of the Commonwealth of Massachusetts nor the Governor of the State of Connecticut can be counted upon to submit to his Legislature a compact involving the rape of two sister States. Despite all their faults, there still survive in these Governors, I trust, some trace of honor."

To clarify all questions at issue over the original compact, I arranged for a noon conference of the six New England Governors with President Roosevelt on January 19, 1938. Later in the day our technical advisers met with representatives of the Federal Power Commission and other flood agencies in an effort to harmonize conflicting views. After pleasant talks with members of Senate and House at dinner at the Mayflower, some of whom I had roasted as the meeting of the New England Council, I left Washington with the impression that the Roosevelt administration now looked with less favor on interstate flood-control projects than a year before. At any rate our compact was dead, and with it died also the absurd dream of a few Congressmen that a regional T.V.A. could be created out of the Connecticut River and its northern tributaries, separated by hills and mountains. Nevertheless, though the compact failed of ratification by Congress, the time and energy spent on framing it were not lost. Wide discussion of the compact by the press throughout New England ushered in a period of good feeling for united action on many other difficult problems almost at hand.

XXXVII. Stormy Weather

Premonitions of a storm brewing over the Highway Department came in the spring of 1937 when Attorney General Daly reported to the old Board of Finance and Control that very high prices were being paid for land in connection with the Merritt Parkway. Subsequently I had a conference with Mr. Daly at which it was agreed that hereafter in closing a land sale or purchase he should make a note to the effect that he approved or disapproved it only "as to form." I requested of him a list of questionable transactions, which was forthcoming. Another list I received from State Comptroller Swartz on whom it was incumbent under a new law defining his duties to examine carefully all highway purchases of land before approving payments. In some instances the price paid for land and buildings was many times in excess of the valuation placed upon the property for taxation purposes.

Having this information, I asked Highway Commissioner MacDonald for an explanation. Prices for land, he said, took a jump as soon as the general route of the Merritt Parkway became known. There were now more holdups than formerly. His purchasing agent, G. Leroy Kemp, a Fairfield County Republican politician, and incidentally a real estate man doing a small business, was, nevertheless, trying to keep prices down to a reasonable level but was having a hard time of it because some owners of property were employing middlemen to negotiate sales for them in order to get as much as they could out of the State. I made the obvious suggestion that an effectual way to deal with holdups would be for the State to exercise its right of eminent domain in a few cases as a general warning of what we were ready to do. I directed him to keep close oversight of all land purchases, as he used to do. Otherwise, I told him frankly, I would approve of none. Himself an honest man in my opinion, the High Commissioner had no suspicion that anyone in his employ might have a crooked mind.

Attorney General Daly was then in the first stages of a thorough investigation of the circumstances surrounding the buying of real estate for the Merritt Parkway. On his assuming office as a judge of the Superior Court in September, the difficult work was carried forward with vigor by his successor, Charles McLaughlin, and an able corps of assistants. Their report, which was submitted to the Governor on January 3, 1938, covered two hundred transactions, in some of which criminal collusion between Kemp and other real estate men was indicated. As the Attorney General's powers were restricted to civil actions, it was decided at once to ask for an exhaustive probe by a Grand Jury of Fairfield County where the crime or crimes, if any, were committed. A few days later I made a formal request for a Grand Jury of Lorin Willis, the State's Attorney of that county, at a conference with Attorney General McLaughlin in his office at the Capitol. It was arranged, to my satisfaction, that one or more members of the Attorney General's staff be placed at the disposal of Mr. Willis to aid him in the Grand Jury proceedings. Events followed fast. The two attorneys immediately called upon Chief Justice Maltbie to discuss my official request. An hour later they came into my office through a line of reporters to inform me that I might announce that all the data collected by the Attorney General to show how the Highway Department had expended $6,000,000 in the purchase of land for the Merritt Parkway would be submitted to a Grand Jury. I left the announcement to the Attorney General, who gave to the press his written report to me. That night and the next morning the startling news was streamlined across the front pages of newspapers all over the State.

The next week Judge Carl Foster summoned, as prearranged, an Extraordinary Grand Jury for the proposed inquiry to appear before him on January 25 for empanelment. It remained for me to await the outcome. A cartoonist sketched a portrait of the Governor seated in his chair at the Capitol and staring, his cigar uplifted, into the long open space before him where no object was visible.

Parallel with Attorney General McLaughlin's investigation into land deals, Public Works Commissioner Hurley, at my request, began a wide investigation into the business methods of the Highway Department. Now a question had previously arisen whether the act creating a Department of Public Works did not transfer to its Commissioner the prime functions of the Highway Commissioner, when it gave the new department jurisdiction over "real assets owned by the State" in all state agencies not specifically exempted by law. As there was in the act no mention of the Highway Department, it was the opinion of Attorney General Daly that the commissioner of Public Works had under the law complete control over all the real assets of the Highway Department, which were interpreted to include road planning, road construction, and road repairs. Commissioner MacDonald was reduced to a subordinate charged mainly with the administration of routine business of a department of which he had been overlord. No dual authority like this, of course, was ever intended by the General Assembly, which assumed that the Highway Department would remain untouched. Since my plea for curative legislation went unheeded by a recalcitrant Democratic Senate bent upon opening the doors and windows of the Highway Department to public view, for months I had to placate two kings, as it were, sitting on the same throne.

On January 6 Hurley brought in a caustic report, cast in the form of a series of indictments of Commissioner MacDonald, his policies, his acts, his engineers, his inspectors, and everyone else connected with him in a department woefully disorganized, wasteful, and inefficient. No good word was said about anybody or anything. Even the beautiful Merritt Parkway was ill designed, ill constructed, and destined to become a dangerous road for travelers to ride over. At once I went over Hurley's charges with MacDonald who was setting the fuse for a counterblast.

In one respect, however, the air was clearing. As early as October, 1937, a case was maneuvered into the Superior Court for an opinion on who was legally in control of the Highway Department. In a concise and lucid memorandum Judge Cornell completely upset Attorney General Daly's ruling which enabled Hurley to climb on the throne, and he was upheld by the Supreme Court to which Hurley's counsel appealed. I was personally interested, as were many others, in the court's interpretation of "real assets." In this instance it held that the term did not include highways and bridges, which, in distinction from state buildings, have no market value. That is, roads and bridges cannot be sold, whereas even the Capitol of the State might be sold to the highest bidder if the General Assembly so ordered. In short, it was the unanimous opinion of the Judges of the Supreme Court that powers of the Highway Commissioner had been in no way abridged by the creation of the Department of Public Works.

MacDonald was now seated again, though not very firmly, on the throne alone. No longer were the Governor and others, like the Federal Bureau of Public Roads in making grants to Connecticut, in doubt concerning with whom they should deal, whether Hurley or MacDonald. That question was now settled to the relief of all of us. I warned Mac-Donald, however, that he was no longer as formerly "monarch of all he surveys" with no one to dispute his expenditures, since under the reorganization legislation he must hereafter submit, as Hurley had done, every project for roads or bridge building to the Governor and his budgetary committee for their approval before letting the contract to the lowest bidder. This rigid control over the Highway Department, which included supervision of the acquisition of land, either by purchase or by resorting to the right of eminent domain, rang the death knell to any further scandals in the construction of the Merritt Parkway.

On February 28 MacDonald appeared in my office with a messenger bearing a report 60,000 words long, in reply to Hurley's, along with a pile of documents on which the report was based. I read MacDonald's letter of transmittal in which he complained, as one hurt, of Hurley's "crudely deceptive and cruelly destructive allegations," and handed out copies of it to reporters whom I let peruse a copy of the report itself in which they quickly discovered the "high lights." I then sat down to a study of the report through the better part of a night.

MacDonald made a hot reply to Hurley's "reckless and unfounded charges," taking them up seriatim. If the Highway Department, he said, was disorganized, that was because Hurley and his aides had terrorized it. If the cost of its administration left for the construction of new roads only a few million dollars out of an annual budget of $20,000,000, that was the fault of the General Assembly which handicapped him by providing insufficient funds. If he had built many waterbound macadam roads, which involved high maintenance costs, that was also because he had insufficient funds for using concrete except upon principal highways.

The controversy flamed high over Hurley's specific charge that the Merritt Parkway, of which 16 miles were nearly completed, was in most respects a poor engineering job. In considering that sweeping charge, I got my first lesson in so-called "pinched bridges." To explain what was meant by "pinched bridges"—a phrase condemnatory and striking enough to light on everybody's lips—a few words are necessary on the design of the Parkway. It is a four-lane highway, two lanes for traffic westward and two for traffic eastward. Between the two pairs of lanes is a strip of cultivated grass and shrubs, in places 21 feet wide, which gradually becomes narrower as one approaches underpass bridges through which the separation line between the two pair of lanes, no longer adorned with shrubs and flowers, is reduced to a 16-inch concrete curb.

Hurley claimed that these underpass bridges were deathtraps. A driver coming to a bridge of this sort would have to make a quick turn in order to escape an abutment and when under the bridge he could not have a clear vision of the road ahead because of the converging lanes. Particularly at night there would be a danger of a smashup between two cars coming in opposite directions because of the almost direct glare of their headlights into the faces of the two drivers. In his report Hurley published a photograph of an underpass bridge and its approaches to make clear his contention. He intimated that an engineer who knew his business would have built wide two-arch bridges so as to keep his lanes straight.

MacDonald replied that before designing the Merritt Parkway he and his engineers had studied other parkways in various parts of the country and had improved upon the type he decided on by making each lane passing under or over bridges two feet wider than elsewhere on the roadway. The fear of deathtraps he declared to be imaginary. A Hurley photograph of bridges and stretches of the Parkway, showing abrupt curves and narrow lanes under the bridges, he denounced as premeditated optical illusions to deceive the public. For comparison with them he exhibited in his report a long rolling Parkway with lanes entering and leaving bridges by gentle, almost imperceptible curves. These photographs, taken in long perspective, in contrast with Hurley's foreshortening, made the

Parkway appear without any blemishes.

The war between pictures did not stop there. All the underpass bridges, about sixty feet in length, were built of reinforced concrete. On one of them there was a crack, of which a close-up photograph was taken for the Hurley report, to give the impression that the concrete was not properly mixed and as a result endangered, in a way not explained, the entire steel-frame structure. To counter this attack MacDonald presented a photograph of the whole bridge which showed a small crack, not in the arch of the bridge, but in an overhead approach. Such a crack, he informed his critic, was often caused by sudden changes in temperature or by deflections over which an engineer has no control.

Again, the Hurley report made much of a photograph depicting a large oak tree so close to the edge of an outer lane that the lane seemed to bend in as if trying to get out of the way. This photograph MacDonald countered with one which showed the tree at a safe distance where it could do no harm either to an automobile or to itself. This spot on the Parkway became a rendezvous for curious people who wanted to see "a road running around an oak tree." Once more, the Hurley report displayed a photograph of a loose top rail of an open bridge, which could be teetered by one hand, as an example of careless inspection before accepting work of contractors. MacDonald retorted that the damage to the rail was done by a stone falling from a truck when the Highway Department was under Hurley's jurisdiction. I teetered the heavy rail by using both hands.

It was all a match of more or less tricky photographs, which entertained the public. A half dozen newspapers sent their own photographers out on the Parkway to take pictures of the scenes in debate. Some of the photographs resembled Hurley's some resembled MacDonald's. I twice drove slowly over the Parkway, stopping at crucial points. On my return, a group of reporters asked me whose photographs told the truth, Hurley's or MacDonald's. "Give me the right kind of camera," I said, "and tell me where to stand or stoop and I will corroborate the truth of both sets of photographs."

In the public interest this wrangling could not be permitted to continue. In fact, just after reading MacDonald's report, I called in Charles J. Bennett, a former Highway Commissioner, in whose ability and integrity

I had perfect confidence, to sift charges and countercharges and to weigh Hurley's plan for reorganizing a department which, it was claimed, was tottering to its foundations. He accepted the task, giving his first attention to a technical study of the Merritt Parkway as an engineering job.

His report, which was supplemented by conferences on the personnel and the entire range of activities being performed by the Highway Department, was concise, cool, and dispassionate. In it neither Hurley nor MacDonald was mentioned by name. He took no sides on the question whether one-arch or two-arch bridges were the better. He was confronted, he said, not with a theory but with the fact that fifty of the sixty bridges of the Parkway were already built or in the process of building. The cost of a radical change in their type would be prohibitive. Nor was any radical change necessary. The underpass bridges would not, as some contended, hold up traffic to the point of congestion, nor "constitute a serious hazard under reasonable driving," for approaches to the bridges were over long radius curves and the roadways through the bridges were considerably widened. Nor did he find any fault with the concrete structure of the bridges. He suggested, however, a number of devices for further safeguards. Every bridge, he held, was a special problem. Of all which were built he criticized by two, one severely and one mildly. Of six bridges for which specifications had been drawn, he approved three underpasses and advised that three overpasses be widened ten feet for reasons which he explained fully. Speaking largely in his conclusion, he said that in his opinion "the Parkway is an excellent piece of construction."

Bennett's same report, which approved, with certain qualifications, the engineering of the Parkway, was favorably received for the most part by press and public. Not so, however, by a rampant group of experts in the art of debunking, who called Bennett a little "passé," and asked me to check up on him by calling into consultation three "nationally known authorities" on road building, on whose opinions, it was said, Hurley had based his sensational report. One of these authorities appeared in my office voluntarily without any summons from me. He seemed to be older than Bennett and not so quick on the trigger. He had designed, a decade before, the bridges of a rather famous parkway over in New York, some of which were of the double one-arch pattern. He condemned utterly the bridges and other features of the Merritt Parkway. I listened and then began to ask questions. I have ridden, I remarked, several times over your parkway, once recently, to see how you managed your arches. I observed that in most cases the radii of the curves leading to your underpasses are so short that my driver slowed down in passing over them and that within the bridges the lanes are no wider, apparently even narrower, than on the open roadway. The one-arch underpasses on the Merritt Parkway were evidently modeled to some extent on yours, but as safeguards against accidents the curves were made longer and the lanes under the arches were made wider than on the open road. If, then, as you say, there have been comparatively few accidents on your parkway, I cannot see how the Merritt Parkway bridges are likely to become, as you predict, scenes of smashups. He did not like this kind of talk. After stating his present views on bridges he took his leave. Neither of the other two "nationally known authorities" ever called on me.

I was now ready to authorize MacDonald to build at once the six bridges which I had held up for Bennett's comment and changes in specifications and to draw up plans for additional bridges. At the same time I ordered him to proceed by condemnation for the acquisition of all land hereafter needed for the completion of the Parkway.

Two or three weeks later, towards the end of March, 1938, the Grand Jury investigating land purchases for the Merritt Parkway indicted Kemp and two real estate brokers, representing land owners, on the charge of criminal conspiracy. It appeared that, instead of purchasing land directly from the owners, Kemp dealt, so far as he could, with the two brokers, one in Greenwich and the other in Stamford, to whom he gave advance information, supposed to be kept a secret, on the route the Parkway was to take so that they might quietly squirm in early as agents of landowners or in some instances buy the land outright for themselves as a safe speculation. The Grand Jury uncovered fifty-odd cases where the brokers divided their commissions about equally with Kemp. Out of these transactions, which, except in three cases, were conducted on a cash basis, Kemp received, during a five-year period, $43,000 and probably more.

His annual salary as a state purchasing agent was $5,000 plus a liberal allowance for expenses. The three conspirators were arrested on bench warrants and released on bail. Kemp soon entered upon a dark and thorny path through the Superior and Supreme Courts which led to the State Prison in Wethersfield, where maximum wages for inmates working in the shops at that time were 10¢ a day.

Indictments out of the way, the Grand Jury made its general report to the Superior Court in sharp criticism of "certain existing practices" in the Highway and other departments which, though "not criminal in nature," should be corrected in the interest of the public welfare. The report was a clear call for the dismissal of Commissioner MacDonald on whom was laid the blame for most of "the waste, extravagance, and incompetence exhibited in the purchase of the right of way for the Merritt Parkway" which might have been acquired at much less cost through condemnation proceedings. Particular blame was laid on him for appointing G. Leroy Kemp "as a purchasing agent for the State without any sufficient recommendations as to his fitness for the position." Among other severe charges against MacDonald were his lack of personal supervision over the construction of the Parkway and his failure to leave proper instructions with his staff during his frequent absences "to deal with important matters requiring prompt attention." Many of the criticisms of MacDonald, it was held, were applicable, in some degree, to his Deputy, who deserved censure though not removal from office as he was acting under the direction of his superior. Next in order for criticism was the well-known Secretary of the Republican State Central Committee, who, it was alleged, received $3,700 out of a brokerage commission for his "friendly services" in easing a sale of land to the State for the Parkway. It was strongly urged that he be no longer retained as publicity agent of the Highway and Health Departments, for which he was being paid in each case $3,000 a year, either under his own name or under the name of a subordinate. In the opinion of the Grand Jury such expenditures wore a sinister look. This political job which I had eliminated from the preliminary budget for 1937–39, was restored without my knowledge in the final budget that came to me from the General Assembly for my emergency signature. Now, by virtue of the authority vested in the Governor by the reorganization legislation, I eliminated the job for good.

On the engineering questions raised by the debate over the Merritt Parkway the Grand Jury felt that it was not qualified to pass judgment. It was, however, convinced that preliminary to all future projects of this kind costing many millions of dollars there should be created "a commission of three representative citizens who would be in actual control of the work to be done and with whom the Highway Commissioner should consult from time to time."

While reading this report I was surprised at the large freedom given to a Connecticut Grand Jury to condemn acts in which they find no criminal intent. Is it, I wondered, quite just to make public the names of men who have a part in acts deemed questionable though declared noncriminal, since people generally, I fear, are apt to infer that all persons whose conduct is censored by a Grand Jury are more or less guilty of some sort of crime. I was surprised, too, that it is within the province of a Connecticut Grand Jury to recommend to the General Assembly specific legislation for the cure of evils which in its opinion exist in a state agency.

I did not censure the Deputy Highway Commissioner, though, if my memory be correct, I asked him many questions in order to ascertain facts about what was going on in his department. The case against MacDonald was different. Starting out as a practical road builder, he developed into a good Highway Commissioner after his appointment to that position. Invariably he surrounded himself with highly trained engineers. Two of his staff graduated from the Sheffield Scientific School while I was a professor there. MacDonald and his engineers built one of the best noncommercial highways in the land. But of late MacDonald had been neglecting his duties and his distress at the loss of full jurisdiction over his department only increased this tendency. I had many talks with him about the matter. It was agreed between us that he would resign after the completion of the first section of the Merritt Parkway scheduled for some time in June. Abruptly the situation was altered by the report of the Grand Jury. On the afternoon of that day reporters thronged my office with inquiries about what I intended to do. By noon tomorrow, I told them, I would have an announcement. Having come to conclusions my mind was at temporary rest.

The next morning I called into my office the Attorney General and a member of his staff for a conference on the removal of Commissioner MacDonald. It was determined, as I desired, that instead of a formal summons for him to appear before the Governor, I should send a mutual friend out to his house to request his immediate resignation. The resignation was promptly received with the Commissioner's thanks for the consideration shown him by the Governor in taking this action. To reporters who were waiting outside in vain for a sight of the Commissioner I simply remarked "MacDonald has resigned." They asked if there would be any further announcement that day. I suggested that they return at six o'clock.

My office cleared of visitors, I called over the telephone Charles Tilden, Professor of Mechanical Engineering at Yale, and gave him the news. Without any preliminary verbal maneuver I told him bluntly that I wanted to appoint Assistant Professor William J. Cox of his staff as MacDonald's successor, today, if possible, before my office was turned into a den of politicians more difficult to quiet than the lions which Daniel tamed with the aid of Jehovah. Naturally Tilden inquired whether I had sounded out Cox on the appointment. I replied that I had not even broached the subject to him, though I had fortified my high opinion of him by the opinions of professional engineers who were well acquainted with his technical knowledge and experience as a civil engineer. "Now I want you to have a talk with him, and if he is disposed to take the position provided it is offered to him, will you kindly make arrangements with President Seymour for his release from college work at the end of the academic year now approaching? At any rate will you and Cox drive up to Hartford this afternoon for a conference at four o'clock, for I hope to settle the question, one way or the other, before the day is over?"

They were in my office near the appointed time. We had an hour's talk. I stretched out before their eyes the extensive highway program which the State had undertaken. "The Merritt Parkway," I said in substance, "is but half finished. It is to be connected with another parkway several times its length. There are many other highways to be built and still more to be widened and otherwise improved to provide for fast-increasing traffic. There must be no more rigging of contracts as charged of the past. No more politics. Here is a labor to challenge the vision, the skill, and the administrative ability of a highway engineer. Any appointment of a Commissioner I may make now, however, will expire on the sixth Wednesday after the convening of the General Assembly next January. But the interim of more than nine months is time enough for an engineer to make good or to fail. With my successor, if I go out, he must take his chances."

The opportunity to make good as a highway engineer on a large scale appealed to Professor Cox. At six o'clock he became the Highway Commissioner of Connecticut.

At length arrived that afternoon in June set for the official opening of a long stretch of the Merritt Parkway from Norwalk to the New York border where it joined the Hutchinson Parkway. Mayor Stack and I cut the ribbon at the Norwalk entrance, both holding the shears, for the passage of a long procession of a hundred automobiles filled with state and county officials. As a symbol of harmony, for one day at least, Cox, Hurley, and MacDonald rode with me in the Governor's car. Without accident we easily negotiated the "pinched bridges," each for variety's sake a little different in its beautiful design, though most were of the same type. When we approached the first of these underpasses I lightly warned the driver to look out for the abutment on his right; it was, in fact, so far away from the roadway that he could not have hit it without deliberate intention. At each town line we stopped to cut another ribbon while a group of citizens stood by watching. The last ceremony was at the junction of the Merritt and Hutchinson Parkways where a 60-foot ribbon was untied by the Governor of Connecticut and Colonel Greene, New York Superintendent of Public Works, representing Governor Lehman. That ribbon was torn into shreds by a riotous crowd before the knot could be undone. Everybody wanted to carry away something in remembrance of the event.

A brilliant sun that afternoon, following a night and morning of showers, brought out all the details of the straight lines and beautiful curves of the Merritt Parkway and all the colors of trees, shrubs, and flowers—

shades of green and red—in the wide central strips between the roadways and along the slopes on both sides of the Parkway. Eighty-give-year-old Schuyler Merritt, after whom the Parkway was named, was there to take part in the ceremony which commemorated his long congressional service to his State. And I could see the face of John MacDonald light up when a representative of Governor Lehman declared that it was "a model highway," and when he heard from the crowds exclamations of praise: Superb! majestic! magnificent! There was no more complaint about "pinched bridges." That became a phrase of a dead controversy.

XXXVIII. Waterbury

Simultaneously with the first disclosures of land purchases for the Merritt Parkway, a blacker cloud of political corruption rose over Waterbury and thence, spreading far and wide, soon enveloped "the land of steady habits" in darkness.

For more than seven years the administration of the municipal affairs of Waterbury had been under the control of T. Frank Hayes, the "reform Mayor," and Daniel J. Leary, "an expert financier." After their election as taxpayers' candidates for office they reduced the tax rate enormously, as they had promised, without inquiry by the citizens of Waterbury on how the feat was accomplished. In 1937, when the city was getting into financial straits, suspicions were awakened that all was not right with Waterbury. At the municipal election in the autumn of that year a coalition of Republicans and independent Democrats ousted Leary by a margin of 33 votes. Hayes barely escaped a similar fate by a margin of 60-odd votes in his favor. The unexpected defeat of Leary provided a way to test rumors about his malfeasance in office.

The interval of doubt was short. The new Comptroller, Sherwood L. Rowland, a Republican, who succeeded Leary on January 1, 1938, reported a fortnight later that he could find no complete records of many large financial transactions during the administration of his predecessor since 1930. Among them were payments for questionable services for which no appropriations had been made by the Board of Aldermen or approval given by the Board of Finance of which Mayor Hayes was chairman ex officio. Vouchers and canceled cheques for these payments were mostly missing.

Waterbury was ablaze with indignation. William J. Pape, the proprietor of two city newspapers, was a leader in ferreting out details of acts which appeared to be criminal. He cooperated with an association of citizens on whose application State's Attorney Lewis of the Waterbury District of New Haven County undertook, with the aid of a New York agency, an audit of the city books. To counter this threat of exposure Mayor Hayes, representing, he claimed, the Board of Finance, gave orders that no further information be made public concerning the records in the Comptroller's office. Nobody paid any attention to his orders. Pape demanded the publication of these records and won out despite the angry protests of the Mayor. Editors of other newspapers joined with him. Day by day revelations of questionable financial transactions became more and more startling. The disclosure that a very large fee was paid by Waterbury to a lobbyist, while Mayor Hayes as Lieutenant Governor was presiding over the Senate and was attempting to block any delving into the records of Leary's office, became a matter of grave concern not merely to Waterbury, but to all the people of the State. The black cloud of political corruption was now hovering over the Capitol in Hartford.

A delegation of Waterbury citizens asked me to have the Attorney General investigate the scandal since it affected both Waterbury and the State. I made it clear to them that under the Connecticut Constitution the Governor could do hardly more than consult with the Attorney General on the proper action to be taken after a thorough probe had been completed by a Grand Jury like the one which was being summoned to deal with the Merritt Parkway. They left my office with the assurance that I would coöperate with them in hastening Grand Jury proceedings if prodding became necessary.

Again events moved fast. On February 4 State's Attorney Lewis reported to the Superior Court that he believed an extraordinary Grand Jury should be impaneled to dig deeper into the evidence his office had uncovered. He took the occasion to disqualify himself and his staff from continuing the inquiry they had begun, on the ground that their residence and business affiliations in Waterbury might lead to charges of partiality. To my complete satisfaction, Hugh Alcorn, State's Attorney for Hartford County, was named special prosecutor in place of Attorney Lewis. On March 8 an Extraordinary Grand Jury impaneled by Judge Inglis of the Superior Court began a task, the scope of which was barely indicated by previous investigations. Its proceedings being kept rigidly secret, press and public wondered what was transpiring in that jury room as political chieftains and leaders of the bar were summoned, one after another, to give information which could be only guessed at. It was observed, too, that some political leaders, among them Leary, who would certainly be called for questioning, were on vacations outside the State in warmer climates for the cure of distempers affecting body or mind. All mysteries were revealed by the press on May 20, the day after the Grand Jury made its dramatic report recommending "the immediate arrest and prosecution forthwith" of twenty-seven persons "on the charge of conspiring to defraud the city of Waterbury and such other charges as the Special Attorney of the State may deem advisable." It was estimated that during the administration of Mayor Hayes Waterbury had been cheated out of "millions of dollars . . . by a powerful, ruthless, and corrupt group of men who had managed the affairs of the city for personal financial gain and political advancement."

The twenty-seven men charged with conspiracy or other offenses ran the gamut of leading city officials from Mayor Hayes downward, who found ready tools to aid them in local and outside lawyers and lobbyists, contractors, brokers, and accountants who would do what they were told to do. On the rim of the group were several prominent lawyers of the State, two of whom were censured by name. The report charged that the police had made no effort to suppress organized gambling in Waterbury which, it was generally believed, was a source of steady income for high city officials. Once I had sent in the State Police to do what the local police were failing to do in the enforcement of state laws against gambling. Mayor Hayes ordered them out. But they stayed on and did a very good temporary job against angry opposition. On their withdrawal gambling became again as vigorous as ever.

The main conspiracy to defraud the city of Waterbury out of millions of dollars, the number of which can never be known, was a cleverly devised maze of disguised financial transactions, which required four men to insure success: Mayor Hayes; his Executive Secretary, Thomas Kelly, to act as his agent in secret negotiations; Carl Olsen, vice-president and treasurer of a bank of which Leary was also vice-president and the largest stockholder, to be on hand with cash when cash was to pass from hand to hand; and Leary himself, who dominated the final scene, to allocate the division of spoils and to destroy all incriminating records.

In the division of spoils on corrupt contracts the conspirators took for themselves in the aggregate immense sums of money in cash. For instance, a New Haven attorney, who over a period of seven years endorsed checks made payable to him amounting to $126,000 for services in attempts to procure lower electric light and power rates for Waterbury, actually received in cash less than $20,000 in accordance with an agreement with Kelly, who kept the rest, part of which, it was shown, went to Hayes, Leary, and Olsen. Again, on the books $75,000 was paid for the rental of trucks to a man who had no trucks to rent. Once more a New York broker, according to the Grand Jury report, was paid $191,000 for only two weeks' actual service in making it "progressively easier" for Waterbury to sell bonds and obtain general credit in the metropolis. Later this man became Leary's partner in floating stock of the Electric Steam Sterilizer Company.

Leary, in an endeavor to extend his activities to the larger affairs of the State, persuaded the Senate chairman of the Committee on Public Health to introduce a bill making it mandatory of equip all public toilets with the electric steam sterilizer, ostensibly as a laudable means for preventing the spread of venereal disease but really as a scheme for creating a monopoly to mulct people out of vast sums of money by compelling them to buy a fake safety device controlled by patents. The bill was quickly whipped through the Senate by lobbyists under the direction of Hayes, a large stockholder in the company. I took the alarm and asked the State Commissioner of Health to test the curiously named machine. He reported that the sterilizer did not sterilize. This news was passed on to the House. Beyond that I informed leaders who called on me that the proponents of the bill seemed to be altogether too innocent of the ways venereal diseases are contracted. The upshot was that House and Senate agreed upon a harmless act requiring that "all public pay toilets must be kept clean and sterile" by such devices as the Commissioner of Health may recommend. The vision of a gold mine in the sky above the gilded dome of the Capitol faded away.

The circumstances connected with the legislative maneuvers over the sterilizer which did not sterilize were investigated by the Grand Jury who discovered that Leary in promotion of his monopoly distributed, two months after the adjournment of the General Assembly, 2,700 shares of the Sterilizing Company to five members—three Democrats and two Republicans. The Grand Jury held that these gifts were gratuities for services rendered in the passage of the bill and were so received. Accordingly the five men were liable to prosecution under the Corrupt Practices Act. Within twenty-four hours of the receipt of the Grand Jury's report I asked the three Democrats to resign at once the offices they held under appointment by the Governor, with the understanding that if they were acquitted of the charges against them while I was Governor they would be reinstated. They promptly complied with my request. When they were brought to trial long afterwards their cases, on motion of the defense, were nolled by the court on the ground that it was an unwarranted inference that their acceptance of the Sterilizer stock two months after the adjournment of the General Assembly was in payment for their activities in favor of the Sterilizer bill itself. The case against one of the Republicans was disposed of in like manner but the other, who introduced the bill and fought hard for it, confessed to a gratuity.

Nothing more astonished the Grand Jury than the revelation of an alliance between the conspirators and two other prominent Republican political leaders to put through the General Assembly of 1935 that sterilizer monopoly. The first step towards the unholy alliance was taken, according to the Grand Jury's report, by Leary in a heart-to-heart business talk with Charles E. Williamson, the prosecuting attorney of the town court of Darien, who in previous times had frequently represented his town or his Senatorial district in the General Assembly. Before taking over the heavy burden Leary wanted to place on his shoulders, Williamson, according to the Grand Jury's report, expressed a desire to confer with his friend Harry Mackenzie. Of course permission was readily granted, for Harry was then second in command of the Republican organization. Harry, it seems, was disposed to share the burden with Williamson, provided there could be agreement on a proper financial consideration. About that there was no trouble. Mackenzie, however, kept as far as he could in the background, while throughout the session of 1935 Williamson took orders nearly every morning on his day's work, which apparently extended beyond special legislation for the city of Waterbury. During the session Williamson received checks aggregating $24,400 which were cashed by Olsen who kept $12,200 for Leary and perhaps Hayes and gave $12,200 to Williamson to be divided equally between himself and Mackenzie. The same arrangement was made for the session of 1937, when $34,000 was split up in the same way. For these transactions Mackenzie and Williamson, who was eliminated from the town court of Darien, faced court action under the Corrupt Practices Act. Ultimately they both took a few months' rest in the New Haven County jail which I was then having put into better sanitary condition than usual by the use of W.P.A. funds granted for that explicit purpose.

Lieutenant Governor Hayes was too hard a nut to crack. With his friends I joined in urging his resignation, without avail. Even the suggestion awakened his indignation. All the charges against him he declared to have no foundation in fact. He had no knowledge whatever, he claimed, of what Leary, Kelly, and Olsen might have been doing. He was not responsible for acts in which he took no part, he said. The trial, which he hoped would come soon, would exonerate him. All this was spoken with the air of an honest man whose honor is hurt. Notwithstanding the evidence which the Grand Jury presented against him, he was entitled under the law to the presumption of innocence until he was proved guilty. In one of my conversations with him we came to a tacit understanding that he would refrain from performing the usual functions of a Lieutenant Governor while his case was in court. That was a very slight scratch on the nut.

The question of calling a special session of the General Assembly for impeachment proceedings against the Lieutenant Governor, the method provided by the State Constitution for the removal of elective officers, was carefully considered by the Legislative Council and many others whom we consulted. There was unanimous agreement that it would be undesirable to suspend or interfere with the court action which had already been taken against Hayes and others on a charge of conspiracy by summoning the Lieutenant Governor before another bar of justice. In any event there was a prospect of a long bitter fight ahead which could not be terminated before the expiration of his term of office in January, 1939. For these reasons the idea of impeachment proceedings was cast aside.

How long and how bitter the court fight was to be no one could then have anticipated. Not until August, 1939, was ex-Lieutenant Governor Hayes convicted in the Superior Court with twenty-two others of conspiracy to defraud the city of Waterbury over which he still presided as Mayor. And not until March, 1941, was the conviction affirmed by the Supreme Court of Connecticut.

The summer and autumn of 1938 were a period of some tension for the people of Connecticut. The Governor of the State had passed the age of seventy-six, an age at which most men are dead. If he should follow in the procession of his generation, then Hayes would take his place at the head of the State. If Hayes should resign in such an emergency, then the President pro tem of the Senate would become Governor. I assured my friends that I was still in good health and likely to pull through the next six months, barring accidents which I hoped to escape by cutting down my speed of travel through the State to fifty miles an hour even where the road was clear far ahead. A newspaper carried a cartoon of a worried-looking Governor for whom prayers ought to be said.

Just after the Waterbury scandal broke, I was invited to address the delegates to the Southern New England Methodist Conference in the South Church at Manchester. I was led by a deacon to the altar and greeted by the presiding Bishop, Herbert Welch. After my speech the Bishop asked me to kneel and blessed me. Obviously I needed it. Not long before that, on my birthday, the Jews of Connecticut founded a scholarship in my name at Yeshiva College of the City of New York, which was celebrating its Golden Jubilee. As my conduct now had the approbation of Jew and Gentile, I felt reasonably safe for time and eternity, though in the outside world a Socialist was damning me as a friend and partner of the Waterbury crowd, and the ranking spokesman of the Republican party was holding me accountable to the Recording Angel for all the alleged sins of Commissioner MacDonald and his man, G. Leroy Kemp.

For a little while my mind was released from political scandals. I attended the memorable Yale Commencement of 1938, where among recipients of honorary degrees I met Walt Disney, whose voice was the voice of Mickey Mouse; Thomas Mann, the world's supreme novelist, who was writing for the *Yale Review*; and John Buchan (Lord Tweedsmuir), Governor General of Canada, who had many amusing stories to tell of his political career. I asked Buchan how he ever found time to do the research for his biography of Augustus Caesar, involving the organization of the Roman Empire. He replied that it was the fulfillment of an ambition of his youth.

That spring and summer New Haven also celebrated its Tercentenary with great éclat under the direction of a committee of which Judge Gilson was chairman. The Yale Bowl, an amphitheater as capacious as the Colosseum of ancient Rome, was the scene of a state-wide praise and memorial service and "a great pageant" displaying the history of the colony. It fell to my lot as Governor to tell the story of the Founding Fathers, the Reverend John Davenport and Theophilus Eaton, and of their famous successors. I was almost equally interested in men whose names time has obscured: the surveyor John Brockett, who laid out the village of New Haven in nine squares, of which the central square was reserved as a civic and religious center, and William Cooper who gave to the Reverend James Pierpont two elm saplings to plant in his front yard, an example to others who eventually made New Haven known through the land as "the Elm City."

XXXIX. Hurricane

On Monday, September 19, I attended the Eastern States Exposition at Springfield. The rain was coming down in sheets and the grounds were thick with mud. The next morning I drove again from Hartford to Springfield through blinding torrential rains to assist in the ceremony of laying the cornerstone of the Connecticut Exposition Building. During a brief lull in the storm I gave a short speech and played with a trowel under the protection of a tent. On my return to Hartford, again through heavy showers, I was troubled in mind by the rapid rise of the Connecticut River, which was spreading over meadows, and by news that other rivers in the eastern part of the State were breaking over their banks. I took preliminary steps towards dealing with another great flood, should Connecticut again be visited by so terrible a disaster as in 1936. Nobody, I think, anticipated that a tropical hurricane in the West Indies might move far enough north to strike New England.

On Wednesday morning, September 21, the situation was outwardly little changed from the day before. I consulted in person or over the telephone with representatives of those state agencies necessary to cope with a flood, not with a hurricane. I asked representatives of Federal agencies to be ready to meet with us in my office not later than Friday morning. I requested the Red Cross to assign Robert Shepard to Connecticut, if possible. I had in mind essentially the old setup of 1936, whose members then became familiar with the problems of a great flood. As yet there were no other indications.

That afternoon I drove to New Haven, through downpours and lulls, to keep an appointment with the Advisory Council of the *Yale Review*, of which I was still the Editor in Chief. We met high in the tower of the Graduate School of Yale University. Towards three o'clock I observed that a violent gale was blowing rain against the windows, some of the rain even coming into the room over the tight-fitting window sills. We looked out and saw trees swaying in the tempest but within sight none were going over. Nervous as I was I went on with the conference, jumping up now and then to view the storm from a window. Towards four o'clock I suggested that two members of the Council who wished to take a train homeward via New York half an hour later would need all that time to get to the station because of the rain and wind. We broke up and went below to the wide covered entrance to the Graduate School where a number of men had taken refuge. They told us of the havoc wrought by a hurricane the last hour—streets blocked by great elms and maples which had been torn out by the roots, wires down, windows smashed and floors deluged by the inrush of water. Through detours my two friends were driven to the station, but they proceeded no farther on the way to New York, for all eastbound trains from Boston were stalled along the line by washouts and flooded tracks. They put up at the nearest hotel for the night. I reached home, a scant two miles away, after a dangerous ride of more than an hour. It was impossible to go on to Hartford that night because no roads could be made passable until morning at best.

During the evening I received messages indicating enormous destruction by the hurricane. Of them one demanding immediate executive action came from police officials of New London, urging assistance of the National Guard in maintaining order and in clearing the streets of wreckage. Great waves had lifted shipping high in the harbor and thrown much of it over the railroad tracks. Hundreds of stores were blown open, exposing their goods to pillage by looters. Fires were blazing up in wrecked buildings on streets near the shore. Fire companies were being held bound in their quarters because of fallen or broken trees lying across exits. Trucks had to precede them to open a way for them through the streets. For a time there was grave danger that a large part of the business district of the city might go up in flames.

I instructed Assistant Adjutant General Wardinski, then alone on duty in Hartford, to call out at once a company of the National Guard composed of men in or near New London. By morning order was restored and fires were brought under control. Though terribly damaged by wind and wave, New London was saved from a conflagration by quick action of its officials.

At daybreak I started for Hartford over the main highway and byroads partially cleared during the night. Along the avenue leading to the Capitol from the south most of the great trees were down, but a narrow pathway had been cut out just wide enough to let an automobile through. In my office my Executive Secretary, Philip Hewes, told me what I would see if I made a tour of Hartford. Of greatest concern was the behavior of the Connecticut River which had inundated the lower east side of the city. Mayor Spellacy said the flood waters of the river were still rising. They were only two feet below the crest of the flood in 1936. Hundreds of men were building up the dike down by Colt's Fire Arms Company with huge piles of sand bags. Thousands of men, women, and children were being evacuated from their houses in the lowlands. If the dike should break it might be necessary to stop all traffic on the outskirts of the city in order to keep the streets free for official business. The Adjutant General had already ordered out several companies of the National Guard for service in the Hartford district; and now, on further request of the Mayor, orders were issued for more Guardsmen to appear at the State Armory for instructions. Next I summoned the Adjutant General for a report on the calls he had received for aid on the National Guard in all hurricane areas; the Highway Commissioner, whose men had been on duty all night, for a report on the extent of their work; the Commissioner of Public Works for what he knew about damage to state buildings and parks; the State Forester for what he had heard about damage suffered by state forests and to consider whether they should be closed to hunters because of the danger from fires. Funds for the purchase of vaccines and various medical supplies were made available to the Commissioner of Public Health. The local Red Cross director reported how families evacuated from Hartford flood areas were being cared for; and the Connecticut Works Progress Administrator stated that hundreds of his men had been coöperating in clearing the streets of Hartford and New Haven during the night and that other detachments were succeeding them. From outside the State Governor Earle of Pennsylvania offered to place at Connecticut's disposal a detail of his state constabulary and air force if needed.

All these conferences were interrupted by telephone messages implor-
ing help of some kind. In a number of districts reservoirs supplying water
to towns had broken and the people were forced to resort to abandoned
wells for drinking water. The residents of New Britain were in terror lest
the dam of their principal reservoir should go. I sent over there three companies of the National Guard to take charge of the situation. A section of
the city which would be flooded if the dam broke was ordered evacuated.
Fortunately the crest of the waters began to fall during the evening. The
dam was holding so well that families living in the endangered district
were allowed by midnight to return to homes which they had feared they
would never see again.

Complaints of looting came in from towns along the seashore and the
Connecticut River Valley. The excited voice of one man over the tele-
phone demanded that martial law be declared in his neighborhood.
I referred him and others who made similar reports to their nearest State
Police barracks, where men were patrolling the roads. I was importuned
to convene the General Assembly in special session to confer upon the
Governor extraordinary general powers to deal with the emergency and
specifically to obtain from that body authority for the immediate construction of another and higher bridge across the Connecticut River.
I replied that there was as yet no agreement on the proper site of the
bridge, and that the Governor already had sufficient powers under the
Constitution as interpreted by his predecessors and confirmed by long
custom to meet the emergency.

Before the day was over Philip Hewes urged city and town officials
who could be reached by telephone to attend the general conference in
my office the next morning with state and Federal relief agencies. That
evening I described over the radio the destruction which followed in the
wake of flood and hurricane, so far as I knew of it, all through eastern
Connecticut to beyond the Great River and along the whole length of
the coast from Stonington to Greenwich. I concluded by requesting iso-
lated communities without telephone connections to send representatives
to the morrow's conference if they were able.

At the conference on Friday my office was crowded with some fifty men from the worst stricken areas. Sitting by me to hear their reports were the heads of the state agencies with whom I had consulted the day before. With us, too, were Robert Shepard of the Red Cross, H. Francis White of the National Emergency Council, and Vincent Sullivan, representing Harry Hopkins, who had assured me yesterday of large assistance in the crisis. My aim in calling the conference was twofold: to coördinate all immediate relief work and to formulate a plan for the gradual rehabilitation of devastated areas in coöperation with such state agencies as might be required.

It was an illuminating conference. When I asked why few or no small villages were represented, someone said, "Because no one can get out of some of them to a highway except on foot, for most bridges are gone and roads are washed out and covered with fallen trees." A man from Vernon broke in to say that the flood had carried downstream ten bridges in his town. Another said that some villages were scant of food and that aviators were dropping supplies to them. "How about that, Highway Commissioner?" I asked. He replied that he had no reliable estimate on the loss of town bridges, but that the flood had broken through many dams and demolished at least nineteen bridges on trunk lines. Two thousand of his men, with all his trucks, he said, were out clearing highways for one-way traffic and building temporary structures across streams. The dearth of drinking water was another problem. Fires were out in New London, but the fire apparatus, the Mayor said, was being used to pump water up to Connecticut College on the hill.

Fortunately the flood in Hartford had reached its crest and the dike was withstanding the strain. And yet, fearing that danger was not over, Mayor Spellacy felt justified in asking for more National Guardsmen. A similar request was made by officials from other parts of the State despite the fact that 12 companies of the National Guard, numbering 900 men, were already on duty. Down the river as far as Saybrook roads were deep with water which had broken over or through banks of the river. When the storm struck Essex a fleet of 200 boats was riding in the harbor. An hour later all but 5 or 6 were sunk or dashed upon the shore or torn into pieces floating down the stream. Spokesmen from coast towns described the terrible destruction along miles of the sea front. Great waves utterly demolished rows of fragile summer cottages. In places nothing was left except the sites on which they were built. More substantial houses and other buildings were unroofed, or put on beam and often blown backward, sometimes two or three hundred feet. We were all aghast at the stories we heard. Robert Shepard promised to stay on to administer relief measures. Vincent Sullivan said that he had authority from Harry Hopkins to send into the hurricane areas 22,000 W.P.A. workers if so many were needed. And Adjutant General Ladd gave assurance that he could send out a thousand more National Guardsmen, to patrol streets and roads wherever state and local police were not at hand in sufficient numbers to maintain order. I requested the city and town officials present to remain on for consultation with these three agencies and the Highway Commissioner concerning their special problems. Then I adjourned the conference to meet on the next Tuesday when I would present a plan for the coördination of all relief work.

George H. Myers, who had given the Yale forest at Union to his *alma mater*, rode with me that far, and we stopped there to see what a cyclone could do to woodlands. Some trees were snapped off, most, I think, were uprooted. Acres of trees lay twisted in a tangle.

The Council, which was called primarily for a conference with Federal relief and rehabilitation agencies, met in the great hall of the Copley Plaza Hotel. Most of the agencies were well represented. Harry Hopkins, who was in California when the hurricane struck New England, at once flew back to Washington and on the morning before the conference took an automobile trip through terribly devastated Rhode Island. He came to Boston not only as chief of the W.P.A. but as spokesman for President Roosevelt. He opened the meeting with an account of what he saw in Rhode Island, paying tribute by the way to the work of the Red Cross there and elsewhere. "I saw homes," he said, "by the hundreds flattened out; hundreds of persons without shelter; people who didn't know where the other members of their families were or whether they were dead or alive." He urged all agencies, Federal, state, and local, to work together first in relieving distress and then in restoring normal life throughout New

England, without quibbling over "who does what." For the purposes designated, he said, all the funds under his control "are yours." That promise was made to 300 state, county, and town officials representing all the States of New England.

Each Governor in turn reported on his own State. No story was so grim as that of Rhode Island, where ten thousand houses had been converted into kindling wood and much of the land on which they were built was washed into Narragansett Bay. Within the last twenty-four hours, the Governor said, a hundred dead bodies had been discovered lying along the shore. The loss of life in Connecticut I estimated to be between 80 and 90, as against only 2 in the flood of 1936. The toll for all New England appeared to be more than 600, with Rhode Island accounting for perhaps 400. In Maine and New Hampshire great forests were blown down. The question rose how to process and save for the market in coming years more than a billion feet of timber.

The Governor of Massachusetts introduced a series of resolutions requesting that all Federal agencies concerned with rehabilitation suspend their hard and fixed regulations in order to cope swiftly with the disaster. The resolutions were passed unanimously after Harry Hopkins spoke in their favor. Finally, just before adjournment, several of us started a discussion on the shortage in food and other necessary supplies in the three southern New England States owing to a truckmen's strike in New York which was holding up all shipments of freight through the city. As soon as the facts of a desperate situation were brought out, a resolution was passed authorizing me as chairman of the Governor's Conference to send an appeal to the strike leaders by way of Mayor La Guardia that food and other household supplies be let through to the devastated areas. Due to the good offices of Mayor La Guardia the ban was lifted. By midnight all necessary supplies began to move freely into New England.

As I made my way slowly back to Hartford that night dangerous stretches of the road were lighted up with brilliant flares and patrols were out to give information on detours and to lend assistance in case of trouble.

I laid before the state-wide conference in my office next morning such information, good and bad, as had come to my office since Friday on the present situation throughout the State, which was supplemented by reports of others. The passage of the flood exposed to view the desolation of river valleys. Pathways cut out to the shore front along the Sound, where miles of sea walls had disappeared, revealed the awful destruction of tidal waves. Not 18 but 38 bridges were destroyed or severely damaged; and 50,000 trees lay flat by roadsides. Commissioner Cox, reporting on washed-out roads, was followed by State Forester Hawes, who said that a preliminary survey of the forests in eastern Connecticut indicated that 50 per cent of trees more than 10 inches in diameter were blown down. The fire hazard he regarded as very great. The stump of a lighted cigarette carelessly thrown into the brush might start a conflagration which would be hard to control. On his recommendation I at once closed the forests to hunting and all inland waters to fishing. He inquired what was to be done with millions of feet of timber that had blown down. I could tell him that before I left Boston the initial step had already been taken towards its salvage by joint action of the New England Governors and representatives of the Federal Government.

Damage to state buildings and parks now appeared to be three times the first estimate. Someone mentioned the precarious Amazon standing on the gilded dome of the Capitol, her wings flapping in the wind and her knees creaking. I replied that she would come down as soon as Commissioner Hurley could determine how best to handle her. By the laughter it was evident that many had in mind the old jest as to whether it is better to have a loose woman hovering over the Capitol or a fallen woman on its grounds.

Tremendous damage, I learned, was done to farmsteads by winds of high velocity sweeping through valleys and over hills. Barns were unroofed; sheds and outhouses were crushed in; cattle were killed by falling timbers—for instance, the barn of a dairy farm near Middletown collapsed, killing 23 cows out of a herd of 27; fences and stone walls were blown over; fruit orchards suffered severely, particularly large apple trees which were broken down or uprooted; and unharvested crops were lying flat in the fields.

By that time relief and reclamation work was in full swing. Detachments of W.P.A. men were dispatched to districts where they were most needed. Health officers with the help of boys from the C.C.C. camps were cleaning up and disinfecting houses still standing. The Red Cross, which took on all available men registered in employment offices, was bringing back families to their homes, feeding and clothing them, repairing and refurnishing houses so as to make them comfortable. Farm bureaus, under the supervision of the State College, were making a survey of rural communities to determine the needs of farmers. Altogether a score of state and Federal agencies were engaged in the restoration of normal activities of every kind.

During the flood of 1936 the Governor's office, it will be remembered, was the clearinghouse of all agencies organized to meet that disaster. But now I felt the need of assistance in dealing with a widespread catastrophe. I appointed Col. Thomas Hewes as Coordinator of Federal and State Agencies. He opened an office in the Capitol where anyone was free to come for information. He also issued a pamphlet which designated local agencies or officials in towns and cities to whom applications might be made for aid. Through this integrated system I was able to keep in close touch with the progress of relief and reclamation in all devastated areas. When the Coördinator had finished his work, I appointed a state-wide committee of twenty-four citizens for the long pull of rebuilding Connecticut.

My hands were still full of business occasioned by flood and hurricane. No one at the conference in my office was ready with an approximate estimate of broken dams (afterwards known to be 50 or more) or could give more than an incidental account of the damage which had been done, other than to roads, by their released waters. Over this lack of knowledge I had a conversation with General Wadhams, Director of the State Water Commission whose prime function, though it had other important ones, was to protect waterways from pollution. Apart from his jurisdiction there was a Board of Engineers, all good and competent men, whose business it was to inspect old dams and to supervise the construction of new dams, under a statute, however, which gave them hardly more than advisory powers. I suggested that a bill be prepared for submission to the next session of the General Assembly. Consolidating the two agencies and making strict control over all dams in the State mandatory. In the meantime, I told him, I was going to ask the engineers to inspect all dams in the hurricane area and to permit no rebuilding or repairs before designs for such work had met their approval for safety. I asked General Wadhams to join me in this effort. The engineers responded gladly. The way was then paved for one united Water Commission with enlarged powers.

At this juncture President Roosevelt happily made available large Federal funds for general flood control in New England by means of dikes as well as reservoirs on any streams where they were necessary in the opinion of state and Federal engineers. Apparently no question was to be raised about electric power and a New England T.V.A. Thus came unexpectedly an opportunity to harness flood waters on a broader plan than was contemplated by the Inter-State Compact which had stumbled through political intrigue to its death. Under the new proposal flood control could be extended to streams outside the Connecticut River watershed to meet the exigencies of frequent devastating floods. On this proposition the New England Governors went into conference with renewed hope of devising plans for permanent control of all waterways within these northeastern States.

From the first days of the hurricane I began visiting the worst hurt cities, villages, and countrysides as fast as ways were open to them. For a comprehensive view of the devastation I took a trip over the hills and plateaus down through valleys and off on crossroads to Norwich and New London and on to Stonington. With me were Colonel Hewes and Works Progress Administrator Sullivan. Along the roads on each side of the mile-long Common of Lebanon giant elms lay torn out by the roots and at the lower end hardly any part of the beautiful church designed by John Trumbull, the portrait painter, remained standing. This church in ruins was the last surviving building shaped by the hand of a great artist. I wondered whether funds could be raised for its restoration.

Descending into the valley southeastward we saw on the left a barn, completely unroofed and resting on its beam, its mounds of hay half spilled over on the ground; then another barn split in two and hay rolling out;

and all along fruit trees stripped of branches and oaks and maples uprooted. On approaching New London we noticed how the leaves of standing trees and shrubbery were wilting and drying up, scorched by the salt spray of immense waves that had blown miles inland.

We went on eastward to Stonington to see the worst that the hurricane could do. Round the harbor and down by the docks the devastation was frightful. Wooden buildings by the shore had all been carried out to sea, leaving no trace behind. With them went sea walls. The fronts of dwelling houses a little farther back were blown completely open, exposing entire interiors. Some houses, half demolished by the wind, had tumbled up against one another. Of others nothing was left but broken frames and scattered boards. All the shipping was lifted by great waves and dropped on land. Sad-faced fishermen were looking over their boats and here and there a fisherman, chewing tobacco, was repairing a boat that could be salvaged.

Near the railway station we visited the scene of prompt and heroic action by the conductor of an eastbound express train of 13 cars having 350 passengers aboard. The train was halted on a causeway between Mystic and Stonington by the lashing of waves. The next wave might overturn it into the sea. The water was already rising to the floors of the train. The conductor immediately ordered all passengers to move forward to the front car, which was uncoupled by a trainman standing up to his neck in water. Most of the passengers obeyed orders. Of those who jumped over-board to save themselves two were drowned. All the others in that single car the engine drew to safety through fallen wires, debris, and a house blown upon the tracks. Soon after the passengers were out of the car a mighty wave threw a fishing schooner out of the water up against it and knocked it over.

Everybody was saying the next day that Connecticut had never suffered so great a disaster. Curious to know how far this might be true, I turned to an old copy of the *American Journal of Science* which contained an excel-lent account of the hurricane of 1815. To my astonishment I saw that the hurricane of 1938 was almost an exact repetition of that of 1815, which originated in the West Indies, came up the Atlantic Coast in the wake of warm rains, and laid waste essentially the same New England area on Saturday, September 23, a mere two days in the same month behind its successor 123 years afterwards.

The devastation wrought by the two hurricanes was, *mutatis mutandis*, the same. If fewer people lost their lives in 1815, it was because there were fewer people to lose their lives and still fewer to build summer houses on the sands of the sea. If there were then fewer fires, it was because lucifer matches were not yet invented and nobody smoked cigarettes. There were then no railroad beds to be washed out, no telegraph, telephone, and electric wires to be blown with their supports into the streets. The largest Connecticut cities were only villages of a few thousand inhabitants. But wind and sea and rivers in flood were there to do their best towards the destruction of whatever stood in the way of their mad career.

As I write I have before me a copy of a letter which Daniel Putnam of Brooklyn, Connecticut, wrote to his daughter the day after the hurricane of 1815: "In short," he concluded, "you can turn your eye no way, but it meets with desolation." This desolation he attributed to "a visitation of Heaven," a very picturesque phrase which I like because of its suggestion that Our Lord came down to earth again to conduct a hurricane either to display his omnipotence or to punish his children for sins of which they were only vaguely aware. But points of view change with time and circumstance. I was a bit ruffled but more amused when a Republican candidate for office attributed responsibility for the devastation of 1938 in large measure not to Heaven but to the Democratic party on the sole ground that, owing to Congressional intrigues, a number of reservoirs on the northern tributaries of the Connecticut River, which were outside the flood area this year, had not been built as I had promised. In reply to this kind of wild talk I gave it as my candid opinion that no legislation enacted by any political party can regulate the whirl of a hurricane or impound the waters of the sea.

XL. My Last Campaign

The Merritt Parkway ghost had been laid, at least temporarily; Grand Juries had helped clean house for both Democrats and Republicans; and now another election was approaching. After due deliberation I let it be known that I was in a receptive mood for the Democratic nomination for Governor once more if that was the will of the party. To this decision I was led by the hope, among others, that the next General Assembly would be favorably disposed towards thorough revision of the accounting system of the State. After rejecting in 1937 a plan for a modernized accounting system which would show the state of the budget day by day, the Assembly had contented itself with a few amendments to existing laws, except in one important instance. It passed an act making mandatory a yearly audit of the books and accounts of the Treasurer and Comptroller. Here was something entirely new. No record could be found that the accounts of the Comptroller had ever been audited by an outside agency!

I was also advocating the extension of mandatory annual audits to all subdivisions of the State under centralized state supervision as an obvious safeguard against dishonesty in local government, whether on a large scale as in Waterbury or on a small scale as had occurred in other municipalities; and a revision of the Lobbying Act of 1937 for better control over lobbyists who had found a hole in the law through which to escape. The time seemed propitious, too, for another effort to take the minor courts out of political intrigue by an amendment to the Constitution. Above all else I wanted to carry forward the reorganization of the state government, involving mergers of related departments, which had been well begun by the General Assembly inn 1937.

The Democrats were in general agreement that their best bet for victory would be to renominate their old state ticket with the exception of their candidate for Lieutenant Governor. Col. Thomas Hewes was finally selected for this place. The Republicans, uncertain about their whole ticket, sent up three trial balloons for Governor to see in what direction the strongest wind might blow. The first to go up was President McConaughy of Wesleyan University, towards whom only a mild breeze blew, because he was not widely known to the rank and file of his party. He came down for the avowed reason that one man could not run a university and the State of Connecticut at the same time. The second man to be sent up was W. J. Pape, as a reward for his services in uncovering the Waterbury conspiracy. He drew a considerable breeze, but he was summoned to the ground, perhaps because he was rather too ostentatious in the display of his moral virtues to hold the entire Republican electorate and to win over enough Democratic votes to make certain his election. The third man who went up into the air, apparently on his own request, was William H. Blodgett, an old war horse of the Roraback machine. While floating around above the earth he attacked my fiscal policy, particularly for the last three years, warning me that "in view of recent revelations in a certain municipality of the State," the public was entitled to know what had happened to the $20,000,000 which the State had received during the last three years from the tax on cigarettes, alcoholic liquors, and small business corporations! Eventually the Republicans nominated Raymond E. Baldwin, Republican leader of the House in 1933, for Governor, and President McConaughy for Lieutenant Governor.

The Socialists, who were backing McLevy, raised high over their heads the slogan, "Don't let the raiders raid again!" Their platform and Jasper's keynote speech at the Convention, both evidently the children of one set of brains, were lively examples of vituperation. I enjoyed the preamble to the platform, in which both Democrats and Republicans were mowed down:

"Year after year, backed by facts, the Socialist party has bluntly denounced the Democratic and Republican parties as political twins acting for private plunder rather than for the public welfare. Today two Grand Juries have stamped those charges as officially proved. Under the lash of their reports the two old parties tremble today—publicly disgraced and publicly indicted. They have forfeited forever the respect and support of the decent people of Connecticut."

In his acceptance speech Mayor McLevy worked himself up into ferocious moral indignation over Parkway and Waterbury corruption. He depicted one after another the lurid scenes revealed by two Grand Juries, and after each picture paused to repeat a refrain which was greeted with tremendous applause, "They didn't know," meaning that the Governor and the Democratic administration didn't know, didn't make any effort to know, and apparently didn't care to know what was going on in Waterbury and the Highway Department.

The question arose in many minds besides my own whether Mayor McLevy and the Republican organization were working together as a double machine to oust me from office. Certainly the Republicans were well disposed towards Jasper. They rarely criticized him. Their National Committeeman said that he always called on the Mayor when he visited Bridgeport. McConaughy remarked that though he disagreed with the Socialist platform he liked "shy, honest Jasper" as a man. And likewise proclaiming that he was not a Socialist, one W. Ben Aurandt, until then in the employ of the Bridgeport branch of the General Electric Company,

formed a "Citizens' McLevy for Governor Organization," intended to convey the impression that great industrial corporations as well as work-men were quite willing to discount a little "harmless socialist" in order to elect honest Jasper as Governor.

Whether or not there was any formal hookup between McLevy and Republican leaders to debunk the Democratic administration, they joined hands towards a common end, which would incidentally benefit both sides. The Republicans could hardly hope to win without the aid of McLevy who would draw more votes from the Democratic than from their own party, and McLevy needed a Republican victory to assure him of the passage of questionable legislation for Bridgeport.

Socialist and Republican camps were thrown into noisy commotion when not only did the A.F.L. officially approve my labor records but Labor's Non-Partisan League, an affiliate of the C.I.O., endorsed me as their can-didate for reëlection. This seemed to my political opponents an amazing thing in view of the fact that I had quelled a sit-down strike by another branch of the C.I.O. only three years before. The question for or against sit-down strikes could not be openly debated on the stump by Republicans because of the halo thrown over my head for putting an end to sit-down strikes in Connecticut. They relied upon Jasper to corral the labor vote.

The Democratic Governor was the game of both parties. I was repre-sented as being the boon companion of Lieutenant Governor Hayes and so must have known what the man was doing long before the exposure of his character by a Grand Jury. Again and again I was asked why I did not compel his resignation—in spite of the fact that a Governor has no com-pulsive power over an elective state officer who performs his duties as laid down by law. The best that could be said of me by any Republican on the stump ran something like this: "No one, of course, can question the per-sonal honesty of Governor Cross—but er—but er–he cannot complain if he is judged by the company he keeps." I rather liked that *but* sentence.

Just as I was held responsible for the Waterbury conspirators and Repub-lican fee-splitters and for the damage done by floods and whirlwinds in the Connecticut River Valley, so the deficit in the general funds of the State which accumulated during the long hard years of the depression was thrown into my lap. The fact that since the Legislature had given me control over the budget I was keeping the current expenses of the government within income was neither admitted nor denied but for campaign purposes ignored. The deficit, which even Roraback did not lay to the Governor, was the thing to play up. It was first lifted without warrant from $12,000,000, the true amount approximately, to $16,000,000 and after that to $24,000,000 by adding an $8,000,000 surplus which, on the authority of the Republican General Assembly of 1931, was expended on a building program for the State's humane institutions. By some juggling with figures, just how I forget, it eventually reached the fantastic height of $29,000,000.

This "appalling deficit" was partly caused, it was alleged, by an unnecessary increase in the number of state employees in order to feed hungry Democrats. The increase in number was recklessly put at 2,700 whereas the correct number of additional employees since 1933, exclusive of the State's institutions, was 1,882, and of these the Federal Government was paying salaries and wages, in whole or in part, of 1,381, thus leaving only 501 new permanent employees whose salaries and wages were paid by the State alone. This increase, I submitted, was extremely moderate in view of the fact of larger services being performed by the State, such as the administration of the Unemployment Compensation Act and a $25,000,000 building program.

The so-called "reformed Republican party," if judged by the policies advocated by its candidates for office, was essentially a reactionary party. In the session of 1937 Republican members of the General Assembly had indeed been true reformers. They forged straight ahead with reorganization and other enlightened legislation which they believed would be beneficial to the citizens of the State, ignoring outside leaders who yelled at them, insulted them, and tried in vain to browbeat them into line with threats or political ostracism. Though the Republican candidates of 1938 insisted that their party should be purged of corrupt bosses, they made no effort to purge themselves of the traditional ideas which had long dominated the Republican party. They went as far as they dared in breaking down the liberal measures of the reformers of 1937. Corrupt and incorrupt alike desired a return to the normalcy of the Roraback regime. "I was not," President McConaughy is speaking, "a very vociferous Republican in the Roraback days. However, it seems to me that the record clearly indicates that the State was infinitely better off when it was under Republican leadership. In those days the State had a record for financial solvency . . . Members of the Republican Senate and House enacted forward-looking legislation for the welfare of Connecticut workers and all other citizens, which made the State known as progressive and social-minded."

Major parts of the reorganization program were attacked. The merit system of appointments, then administered by a most competent non-political Personnel Director, was "fixed," President McConaughy "strongly felt," by the Democrats for their own benefit. He declared that, despite the loud talk about economies resulting from reorganization, there had been "not a single definite demonstration of a dollar saved for the State." Yet the Supervisor of Purchases had demonstrated that he had saved the State $1,500,000 the first year and the Budget Director had conservatively estimated that rigid control of expenditures had saved the State almost a million more in the same period.

The Republicans also charged that the entire building program "had been bogged down by inefficiency and politics." Mr. Baldwin said that the program was still "largely on the drafting boards," and President McConaughy gave it as his opinion that if the truth were made known "not a brick has yet been laid." To prove it the Republican organization sent a pair of professional photographers into the field to take pictures. At the new Training School for Defectives in Southbury the photographers set their camera at an angle which excluded from vision buildings going up and showed only a terrain torn by steam shovels for the construction of roads and tunnels. Prominent over the débris, however, was a sign "P.W.A. Project." At Rocky Hill where buildings for a Veterans' Home were under way the photographers were unable to find a satisfactory angle for their camera: so they let it play over a stretch of woods in the foreground which lay tangled and twisted by the hurricane and called the scene "The Site of the Veterans' Home." At the State Hospital for the Insane in the suburbs of Middletown they found what they wanted in an ugly little frame house undergoing repairs not far away but having no connection whatever with the state institution. As a matter of fact, buildings for twelve institutions involving contracts amounting to $8,000,000 or more were rising in all stages of construction up to completion; while architects and their assistants were working full speed on designs of other buildings so that contracts might be let for their construction by January 1, 1939, in order to qualify for all the grants, totaling $12,000,000, by the Federal Government, a large part of which had been made in recent months. Ten thoroughly misleading photographs, which, it was asserted, were "the only claim to progress in the $25,000,000 building program," were reserved for exhibition in the press the day before election, thus leaving no time to show up their fraudulent character. The advertisements closed with the slogan: "Stop This Waste. Vote Republican."

Much legislation, somewhat apart from reorganization, was subjected to both rear and frontal attack. Of this a conspicuous example was the semiannual inspection of motor vehicles, then mandatory under the law, which in the first year of its application had decreased fatalities on the road by 8 per cent. The issue came into the campaign in an amusing way. A poultry farmer, by name Robert Morris, living on a highway in Fairfield County, displayed on a post erected in front of his house a sign which read "Sign here to Stop Car Inspection." During the first day, it was said, nearly a hundred automobilists stopped and signed their names in a big book attached to the post. There would have been many more signatures, the farmer said, had not the threat of a sprinkling rain compelled him to take the book into the house to keep it dry. This was the origin of a mammoth petition containing ultimately, it was claimed, 60,000 names, for the repeal of the obnoxious State Inspection Act, which "gets nowhere in avoiding accidents." Whether the 60,000 signatures were all genuine is immaterial, for with the passage of weeks the madness grew. The political campaign had hardly got into swing when I saw in my travels through Fairfield County hundreds of automobiles plastered with legends against inspection and banners flying in front or back.

The Republican candidate for Governor found in this surge of hostility against inspection a new issue and he made the most of it. He set up the claim that inspection as then conducted was so casual as to be of no value, that drivers "doctored up" their automobiles before they entered inspection lanes, and that only 2 per cent of accidents on the road were attributable to faulty mechanism. Before the campaign was over he came out against any inspection whatever. I replied that even though inspection might at times be hurried, something was gained by a check-up twice a year to show that an automobile was in reasonably good condition when let loose on the roads with a half million other cars, and that there was no way to determine what percentage of accidents were caused by mechanical defects. Is it not, I asked, the first principle in dealing with machines that they be kept in as good condition as possible? How about airplanes, railroad cars, and elevators? Would you let them go uninspected because only a small percentage of accidents are due to defective machinery? Is not a single life worth saving, whether it be the life of a Democrat or a Republican?

One eulogist of palmy Republican days raised in a roundabout way the question of my mental and physical competency to continue longer in the office of Governor because of my age, insinuating that if reelected Governor I intended to resign in favor of the Democratic candidate for Lieutenant Governor. This question of age was soberly discussed in a long editorial in a leading newspaper, to the conclusion that the Republicans should be congratulated for choosing candidates whose ages, all added together, fell 10 per cent below the combined ages of the Democratic candidates. Unable to take the difference seriously, I countered with a disquisition on the dangerous ages in the life of man as I had personally observed them. The most dangerous age of all lies, I clearly proved, between fifty and fifty-five when my father and his father died, and also most of the boys and girls with whom I grew up over in Mansfield. In extemporaneous speeches I warned my implacable critic, then at the most dangerous age of fifty-one, who first brought the subject of age into the campaign, that he failed to consider the public interest when he offered himself as candidate for an office which would not expire until 1940 when he would be fifty-three years old, the exact age when my hitherto robust father died. If a man passed the age of fifty-five, I held, he was good for seventy, when comes another critical period of a half-decade during which my maternal grandfather died. But my family history, direct and collateral, gives abundant evidence, I could truthfully say, that all the men and women of my blood who survive their seventy-fifty year, as I have done, are likely to live on in the full vigor of youth until the high eighties and sometimes into the nineties, less often just dipping over a century! After a full century of life they had to take their chances. All this family history, I assured my audiences, was carefully scanned before I accepted, at the age of seventy-six, another renomination for Governor.

The strategy of Republicans and Socialists was to put me on the defensive and to keep me there. They had a way of raising minor issues, then dropping them for a few days for new issues, and later returning to the old ones. That question of honesty in government was always recurring. Mayor McLevy let it be known that he had no doubt about his own rugged honesty. Such Republicans as spoke for themselves went no further than to say that they believed they were honest. This gave me an opportunity to discuss the difference between a certainty and a belief qualified by some reservations. Are you not protesting your honesty too much, I asked, in classifying yourself with the angels? Do you Republicans really believe in your slogan "For Recovery—Bring in the Republicans?" Are you not insulting the intelligence of the people of Connecticut in declaring that the mere election of Republican state officials and a Republican United States Senator and Representatives in Congress will restore industrial prosperity throughout the State and the nation? You must know, if you observe and read, that great manufacturing plants in the State are now running on two or three shifts of workers a day and that the chairman of General Motors last week called back 35,000 employees who had been laid off and added as he did so the comment that in his opinion the recovery of business was now here to stay. This return to prosperous days, I submitted, was being accomplished without assistance from the Republican party in Connecticut, a remnant of the old Roraback machine.

In a straight contest between the Democratic and Republican parties I felt reasonably certain of reelection. There was, however, fear that Mayor McLevy might upset the applecart. If he received no more than 25,000 votes I felt fairly safe, but if the number should run up to 50,000 the election would probably go to Mr. Baldwin. But I sensed no imminent danger of defeat until a fortnight before election day when the president of a large manufacturing company informed me that nearly all his employees from top to bottom appeared the day before wearing McLevy buttons. Similar news came from all industrial areas west of the Connecticut River. Labor organizations, it was apparent, had been persuaded to go over to McLevy on the assurance that he could be elected. Not until later did I learn that W.P.A. workers engaged on state building projects were also displaying McLevy buttons. Old Guard Democrats in Hartford, Fairfield, and New Haven Counties, I well knew, were lukewarm towards my candidacy, but they always had been. I could count for support on a large majority of Democrats and Independents. But would their number be sufficient to carry me through against Republicans, Socialists, and disaffected Democrats who were working for my defeat, whether separately or in concert I had no means of ascertaining?

A man who accepts nomination for an office is to some extent responsible for defeat. He is under obligation to his supporters to win if he can. Obviously the thing for me to do was to cut down, if possible, McLevy's probable vote where he was strongest. Waterbury was conceded as lost by the Democrats to McLevy because Hayes still hung on as Mayor. A big Democratic rally was arranged there, which went off well. On an afternoon I also appeared unannounced at a large meeting of Russians who were undecided whether they should remain in the Democratic fold or go over in a flock to McLevy. I had a good time with that group. Honest Jasper was destined to carry Waterbury by only 413 votes. Then I bearded the lion in his den. A canvass of Bridgeport seemed to show that neither the Democrats nor the Republicans would be able to muster more than 8,000 votes at most, while all the rest, towards 30,000, would be cast for McLevy. Early in the campaign I had attended a Democratic rally in Bridgeport. At that time I ignored McLevy on the advice of party leaders so as not to be drawn into a controversy apart from the main issues between Democrats and Republicans. Now ten days before the election I visited Bridgeport twice. I addressed another general rally. I conferred with influential men in various racial groups and made short speeches to a number of good audiences which they brought together for me. I told them all what I stood for in the way of social legislation. I then struck out against Mayor McLevy who was equivocating on slum clearance for Bridgeport, a subject near the heart of many of its citizens. "As you all may know," I said in substance, "Father Panik in association with others was a pioneer in a project for low-cost housing and slum clearance in your city. He was the first to broach the matter to me, and on our recommendation the General Assembly in special session passed a bill permitting any municipality in the State to set up a Housing Authority for the purpose you all want. Your Mayor is now asking you to vote the Socialist ticket on the claim that he and his party were the pioneers in legislation for ridding Bridgeport of its slums. Just read again the platform of the Socialist party and you will see that McLevy and his party now stand for low-cost housing only 'wherever needed on terms consistent with the interests of the citizens as a whole.' Notice that qualification, 'consistent with the interests of the citizens as a whole.' It is said that his fellow Socialists pleaded with him to omit that nullifying phrase and he said 'nothing doing.' Property owned by a Housing Authority, you probably know, is nontaxable under the law. It looks as if your Mayor is more interested in taxes on your slums than in clean and healthful living places for people who are poor or of moderate means."

After this McLevy roared louder than ever against a Governor who shut his eyes to political corruption. But when the Democratic votes of Bridgeport were counted a few days later they rose from an estimate of 8,000 to over 14,000 and McLevy lost to the Democrats one of the three State Senators he expected to elect.

As in two previous campaigns, the Republicans had up their sleeve a card to be played towards the end of the political game. In 1930 they made use of a radical Irish leader who claimed that I was an enemy of Ireland. In 1934 they made use of a radical labor leader who undertook to hold me responsible for the actions of a Republican Lieutenant Governor in calling out the National Guard to quell a strike while I was out of the State. This year they decided to resurrect by legal action the Union party of 1936 as a scheme for drawing votes away from Cross to Baldwin.

Most people, I daresay, have forgotten the origin of the Union party of 1936. In June of that year, to be brief, Congressman William Lemke of North Dakota, an implacable Republican enemy of President Roosevelt, announced from Washington that he would be the candidate for President of the United States on the ticket of the Union party which he "had been instrumental in establishing officially." On the evening of this announcement Father Coughlin, speaking over the radio in a nationwide hookup, for his organization, the National Union for Social Justice, comprising, he said, 8,000,000 members, endorsed Lemke's candidacy. Henceforth the Union party became popularly known as Father Coughlin's party. Among many measures recommended in its platform were a repudiation of the national debt and a provision for a pension system which would guarantee "a comfortable living for all above sixty years of age." In the heat of the campaign Father Coughlin called President Roosevelt "a betrayer and liar" and "a double-crosser." The designation of the Union party got on the Connecticut state ticket that year with two nominees, one for President of the United States and another for Congressman at Large, with supplementary nominations for Congressmen in various districts. It was a queer looking ticket with five blank spaces having no nominees for the usual state executive officers.

This old Union party having been knocked into smithereens by President Roosevelt's reëlection, the Republicans, perhaps abetted by a small group of Democrats, prepared to use its designation on the state ballot of 1938 for their own purposes. They presented a list of nominees to the Secretary of State who refused to place some of them on the ballot, mainly for the reason that he had received no special nominating petitions from them as required by law. One of the names turned down by the Secretary of State was Albert Levitt, nominee for Judge of Probate in the town of Redding. Thereupon Levitt, describing himself as attorney for the Union party, appeared before a Judge of the Superior Court on November 1, just a week before the election, and asked for a peremptory writ of mandamus to compel the Secretary of State to place on the state ballot all the names he had rejected as not complying with the law. The writ was immediately served and obeyed. The completed ticket was a perfect "draw-away scheme," headed by Baldwin for Governor and McConaughy for Lieutenant Governor, along with an endorsement of four Republican candidates for Congress. The rest of the ticket included some Democrats who were on it without their consent. The Republicans saw to it that there would be no time for an appeal to the Supreme Court to set aside as an error the decision of the Judge of the Superior Court. The new-fledged Union party had no connection with the Union party of 1936 except in name. Not sensing the fraud, the followers of Father Coughlin would nevertheless think, as seems to have been intended, that the Connecticut Union party had been blessed by the priest of the Shrine of the Little Flower. And a few nests of disgruntled Democrats, knowing the fraud, would be happy over a chance to get back at the Governor who had failed to give them the jobs they had asked for.

I voted early on election day in New Haven and drove immediately to Hartford. All day friends and telephone calls came in to inform me how the voting was going on in different parts of the State. In the large cities Democrats were heavily cutting me for McLevy and to a less extent Republicans were cutting Baldwin for me. I repeated my old remark that if McLevy received 50,000 votes I would go under. I dined with Mansfield friends and others at the home of Fannie Dixon Welch over in Columbia, where the first election returns we received showed me running ahead. Disturbed, however, by the large vote cast for McLevy I hastened back to Hartford where I sat for an hour or two by the radio of the *Hartford Times*, and then migrated to the studio of the Travelers Insurance Company (WTIC). There, surrounded by tabulators and newspaper correspondents, I awaited the outcome. McLevy's vote kept climbing and climbing until it reached the height of more than 160,000. And yet, despite all that, Baldwin and Cross were running nip and tuck. One moment Cross was elected and the next moment it was Baldwin. When by three o'clock in the morning the returns were mostly in, Cross was leading Baldwin by a few hundred votes on the straight Democratic-Republican tickets. But Baldwin more than offset this number by 3,000 votes which he received on "the draw-away" Union party ticket. At once I conceded his election in a brief radio address to the citizens of the State and in a personal

Governor Cross Leaving the Capitol on the Inauguration of His Successor.
Courtesy of the Hartford Times.

congratulatory telegram scribbled with pencil on a scrap of paper. For
that scrap of paper with erasures and emendations there was a scramble
among the correspondents which was quieted by having it photographed.

Then I walked through the cool November air over to my room in
the Hartford Club, raised a window to clear my lungs completely of the
foul air of six weeks of political abuse, took a very hot bath, and slept
soundly until the telephone bell rang to call me to breakfast at the accustomed hour.

I spent the morning in my office at the Capitol. Friends, telegrams, and telephone calls poured in to express surprise at the outcome of the election or to commiserate with me over my bad luck. Many urged that I contest the election. My invariable reply then and later was that a contest would be against the public interest. Whether the Union party was on the ballot legally or illegally now made no difference, for some hundreds of citizens had voted its ticket, naturally assuming that there was no question about its legality. In the circumstances I said I could take no part in an effort to disenfranchise those hundreds whoever they may be. Should the case be appealed to the Supreme Court, there would be no way to prove

Crystal Caverns, Bermuda, March 1939. Mrs. Barlow and her daughter Catherine A. Turner [Carper] with W.L. Cross.
Wilbur Lucius Cross Papers (MS 155), Manuscripts and Archives, Yale University Library

that anyone who voted for Baldwin on the Union ticket would have voted for me had there been no Union ticket. In the afternoon, I drove through more fresh air to New York to address the National Institute of Arts and Letters at the Hotel Plaza and to attend the next morning the annual meeting of the American Academy of Arts and Letters, of which I was then Chancellor. Before leaving Hartford I released my last Thanksgiving Proclamation which I had held back for several days to keep it from being kicked about in the political arena for good or for evil.

A Proclamation
By His Excellency Wilbur L. Cross, Governor

As the colors of autumn stream down the wind, scarlet in sumach and maple, spun gold in the birches, a splendor of smoldering fire in the oaks along the hill, and the last leaves flutter away, and dusk falls briefly about the worker bringing in from the field a late load of its fruit, and Arcturus is lost to sight and Orion swings upward that great sun upon his shoulder, we are stirred once more to ponder the Infinite Goodness that has set apart for us, in all this moving mystery of creation, a time of living and a home. In such a spirit I appoint Thursday, the twenty-fourth of November, a day of

Public Thanksgiving

In such a spirit I call upon the people to acknowledge heartily, in friendly gathering and house of prayer, the increase of the season nearing now its close: the harvest of earth, the yield of patient mind and faithful hand, that have kept us fed and clothed and have made for us a shelter even against the storm. It is right that we whose arc of sky has been darkened by no war hawk, who have been forced by no man to stand and speak when to speak was to choose between death and life, should give thanks also for the further mercies we have enjoyed, beyond desert or any estimation, of Justice, Freedom, Loving-kindness, Peace—resolving, as we prize them, to let no occasion go without some prompting or some effort worthy in a way however humble of those proudest among man's ideals, which burn, though it may be like candles fitfully in our gusty world, with a light so clear we name its source divine.

Former Governor Cross at his nephew Leon Dimock's turkey farm, previously the home of grandfather Gurley, 1947.
University of Connecticut Photograph Collection, Archives & Special Collections, University of Connecticut Library

Index